"FREEMASONRY" AND RITUAL WORK

THE MISRAIM SERVICE

RUDOLF STEINER (1904)

"FREEMASONRY"
AND RITUAL WORK
The Misraim Service

Letters, Documents, Ritual Texts, and Lectures from
the History and Contents of the Cognitive- Ritual Section
of the Esoteric School : 1904-1914

Documents of a New Beginning
after the First World War : 1921-1924

Translated by John Wood
Introduction by Christopher Bamford

RUDOLF STEINER

SteinerBooks

CW 265

SteinerBooks
Anthroposophic Press

610 Main Street
Great Barrington, Massachusetts 01230
www.steinerbooks.org

Original translation from the German by John Wood. First published in English by Etheric Dimensions Press, Switzerland and Scotland, 2005; edited by Paul Emberson and associates. Foreword to the British edition copyright 2005 by Paul Emberson.

This book is volume 265 in the Collected Works (CW) of Rudolf Steiner, published by SteinerBooks, 2007. It is a translation of the German *Zur Geschichte und aus den Inhalten der erkenntniskultischen Abeilung der Esoterischen Schule 1904-1914* published by Rudolf Steiner Verlag, Dornach, Switzerland, 1987.

Library of Congress Cataloging-in-Publication Data

Steiner, Rudolf, 1861-1925.
  [Zur Geschichte und aus den Inhalten der erkenntiskultischen Abteilung der esoterischen Schule, 1904-1914. English]
  Freemasonry and ritual work : the Misraim service / Rudolf Steiner ; translated by John Wood ; introduction by Christopher Bamford.
     p. cm. — (The collected works of Rudolf Steiner ; 265)
  "Letters, documents, ritual texts, and lectures from the history and contents of the cognitive-ritual section of the esoteric school, 1904-1914; documents of a new beginning after the First World War, 1921-1924."
  Includes bibliographical references and index.
  ISBN 978-0-88010-612-2
  1. Anthroposophy. 2. Freemasonry—Rituals. 3. Occultism. I. Title.

BP595.S894Z87 2007
299'.935—dc22
                              2007004591

Printed in the United States of America

CONTENTS

II.

THE CONTENTS OF THE COGNITIVE-RITUAL SECTION

Explanation of the Ritual Texts

Sketches and Explanations of Ritual Objects

Contents   ✳   ix

Explanation of the Temple Legend

Appendix

III.

DOCUMENTS OF A NEW BEGINNING AFTER
THE FIRST WORLD WAR

From the new beginnings after the First World War until the refounding of
the Esoteric School as "the Free High School for Spiritual Science."

Documents

A Note about the British Edition

This volume contains the wording of various rites, of Freemason origin, adapted by Rudolf Steiner and initially performed from January 1906 onward as the "Misraim Service" in the Esoteric School of the Theosophical Society in Germany. The wording is taken in the main from Steiner's own written records. The book contains also the surviving part of the instruction he gave about the rites, reproduced as far as possible from his pupils' often scanty notes. Sundry sketches of ritual instruments and furnishings are included, as are copies of relevant notes made by Rudolf Steiner himself. Together these comprise part of the esoteric core of his teaching, reserved for his most advanced pupils in the Esoteric School, up to the outbreak of the Great War in 1914. These ritual texts shed a most interesting light on Steiner's first steps in the renewal of the Mysteries.

Although the book contains a wealth of material, it covers only a fraction of the instruction given by Rudolf Steiner in the upper levels of the school. Few details of the teaching and the rituals in the higher grades have come down to us. None of it was intended for publication at the time. Pupils were strictly forbidden to divulge any aspect of the esoteric work outside their circle. After Rudolf Steiner's death his wife and executrix, Marie Steiner, was brought into such acrimonious conflict with the remaining leadership of the Anthroposophical Society that she felt compelled to publish virtually everything in her possession, for fear of being accused of holding back esoteric treasures for her own personal use. Events showed her fears were probably well founded. It thus came about that Rudolf Steiner's interdiction was not followed. The German edition of this volume was compiled and published in 1987 by the executors of Rudolf Steiner's literary estate.

We English-speaking readers owe a special debt of thanks to the late John Wood for his lucid and scrupulously accurate rendering in English of this, and other volumes of Rudolf Steiner's esoteric works, as also to his able helper and proof-reader, Marguerite, his wife. Translating works of this nature, magnitude and style is no slight task. John and Marguerite have avoided Anglicizing the text, remaining faithful to the German publisher's formulations, which may occasionally seem awkward to the English mind. It was John's express wish that his English translation of this particular work be edited and published by the Etheric Dimensions Press, to whom he gave full discretionary powers to make such amendments as they deemed appropriate.

The German edition has extensive commentaries by the editor, Hella Wiesberger, describing the historical context of the Misraim Rites within the Esoteric School, and dismissing suggestions that Rudolf Steiner was a Freemason in the usual sense. She also enlarges on some of the references he made to persons and events, and sets out her understanding of his reasons for creating, in the particular way he did, what she prefers to call a "cognitive cultus" (*Erkenntniskultus*). Hers is a modern approach, the esoteric subject matter being sorted, classified, annotated, cross-referenced and indexed. A detailed table of contents is provided, as well as a chronological register of lectures referred to in the text and other reference tools.

The British publishers are most appreciative of the vast work accomplished in compiling the German edition. The subject matter is presented clearly and logically. Yet they do have reservations about the views put forward by its editor. It seems to them that, in the endeavor conclusively to demonstrate Rudolf Steiner's independence from any Freemason Order, and the sovereign nature of his work in the Esoteric School, some of the reasons why he did choose to link the school's ritual activity to existing Misraim Rites, specifically, have been overlooked. The German editor has also tended to interpret the Misraim Service of those early years unchronologically, in terms of certain remarks made much later by Rudolf Steiner, after the War, in quite different contexts.

For these and other reasons the British editors would have preferred to omit parts of the commentaries. They would have been happier also to present the esoteric subject matter in a manner they feel would be more in keeping with its meaning. But to have done so would have entailed major changes and might have given offense to those who look upon the Rudolf Steiner Press in Dornach as an authority in matters of spiritual science. After much heart-searching they have, therefore, retained Hella Wiesberger's presentation. What follows is thus an integral English version of the German edition. Rudolf Steiner's communications form its essential content.

These words should not be taken as a criticism of Hella Wiesberger and her team, who, in compiling the twelve or more comprehensive tomes of material from the first and second esoteric schools, have performed a monumental task. If the above remarks stimulate the reader to reflect on these questions and make his or her own judgement, then the purpose of this foreword will have been fulfilled.

Paul Emberson

INTRODUCTION

CHRISTOPHER BAMFORD

1.

As noted by Paul Emberson, co-publisher and editor of this English language edition, the present volume is essentially a compilation of available materials and already contains compendious, detailed, and rich material—both introductory and exegetical—from the hand of its German editor and compiler, Hella Wiesberger, who performed a truly marvelous service in making these texts available. As Emberson also notes, however, there are areas Frau Wiesberger did not chose to explore. Among these areas, perhaps the most interesting is the reason that Rudolf Steiner decided to link the ritual activity of the Esoteric Section of what was then the Theosophical Society to Freemasonry and to the Memphis-Misraim ("Egyptian") Rites, rather than to any other Freemasonic lineage. Underlying this is the question of ritual itself: What is it? And why is it an essential human activity?

In a general sense, the answer to the question of Freemasonry is clear. As Steiner began to establish his esoteric mission, he wished to connect his spiritual work and mission to those currents whose wisdom and dedication had prepared the ground for what he knew to be his task. As a matter of conscience and an expression both of gratitude and continuity, he wanted to acknowledge all who had preceded him and to relate himself to them in his characteristically free, creative, conscious, and independent manner. At the same time, since nearly everyone else active in the spiritual revival at the turn of the twentieth century had some Masonic connection, by undertaking his own "Masonic" work, Steiner put himself in a position where he would potentially have influence in the orientation of the revival.

He also understood the centrality, and even necessity, of ritual as the archetype and paradigm of embodied spiritual activity that actually worked with the spiritual world, and he recognized that Freemasonry offered the preeminent spiritual, nonreligious (nonsectarian), communitarian model, whose archetype was the "Temple" at all levels—human, earthly, cosmic, and divine. He knew, too, that Freemasonry—no matter how hollow it appeared—was a chief repository, if not *the* chief repository, of the esoteric, ritual tradition and initiation still active in the West. In addition, most of the guiding spirits in the recent development of the West had been Masons, among them, Haydn, Mozart, Goethe, Lessing, the Founding Fathers of the American Constitution, and many of the great esotericists of the nineteenth and early twentieth centuries, including Madame Blavatsky and the early Theosophists. Freemasonry, in other words, had played an important role in the evolution of consciousness that marks the modern era.

For these reasons, though he never became a Mason, Rudolf Steiner in 1905 sought and received, on the basis of his self-evident, extraordinary initiatory status, a formal patent from the "Great Orient of the Scottish Ancient and Accepted Thirty-Three Degree Rite of the Order of the Ancient Freemasons of the Ancient and Primitive Memphis-Misraim Rite" to direct his own "order" under the name Mystica Aeterna. He received his charter from Theodor Reuss of the Ordo Templi Orientis or O.T.O. Steiner, however, was never at any time a member of, or had anything to do with, the O.T.O. He was simply given the right to use the name Misraim. Reuss himself had received permission to operate the Memphis-Misraim Rite from John Yarker, who, some twenty years previously, had initiated Madame Blavatsky into the same order.

In due time, Mystica Aeterna became the "Cognitive-Ritual Section" (also called the "Misraim Service") of the Esoteric School of the German Section of the Theosophical Society and is the subject of this book. The "Masonic" phase in Rudolf Steiner's life and work passed, but as with everything else that he took up, it remains

transformed and alive in many ways in Anthroposophy as he
handed it down to us today.

2.

As for modern Freemasonry, its origins are lost in the mists of
time. Practically every imaginable source has been proposed, from
the Druids of megalithic Britain to Pharoanic Egypt and beyond.
John Yarker even traced the origins back to the fall of Atlantis, thus
making Freemasonry the bearer of the primordial wisdom of the
Rishis or Sages who seeded post-Atlantean culture. Not surprisingly, therefore, Michael Baigent, responding to this luxuriant confusion, concludes: "There is no Origin.... It is a mythical beast."

On all the evidence, however, several distinct spiritual influences seem to feed into the arrival of Freemasonry on the historical stage in the late seventeenth century. At the very least, one can
discern the presence of the following: the echo of the ancient mysteries, Egyptian Hermetism, and so-called Gnosticism; ancient and
medieval guild or craft initiations; monastic culture; the learning
of the cathedral schools; the traditions of the Knights Templars
and the Cathars (Manicheans); Jewish kabbalah; alchemy; certain
streams of Islamic (especially Ismaeli) and Celtic esotericism;
Renaissance Hermetism; and Rosicrucianism.

3.

The guilds originated in the traditional idea that every occupa-
tion is a "priesthood" and that every human being is a kind of
priest, who, made in the image of the creator, is analogously a creator or "maker." To be a craftsperson or an artist (no distinction
originally being made between the two) was therefore to perform
a sacred, priestly, quasi-divine function. Hence, very early, groups
arose that practiced particular activities, each possessing its own
rites of initiation. These rites or rituals expressed the qualitative,
cosmological significance of the activity in question, but since cosmology, like the cosmos, is one, all rites were interrelated as specific aspects or applications of the religion of the time. Because of
the correspondence of microcosm and macrocosm, the rites were
also means of perfecting the individual craftsperson and acted as

supports for his or her inner development. Such initiations were not so much a question of "esoteric" learning or praying as of realizing *through the work* the full humanity of the maker and his or her society.

In the simplest sense, all true rites, like symbols, are the earthly reflection of the language of the spiritual world. As Rudolf Steiner frequently stresses, rightly perceived earthly phenomena are the sensible trace or expression of transcendent, spiritual realities. In this sense, the world as given is already sacramental—the visible sign of an invisible presence. It is up to us to realize it, and the process of so doing is called ritual.

As humanity, we are the bridge that unites visible and invisible worlds. By our uprightness, which is the bearer of our thinking, feeling, and willing, we symbolize ("draw together") the whole. Moving and acting through space—thereby creating it—we define the six directions, while through our center (the "seventh" direction), we have potential access to affect all worlds to make them one in harmony, wisdom, and power. Actualizing this potential, human beings have therefore always sought to conform their actions with—and thereby participate in—the creative realities of the spiritual world, knowing that in so doing they assumed the full dignity of their bridging status as spiritual-physical beings to become coworkers in the divine work of creation.

Put another way, human actions become real—and the fullness of the Earth is realized—to the extent that human beings participate in a transcendent reality. As Christ says, "I have given you an example, that ye should do as I have done to you" (John 13.15), that is, "Love one another, as I have loved you" (John 15:12). In other words, as Hindu texts commenting upon the Vedas put it: "We must do what the gods did in the beginning" (*Satapatha Brahmana*), or "Thus the gods did; thus men do."(*Taittiriya Brahmana*). Such imitation of divine realities is ritual. Initiation and ritual, in fact, not only imitate divine realities but also incarnate them, because true imitation is union or identity.

In ritual, the spiritual world provides the pattern, archetype, or prototype, and we reenact it. By our imitation, we participate in spiritual reality and are transformed. At the same time, we transform it: we spiritualize the world so that it becomes truly, consciously sacramental. Therefore Yahweh tells Moses (Exodus 25:9): "According to all that I show thee, after the pattern of the tabernacle ... even so shall ye make it." This pattern, broadly speaking, is the "order" of the universe, which in Sanskrit is *rita*, from which we derive our word "ritual." Such order, the divine activity through which the world is produced, is closely related to *measure* and measure to geometry (and hence to architecture), for as Plato said, "God geometrizes always." Thus, while every initiation and rite will have such a cosmological component, the builders' or masons' initiation will be privileged in this regard.

There is also inevitably a "magical," theurgic aspect to ritual, as became manifest in the Renaissance when it was revealed— through the translation of the *Corpus Hermeticum*, the core texts of the Hermetic tradition—that the ancient Egyptians made statues "ensouled and conscious, filled with spirit and doing great deeds; statues that foreknow the future and predict it by lots, by prophecy, by dreams, and by many other means; statues that make people ill and cure them." In other words, a ritual act, besides invoking the invisible in the visible, can draw down and, in a sense, "create" spiritual realities.

4.

Precisely how the medieval guilds arose is unknown. Some trace the origin to certain clubs or societies called *collegia* (Greek, hetaira) existing in the ancient world. Perhaps migrating from Egypt, where they would have been part of the temple hierarchy, *collegia* first appear in Greece as citizen groups formed around a god or hero, such as Dionysius, Isis, or Orpheus. Such groups, led by an architect initiated in the temple, constructed the first theaters associated with the Dionysian rites. We know from Strabo, the ancient geographer, that the *hetaira* were organized in different communities and had particular rites of initiation and symbols of recognition and greeting. We may also note, however, that Greece, breaking with the temple traditions of the Egypto-Chaldean period, had already begun the process of democratization by which initiation and the search for enlightenment and redemption were increasingly freed from the constraints of priesthood and sacred geography, and opened to all, everywhere.

In Rome, *collegia* were traced back to Numa Pompilius, the second king of Rome (c. 717-673 B.C.E.). Under Servius Tullius (578-535 B.C.E.), the sixth king of Rome, they were organized into "centuries" in three groups: carpenters and masons; metalworkers; and musicians. The *collegia* were part club, part cult and, in many cases, also burial societies. In time, however, they became predominantly trade associations. They proliferated during the Roman Empire and were carried to its farthest boundaries until scattered by the barbarian invasions. It is unknown whether they survived and, if so, how many did so, though it is likely that some vestiges must have remained to form the groups of artisans who built the first churches and monasteries. This much is more or less fact. The rest of the story is more hypothetical.

A common hypothesis concerns the "Comacini." It is said that, when Italy was overrun and the Roman collegia were suppressed, the architectural college of Rome sought refuge to the north, around Lake Como—hence "Comacini." The expression "magistri Comacini" first appears in the code of the Lombard king Rotharis (636-652). They are mentioned as master masons able to make contracts and subcontracts for building works and permitted to bring with them fellow "collegantes," or guild members, as well as serfs or servants. It is also known that retinues of craftspeople accompanied Christian missionary monks traveling northward and westward—for example, Saint Boniface (c. 672-754) who went to Germany and Saint Augustine of Canterbury (d. 604) who went to England. Some of them may well have been Comacini mason architects and builders (many of whom were also monks). If this was so, they provided the basis of what would become the monastic building associations, whose skill and understanding would lead to the architectural triumphs of the Romanesque and Gothic periods. It has also been proposed that the Comacini remnants met the remnants of other *collegia*, who had come to Britain and had been absorbed into the legendary Celtic *culdees* ("Friends of God"), thus providing Freemasonry with its first Druid connection.

Confirming this general picture, the earliest known Masonic document (c. 1390) the Halliwell Manuscript, or "Regius Poem"— the first of the so-called Old Charges (ancient documents upon which the Masonic constitutions are based)—claims that masons arrived in England in the reign of Alfred the Great's grandson, Athelstan (c. 895-939), the first king of all England. The Regius Poem is interesting for other reasons. Internal evidence indicates that a priest wrote it, and it places the source of Masonry in geometry, which is said to be synonymous with masonry and invented by Euclid in Egypt. This reference to Egypt at the very source of Masonry is interesting, since, as we shall see, Rudolf Steiner chose to align himself with "Egyptian Masonry." Equally interesting is the fact that, at the time of his most intense involvement with the Masonic tradition, Steiner gave his most profound lectures on number and geometry (see Rudolf Steiner, *The Fourth Dimension*). The text tells us:

> The clerk Euclid on this wise it found
> This craft of geometry in Egypt land
> In Egypt he taught it full, wide.
> In diver lands on every side.

After mentioning the introduction of geometry/masonry into England under Athelstan and going through many moral and practical injunctions, the manuscript turns to the Seven Liberal Arts (grammar, rhetoric, logic, arithmetic, geometry, music, astronomy), also here claimed to be taught by Euclid "through the high grace of Christ in heaven."

> These be the sciences seven
> Whom useth them well he may have heaven.

Thus, we are brought into the influential orbit of the so-called twelfth-century renaissance, exemplified by the ecclesiastical and cathedral schools, preeminently those of Paris and Chartres. This is not surprising. The great cathedrals, which were being built concurrently, were marvels of the very same cosmological and theological teaching, whose groundwork was being laid in the renewal of Pythagorean and Platonic thinking in the schools. At the same time and in the same places, the Seven Liberal Arts were being reimagined as an initiatory path of the soul, rather than as a mere cultural preparation. A key text, which would have been known to the English Masons, as it was to Chaucer, was Alain de Lille's *Anticlaudianus*. Alain de Lille (1128-1202) may well have even spent time in England. In this work, Nature, realizing that her works are defective, longs to create the perfect human being. She calls the Virtues to her aid, and they, along with the Seven Liberal Arts, contribute to the perfecting of human nature.

The next earliest "guild" Masonic manuscript is the Matthew Cooke Manuscript (c. 1450). Although this text was not published until 1861, its content was certainly known to the earliest (speculative) Freemasons (1720-1723) and formed part of the original constitutions. It begins, again, by invoking the Seven Liberal Arts, "which seven *exist only through geometry*." The primacy of geometry is confirmed by another manuscript discovered by Locke in Bodleian Library in 1696 and attributed to King Henry VI (1422-1470). First published in 1748, it defines Freemasonry as "the knowledge of nature and the comprehension of the forces within her" and derives it from *Pythagoras*, who, after spending twenty-two years in Egypt, founded his school, the first "Lodge," in Crotona, Italy. Implicit in this manuscript is the conception of geometry itself as the "Royal Art," by which the "rough stone" becomes the "cubic stone of mastery." The identification of geometry as the fundamental science goes back at least to the second-century Neo-Platonist Maximus of Tyre.

In the Cooke manuscript, geometry is first described as "teaching us all about mensuration, measures and weights, of all kinds of handcrafts." Its origin is here traced back, as in Genesis 4, to the line of Cain, for it was Cain who built the first city:

Before Noah's flood, by direct male descent from Adam in the seventh generation, there lived a man called Lamech who had two wives, called Adah and Zillah. By the first, Adah, he begat two sons, Jabal and Jubal. Jabal was the first man that ever discovered geometry and masonry, and he made houses and he is called in the Bible the father of all who dwell in tents or dwelling houses. And he was Cain's master mason and governor of the works when he built the city of Enoch, which was the first city ever made and was built by Cain, Adam's son, who gave it to his own son Enoch.... And at that place was the science of geometry and masonry first prosecuted and contrived as a science and as a handicraft. And so we may say that it is the first cause and foundation of all crafts and sciences. And also this man Jabal was called the father of shepherds.... He was the first that made partition of lands, in order that every man might know his lands and labor for himself....

And his brother Jubal or Tubal was the inventor of music and song.... He discovered that science by the sound of the weights of his brother, Tubal-Cain's hammers....

You must know that this son Tubal-Cain was the founder of the smith's craft and of other handicrafts dealing with metals ... and his sister Naamah discovered the craft of weaving, for before her time no cloth was woven.

Readers of Rudolf Steiner will recognize this story and know that throughout his career, from *The Temple Legend* to the end of his life, he aligned himself and Anthroposophy with the line of Cain rather than Abel (who represents the priestly lineage), thereby also placing himself in the "Masonic" lineage.

The text goes on to tell how, in expectation of the Flood, the descendents of Cain wrote their science on two pillars, which were discovered only many years later, one by Pythagoras and the other by Hermes, who taught the sciences inscribed thereon. Paying no heed to chronology, our author tells us how Noah's son Ham, who was the father of Nimrod and who "began the Tower of Babel and taught his workmen the craft of masonry," carried on the tradition. Following that, many cities, temples, and dwelling were built "and in this manner the craft of masonry was first instituted and charged as a science." As for Euclid, he was an Egyptian (!), and the Egyptians learned the Liberal Arts, above all geometry, from Abraham. But the Children of Israel must have forgotten it, for it is said that, when they were exiled in Egypt, they learned the masonic crafts from the Egyptians and thus were able to construct the Temple of Solomon. No mention is made of Hiram Abiff, who was later considered the master constructor of Solomon's Temple, but who does not (at least openly) enter Masonic teaching until the 1720s, thus making it quite possible, as Steiner asserts, that it was "a secret known to the Rosicrucians." By then, of course, masonry was only speculative and no longer, as among the guilds, primarily operative.

5.

One way of considering the conundrum of origins is to think of it in terms of the evolution of consciousness. From this perspective, the fifteenth century witnessed what Rudolf Steiner called the birth of the age of the "consciousness soul"—our own modern/postmodern age—while the previous three centuries saw both what we might call the "sunset effect," or flowering of the previous "intellectual soul," in the high cathedral culture of the Middle Ages and a foreshadowing of what was to come in various groups and movements, which would provide the esoteric counterstream, or corrective, to the materialism and egotism that is the shadow of our age. In other words, various other influences converge into the vessel provided by the medieval masons to create modern Freemasonry. Here, two points may be noted. First, whatever the source of Masonic wisdom, the evidence of the great cathedrals alone reveals beyond a doubt that, from the Romanesque through the Gothic periods, the Middle Ages was near miraculously endowed with architects, masons, and sculptors learned in the symbolic languages of esoteric tradition. Going beyond the cathedrals, the beauty of the period, extending into the vibrant joy expressed, for instance, in the Books of Hours, demonstrates a widespread and high level of initiatory knowledge. Second, there are no overt initiatory rituals or secret doctrines in the "Old Charges." Essentially, the path of the mason seems to have had but three aspects: moral development; inner, "gnostic" development through the Seven Liberal Arts, and the practice of the Christian religion. That is, while guild masonry certainly seems to have been the chief vessel of what would become Freemasonry, other streams contributed to its formation or creation in modern times.

6.

The Templars are often mentioned in this context, though without any clear documentary evidence. The idea of a Templar origin, in fact, appears only quite late—after the founding of Freemasonry properly so called in 1717—in the famous 1737 oration by the "Chevalier" Andrew Michael Ramsay, who claimed that Free-masonry arose in the Holy Land during the Crusades as a "society of knights, who devoted themselves to the purpose of rebuilding the sacred edifices which had been destroyed by the Saracens." What evidence Ramsey had or whether his motive was simply to give the organization a factional aristocratic and chivalric coloring is unclear. It is equally unclear whether he was referring to the Knights Templars, the Hospitalers of Saint John, or an associated group of "crusading masons." No matter, because from that point on the "Templar" legend took hold, and Templar grades began to proliferate. One must trust such things.

"Nine distinguished and venerable men," led by Hughes de Payen, formed the "Militia of the Temple" in Jerusalem in 1118. Initially, the order was under the auspices of the Patriarch, sixty-seventh in line from the Apostle John, the Beloved Disciple. (The Templars would always revere Saint John and see themselves as a Johannine order.) A tenth person, Hughes, Comte de Champagne, who had donated the lands of Clairvaux to Saint Bernard, joined them in 1126. Vowed to poverty, chastity, and obedience, the Templars' mission was to secure pilgrim routes and to protect pilgrims. At first, having no rule of their own, they lived under the

Rule of Saint Augustine, but in 1128 Saint Bernard instituted a separate rule for the "New Knighthood." Under his aegis, the Templars began to expand and prosper, not only in the Holy Land, where they began excavation of Solomon's Temple (in search perhaps of the Ark of the Covenant), but also throughout the Christian world. This was at the same time as the masonic guilds began to emerge.

The Templars, guardians of the Holy Land, keepers of the secret of the Temple, and protectors of the faithful, were great builders of churches as well as fortified buildings and castles (called *Kraks*). Countless Templar centers were constructed from the Middle East to the north of Scotland. Initial architectural guidance would certainly have come from the monastic tradition. Saint Bernard, after all, was himself a master architect. Very soon, however, they seem to have assumed the responsibility themselves and formed bands of "servants," craftsmen—operative masons and others—who worked with them under a "master builder." Their role in the building of the great cathedrals is unclear.

In the Holy Land, the Templars established close relationships with certain esoteric Islamic, especially Ismaili, Sufi orders—above all, the Qarmatians, the Assassins, and perhaps the Ikhwan al-Safa or Brethren of Purity (or Sincerity). The first was a communitarian religious and social reform movement, which spread through workers groups organized in corporations through lodges. Founded by Hamdan al-Qarmat around 880, it mixed speculative and apocalyptic elements and espoused reason, tolerance, and equality. A universalistic, "socialist" movement, Qarmatian communities were based on voluntary gifts from members and held all property in common. The communities were esoteric and initiatory, but not secret. There was a seven-degree initiation.

The Assassins (deriving from the Arabic *assas*, meaning "guardian") were also an Ismaili offshoot. An austere, initiatory military order, like the Templars, they took as their mission the spiritual guarding of the Holy Land, the Mystical Mountain.

The Ikhwan al-Safa, who have also been connected with Christian Rosenkreutz's legendary journey to the East, were Sufi wisdom philosophers who came together in "a kind of Masonic Lodge" around Basra in the tenth and eleventh centuries. Organized in grades, they synthesized the ancient wisdom streams of Hermetic, Pythagorean-Platonic, and Gnostic thought with the "Religions of the Book"—Torah, Gospel, and Qur'an, transmitting what they learned in an encyclopedia of the sciences consisting of fifty-two epistles, from arithmetic, geometry, astronomy, and music to cosmology, the sciences of nature, psychology, epistemology, intelligible realities, theology, and others. The emphasis was universal:

> We have drawn our knowledge from four books. The first is composed of the mathematical and natural sciences established by the sages and philosophers. The second consists of the revealed books of the Torah, the Gospels, and the Qur'an, and the other tablets brought by the prophets through angelic revelation. The third of the books of Nature, which are the ideas in the Platonic senses of the forms of creatures actually existing, from the composition of the celestial spheres, the division of the Zodiac, the movement of the stars ... to the transformation of the elements, the members of the mineral, plant, and animal kingdoms, and the rich variety of human industry. The fourth consists of the divine books which touch only purified people and which are the angels who live in intimacy with chosen beings, the noble and purified souls.

In a word: "The Brethren of Purity believe that the Truth is one without it being the private work of anyone. God has sent his spirit to all humanity, to Christians as to Muslims, to blacks as to whites." Clearly, a Sufi influence is not out of the question.

Whatever the historical justification of connecting Freemasonry with the Templars, it is clear that the military orders (as well as the Crusades) introduced several important elements into the Western tradition. Chief among them would probably be the guiding star of the Temple of Jerusalem—its mystical construction, the cosmic catastrophe of its destruction, and the perennial hope and promise of its rebuilding. No sooner had the Templars arrived in Jerusalem than they hastened to the Temple Mount and began excavations. What they found in the secret room unearthed in 1188 remains unknown. We do know that they formed a lay chivalric order of profound spirituality, universality, practical accomplishment, and financial success, which was one of the causes leading to their destruction.

Historically, the First Temple (Solomon's) was constructed around 960 B.C.E. and destroyed around 586 B.C.E.; the Second Temple was built 535-515 B.C.E. and destroyed in 70 C.E. Ours is the task of rebuilding the Temple. It is the Knights Templars—not necessarily the literal Knights Templars but all those whose souls resonate with the "image" of the Temple—who assume personal responsibility for this task and therefore take as their way the way of the Temple. In so doing, they constitute an imaginal lineage going back to the First Temple and beyond that to the Master Architect and Builder of All. They are those who become the question: *How is the Temple to be rebuilt?* Modern spiritual movements, from Freemasonry to Anthroposophy, address this question.

A possibly direct filiation lies through Scotland. Considerable literature exists proposing that, after the destruction of the order in 1307-1314, those who escaped execution dispersed, many fleeing to join their fellows in Scotland, where a long-standing connection already existed and would be further cemented. Hughes de Payen, founder of the order, had visited Scotland as early as 1128, receiving a land grant from King David I, the first anywhere to the Templars. There was also a connection with Saint Bernard (author of the order's rule) and the Cistercians, leading to the creation in 1137 of a teaching Lodge of Masons to build Melrose Abbey. After their reception by Robert the Bruce, the Templars are said to have formed a close association with Masons as well as aristocrats such as the Sinclairs of Roslin, patrons and builders of the celebrated Roslyn Abbey. Quite apart from the Templar connection, there is documentary evidence suggesting the origin of Freemasonry in Scotland: the earliest use of the word "Lodge," the earliest record books for such, the earliest examples of "non-operative (speculative) masons," the earliest connection with specific moral ideals, the earliest reference to the secret Mason Word, and the earliest references to Masonic catechisms as well as degrees or grades. From Scotland, Freemasonry would have descended to England and thence to continental Europe.

There is another, perhaps even more important Templar contribution. The Templars certainly represented, if not the first, the most dazzling example of a lay initiatory order whose spiritual path was individual, chivalric, and clearly in the world. The ethos of the Crusades and a sense of personal responsibility for the places hallowed by the Incarnation provide the outer context of their formation. What was inwardly at play? The mysterious *Baphomet*—the abominated "goat-bearded," "clover-hoofed" devil-idol they were accused of worshipping—gives some clue.

Who or what Baphomet might have been has been variously interpreted. The name has been considered, for instance, as a corruption of the word "Mohammed"; as the altered form of an Arabic word meaning "Father of Understanding"; as confounded of two Greek words, *baphe* (baptism) and *metis* (wisdom), implying initiation; and as referring to Sophia, the divine feminine (an association with which Rudolf Steiner concurs in *The Temple Legend*, Lecture 12). The image, for its part, has been variously described as the head of John the Baptist or as an idol with a human face or with the head of a goat (or a cockerel) and the body of a man (or a woman). It has been aligned with phallic worship and sexual rites and associated with Pan, Mendes, and other goat gods. Perhaps the best explanation is that it was, in fact, "a complete emblem of the secret traditions of the Order" (Fulcanelli).

Used outwardly as an esoteric glyph, a seal of chivalry, and a sign of recognition and reproduced on jewelry and on the walls of the Templar commanderies and the tympanums of their chapels, the image was composed as follows: The face was an isosceles triangle (apex down), the hieroglyph for Water, and the nose was a similar triangle (apex up) at its center, the hieroglyph for Fire. At the base of the larger triangle was the symbol H, or the

Greek ETA, indicating the universal Spirit—the mouth. Above, to the left and right, were the symbols for the Sun and the Moon—the eyes. Below was the cross placed on a globe (the double hieroglyph of mercury and sulfur, active and passive) radiating vertical lines—the beard. Thus, the Baphomet may be seen as an alchemical, Hermetic symbol and, equally important, as authorities have pointed out, a Manichaean one.

7.

The Manichaean relation is significant. In this regard—apart from the Templars, who in some sense constitute a "Knighthood of the Light"—mention should be also be made of the Cathars, most explicit transmitters of the Manichaean tradition. Rudolf Steiner makes the connection clear in his lecture on the Manicheans in *The Temple Legend.*

In this cycle, given synchronously with the formation of the Cognitive-Ritual Section, Steiner's focus in *The Temple Legend* is the relationship of Theosophy (Anthroposophy) to the esoteric stream represented by Freemasonry. In the process, he links Manichaeism as "a mighty spiritual current" to the medieval Albigensians, Waldenses, and Cathars as well as to the Templars and Goethe—and to Anthroposophy itself. Freemasonry, he says (according to Mathilde Scholl's abbreviated notes), belongs to this stream, though, as he puts it, "through an extraordinary concatenation of circumstances," it "united with the Rosicrucians." Two years later, in *An Esoteric Cosmology,* he attributes "Christian esotericism" as such—Anthroposophy itself—to Manichaeism and its founder Mani, who considered himself an incarnation of the Holy Spirit. Therefore, not surprisingly, the cycle of *The Temple Legend* follows the evolution, or progressive realization, of human freedom expressed through individual conscience, responsibility, and creativity. Thus, it begins on Pentecost as the festival of "Christ"—His Spirit, the Holy Spirit, who is quintessentially the free spirit, the spirit of freedom—"in us."

Against this background, Steiner turns to Manichaeism. He calls it "a more important spiritual current than Rosicrucianism." In his words, "Mani's intention was to create a spiritual current which goes beyond the Rosicrucian current, which leads further than Rosicrucianism." Manichaeism does so because it flows over into the next epoch, the Sixth Epoch, helping to create it. Mani himself, called "the widow's son—a key term in Freemasonry, later applied to Hiram Abiff—was born in Lower Mesopotamia, present-day Iraq, in 216 C.E. and died, after being tortured, in 277. As for the designation "widow's son," Steiner explains:

> In all esoteric teachings, the soul was always known as the "mother; the instructor was the "father." Father and mother, Osiris and Isis, are the two forces present in the soul. Osiris, the instructor, represents the divine that flows directly into the human being. The soul itself, Isis, is the one who conceives, receives the divine into itself. She is the mother. [But then, in the course of evolution] the father withdraws. The soul is widowed. Humanity is thrown back onto itself. It must find the light of truth within its own soul to act as its own guide. Therefore, Mani calls the feminine element ... no longer confronted by the divine fructifier, the "widow." And thus he calls himself "the widow's son."

At twelve, Mani received the first of a series of calls from his angel, which he called his "inseparable" twin. This was his Higher Self, or "I," his true identity in and as "the Holy Spirit," which he was able to access or incarnate while on Earth. In this state or from this being—his higher or cosmic self united with the divine Human—Mani was to learn the secrets of creation and evolution.

The greatest of these secrets concerned the Light and the Darkness—good and evil. At the beginning of creation, as a consequence of the Creator's experiencing a moment of doubt, the Spirits of Darkness came into being and sought to invade the Kingdom of Light. They reached the very borders of the kingdom but failed to enter and remained there, poised and ready. They had to be removed—"punished." But how was the Creator, who knew only goodness, to act in such a circumstance? His Kingdom of the Light knew only goodness and love. With what could it punish? There was no "evil" or violence in it. The Kingdom of the Light—the Spirits of the Light—had therefore only one choice: to give themselves wholly to the darkness in love. So they took a part of their own kingdom and embraced the darkness, merging and mixing with it. The result was a mixed kingdom, of interpenetrated light and darkness, in which a leaven was at work, a ferment of light waiting to be released. Creation followed—a whirling dance of light and darkness, evolving into a materialized world, containing death. Again, danger loomed, for unless death and darkness could be overcome, creation would ultimately destroy itself. What to do? In response, the Light created humanity in its image and likeness and sent it forth to Earth, to the mixed kingdom of light and darkness, life and death, to separate the light from the darkness through its own being—through love and forgiveness freely given in individual acts of responsible conscience. "The profound thought here," Rudolf Steiner says, "is that the kingdom of darkness has to be overcome by the kingdom of light, not by means of punishment, but by gentleness, mildness, meekness; not by resisting evil, but by uniting with it, in order to redeem evil as such. Because a part of the light enters into evil, the evil itself is overcome."

Mani's complex vision includes a vibrant, imaginal, dramatic cosmology of spiritual beings. At its heart lies the greatness of humanity as a divine spark connected to—and in potential identity with—the archetypal or primal Humanity. As such, humans were created as beings of light, given the mission to aid the divine in the illumination of the world of matter, just as Steiner speaks of humanity's mission to turn wisdom—the sparks in creation—into love so that the Earth may become a Sun. That is to say, for the Manichean, the world as we see it is spiritual: it is light, but mixed with darkness. The Sun, the stars, and the Earth—all were spiritual. The task of the Manichean was to engage every perception, every thought, every feeling, and every cognition and through love—the only means available to the Good, the divine spark—to overcome the darkness, transform it, and release the spark of divinity.

Mani's mission was to bring this reality into the world. He saw himself as the universal successor to Zoroaster, Buddha, and Christ as well as to certain Gnostics and to Enoch, Shem, and Saint Paul. Mani incorporated the essential teachings of these pasts into his enchristed universal teaching, permeating them with the Holy Spirit, the Anthropic "I."

"The writings, wisdoms, apocalypses, parables, and psalms of the earlier churches are from all parts united in my church to the wisdom which I have revealed to you," he wrote. "As a river is joined to another river to form a powerful current, just so are the ancient books joined in my writings; they form one great wisdom, such as has not existed in preceding generations."

For Rudolf Steiner, "Mani is the one who prepares that stage in human soul development when human beings will seek for their own soul-spirit light." This is the sovereignty of conscience—the divine spark. Steiner says that all that comes from Mani is an appeal to our own spirit light of soul and, at the same time, a rebellion against anything that does not conform to our own conscience. He sets Mani very high and connects him with a series of important incarnations, beginning with the profoundest element of Egypt—what he calls the "Hermetic Initiation." He tells us that it was the individuality of Mani who, as the Disciple of Sais, lifted the veil of the statue of Isis, which no mortal had ever done. This individuality next incarnated as one of the Three Magi, Caspar, who came from Africa and presented the infant Jesus with myrrh, the symbol of death and resurrection. Soon afterward he died, to be reborn again almost immediately as the son of the Widow of Nain, whom Christ raised from the dead (Luke 7:11-15). Then, in the fourth century, Steiner tells us that a counsel of initiates (including Skythianos, Zoroaster, and the one who in that age reflected the Buddha) gathered around the Mani individuality, who was the greatest of those present, according to Steiner. Their task was to determine how the wisdom of the pre-Christian ages could flow once again into human evolution. Before this could truly begin to happen, another incarnation was required.

Mani was born as the historical Parzival, who comes to Christ through his own inner forces. His is a Sophianic initiation. Before he can learn to ask the Fisher King Amfortas "What ails thee?" he himself must become the question. He must learn that what ails Amfortas ails him too, and everyone else: there is no separation between human beings. Parzival thus learns to become his brother's keeper, the keeper of the Earth and stars, because he knows that he is all of these: one body, one substance, one spirit, all responsible for all. He learns this from inborn womanhood—the Isis-Sophia being, represented by all the female characters, who teaches him the transformational power of grief, faith or radical openness, love, and reverence. Finally, it is Mani who, in 1459, initiated Christian Rosenkreutz and orchestrated the pouring into him of the now Christened wisdom of the Rishis and the ancient sages of our present earth phase.

From this picture, we can sense the spirit of Mani (in all its manifestations, including the Parzival Grail) casting a light over the evolution of consciousness with the experience of the "I," achieved through a purification of the soul and giving rise to a new heart's sense that "love conquers all"—a radical openness to the divinity of the "other." We can see it also in the development of the idea of "natural law," which asserts the universality of humanity. Thus, every human being is made in the image and likeness of God, and the Earth and its fruits are given in common to all humanity, to humanity as a whole and to every human being in his or her place. These are "the common possession of all things and the identical liberty of all" from which follow universal human rights and the duty of each to care for all (particularly the poor, the less fortunate), to respect all, to be responsible for all. All this flows into the great channel of Freemasonry—and Anthroposophy.

8.

Besides guild masonry and the Manichaean stream, mention should also be made, before reaching the sea change represented by the Renaissance, of alchemy. Alchemy is the primordial, initiative, and mystery science, at once natural and supernatural, of the redemption of matter, fallen with humanity and hence only redeemable with it. Derived from the most ancient revelations, alchemy—as the dual process of the spiritualization of matter and the materialization of spirit—is present and recognizably kin in all civilizations, including China and India. Reaching the West through Egypt and passing into the Hellenistic world and thence into Islam, it entered medieval Christendom sometime before 1182 C.E., the date of the translation of Morienus's *Testament of Alchemy*, the first Islamic alchemical text to be translated. Once arrived, alchemy underwent a rapid process of re-imagination (reinterpretation) and transformation to become the "sacred science" par excellence of Christianity—the cosmological and metaphysical universalization of the celebration of the Mass, the magnum opus of the Mystery of Golgotha. In the words of one commentator, Maurice Aniane: "The true role of the alchemist was to celebrate analogically a mass whose species were not only bread and wine, but also all of nature in its entirety." As such, from its beginnings, alchemy permeated every aspect of medieval spiritual culture, from its buildings and artworks to its cosmology, theology, and metaphysics—as it was to continue to do into the Renaissance and beyond, up to and including Anthroposophy, which, in a sense, is alchemy for our time.

And yet alchemy has always been difficult to find. Its "esoteric" nature—the fact that only those who have done the requisite inner development can experience its realities and understand its principles—makes it difficult to trace. There is also the fact that, while the processes are universal, each alchemist's experiences are individual and unique. Nevertheless, the evidence of its early ubiquity in the currents that flow into Freemasonry is difficult to refute. Texts proliferate throughout the Middle Ages, and the greatest medieval thinkers—Albertus Magnus, Thomas Aquinas, Raymond Lully, Roger Bacon, and others—address the subject. Above all, its symbolism is in the great mason-built cathedrals, in the dwellings of philosophers, among the Templars, in the Grail, and, indeed, everywhere.

9.

Thus we reach the Renaissance, which may be said to have begun with the journey to Italy from Misra in Greece of the octogenarian sage and initiate Giorgio Gemistos, known as "Plethon" because he was thought to be the reincarnation of Plato. A larger-than-life figure, Plethon effectively transformed European culture. He came as adviser to the Orthodox delegation to the last ecumenical Council of Florence/Ferrara in 1438-1439. Although Plethon spent some time at the council, he spent most of his time with Cosimo de Medici. Convinced that there was a universal Cosmic Solar Religion going back to primordial times and uniting all religions, he fired Cosimo with the idea of a lineage of ancient theologians reaching back into prehistory. His version began with Zoroaster, Hermes, and Orpheus, and included Eumolpus (legendary founder of the Eleusinian Mysteries), Min (or Misraim, first king of Egypt), Minos, Numa, and even the Brahmans of India, the Magi of the Medes, the Druids of Ireland, and many others—ending with Pythagoras, Plato, and the Neoplatonic philosophers.

At the same time, as if by some miraculous coincidence, Plethon happened to be traveling with a trunk of ancient texts unknown in Europe. It seemed that he had with him not only the entire wisdom of Greece but also that of Egypt and ancient Persia! Bit by bit, Plethon lent Cosimo these texts to read. The result was that, almost beside himself with excitement, Cosimo "conceived in his noble mind a kind of Academy" and, about 1450, asked the son of his favorite doctor to organize it and start translating the texts of the ancient theologians Plethon had provided. Thus the Platonic Academy of Florence came into being, and Marsilio Ficino initiated his epoch-making translations, beginning with the Egyptian wisdom of *Corpus Hermeticum* and the *Chaldean Oracles* (attributed to Zoroaster) and including the complete works of Plato, Plotinus, Iamblichus, Porphyry, Proclus, and others.

Plethon's influence was enormous: Paracelsus and Renaissance alchemy, Columbus (who sailed with a map inspired by Plethon), Nicholas of Cusa (initiated into "divine ignorance" on a sea voyage from Greece, on which, providentially, he met Plethon on his way to Florence), Giovanni Pico della Mirandola (the founder of Christian Kabbalah and the author of the celebrated "Oration on the Dignity of Man"), the magus and proto-Rosicrucian John Dee, as well as Giordano Bruno, the Rosicrucians and, indeed, Freemasonry itself are unthinkable without his mission.

It was Plethon who publicly introduced the project of the Christianization of ancient wisdom. Plethon pushed the idea of ecumenicism to the bounds of heresy, upholding the universality of all forms. His position was, to adapt a current slogan, "to think religion globally and embody it locally." At the same time, he provided a symbolic language, centered on fire as the omnipresent all-luminous substance, pure luminescent Spirit, the nature and source of all created things. All things were filled with tongues of flame, descended from a single fire, the quintessence and medium of all magic and of alchemy.

The consequences of this initiation were far reaching. Nevertheless, generally speaking, what Plethon achieved built upon what flowed from the Middle Ages. Yet mention should be made of still one other consequence of the "Plethonic" revolution: the reinforcement of the theurgic, or magical, aspect of ritual. What it reinforced, of course, was the Christian Mass, with its incantatory words of consecration, music, incense, lights, and wine, culminating in the supreme magical act of the transubstantiation of the Eucharistic host. The Mass was, in a sense, always the model and archetype of ritual and initiation in the West (and, later, because of this, always a problem for Freemasonry), but prior to this moment it had been held apart as beyond comparison.

Plethon's teaching and the translation and the availability of Hermetic and Neoplatonic texts on magic and theurgy—such as Proclus's *On Sacrifice and Magic*, Iamblichus's *On the Mysteries of the Egyptians*, and the *Corpus Hermeticum*—changed the situation. The Mass remained privileged, but its layers of meaning could be seen as infinitely expandable. At the highest level, then, alchemists could begin to conceive their work as priestly: celebrating a species of Mass in which the host was not just bread and wine but nature as a whole. At the same time, the Renaissance "Mages," learning to live in a universe filled with spiritual, cosmic, astral, planetary, and other beings, developed complex ways of ritually interacting with them that ran the gamut from music, song, incense, herbs, stones, and talismans to explicit practices of ritual magic.

10.

Rosicrucianism lands on the historical stage in 1614 with the publication of the *Fama Fraternitatis*, or "Report" announcing the Brotherhood of the most praiseworthy Order of the R.C. Written in German and "Addressed to the Learned in General and to the Governors of Europe," the document called for scholars, scientists, artists, and mystics to unite in the cause of a "general reformation of things divine and human." Two more texts followed: the *Confessio Fraternitatis* and *The Chemical Wedding of Christian Rosenkreutz*, which made clear the alchemical, Hermetic foundation of the movement. The result was a fury of activity calling for a "general reformation" or great transformation of all aspects of culture. This lasted for about twenty years, until the Thirty Years War put an end to the promise of a new age or deferred it to some indefinite future.

The texts told the following story. C.R.C., the founder, was born in Germany in 1378, perhaps into a Cathar household. In 1383, when he was five years old, his parents sent him to a cloister, where he learned Latin and Greek. Soon thereafter, still young and full of passion, he set forth on a pilgrimage of initiation to the Holy Sepulcher in Jerusalem. Passing through Cyprus, he came to Damascus, where the learned sages of Persia and Iraq, fleeing the Mongol invasion, had sought refuge. So many saints, philosophers, alchemists, and physicians were gathered there that Rosenkreutz gave up the idea of going to Jerusalem and decided instead to stay and learn Arabic. After three years of study, he moved to Damcar in Arabia, where he translated into Latin the *Book M* (*Mundus*, World). There he met with many scientists, astrologers, theologians, and mathematicians—which sounds like the Ikhwan al-Safa. Accepting this story at face value and remembering that the Templars may likewise have met with the Brethren of Purity and studied their summa of the sacred sciences in fifty-two epistles, we may assume some connection between the two manifestations.

After great inward transformation and much learning, especially in the "transmutation of metals" (alchemy), C.R. finally turned toward home, passing by Egypt and Fez in North Africa. Wherever he went, he continued to meet with the local sages, who initiated him into their wisdom. Arriving at last in Europe, he sought to gather around him scholars and scientists to transmit what he had learned. Failing to do so in Spain, he returned to Germany, where, after a while, he began to teach. He formed an order of eight brothers. Together, they created a universal symbolic language, healed the sick, and built a house called Sancti Spiritus (Holy Spirit). When the time was right, the eight then dispersed to continue their research and spread the word. For this purpose they agreed to the following "Rules":

1. To have no other profession than to cure the sick, and that *gratis*
2. To wear no special attire, but to conform to the customs of the land
3. To meet every year at Christmas in the house Sancti Spiritus;
4. To find a successor to take their place after they died
5. To take the word C.R. as "their seal, mark and character"
6. To remain secret for one hundred years.

One hundred and twenty years after his death, as Christian Rosenkreutz had requested, his tomb was opened. This was in 1604. Hence, he must have died in 1484, at the age of one hundred and six. To this story, Rudolf Steiner adds a prequel. Sometime in the thirteenth century, at an unknown location, twelve initiates, who had received all ancient and contemporary wisdom, united to aid humanity and formed for that purpose a "spiritual lodge." A thirteenth then came to them as a youth and grew up under their care and instruction. Enormously gifted, delicate, and sensitive, his spiritual forces grew exponentially, and as they did so, he found himself physically wasting away. Finally, he lay as if dead. The twelve gathered around him. All the wisdom of the ages flowed from them into him. As he returned to life, it was clear from what he said that all that they had given him had been permeated with Christ—Christ filled.

Shortly thereafter the thirteenth died, soon to be reborn as C.R.C., founder of the Order of the Rosy Cross.

11.

Historically speaking, the Rosicrucian Movement represents the culmination of the impetus of Hermeticism, Christian Kabbalah, and universality set in motion by Gemistos Plethon and framed— against the background of the Reformation—by Joachim of Fiore's apocalyptic historical vision of the coming of the Age of the Spirit. Into it flowed the esoteric traditions. This then streamed together—above all in Britain—with (operative) craft masonry, which was in the process of becoming (speculative) modern Freemasonry.

12.

Again, the evidence is sparse. The story appears to begin in Scotland. The existence of Masonic lodges, used for more than storing tools, is documented from at least the fifteenth century. About a century later, in 1583, James VI of Scotland (also James I of Great Britain) appointed William Schaw to be Master of the Work and Warden General with the commission of reorganizing the Masonic craft. In 1598 he issued the so-called Schaw Statutes, setting out the duties of Masons both to the lodge and to the public. In 1599, he drew up a second statute, which referred for the first time to the existence of esoteric knowledge within the craft of stone masonry and revealed the existence of a "Mother Lodge"— Kilwinning. For this reason, Schaw is therefore reputed to be the father of modern Freemasonry. Evidence of this lies in the fact that by the late sixteenth and early seventeenth centuries, men who were not masons were being admitted to the Scottish

Lodges—that is, "speculative masonry" was evolving out of its "operative" vessel.

It is also known that the Scottish Masonic lodges were aware of the Rosicrucian texts. A manuscript translation exists that is dated 1633, done by a collector of alchemical texts, Lord Balcarres, whose daughter married Sir Robert Moray, who had been initiated into the Lodge of Edinburgh in 1641 and designed an elaborate mason's mark (a pentagram) for himself. Moray later became the patron of Thomas Vaughan, who published the first English translation in 1652 and was also one of the founders of the Royal Society. In the same vein of vague connections, the earliest reference to the "mason's word" is also connected to Rosicrucianism:

> For we be Brethren of the *Rosie Crosse*,
> We have the *Mason Word* and second sight.

In England the first clear reference to Masonry (which probably migrated from Scotland) is by the antiquarian, mathematician, astrologer, and student of alchemy Elias Ashmole, who also had "Rosicrucian" aspirations. In 1646, Ashmole wrote in his diary that at 4:30 in the afternoon of October 16, he was "made a Freemason at Warrington in Lancashire." Nothing else is said, and the next mention by Ashmole is not till 1682. It is important to recognize that, though related, and mutually influencing each other through the next two centuries, the Rosicrucian and Masonic movements are by no means identical. Rosicrucianism seems to have "midwifed" modern Freemasonry and, from time to time, influenced it in the direction of Hermeticism (alchemy) and esoteric Christianity. Or, as Steiner seems sometimes to suggest, Freemasonry (a "Scoto-English" creation) was an attempt, as it were, to "steal" or co-opt the German Rosicrucian impulse from becoming the guiding spirit in the unfolding of the Consciousness Soul Epoch, which would therefore become the Anglo-Saxon rather than the Germano-Central European Epoch. The esoteric background here is vague. Speaking of the spiritual evolution of the consciousness soul, Steiner says:

To know how things stand, one must at least begin to understand this "British"—or British-tinged—occultism. This occultism is absolutely present. What people know of all sorts of high grades of Scottish Freemasonry is actually only the external side of this occultism—the side shown to the world. Comprehensive and working occult schools actually stand behind this external side. These are schools that have taken up the ancient occult traditions and the ancient occult stream to a much higher degree than is the case among similar groups in Central Europe. In Central Europe we strive more and more to allow knowledge of the spiritual world to rise up out of our own spirituality. In the British tradition, they have preferred to lean on what has been traditionally handed down from the more ancient occult schools. In fact, going back to the beginning of the seventeenth century, we find particularly in England, Scotland, and Ireland (less in Ireland *but all over Scotland*) such occult societies. In these societies, they continue to propagate ancient occult knowledge, while transforming it in a certain way....

The important thing to note is that at the beginning of the seventeenth century, a certain soul incarnated in the British Isles, who did not work outwardly in a very significant way but worked nevertheless in a most stimulating way. This person incarnated in a British body in which there was more French and Scots blood than English blood. From this soul actually came forth what gave the impulse in Britain not only for external spiritual life but also for *occult* life....

In British occult life they knew the significance of the physical body. They made the etheric body least active and regarded the physical body as an instrument of all spiritual life. Because of this, in their occult schools one could not experience very much from the spiritual world. But the ancient traditions were very well preserved. The occult schools preserved what had been handed down by ancient clairvoyance, and they sought to permeate this with concepts. Thus an occult science arose that really only worked with the experiences passed on by what had been seen by clairvoyance in the previous post-Atlantean periods. In these schools, they penetrated what had originated in clairvoyance with purely physical concepts derived from thinking with the physical body. In this way, an actual occult science arose that covered all domains of life.

13.

Besides Ashmole, other references throughout the century contribute to the general impression that speculative Masonry (quite apart from the Rosicrucian connection) was on the rise: one Randle Holms III reports being "made" a Mason in a lodge in Chester in 1665, while Robert Plot's *Natural History of Staffordshire* (1686) mentions the "Society of Free-Masons" spread all over the nation. In the same year, John Aubrey, in his *Lives*, refers to the Fraternity of Adopted Masons or Freemasons.

By 1717 Freemasonic activity had increased to the point that four London lodges, made up of craftsmen and merchants, none of very high standing, assembled on June 24, Saint John's Day, at the Goose and Gridiron Ale-House in Saint Paul's Churchyard to form a Grand Lodge. From such modest beginnings, modern Freemasonry dates. There was a tradition of clubs, groups of friends meeting for pleasure, with drink and song prominent in their activities and perhaps some serious conversation and ritual thrown in. This social aspect certainly played (and continued to play) a role. But something more serious was also afoot. They elected a Grand Master, chose symbolism based on the mason's craft—compass, square, and so on—and added an element of secrecy (and a "secret" history.) About the first Grand Master, Antony Sayer, little is known. The second, George Payne, began to establish rules and standards and to research the early history of Masonry and the Old Constitutions. General Regulations were produced, manuscripts began to be collected, but no comprehensive account of the craft emerged.

The third Grand Master, The Reverend John Theophilus Desaguliers, was more impressive. A lawyer, medical doctor, mathematician, chaplain to the Prince of Wales, a fellow of the Royal Society and its curator and demonstrator, and a minor celebrity for his lectures on Newtonian science, Desaguliers transformed the range of Masonry. Scientists, enlightened minds of all kinds, and, above all, the aristocracy now began to take an interest. A Scottish clergyman, James Anderson, was commissioned to revise the constitutions. This he did (though how much was his and to what extent he was simply carrying out Desaguliers's enlightenment agenda is unknown). Published in 1723, the *Constitutions* contained the first account of the legendary prehistory of Masonry as well as "New" Charges, the first of which read:

> A *Mason* is oblig'd by his tenure to obey the moral Law; and if he rightly understands the Art, he will never be a stupid Atheist or an irreligious Libertine. But though in ancient Times Masons were charged in every country to be of the Religion of that Country or Nation, whatever it was, yet 'tis now thought more expedient only to oblige them to that Religion in which all Men agree, leaving their particular Opinions to themselves; that is, to be *good* Men *and true,* or Men of Honor and Honesty, by whatever Denominations or Persuasions they may be distinguish'd; whereby Masonry becomes the *Center of Union,* and the means of conciliating true Friendship among Persons that must have remain'd at a perpetual distance.

Three points stand out in this apparently innocuous statement. First, Freemasonry has a moral basis. At some level, when it began, it was a kind of "ethical culture" club. Second, as with the second Rosicrucian law ("To wear no special attire, but to conform to the customs of the land"), the Mason is bound to no particular "religion" but only to "the religion in which all men agree," that is, belief in a Supreme Being, whatever form that might take. Third, as it "conciliates true friendship" among those at a distance, it is potentially international, if not global. Here we see the potentially political implications of Masonry in the age of the absolute State.

We may also note a certain tension between Christ and Freemasonry that continues up to the present. "The religion in which all men agree" implies a "Deist" or Unitarian piety, rather than a Trinitarian (Christ-conscious, if not Christ-centered) Christianity. There were practical reasons for this. Then, as now, the Incarnation seemed to pose insurmountable difficulties for universalism. If you wished to unite people of different religious convictions, what choice did you have? Everyone could agree upon the vague notion of a "higher power." At the same time, one can justifiably suspect a kind of capitulation to scientism in this posture. The great Newton (and many members of the international scientific fraternity were Deists. To admit the Incarnation as a scientific reality would—at the very least—have rendered the growing paradigm of modern science invalid. The contrast with Rosicrucianism—*Ex Deo Nascimur, In Christo Morimur, Per Spiritum Sanctum Reviviscimus*—could not be more different and indicates where Steiner stands on this question. As he put it in the title of a well-known lecture, "Christianity began as a religion but it is greater than a religion." The deed of Christ on Golgotha is for the Earth and all humanity: it is a divine-cosmic, universally transformative, creative and ongoing act.

In Anderson's history, Masonry becomes the repository of humanity's moral and scientific genius. He traces Masonic history from Adam, the first Mason, who was created in the image of "the Great Architect of the Universe" and had the Seven Liberal Arts—and especially geometry—inscribed in his heart. Thereafter, all the great figures throughout the ages from the Old Testament through Greece and Rome and the Middle Ages are described as Masons, Master Masons, and Grand Masters! However absurd this might sound today, it was quite restrained compared with what would follow.

14.

Soon the movement spread, taking root in France in 1725-1730. It grew rapidly—a Grand Lodge was founded in the 1730s, becoming in 1773 the Grand Orient de France. As Freemasonry changed, the Grand Orient changed. Whereas in England, Masonry had an egalitarian and ethical emphasis, in France mystical, esoteric, and chivalric themes began to predominate, highlighting a tension in the movement from the beginning. On the one hand, in defiance of nationalism, sectarianism, and dogmatism, all human beings were brothers united in a common devotion to "the Great Architect of Universe." Here Masonry promoted democracy and tolerance. On the other hand, Masonry also endorsed the belief in an ancient wisdom tradition, handed down by initiates and embodied in secret rites and symbols, accessible only to an elite. This dichotomy, which developed within the first twenty years, would run through Freemasonry throughout the next two centuries. Underlying this dichotomy was another: in the premodern period all the currents feeding into Freemasonry, including that of operative (Pythagorean) masonry, were concerned primarily with the "Great Work" of the moral, spiritual, and psychological inner development and perfection of the *individual*; with the Freemasonic turn into the modern age, the emphasis shifted to the social and collective, to *humanity*—in other words, to the evolution of consciousness, rather than individual perfection. This led to confusion at many levels, as individual perfection increasingly took a secondary place to social and political considerations.

At the same time, two changes occurred. First, there was the esoteric legend of Hiram Abiff, architect of Solomon's Temple—a "secret known to the Rosicrucians" according to Rudolf Steiner. Whether Anderson, Desaguliers, or someone else introduced this founding myth is unknown. It must have occurred sometime between the first edition of Anderson's *Constitutions* (1723), where it remains unmentioned, and the second edition (1738), where it plays a considerable role. "When the legend of Hiram's death was first incorporated into our older traditions is not easy to decide," according to the Masonic historian Robert Speke Gould, "but in my judgment it must have taken place between 1723 and 1729." The first reference is 1730 by Samuel Prichard, whose *Masonry Dissected* revealed the rituals for the first time. Previously, the founding story had involved Noah.

Prichard, referring to Hiram as "Grand Master Hiram" tells the stories of both Noah and Hiram. According to Prichard, the order was founded with the building of the Tower of Babel, handed down by Euclid the Egyptian to Hiram, Master Mason of King Solomon. Generally speaking, however, in Masonic literature, no origin for Hiram exists. Among other attributions, it has been purported to be a true story, a retelling of the Osiris legend, or an allegory of Adam's expulsion from Paradise, of the death of Abel, of the death of Christ, of resurrection in general, and of the persecution of Templars. Confirming Rudolf Steiner's conviction of a Rosicrucian origin, there is the idea put forward by Johann Gottlieb Buhle in his Historico-Critical Inquiry into the Origins of the Rosicrucians and Freemasons (1804), which Steiner probably knew, that "older Freemasons" (i.e., Rosicrucians) had an acronym, H.I.R.A.M: Homo Iesus Redemptor Animorum (Human Jesus Redeemer of Souls.)

Second, there is the famous *Oration* (1737) in Paris of the Scot Andrew Michael ("Chevalier") Ramsay, who, uniting a chivalric (Templar) origin in connection with Scotland, gave rise to the idea of "Higher Grades," which would in turn create the split between "blue" Masonry, with its craft degrees, and "red," so-called Scottish, preponderantly chivalric Masonry with mystical, esoteric degrees, based on an elaboration of the story of Hiram Abiff's death and extending far beyond the craft degrees. Further complicating the picture, interacting with red Masonry were various esoteric currents represented by such figures as Martines de Pasqually, founder of the "Elect Cohens" and his disciple, the Unknown Philosopher, Louis Claude de Saint- Martin, frequently invoked by Rudolf Steiner, following whom "Martinism" arose.

In his *Oration*, Ramsay stated 1) that the ancestors of the Masons were the Crusaders and that the Order had been established in the Holy Land; 2) that its purpose was to unite individuals of every nation into a brotherhood, both to rebuild the temples in Jerusalem and to bring about a return to the true principles of Sacred Architecture; 3) that the Order was also somehow connected with the ancient Mysteries of Demeter, Isis, Athena, and

Artemis; 4) that the bond of union went back to the ancient religion of Noah; 5) that therefore the Order was being restored, rather than founded; 6) that they agreed upon certain words and secret signs by which to recognize each other and adopted symbolical ceremonies for initiation; 7) that as the Crusades waned, they returned to their several countries and established lodges there; and that 8) in this manner the Mother Lodge of Kilwinning in Scotland came into being in 1286.

In the half century following Ramsay, Freemasonry proliferated in both orders and grades, spreading into Germany and eastward into Central Europe, as well as south into Italy and Spain. In Germany, for instance, following the first recorded lodge in Hamburg in 1737, Masonic and Para-Masonic rites proliferated luxuriantly. By the 1750s there were lodges all over Germany—but without a central single authority. For a time, the so-called Strict Observance, founded in the 1760s by Baron Hund dominated the scene. But there were many other manifestations, including the "Golden and Rosy Cross" and other Rosicrucian-inspired orders, some of which seem to have predated Masonry as such.

Thus, the first century of Freemasonry presents a massive, complex history, filled with fascinating figures, many of whom are worth further study. The task of this introduction, however, having outlined something of the nature of Freemasonry, is to look at why Rudolf Steiner might have chosen the Memphis-Misraim Rite—that is, a stream with an apparently "Egyptian" emphasis rather than, say, a Rosicrucian, Alchemical, or Templar one.

Certainly, Egypt, as the font of wisdom, has always been a name to conjure with. Egyptomania in this sense is not a new thing. The ancient Greeks already had it. For Pythagoras and Plato, Egypt was the source of what they knew, as it was in some measure for Israel also. Moses, legend had it, if he was not actually an Egyptian, certainly learned from his captors. The same was often thought to be true of the other compilers and authors of the Old Testament itself, which was thus also seen as a transformation of Egyptian wisdom. Hellenistic times likewise unfolded, as it were, within a Hermetic, Egyptian frame. The trend continued somewhat into the Middle Ages, but much diluted and with little to go on, in the form of either texts or common knowledge. But all that changed with the Renaissance, which, as the historian Frances Yates and others have now shown, represented not so much a rebirth of classical (Greek and Roman) learning as an infusion of a more ancient teaching, especially Egyptian and Hermetic. All this accords with the ideas of Rudolf Steiner, for whom our own historical moment echoes and repeats at a higher level the Egyptian cultural epoch. What humanity experienced in Egyptian times—that humanity is a cosmic organ—rises today as an unconscious memory in humanity.

15.

"Egyptian Masonry" is another tangled tale, confusing an already confused picture. Jean, l'Abbé Terrasson, in his novel *Sethos* (1731), as well as the Chevalier Ramsay, in his novel *Cyrus* (1727), had already suggested a Pharoanic filiation for speculative Masonry. Before that, Christian Rosenkreutz had included Egypt on his "noble travels." In *Oedipus Aegyptianicus* (1652-1655), the Jesuit Athanasius Kircher, the "master of a hundred arts," claiming to be able to read hieroglyphs and stating that Adam spoke ancient Egyptian and that Hermes Trismegistus was Moses, initiated the esoteric study of Egypt as the primal source of all wisdom. Thus "Egyptosophy" was born and increased in influence throughout the eighteenth century (culminating perhaps in Napoleon's military expedition in 1798-1799, which brought back to Europe, among other priceless artifacts, the Rosetta Stone). By the 1760s various treaties on Egyptian initiation were circulating.

But the story really begins with the enigmatic and mysterious Joseph Balsamo, known, among other names, as Alexander Cagliostro (1743-1795), "the best abused and most hated man in Europe." Whether Cagliostro was, in fact, Joseph Balsamo, however, remains an open question. Madame Blavatsky thought he was not. In his *Memoirs*, he claims to know neither the names of his parents (having been left an orphan at the age of three months) nor where he was born. He had been told Malta, but his earliest memories were of the holy city of Medina, where he was called Acharat and lived in the palace of the Mufti. There, though the outward religion conformed to Islam, "the *true* religion" was imprinted in his heart. Attached to him, as a servant, was an adept, Althotas. When he was twelve, having learned many languages and received instruction in various sciences, he and Althotas left Medina for Mecca. They stayed there a number of years. On the day of his departure, the Sherif (in whose palace they had lived) famously remarked, "Nature's Unfortunate Child, adieu." Althotas, still according to the *Memoirs*, then accompanied Cagliostro to Egypt and other distant mystic points for further initiations, until they finally arrived in Malta, where Althotas died and legend, to a degree, becomes history. Thus legends arise:

> I am of no time and no place. Outside time and space, my spiritual being lives its eternal existence. If I immerse my thought going back through the course of the ages, if I spread by spirit toward a mode of existence far distant from what you perceive, then I become what I desire. Consciously participating in absolute being, I regulate my actions according to the milieu that surrounds me. My name is my function, and I choose it, as I do my function, because I am free. My country is wherever I am....
>
> Here I am: noble and a traveler. I speak, and your soul shudders to recognize ancient words. A voice in you that has been silent for a long time responds to my words. I act and peace returns to your hearts, health to your bodies, hope and courage to your souls. All human beings are my siblings. All countries are dear to me. I travel everywhere, so that everywhere the spirit can descend and find a way to you.

An initiate, a "Noble Traveler" (the rank has Rosicrucian overtones) like the Comte de Saint Germaine, with whom he was associated and whose student he was even reputed to be, Cagliostro has been reviled as a charlatan, a rogue, and general trickster. He was the last person to die a prisoner of the Inquisition. This is perhaps the price initiates must pay—to be mocked and arbitrarily denigrated by the establishment. Witness Thomas Carlyle:

> Count Alessandro di Cagliostro, Pupil of the Sage Althotas, Foster-Child of the Sherif of Mecca, probable Son of the last King of Trebizond; named also Acharat and Unfortunate Child of Nature; by profession healer of diseases, abolisher of wrinkles, friend of the poor and impotent, grand master of the Egyptian Mason-lodge of High Science, Spirit- summoner, Gold-cook, Grand Cophta, Prophet, Priest, and thaumaturgic moralist and swindler; really a Liar of the first magnitude, thorough-paced in all provinces of lying, what one may call the King of Liars.

Giuseppe (Joseph) Balsamo appears to have been born in Palermo, Sicily, in 1743. (Forty-four years later, Goethe, visiting Palermo, looked up his family tree and thought Cagliostro important enough to dedicate ten pages of his *Italian Journey* to him—pages that Steiner would have known well.) Educated first at the Seminary of Saint Roch at Palermo, he proved too much for the good fathers (he ran away often) and was transferred to the Convent of the Benfratelli at Cartagirone. He was given the task of novice assistant in the apothecary, where his superior, Father Alberto, a master chemist, initiated him into the mysteries of alchemy. Cagliostro, barely a teenager, thus learned how to distil and sublimate, to make tinctures and medicines, and he heard for the first time about the Philosopher's Stone. But his wild nature again proved too much, and soon he found himself working as an artist and dreaming of becoming an alchemist on the streets of Palermo. He stayed there until about the age of seventeen, when he found his way to Messina. There, legend goes, he met the great Hermetic—and, some say, Manichaean—adept Althotas (according to Eliphas Levi, "Messenger of Thoth"), who took him to Egypt. This was the first leg on a pilgrimage of knowledge, echoing the Templar connections and similar to that of Christian Rosenkreutz. Whatever the factual basis of any of this story, they (or Joseph Balsamo at least) finally reached Malta, where they visited Althotas's great friend, Manuel Pinto de Fonseca, the Grand Master of the Knights of Malta.

According to some sources, on this first visit to Malta (1766-1767), Cagliostro worked closely with Pinto in his alchemical laboratory. If, when, and where he achieved the Great Work is unknown. Possibly, he also became a Freemason, being initiated into the Lodge of Saint John of Scotland of the Secret and the Harmony. The question arises because he was also initiated in London in 1777 into the Rite of the Strict Templar Observance. In any case, a certain Chevalier Luigi d'Aquino of Naples, the brother of the Grand Master of Neapolitan Masonry and a member of the Naples Secret and Harmony Lodge, was in the habit of visiting Malta during this period and brought back to Naples a mysterious series of three very high grades apparently inspired by Egypto-Hellenistic Hermetism—the Arcana Arcanorum. These were later integrated into the Misraim Rite, whether by him or someone else is not known. One source has him doing so as early as 1788, which would more or less make him a founder of the Misraim Rite. In any event, on one of these visits, d'Aquino met Cagliostro and invited him to travel to Naples with him, where he initiated him into the Arcana Arcanorum.

After a period in Italy, Cagliostro began to travel: England, Holland, Germany, France, Russia, and back and around again. Wherever he went, he went as a Freemason as well as a wizard. He frequented the highest grades, accumulating initiations and meeting the most initiated, the greatest, including Sainte Germaine. Scandal, surprise, wonders, healings, and wisdom accompanied him. Alchemist, thaumaturgist, political revolutionary, and perhaps in some measure charlatan, Cagliostro was a force to be reckoned with. The years leading up to the French Revolution were difficult times for the absolutist states. Democracy, republicanism, the sanctity and freedom of the individual were stirring. Cagliostro stood at the forefront of the movement of consciousness for progressive social change. In his Letter to the French People (1786), he denounced all abuses of power, expressed anger against the queen and hatred for those in power, and prophesied the demolition of the Bastille, a General Assembly, the suppression of Orders under the King's private seal: in a word, he anticipated the French Revolution, although he hoped it would be peaceful and transpire patiently and prudently. Notwithstanding, he was declared a public danger.

16.

Cagliostro founded "Egyptian Masonry" on December 24, 1784, in Lyon, France. (Evidence, however, exists that for several years previously, beginning in 1778, he had been teaching the Rite. Lyon was a hotbed of Masonic activity. Martinism, mesmerism, and Swedenborgianism were all practiced. Louis Claude de Saint-Martin himself was there. When Cagliostro arrived, everyone rushed to meet him. There was a whirlwind of discussion, much exchange of ideas. The magus taught and did healings. The dead appeared. He demonstrated clairvoyance and practiced mesmerism (hypnotism). Lyon was at his feet.

Cagliostro accepted students. With twelve fellow Masons, he founded Mother Lodge Wisdom Triumphant. He agreed to renew Masonry—by returning it to its Egyptian sources—and announced the catechism and rituals of Egyptian Masonry, promising physical, soul, and spiritual regeneration. He would be the Grand Cophta. Cagliostro asserted that the tradition stemmed from Enoch and Elijah (Elias) and taught that the Philosopher's Stone was no fable and that humanity could regain its innocence, forfeited by Adam at the Fall. Women were admitted, and the Lodge was dedicated to Saint John. The power to command angels was promised. All religions were tolerated: a belief in God was the sole condition of initiation. In the words of one historian, "Cagliostro's Rite certainly far surpassed all previous systems in its richness, its initiatory and theurgic capacity through the practice of alchemy and the search for spiritual immortality, although it was however Egyptian only in name."

In 1789 Cagliostro tried to introduce his Rite in Rome, perhaps seeking recognition and acceptance from the Roman Catholic

Church. This act of folly led to his imprisonment by the Inquisition, in whose jails he died a martyr in 1795. His "Egyptian Masonry" endured a few more years under his successor, the second Grand Cophta, François de Chefdebien d'Armissan (1753-1814), after which it apparently disappeared. But the idea did not die. Others began to defend the Egyptian origins of Freemasonry, and rites began to proliferate.

17.

The actual Memphis-Misraim Rite begins with the story of the Misraim Rite. The word itself has levels of meaning. In the Old Testament, the founding ancestor of the Egyptians is Misraim, the second son of Ham. This Misraim, according to the history of the Order, worshipped under the names of Osiris, Adonis, or Seraphis and known to profane history as Menes, was the legendary first king of Egypt. From this Misraim, then, the order was said to derive. It begins in Italy, perhaps in Venice in 1788 in Socinian (anti-Trinitarian, rationalist) circles under Cagliostro's influence and patent. (Sir Martin Folkes [1690-1754], a British antiquarian, high Mason, and president of the Royal Society, apparently founded a lodge in Rome in about 1740, which was called Misraim, thus asserting the Judeo-Egyptian provenance of Masonic initiation.) From Venice, it appears to have spread rapidly to Milan, Genoa, and Naples, arriving and developing in France in 1810-1815. The first historically attested Lodge was founded in Paris by the Bédarride brothers, who came of an old family of Sephardic Jews from Cavaillon (between Aix-en-Provence and Avignon). Members of Napoleon's military, initiated in Italy, probably in Naples, they were Masons and founded many military lodges. They would have been learned in the Talmud and the Zohar as well. Their father, Gad Bédarride, may well have met and been initiated by Cagliostro himself.

Following the establishment of the Paris Lodge, the Misraim Rite rapidly proliferated, developing a profusion of grades, leading to the distinctive and mysterious Arcana Arcanorum—secret

Hermetic, Egypto-Hellenistic teachings apparently brought from Malta to Naples by the Chevalier d'Aquino and Cagliostro around 1770. They are said to form "the whole philosophical system of the true Misraim Rite" and furnish "an extended explanation of the relationship of humanity and the divine through the mediation of celestial spirits." They are so secret, however, that nothing is known of them.

The Misraim Rite also seems to have had a politically revolutionary tenor, which led to an affiliation with the Carbonari (Italian "charcoal burners"), the Freemasonry-type secret (initiatory and revolutionary) society, originating in Naples (1808-1815) and dedicated to political freedom, following the principles of the French Revolution. The Carbonari were forerunners of the Risorgimento, the great movement of Italian cultural nationalism and political activism, into which they were gradually assimilated. Led initially (1831) by Guiseppe Mazzini and his Giovine Italia ("Young Italy"), a secret society with a republican, anticlerical program, the Risorgimento would eventually unite Italy and free it from the yoke of foreign powers. It would do so under Victor Emmanuel II of Sardinia, with the aid of Giuseppe Garibaldi.

Garibaldi, according to Rudolf Steiner's karmic research, was a key figure of modern times—a reincarnated initiate of the Hibernian Mysteries. In his account of his life and his karmic connections, however, Steiner does not mention two interesting, if perhaps minor, details. First, Madame Blavatsky had a close connection with Garibaldi (and the Carbonari). Dressed as a man, she fought alongside him and was severely wounded at the Battle of Mentana (1867). She was picked out of a ditch for dead—a near-death experience that, according to Colonel Olcott, was critical in her development. As with everything else connected to Madame Blavatsky, the details are shrouded in mystery. She kept them to herself. On one occasion, she said, "The Garibaldi alone know the whole truth.... What I did, you know partially; you do not know all." On another occasion, she said: "Whether I was *sent* there, or found myself there by accident, are questions that pertain to my private life." Second, it was Garibaldi, a Mason of high standing and a member of the Memphis Rite, who fused the two Rites—of Memphis and Misraim—becoming the honorary first Grand Master of the Ancient and Primitive Rite of Memphis-Misraim in 1881.

In this tale of mysteries surrounded by mysteries, the origin of the Memphis Rite is itself shrouded in legend from the beginning. The likely story tells that it was founded in 1815 in Montauban, France, by one Gabriel Mathieu Marconis de Negre (1795-1868) and a certain Samuel Honis, native of Cairo—whence he brought the Rite. According to legend, it was said to derive from the Templars:

> Who received it from the Brothers of the Orient, whose founder was an Egyptian Sage called Ormus, converted to Christianity by St. Mark. Ormus purified the doctrine of the Egyptians according to the precepts of Christianity. Around the same time, some Essenes and other Jews founded a school of Solomonic science around Ormus. Until 1118, the disciples of Ormus remained the sole depositories of ancient Egyptian wisdom, purified by Christianity and Solomonic science. This was the teaching they communicated to the Templars.

A more sanguine account has it arising out of the experience of Masons who accompanied Napoleon to Egypt and, encountering there living remnants of various esoteric and Gnostic schools, incorporated them into already existing rites. From this point of view, it is a synthesis of various, earlier primitive rites. What makes the early history even more difficult is that, though apparently founded in 1815, it does not fully appear until "refounded" by Jacques-Étienne, the son of Gabriel Mathieu Marconis, in 1838-1839, at which time it appeared to be a schism of the Misraim Rite (of which Jacques-Étienne had been a member). Therefore it is described as a variant of the Rite of Misraim. It takes Egypto-Hermetic (or alchemical) tradition and fuses it with Templar and chivalric elements. It always attracted personalities in search of an ideal. In London, where numerous English lodges worked the Rite in French, the doors were always open to Republican figures. It was in London, then, that Garibaldi became an honorary member.

18.

If a name carries a spiritual meaning, the designation "Memphis," while invoking ancient Egypt in general, has further, quite specific resonances. There were four teaching or theological centers in Egypt: Heliopolis, Memphis, Thebes, and Hermopolis, where the first three were connected under the aegis of Thoth. Heliopolis revealed the "theology" of creation—the creative act of Atum and the eight gods (the Ogdoad), Thebes defined the process of genesis, while Memphis (which interests us) focused on the generative work of Atum in the form of Ptah (Vulcan). Ptah is the primordial active Fire—the fire fallen ("coagulated") in earth, the fire that is the marriage between heaven and Earth—through whom all beings and things come into being. This is the creative fire, the seed or consciousness in all things; it "partakes of what is below through its root, and it partakes of what is above through its source." Ptah, we may say, is the immanent artist of the *fiat lux* through whom the Word made all things.

19.

The person who did most to promote and unite the Memphis-Misraim Rite (and whose name is forever associated with it) was the Englishman John Yarker (1833-1913), a man of "significant character," according to Rudolf Steiner. Born in Westmorland, he and his family moved to Lancashire, where Yarker started an import-export business, in the service of which he traveled extensively—to the United States, Cuba, and the Dutch Indies, among other places. At age twenty-one, he became a Mason under the auspices of the Grand United Lodge. But "fringe masonries" always attracted him, and very quickly he accumulated memberships and initiations in many different orders. In 1871 we find F. G. Irwin proposing his candidacy for the Societas Rosicruciana in Anglia (SRIA), and by 1891 we find him an honorary member of the Rosicrucian Metropolitan College. In 1877 (November 24), he initiated Madame Blavatsky into the highest adopted (i.e., women's) degree ("crowned princess") of the Memphis-Misraim Rite. Later, in 1879, he became an honorary member of the Theosophical Society. It is unknown whether he was a member of the Golden Dawn, but he certainly studied with the occultist Papus (Dr. Gérard Encausse) in Paris (where he also received a charter to bring Martinism to England) and was certainly a friend of William Wynn Westcott, one of the leading lights in the renewal of so-called Rosicrucianism in England. How many other groups he was associated with is unknown, but certainly there were many more, among them the Memphis Rite.

The actual process of the fusion of the two rites is confusing. Both existed. Somehow, it seems, Yarker became English Grand Master of the Misraim Rite in 1871. Meanwhile—and this is more certain—at around the same time, he became the British representative of the American Grand Master of the Sovereign Sanctuary of Memphis, Harry J. Seymour, who gave him the charter for England and Ireland. The first fusion took place in Naples in 1880 at a gathering of the Memphis Rite. Yarker delegated Giambattista Pessina, who seems to have collected Egyptian lineages, to represent him. Although he was not present in person, clearly he was present in spirit. Some kind of initial fusion then occurred under the primary influence of Garibaldi, who was made first international Grand Master (Hierophant). The full consecration of the union occurred gradually over the years. In 1902 John Yarker himself became the Grand Hierophant (international Grand Master) of the conjoined Egyptian Rites. Thus it was he who gave Theodor Reuss the charter, which Reuss then passed to Rudolf Steiner, who received it with gratitude but without any illusions. He understood and stressed, when the occasion presented itself, that the affiliation with Memphis-Misraim was purely spiritual. As far as he was concerned, the phenomenal trace was moribund, if not dead.

Linking himself formally with all that flowed into and through Freemasonic tradition—with the spiritual impulses and beings that this tradition sought to manifest on Earth—Rudolf Steiner felt justified in creating a new vessel into which these impulses could descend once again and be renewed, for his time and into the future.

20.

Undoubtedly, the tradition outlined here is Steiner's tradition of "initiation science." The confluence of the ancient Mysteries, Hermetic or alchemical sacred science and cosmology, the Christian-Manichaean principle of freedom and love, and the identity of the human-earthly, cosmic, and divine Temples under-lie all of Anthroposophy.

As for Egypt, it was always close to Steiner's heart. His first recorded Christmas Lecture (December 21, 1903) related the mysteries of the divine birth to the "Festival of the Spiritual Sun in the Egyptian Mysteries." As stated, our age, the so-called fifth post-Atlantean epoch, is a recapitulation at a higher level, "a sort of reawakening," of the Egyptian epoch. In the lecture cycle *Egyptian Myths and Mysteries*, Steiner gives many instances of the places where this repetition or recurrence may be seen, but what he says about Hermes Trismegistus is perhaps most interesting in the light of the Hermetic echoes we have been following:

A new teaching, a wholly new method, became necessary in Egypt. In ancient India, human beings troubled themselves but little about how what happened in the spiritual world was imprinted on the physical plane—about the correspondence between human beings and the gods. But in Egypt something else was needed. In Egyptian initiation, pupils had not only to see the gods, but also to see how the gods moved their hands in the writing the starry script and the evolution of all physical forms. The ancient Egyptians did have schools entirely on the model of the ancient Indians, but they also learned how spiritual forces were correlated with physical forms. Thus they were taught new subjects. In India, pupils were shown the spiritual forces clairvoyantly, but in Egypt they were also shown the physical correspondence of those spiritual deeds.

They were shown how every member of the physical body—
for example, the heart—corresponded to a spiritual act or
work. The founder of this Egyptian school ... was the great initiator Hermes Trismegistus. It was he, Thrice Great Thoth,
who first showed human beings the entire physical world as
the handwriting of the gods.

Thus, insofar as Anthroposophy—and the work of the
Cognitive-Ritual Section—centers on the spiritual practices that
lead to and embody in deed and word the realities of "reading in
the Book of Nature" and "deciphering the Cosmic Script," they
may be seen under the sign of and renewing the original Hermetic
Revelation. Hence, the rubric "Egyptian Masonry."

21.

It cannot be emphasized enough that Rudolf Steiner's relationship to esoteric traditions, such as Freemasonry, was unique
among the esotericists of his time. Deeply versed in their sacred
deposits, an adept of their teachings, he understood that the
needs of our time require a new approach. Conscious of the
absence of the gods and the reality that we are all now widow's
sons and daughters, he knew that all the great spiritual currents
flowing into the present from ancient India, Persia, Egypt, and
Greece call upon us to renew them out of humanity's evolving consciousness of the "I." Although he had deeply meditated and,
indeed, realized all the esoteric mysteries, he saw his task not as
safeguarding these treasures, but as transforming them out of and
for the sake of their and our future. Therefore, although one may
speak of him, for example, as an alchemist, a Christian mystic, or
as the bearer of the essence of Freemasonry, he was always, in fact,
truly *sui generis*: entirely his own person.

According to an auditor's notes to the lecture on Manicheanism
in *An Esoteric Cosmology* (given in Paris in 1906), Rudolf Steiner
said:

The difference between esoteric brotherhoods before and after Christianity is that *before* the advent of Christianity their chief mission was to guard the sacred tradition. *Afterward*, it is to form and mold the future. Esoteric science is not abstract and dead, but active and living.

Rudolf Steiner's relationship to Freemasonry, as it was to all the teachings to which he was heir, is always *active and living*. He is not "guarding" sacred tradition, *he is forming and molding the future*— and he calls upon us to do so too.

BIBLIOGRAPHY

Ambelain, Robert, *Franc-maçonnerie d'autrefois: cérémonies et rituels des rites de Misraïm et de Memphis*. Paris: Robert Laffont, 1988.

Baigent, M. and R. Leigh, *The Temple and the Lodge*. London: Corgi,1992.

Brault, Eliane, *Le Mystere du Chevalier Ramsay*. Paris: Editions du Prisme, 1973.

Caillet, Serge, *La Franc-maçonnerie égyptienne de Memphis Misraim*. Paris: Dervy, 2003.

Churton, Tobias, *The Golden Builders: Alchemists, Rosicrucians, and the First Free Masons*. London: Signal Publishing, 2002.

Cooper, Oakley, Isabel, *Masonry and Medieval Mysticism: Traces of a Hidden Tradition*. London: Theosophical Publishing House, 1977.

Frick, Karl R. H., *Die Erleuchten. Gnostisch-theosophische und alchemistisch-rosenkreutzerische Geheimgesellschaften bis zum ende des 18. Jarhunderts*. Graz: Akademische Druck- und Verlaganstalt, 1973.

———, *Licht und Finsternis. Gnostisch-theosophische und fraumaurisch-okkult Geheimgesellschaften bis an die Wende zum 20. Jarhundert*. Graz: Akademische Druck- und Verlaganstalt, 1975-8.

Fulcanelli, *The Dwellings of the Philosophers*. Boulder: Archive Press and Communications, 1999.

Galtier, Gérard, *Maçonnerie Egyptienne Rose Croix et Néo-Chevalerie: Les Fils de Cagliostro*. Paris: Editions du Rocher, 1989.

Haven, Marc, Le Maitre Inconnu, *Cagliostro: Étude historique et critique*. Paris: Paul Derain, 1966.

Henderson, G.D., *Chevalier Ramsay*. London: Thomas Nelson, 1952.

Jacobs, Margaret C., *Origins of Freemasonry: Facts and Fictions*. Philadelphia: University of Pennsylvania Press, 2005.

King, Frank, *Cagliostro: The Last of the Sorcerers*. London: Jarrolds, n.d.

Le Forestier, René, *L'Occultisme et la La Franc-maçonnerie Écossaise.* Milan: Archè. 1987.

Mackenzie, Kenneth, *The Royal Masonic Cyclopedia* (1877). Kila, Montana: Kessinger Publishing, n.d.

McIntosh, Christopher, *The Rose Cross in the Age of Reason: Eighteenth Century Rosicrucianism in Central Europe and its Relationship to the Enlightenment.* Leyden: E.J. Brill, 1992.

Naudon, Paul, *Les Origines religieuses et corporatives de la Franc-maçonnerie.* Paris: Dervy, 1972.

Reghini, Arturo, *Les Nombres Sacrés dans la tradition Pythagoricienne Maçonnique.* Milan: Archè. 1981.

Ribadeau Dumas, F., *Cagliostro.* London: Allen and Unwin, 1967.

Stevenson, David, *The Origins of Freemasonry: Scotland's Century 1590-1710.* Cambridge: Cambridge University Press, 1988.

—————, "James Anderson: Man and Mason," *Heredom,* Volume 10, 2002.

Steiner, Rudolf, *An Esoteric Cosmology.* Blauvelt: Garber, 1988.

—————, *From the History and Contents of the Esoteric School.* Great Barrington: Steinerbooks, 2006.

—————, *The Secret Stream: Christian Rosenkreutz and Rosicrucianism.* Great Barrington: Anthroposophic Press, 200?

—————, *Spiritualism, Madame Blavatsky, and Theosophy.* Great Barrington: Anthroposophic Press, 2001.

—————, *The Temple Legend: Freemasonry and Related Occult Movements.* London: Rudolf Steiner Press, 1997.

Ventura, Gaston, *Les Rites Maçonniques de Misraïm et Memphis.* Paris: Maisonneuve & Larose, 1986.

—————, *A New Encyclopedia of Freemasonry.* Philadelphia: The David McKay Company, n.d.

Waite, A.E., *The Secret Tradition in Freemasonry.* Kila, Montana: Kessinger Publishing, n.d.

Wallace-Murphy, T., and Marilyn Hopkins, *Rosslyn: Guardians of the Secrets of the Holy Grail.* Boston: Element, 1999.

Woodhouse, C.M., *George Gemistos Plethon, The Last of the Hellenes.* Oxford: Oxford University Press, 1986.

Yarker, John, *The Arcane Schools.* Belfast: William Tait, 1909.

Many websites were also used. Especially useful was:
Grand Lodge of British Columbia and Yukon: http://freemasonry.bcy.ca

The basis of Anthroposophical spiritual science is contained in the published works of Rudolf Steiner (1861-1925). In addition to this Rudolf Steiner held many lectures and lecture courses both for the general public and for members of the Theosophical Society—later Anthroposophical Society—between 1900 and 1924. The title *Theosophy* was always used by him in the sense of Anthroposophical spiritual science. For this reason the German Section of the Theosophical Society was renamed the Anthroposophical Society, upon his advice, when it became an independent body in 1912/1913. Alongside the work of publishing and lecturing Rudolf Steiner also taught in his Esoteric School. This was made up of three sections from 1904 onwards until, at the outbreak of the First World War in 1914, it ceased to function. Not until ten years later did Rudolf Steiner make preparations to reintroduce the Esoteric School. It was intended as the "Free High School for Spiritual Science at the Goetheanum" containing three classes and several scientific and artistic sections. As a result of his early death, however, he was only able to fulfil a part of his intentions.

From the beginning he appointed Marie Steiner-von Sivers (1867-1948) as the legal trustee of his literary estate and overseer of the shorthand notes and other texts of his many lectures and to prepare them for publication. Marie Steiner established the *Rudolf Steiner-Nachlaßverwaltung* (Executorship of Rudolf Steiner's Estate) a few years before her death to continue the work that she had begun and to prepare above all for the publication of the complete works. According to her instructions the esoteric work of Rudolf Steiner was also to be included in this collected edition, a task which she had already begun.

The documents here presented apply to the outer and inner history of the Cognitive-Ritual Group, which formed the second and third sections of the Esoteric School 1904-1914. Whereas in the First Section of the Esoteric School instructions were given for the inner development of the individual pupil (see volume 264 of the Collected Works: *From the History and Contents of the First Section of the Esoteric School 1904-1914*), this volume deals essentially with the ritual itself. Membership in the Esoteric School, however, always presupposes an intimate knowledge of Anthroposophy as a science of the spirit.

The present document includes all the relevant writings of Rudolf Steiner, Marie Steiner-von Sivers and others, not excepting notes made by those taking part in lessons and instructive sessions that have a bearing on the Cognitive-Ritual, all of which are in the possession of the executors of Rudolf Steiner's will (*Nachlaßverwaltung*). The inserts enclosed in round brackets ( ) appear thus in the original text. Inserts within square brackets [ ] are additions made by the German editor or the translator. The letters CW stand for the "Collected Works" (of Rudolf Steiner's literary works). The bounteous store of material at our disposal certainly provides us with a fairly comprehensive glimpse into the way in which the esoteric work was carried out, but it does not supply us with a fully comprehensive reconstruction of proceedings, owing to the fact that certain of the connecting links and essential pieces of information, which could have thrown light on the practical details, have not been preserved. For this reason we have attempted, through our copious introductory remarks and comments, to establish the historical and material connection of these things to Rudolf Steiner's whole life's work. To further elaborate the history and essential nature of Freemasonry on account of Rudolf Steiner's connection—for reasons of esoteric-historical continuity—with a society of High-Degree Masons (this circle belonged nominally to a chapter of Memphis-Misraim-Masonry)—does not lie within the scope of the present volume. For Rudolf Steiner's spiritual sources—even though the symbols he made use of in his Cognitive-Ritual bear some resemblance, as he clearly explained, to many elements of traditional Masonic rituals—did not lie with this traditional esotericism, but sprang from his personal cognitive connection to the world of the living spirit. This is made quite clear by the perusal of the documents presented here, as also by that of the whole of this book.

Three points need special emphasis:

1. Rudolf Steiner's main intent was to make esotericism and also ritual-symbolism understandable again to the general public. On the day after Rudolf Steiner and Marie von Sivers (Marie Steiner) had established their connection to the Misraim current, thereby providing continuity, he expressed to her concerning the task of renewing and reshaping the ritual-symbolism that lies at the heart of spiritual life: "this shall be our ideal: to create forms that will express the life of soul. For an epoch that is unable to behold any forms or create them out of inner vision will of necessity see the spirit fade to a meaningless abstraction (...). So the work for the future will consist of shaping the religious spirit into something of beauty that will appeal to the senses." (See the letter November 25, 1905, p. 84 of the present volume). In this sense new esoterically artistic forms were created one after another. (See among other things: *Rosicrucianism Renewed: The Unity of Art, Science, and Religion* [CW 284] *(Bilder okkulter Siegel und Säulen. Der Münchner Kongress, Pfingsten 1907 und seine Auswirkungen); The Four Mystery Plays* [CW 14]; and *Ways to a New Style of Architecture* [CW 285] *(Wege zu einem neuen Baustil)*, about the architectural, plastic and color forms of the Goetheanum building.) The secrets of the sounds of speech, which until 1914 had formed the content of instruction in the higher degrees, were used on the Goetheanum stage as the art of speech formation and eurythmy and in curative eurythmy as a therapeutic measure.

2. Rudolf Steiner considered the World War of 1914-1918 to be a deeply significant turning-point for the whole consciousness of the age. Out of the recognition of this fact he explained at the outbreak of war in the summer of 1914 that the time for the cultivation of the cognitive-ritual work, as it had been practiced up till then, had now run its course (See p. 114). What he meant by that becomes clear from the following statement about Freemasonry: "At the present time such things as these are no longer appropriate. What is it about them that we have mainly to reject? We have to reject their exclusiveness. This very soon creates a spiritual aristocracy that should not exist, and the democratic principle that must come into its own more

and more is thoroughly opposed to the Freemasonry Societies, just as it is opposed to the exclusive priesthood" ("Lecture to Workmen at the Goetheanum," June 4, 1924).

3. With that was not meant that the symbolic-ritual practices should no longer be used at all, for, two years after the dissolution of the Cognitive-Ritual Working Group, he indicated that one of the tasks of the present time was to enter with understanding into ritual symbolism, so that the things pertaining to humankind might not be entirely lost and people in the future finding a record of them might be able to understand them (Berlin, June 20, 1916). Again, after a further two years, the following statement was made: "In order to preserve the continuity of human evolution it is necessary today to link up, as it were, with ritual and symbolism" (Dornach, December 20, 1918). However the form they take must undergo appropriate change. He took this in hand when, at the turn of the year 1923/24, he reorganised both the Anthroposophical Society and the Esoteric School.[1] Owing to his serious illness, which started in September 1924 and led to his death in March 1925, he was unable to transform the symbolic-ritual, respectively cognitive-ritual, method of working into a form compatible with a modern consciousness of our age.

Hella Wiesberger

---

1. See: *Die Weihnachtstagung zur Begründung der Allgemeinen Anthroposophischen Gesellschaft 1923/24* [The Christmas Meeting for the Founding of the General Anthroposophical Society] (CW 260) as also: *Die Konstitution der Allgemeinen Anthroposophischen Gesellschaft und der Freien Hochschule für Geisteswissenschaft. Der Wiederaufbau des Goetheanum* (CW 260a).

INTRODUCTION TO THE GERMAN EDITION

HELLA WIESBERGER

Concerning the Spiritual-Scientific Meaning of Ritual

In order to elucidate the connection that Rudolf Steiner's cognitive-ritual work, here delineated, bears towards the rest of his life's work it is necessary to take account not only of the outer history of his working methods, but also from the start to make clear what was for him the meaning and significance of ritual as such.

*

From anthroposophical knowledge we are informed that in olden times humankind was endowed with an instinctive clairvoyant consciousness and that the human being as well as the whole of nature were motivated, formed and supported by the creative powers of a divine-spiritual world. This consciousness grew ever fainter in the course of time until it disappeared completely when the reasoned thinking that is directed solely towards the laws of the physical world was developed. This was necessary because it was only thus that humankind could become spiritually independent of the creative powers of the universe and so be able to gain inner freedom from them. We are now faced with the task of developing a new connection to the spiritual world out of our free and independent intellect.

It was this fact that made it the main aim of Rudolf Steiner's life to prepare modern intellectual thinking to become an instrument for comprehending the spirit. That is why the opening sentence of his *Anthroposophical Leading Thoughts* begins:

Anthroposophy is a path of knowledge to guide the Spiritual in the human being to the Spiritual in the Universe.[1]

---

1. *Anthroposophical Leading Thoughts* (CW 26).

The practical steps for following this path are set out in the whole body of Rudolf Steiner's work, but foremost in his basic works: *Intuitive Thinking as a Spiritual Path,* otherwise known as *The Philosophy of Spiritual Activity (The Philosophy of Freedom)* and *How to Know Higher Worlds.*

Self evident as it was for people of the ancient civilizations to make use of symbols and to practice rituals in order to give form to their social life, with the fading of their connection to the divine spiritual world the understanding of the meaning of their rituals also disappeared. And so for modern abstract intellectual understanding, which has become increasingly the all-powerful world-embracing influence during the course of the twentieth century, the surviving ritual traditions now stand for little more than incomprehensible relics of a bygone age. Nevertheless present ritual needs do not arise out of the intellect but from other layers of the human soul.

With that the question arises as to what it was that induced Rudolf Steiner, as a thoroughly modern thinker, to cultivate ritual forms in his Esoteric School and to make use of them later in other contexts. In order to give due consideration to this question the whole depth and expanse of his spiritual-scientific views on the essence and the task of ritual in human and earthly development would have to be made clear. As this is beyond the scope of the present work we can only refer to a few important aspects pertaining thereto.

The Understanding of Ritual Is Based on Spiritual Insight

> We need a harmony between knowledge, art,
> religion and morality ... for our complicated
> social life that is threatening to spread chaos
> through the world.[1]

Rudolf Steiner's basic conception of ritual was founded on his spiritual insight trained according to modern methods of acquiring spiritual knowledge. In this the spiritual content of the world is revealed as "the basis and underlying principle of all existence,"[2] and by its nature instils an experience which is at the same time conscious, artistically sensitive and pious. As long as humanity lived in a condition of instinctive clairvoyance civilization was supported by a uniform scientific, artistic and religious spiritual insight. "What was known to human beings was incorporated by them into the material world; they turned their wisdom into something artistically creative. And while the pupils of the Mysteries vividly experienced what they thus learned as the Divine-Spiritual pulsating through the world, they offered up their religious rites, a sacred art, as it were, transformed into a ritual."[3]

For the advancement of humanity it was necessary that this unified experience should become split up into three separate currents, those of art, science, and religion. During the course of further evolution these three sides of human nature moved ever further apart and have lost all connection with their common origin. The result of this has been that cultural and social life has become ever more chaotic. In order for new forces of direction to become active again the three "ancient sacred ideals" of art, science, and religion must be born again out of the modern knowledge of the spirit. Rudolf Steiner regarded this as the primary concern of Anthroposophy, and he used to refer to it, especially on important

---

1. Ilkley, August 5, 1923.
2. "The world of ideas is the basis and underlying principle of all existence." Published in *Wahrspruchworte*, (CW 40).
3. Berlin, March 5, 1922.

occasions within the Anthroposophical Movement, as for instance at the first performance in the Goetheanum.[4]

In the sense of the words spoken on that occasion: "Those who begin to decipher nature's open secrets through clairvoyant insight so that they have the urge to express them in ideas and shape them in artistic forms will also feel the need to venerate them from the innermost depths of their heart through religion. For them religion becomes the handmaiden of science and art."[5] Rudolf Steiner had always felt impelled to elaborate the results of his spiritual vision not only by means of science, but also through art: through a depiction of spiritual truths. For "pictures lie behind everything that surrounds us; it is these pictures that are being referred to when people speak of spiritual primal causes" (Berlin, July 6, 1915). Because it seemed important to him, just on account of the social life, to shadow forth the spiritual not only in scientific terms, but also in visible form, for that reason everything that characterizes the Anthroposophical conception of life had to be embodied in the representative piece of work, the Goetheanum building (Dornach, January 23, 1920). After we had been bereft of the Goetheanum on New Year's Eve 1922, Rudolf Steiner expressed what he had intended it to show to the world in the following rather concise formula:

> The Goetheanum was perceived as a bodily symbol for that which the three main interests of humanity seek to build up in the depths of the soul. These three are the morally religious, artistic and scientific interests.[6]

The work carried out in the cognitive and artistic field of interest is plain to see, but how is it in the case of religion? Though this is not so evident it can nevertheless be characterized on the one

---

4. Dornach, September 26, 1920.

5. Rudolf Steiner's report of his address on September 26, 1920, at the opening of the first High School Course at the Goetheanum. *Waldorf News Letter,* March 1921.

6. In a sketch for an article about the first Goetheanum after it was destroyed by fire on New Year's Eve 1922.

hand as a keenness of soul for the spirit lying behind what is material (Mannheim, January 5, 1911), on the other hand it can be epitomized by the oft-recurring statement that the inherently religio-moral influence of Anthroposophy cannot contribute to religion in a confessional sense; that spiritual-scientific endeavors are not a substitute for religious practice and a religious life; and that one should not make Anthroposophy into a religion although it can be in the highest degree a supportive base for religious life (Berlin, February 20, 1917). Anthroposophy as a science of the supersensible and the Anthroposophical Society as its physical base should not be bound to any particular religious confession, for in its essence it is interreligious by nature. Its most central piece of knowledge, that of the significance of the Christ-Spirit for human and earthly evolution, does not rest on the doctrine of the Church but is based on initiation-science from which all religions have sprung. It was in this sense that Rudolf Steiner once characterized the task of Anthroposophical investigation as that of identifying the thread of truth common to all religions, thereby bringing about the mutual understanding among the various religious currents throughout the world (Berlin, April 23, 1912).[7] From this it follows logically that from an Anthroposophical point of view practical religious exercises carried out within a confessional context must remain a private concern of the individual. That was also to be found laid down in the statutes of the Society from the beginning.[8]

---

7. This is also one of the aims of the Theosophical Society. (The second of the three principles runs thus: "Through investigation of the central truths of religions, sciences, and the worldviews of all ages and peoples to lead humankind to a higher understanding.")

8. Already in the Statutes of the Theosophical Society, and then also in those of the Anthroposophical Society, it is laid down from the start that the membership is not dependent upon a religious confession.

The Ideal of Turning the Whole of Life into a Sacrament

> Sacramentalism is an expression of human dealings fired by sanctity.[1]
>
> What formerly only took place at the Church altar must become the prerogative of all humanity.[2]

The capacity of being able to experience how spirit becomes visible in ritual practices had to disappear, for it is an evolutionary principle that faculties must cease before they can be newly won on a different level. For that reason every development occurs in a sevenfold rhythmic process, evolving during the first four stages and regressing during the last three. The result of this is that the third, second and first stages are passed through a second time, but now with the addition of what was newly acquired up to the fourth stage. For earthly humanity what is newly acquired is the "I" or individuality, which develops during the evolutionary phase through birth and death and in the regressive phase becoming spiritualized towards freedom and love. The latter, however, necessitates the sacrifice of egoism which was a consequence of developing individuality and the sense of freedom.

Many references to this micro-macrocosmic development are to be found throughout Rudolf Steiner's work. This is made particularly clear by the following because they are in the form of diagrams (pp. 11 and 12) and meditations:

Translation of handwritten notes (page 11):

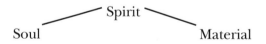

Soul   Spirit   Material

Evolution is expansion of the Spirit on the outside of the Material

Involution is the contraction of the Spirit in the inner part of the Soul

    No Evolution is possible without at the same time a corresponding Involution

    No Involution is possible without a simultaneous corresponding Evolution

---

1. Cologne, December 27, 1907.
2. Dornach, November 27, 1916.

Geist

Seelisch   Stofflich

Evolution ist Expansion des Geistes im Äußeren des Stofflichen.

Involution ist die Contraction des Geistes im Inneren des Seelischen.

Es ist keine Evolution möglich, ohne gleichzeitige entsprechende Involution.

Es ist keine Involution möglich, ohne gleichzeitige entsprechende Evolution.

Page of notebook, Archive No. 593

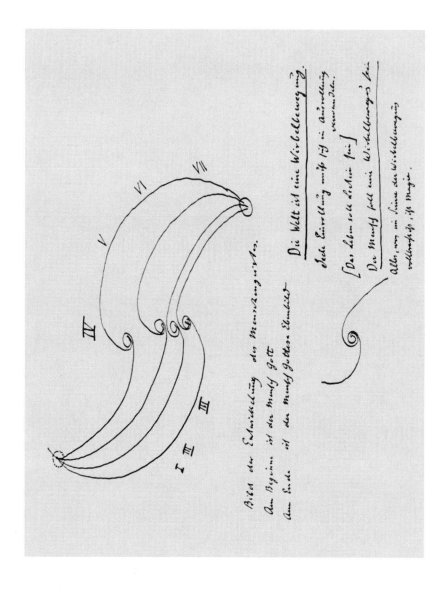

Page of notebook, Archive No. 712

✳ ✳ ✳ ✳ ✳

Translation of handwritten notes (page 12):

> Picture of the evolving human spirit.
> To begin with the human being is God
> At the end the human being is God's likeness.
>
>> The world is a spiral movement.
>> Every inward spiralling must become an outward spiralling.
>> [Life must be a lesson].
>> The human being must be a spiralling movement.
>> Everything performed in the sense of a spiral movement is magic.

✳ ✳ ✳ ✳ ✳

Handwritten entry in a notebook from 1903 (Archive No. 427):

Striding you move through the power of thought on the flow of separate existence and follow seven guiding powers under the leadership of truth: earthly desire drags you down, putting the guiding powers under the dominance of disbelief; the spirit uplifts you, raising the seven to the reverberating sun.

1. In separateness discover the law: for the law wove the first of the seven into the material.

2. In movement discover life: for life cast the second of the seven into the material.

3. In desire discover the person: for the person stamps the third of the seven into the material.

4. In thought discover your Self: for the fourth of the seven gave its Self to your "I."

5. In your desire discover renunciation: for through renunciation the fifth of the seven sacrificed its Self so that you might exist.

6. In your movement discover heavenly peace: for heavenly peace was sacrificed by the sixth of the seven so that you might be animated as an individual.

7. In your separateness discover your eternal law: for as eternal law the seventh of the seven created your Self and will lead it as eternal law out of separateness.

✳ ✳ ✳ ✳ ✳

The power of involution was born in humankind when Christ, Who brought about the cosmic-human evolution-involution process in the world, appeared historically and became the leading spirit of the Earth through His great sacrifice on Golgotha:

> The fact that human beings can regress to a consciousness of their spiritual connection [to the cosmos], is to be attributed to the Mystery of Golgotha. But what one owes to the Mystery of Golgotha must be searched for out of one's own free inner impulse. Christianity presupposes freedom (Dornach, February 11, 1920).

Since the regression of consciousness must come about from the present day onwards, it becomes necessary for ritual and the sacraments to be introduced into the element of freedom within Christianity. That is to say that increasingly towards the future it will not be a case of the one making a sacrifice for others, but of all humanity collectively going through the experience of becoming similar to Christ, to Him who descended to the Earth as a Being from the Sun (Dornach, December 23, 1922). Freedom, individualism in religious matters and in sacramentalism does not signify for spiritual science that everybody should have their own religion—that would lead to a total fragmentation of humanity into single individuals—but that through acceptance of anthroposophical knowledge a time will come, "however distant it might be," in which humankind will become ever more deeply stirred by a knowledge of the inner world of truth. And thereby "in spite of all individuality, in spite of the fact that everyone will be able to find the truth within themselves, agreement will prevail"; amidst strict maintenance of freedom and individuality one will be able to work together in free association (Berlin, June 1, 1908).

In this sense, reference was continually made to the fact that what had hitherto only been performed at the Church altar must be embraced by all humankind, that all human activity must become an expression of the supersensible. Especially since the First World War it was more and more strongly emphasized how important it is for the whole of society to regain a harmonious relationship to the cosmos lest humankind be condemned "to develop ever greater disharmony in social life and to spread ever more war materials over the earth." One will not acquire improved cultural powers as long as one only serves human egoism, especially in the fields of technology and science, alongside a segregated religion, and so long as experiments at the laboratory table are not carried out in deep reverence for the great "world principle." "The laboratory table must become an altar" we constantly hear.[3]

That it will be a long path in which tolerance will have to be practiced, both on the part of those who need to cultivate the old tasks and those who are preparing for the new ones, that is abundantly evident from the following statements:

> True as it is that with regard to spiritual life a totally new age is about to dawn, so it is also true that the way to Christ, which for many centuries has been the right one, will continue to be that for centuries to come. Things merge only gradually into one another. But that which used to be right will gradually change into something else when humankind is ripe for it to happen. (Karlsruhe, October 13, 1911) [*From Jesus to Christ*].

> Those who think that, through the deep understanding that their innermost soul has of Christ—the Spirit of Golgotha—they can hold direct intercourse with the Christ, must look with

---

3. Heidenheim, April 29, 1918. See also *The Spiritual Guidance of the Individual and Humanity* (CW 15); Dornach, November 27, 1916; Zurich, October 9, 1918; Dornach, December 30, 1922.

understanding upon those who need the positive declarations of a confession of faith, and who need a minister of Christ to give them comfort with the words "Thy sins are forgiven thee." On the other hand there should be tolerance on the part of those who see that there are people who can be independent. This may be all an ideal in the Earth existence, but the Anthroposophist, in all events, may look up to such an ideal (Norrköping, July 16, 1914) [*Christ and the Human Soul*].

But it was not only in connection with the individual human being that the importance of ritual was mentioned, but in connection with the whole of humankind's and the Earth's evolution. In lectures held at the time when the Movement for Religious Renewal, The Christian Community, was founded and the remark was made: "the Mysteries lie hidden in the ritual and will only be revealed in their true significance at a time in the future"—the "Mysteries of the Future"—on that occasion it was said that a time will come when the Earth will no longer exist; all the substances of which at present the kingdoms of nature and our human bodies are composed will be turned to dust in the universe. And all the processes that have been activated by mechanical techniques will belong to the past. But through the fact that the right rituals have been enacted, which proceeded from a "true understanding of the spiritual world," elementary spirit-beings connected with the progress of the Earth can be summoned to the aid of these degenerative processes in nature and cultural life and will enable the Earth to arise anew from destruction (Dornach, September 29, 1922) [*Supersensible Influences in the History of Humankind*].

Further confirmation, of far-reaching implication for the whole of human and cosmic evolution, to support the statement that the Mysteries of the future lie with ritual is given by the results of that spiritual research, which reveal that the divine-spiritual of the cosmos will undergo a profound change in the future by working with the free human being endowed with self-consciousness: "It will be no longer the same being as before when it shines forth from humankind. The Divine-Spiritual, in passing through humankind, will experience a being that had not previously been revealed."[4] For this new way of revelation of the cosmic Spirit-Being the relevant forms of culture will only be created in the future, for the essence of a true ritual consists in the fact that "it is a copy of what is taking place in the spiritual world" (Dornach, June 27, 1924).

The prerequisite to all that is the spiritualization of thinking. Only when one makes that one's starting point will one be able to turn all one's deeds into acts of sacrament. Then out of a knowledge of spiritual realities the ancient ceremonies will undergo a change, because no symbols are needed where reality is concerned. (Karlsruhe, October 13, 1911 [*From Jesus to Christ*] and the lecture to the workmen in Dornach, September 10, 1923).

The change in the ceremonies here referred to is the change in the Christian sacraments, which, according to the traditional view, enshrine the meaning of Christianity, but actually have their origin in the ancient Mysteries. It was only in the sixteenth century at the Council of Trent in 1546, when the Vulgate Bible was pronounced the only authentic translation, that the Latin "Sacramentum" replaced the Greek "Mysterion." The concept "sacrament," however, was already contained in ecclesiastical parlance since the time of the Church Father Tertullian in the second century. But in respect of number, significance and effect this interpretation was certainly variable until, at the Council of Ferrara-Florence in 1439, the Roman Catholic Church fixed the number of sacraments to seven (Baptism, Communion, Confession, Confirmation, Marriage, Ordination and the Last Anointing) and proclaimed as dogma that the sacraments, initiated by Christ, are rituals consisting of a visible element (*materia*) and a form of words (*forma*) through which a sacramental grace can be conferred.

When, on the other hand, the Evangelical Church only recognized two sacraments, Baptism and Communion, this arose from the fact, as Rudolf Steiner explained (in a lecture in Dornach, October 2, 1921), that by the time of the Reformation one had lost

---

4. See "The Future of Humanity and Michael's Deeds," *Anthroposophical Leading Thoughts* (CW 26).

the awareness of the inner numerical constitution of the world. For the idea of the seven sacraments sprang originally out of the ancient knowledge of the evolutionary and involutionary processes controlling the whole of existence. With the seven sacraments, therefore, the seven stages of life through which one passes, including the social life, in which one develops partly evolutionary and partly involutionary values, should have the corresponding opposite values added to them. The seven stages of human life are: birth, strength (maturity), nourishment, procreation, recovery, speech, transformation. They can be characterized as follows: the involution within the birth forces is the process of death, which comes into play when birth takes place: it is to be sanctified by the sacrament of Baptism. The whole process of becoming mature, including puberty, is to be sanctified by the sacrament of Confirmation. The process here specified as nourishment is the embodiment of the soul-spiritual into the bodily-physical, that is to say, between the soul-spiritual and the bodily-physical the right rhythm has to be established so that the soul-spiritual does not sink to the level of the animal but also does not lose itself in otherworldliness. The involution, which is part of the evolutionary process, is to be sanctified by the sacrament of Holy Communion. Along with this rhythmical vacillation process between the soul-spiritual and the bodily-physical is the possibility of always being able to go back in time through the power of memory. For development to be complete there must be a recollection of the previous events that one has experienced. The involution belonging to the power of memory which evolved out of our inner being, is to be sanctified by the sacrament of Confession, which includes the searching of conscience, repentance, and the resolve to atone for past sins by undertaking penance, either self-imposed or laid down by a priest, in order that the act of memory becomes Christianized and simultaneously raised into the moral sphere. With these four processes here characterized the events of evolution since humanity's birth have been exhausted. The act of memory represents a strong intensification; evolution and involution are already drawing nearer to one another. Death is a natural involutionary event. The corresponding sacrament is the Last Anointing. As formerly the natural events of life stimulated the physical-bodily nature, so now the soul-spiritual life must be stimulated by the Last Anointing, which was regarded by the old nature wisdom as an ensouling process. "Expressed through rhythm the physical-bodily nature disappears at death, the soul-spiritual regains its form." That is what is understood by transformation.

As at death our individual life comes to an end, the two missing stages and sacraments must relate to something that is not of an individual nature. An interchangeable relationship between humanity and the divine-spiritual world, which is unconscious to ourselves, exists in every human being. If that were not the case we would never be able to find our way back again. But there exists a deeply hidden involutionary process within us, "much more hidden than what takes place inwardly when with one's organism one passes through death." It is a process that never comes into our consciousness during the course of an individual life. The evolutionary process that is equivalent to this involutionary one is to be seen in the sacrament of Ordination, which corresponds to what is called "speech."

What is represented by the seventh sacrament is a picture of the soul-spiritual within the physical-bodily nature as it comes to expression in man and woman: "One would have to say that the descent to Earth is circumscribed by a certain boundary. The woman does not completely reach this boundary; the man, however, overshoots the mark. Therein lies the real contrast on the physical-bodily side." Because each possesses a certain imperfection there is a naturally occurring state of tension present. "When we look for the sacrament equivalent to this we find it in the Marriage Ceremony."

This basic idea of Christian esotericism in connection with the sacraments—that we enter life as an imperfect being, that we acquire evolving qualities on the one hand, involutionary ones on the other, to which, in order to perfect our development, opposite qualities are added by means of the sacraments—is no longer understood. Today, however, it is very necessary for us to acquire involutionary qualities.

*Spiritual Thinking as Spiritual Communion,
as the Beginning of a Cosmic Ritual That Is Right
and Fitting for Humanity Today*

> The first beginning of what must come to pass if
> Anthroposophy is to fulfil its mission in the world is
> that our whole relationship to the world must be
> recognized to be one of cosmic ritual or cultus.[1]

Rudolf Steiner starts with Communion when he tackles the spiritualizing of the form of the sacraments, which is justified from the point
of view of the law of evolution by the fact that in the sacrament of
Communion we have the involutionary opposite force to incorporation of the soul-spiritual in our physical being. As the last stage in the
process of incorporation is the binding of the thinking to the physical brain, so in the regressive, spiritualizing process intellectuality has
to be introduced into this thinking, which is now physical.

Rudolf Steiner starts from this point already in the first of his publications: *A Theory of Knowledge Based on Goethe's World Conception* (1886).
Here he demonstrates the fact that pure thinking, that is thinking
not based on the senses, unites with world spirituality, which he then,
one year later, describes as Communion.

> Whoever accredits thinking with the capacity of grasping what
> goes beyond sense perceptible objects must also of necessity
> acknowledge the existence of such objects. But the objects of
> thinking are ideas. When thinking grasps an idea it merges with
> the primal ground of existence; what works outwardly enters
> the human spirit; it identifies completely with objective reality.
> The becoming aware of an idea in its reality is the true com-
> munion of humankind. Thinking has the same significance for
> ideas as the eye has for light and the ear for sound. It is an
> organ of comprehension.[2]

---

1. Dornach, December 31, 1922. *Man and the World of Stars,* pp. 184, 186.
2. Introduction to second volume of *Goethe's Scientific Writings* in the Kürschner
edition, p. IV.

As the content of Anthroposophy is nothing else than what can be investigated in this way out of the world of ideas, that is the world of spiritual reality, and is naturally of a morally religious nature, it is not surprising that even in the early years it was said that by its teachings the whole of life right down into its everyday details would be sanctified and become a sacrament and that this was even the deeper meaning of its existence (Berlin, July 8, 1904). It also becomes clear why it is said in the lectures (*Man and the World of Stars* [CW 219]), which are so important for our present theme, that the spiritual Communion experienced through spiritualized thinking is the "first beginning of what must come to pass if Anthroposophy is to fulfil its mission in the world" (Dornach, December 31, 1922).

How the sacrament of Communion can become reality through the symbol of the Last Supper is described in the lecture given in Kassel, July 7, 1909: "Humanity is only at the beginning of Christian development. Its future lies in the recognition that the Earth is the body of Christ. For through the Mystery of Golgotha a new center of light was created in the Earth; it was filled with new life right into the structure of the atoms. That is why Christ could say as He broke the bread made of the grain from the Earth: 'This is My body.' And what He could say to them as He gave them the juice of the grape—the sap of a plant: 'This is My blood'." And it continues thus: "Because He had become the soul of the Earth He could say of the solid substance, 'This is My body'; and of the plant's fluid, 'This is My blood'—just as you say of your body, this is my body; and of your blood, this is my blood. And those who are able to grasp the true meaning of these words of Christ create for themselves thought-images that attract the body and the blood of Christ into the bread and the wine, and they unite with the Christ Spirit. *In this way our symbol of the Lord's Supper becomes a reality.*"[3]

Nevertheless, it thus continues: "Lacking in our hearts the thought that unites us with Christ we cannot engender the force

---

3. *The Gospel of St. John in its Relation to the Other Three Gospels,* particularly the Gospel of St. Luke, pp. 225/226.

of attraction that draws the Christ Spirit to us at Holy Communion; but by means of such a thought-form the attraction is generated. For those, then, who need the outer symbol in order to perform the spiritual act—that is, to unite with the Christ—Communion will be the way until such time as their inner strength will have grown, and they are so permeated by the Christ, that they can dispense with the outer physical agency. The sacrament of Communion is the preparation for the mystical union with the Christ, the preparatory schooling. That is the light in which we must see these things. And just as everything evolves from matter upwards towards spirit under the Christian influence, so those things that existed primarily as a bridge must grow and develop under the influence of Christ. The sacrament of Communion must rise from the physical to the spiritual plane if it is to lead to a true union with the Christ. One can do no more than hint at such matters, for only if they are received with a full sense of their sacred nature will they be rightly understood."

In the same sense, from the lecture given in Karlsruhe on October 13, 1911, we learn that: "By means of meditations, concentration exercises, and all that we can acquire as knowledge of higher worlds, we become ripe in our being to experience not merely thought-worlds, not merely worlds of abstract feelings and perceptions, but to permeate ourselves inwardly with the element of Spirit; thereby thoughts, meditative thoughts, will be able to live in us; they will even be the very same, only from within outwards, as the symbol of the Holy Communion, the consecrated Bread, has been from without inwards."[4] Friedrich Rittelmeyer recounted in his memoirs, *Rudolf Steiner Enters My Life*, that when Rudolf Steiner was asked: "Is it not possible to receive the Sacrament without bread and wine, only in meditation?" he was answered: "It is possible. From the back of the tongue it is the same."

In the lecture given in Dornach, December 31, 1922, which starts with the words "Spiritual knowledge is a veritable Communion, the

---

4. *From Jesus to Christ*, Lecture 9, p. 124, Rudolf Steiner Publishing Co., 1956.

beginning of a cosmic ritual that is right and fitting for the person of today," a ritual "that can also grow," it is suggested that the Communion with the World-Spirit can be further deepened. In other connections it is also suggested that a certain sacrificial offering has to be brought so that one can go beyond the general experience of Spiritual Communion and arrive at truly cosmic knowledge. What has to be sacrificed in this case is indicated by the technical expression "the sacrifice of the intellect." But under this heading it is not in any way meant that one should forego thinking as such, but rather that one should renounce egoism and self-will in thinking, which consists of the arbitrary linking of thoughts. Explanations about this are contained in two lectures from 1904 and two lectures from 1923 and 1924.

The two lectures from 1904 are, to be sure, only preserved in very imperfect copies and have therefore not yet been published. For that reason the part that concerns us here is quoted verbatim. In the lecture of June 1, 1904, it is stated that in order to decipher the akasha record to investigate cosmic evolution certain preliminary conditions have to be met, one of which is the following:

> ... to put one's own thoughts at the disposal of this Principle, this Power, and these Beings whom, in Theosophical parlance, we call the Masters.[5] For ultimately it is the Masters who have to give us instructions to enable us to read in the akasha record. It is written in symbols and signs, not in words of an existing language or one that has existed. As long as one only uses the power that one usually applies to thinking—and everyone who has not been specially trained for this purpose uses this power— one cannot read the akasha record.
>
> If you ask: "Who is thinking?" you will have to say: "I think." You connect together object and predicate in forming a sentence. So long as you yourself connect the single concepts you are not able to read in the akasha record. You are unable to read

---

5. In connection with the Masters see *From the History and Contents of the First Section of the Esoteric School 1904-1914* (CW 264).

because you connect your thoughts with your own ego. You have
to obliterate your ego. You have to renounce all your own opinions. You have to merely put forward your ideas for the connection to be made by forces outside yourself, by the spirit.

Thus it is renunciation—not of thinking itself, but of connecting the single thoughts yourself—which is necessary for you to
be able to read in the akasha record. Then the Master can come
and teach you, with the help of the outer spirit, to surrender
your thoughts to the universal World-Spirit, so that He can show
you what happened in history. Then it is not you who judge the
facts, but the universal World-Spirit who speaks to you. And you
place your thought-substance at His disposal.

Now I have to say something that may awaken prejudices. I
have to say what it is that is necessary today before one can eliminate the ego in order to be able to read in the akasha record.
You know that one looks askance today at what the monks practiced in the Middle Ages—namely the "sacrifice of the intellect."
The monks did not think in the same way as a modern investigator thinks. The monks had a kind of sacred science, the
sacred theology. One did not have to decide about its content.
One therefore said that the theologist of the Middle Ages must
use his judgement in order to expound and defend the given
revelations.[6] Whatever one may think of it today, that was a strict
schooling in the sacrifice of the intellect for the sake of a pre-
established content. We will not consider if it is a good thing or
a bad thing according to modern ideas.

This "sacrifice of the intellect" performed by a monk of the
Middle Ages led to the elimination of personal judgement
based on the ego. It enabled him to learn how to place the intellect in the service of something higher. Through reincarnation
the effect of his former sacrifice resulted in him becoming a

6. Concerning the two sorts of truth in modern spiritual science—that based on
knowledge and that from revelation—see the lecture given in Liestal, October
16, 1916, in *Philosophy and Anthroposophy* (CW 35); also the study by Hans Erhard
Lauer *Erkenntnis und Offenbarung in der Anthroposophie*, Basel, 1958.

genius in observation. If higher vision was then added to this then he was able to direct his thoughts upon facts observable in the akasha record (Berlin, June 1, 1904).

In the lecture held a few weeks later we read:

... the further one proceeds along the path of knowledge, the more necessary it is to acquire devotion; one becomes more and more devotional. Out of this devotion then flows the strength to acquire the very highest knowledge. Those who manage to forego making their own thought combinations will gain the ability to read in the akasha record. One thing, however, is necessary: that one eliminates one's personal ego to such an extent that it makes no further claim to combine the thoughts itself.

This is not at all easy to understand, for a person claims the right to be allowed to combine the predicate with the subject. As long as one continues to do that, however, it is impossible for one to really study esoteric history. When, unselfishly—but also with clarity and consciousness—one lets thoughts rise up within one, then an event occurs, which, from a certain point of view, is well known to all esotericists, namely, that the ideas, the thoughts, which one previously formed into sentences and opinions according to one's own views, now form themselves out of the spiritual world, so that it is not I who forms opinions, but opinions are formed in me. It is then the case that one has offered oneself up so that a higher self speaks out of the Spirit through one's ideas.

That is—esoterically conceived—what was called "sacrifice of the intellect" in the Middle Ages. It signifies the relinquishment of one's own opinions, one's own conviction. So long as I make my own thought combinations and do not place my thoughts at the disposal of higher powers who simultaneously inscribe them into the tablet of the intellect, for so long I am not able to study esoteric history (Berlin, July 25, 1904).

The concept "sacrifice of the intellect" appears again in the two lectures, Penmaenmawr, August 31, 1923 (*Evolution of the World and of Humanity*) and Prague, April 5, 1924 (*Karmic Relations, Vol. V*).

Here it is in connection with the results of investigations into the lost manuscript of a dramatic epic poem from the first four centuries of the Christian era. This poem was written by the mystery teachers of that time, because they foresaw that people in the future would develop their intellect more and more. This would bring them freedom, but at the same time would take away their clairvoyance. They would thereby experience a great crisis through the fact that their understanding would no longer extend to those regions out of which the actual deeper foundations of human and earthly evolution and the cosmic significance of Christianity could be understood. This foresight aroused in the mystery teachers the greatest anxiety as to whether humankind would be able to gain sufficient maturity to receive what had come into the world through the Mystery of Golgotha. For that reason they clothed their message, "that to be able to understand the cosmic significance of Christ a sacrifice of the intellect was necessary," in a mystery drama,[7] that lost epic drama we have already mentioned. In a thrilling manner the scene is depicted in which a young hero gains clairvoyant insight into the cosmic significance of Christianity by his willingness to sacrifice his intellect. And these mystery teachers wished by means of this poem—the greatest poem inspired by the New Testament—to present to humankind, in a kind of credo, the challenge of the "sacrificium intellectus." For if humankind is to find the connection with what has come into the world through the Mystery of Golgotha, this "sacrificium" must be practiced by all who are striving for a spiritual life, to acquire learning: everyone who aspires to learning, who wishes to gain wisdom, must develop a sense for ritual and sacrifice. "For sacrifice is a law of the spiritual world" (Berlin, February 16, 1905). "There must be sacrifice; without sacrifice there is no 'becoming,' no progress" is what is recorded in notes of a Class Lesson in Basle, June 1, 1914.

---

7. The expression "mystery drama" was used by Rudolf Steiner in a notebook entry to the lecture in Prague, April 5, 1924, Archive No. 336.

In an artistic form the "sacrifice of the intellect" is shown in Rudolf Steiner's third Mystery Drama: *The Guardian of the Threshold.* In a spiritually dramatic moment in the play the spirit-pupil Maria—with the help of her spiritual teacher Benedictus, who, in this scene taking place in spirit land, is dressed characteristically in priestly robes—makes her sacred vow in front of Lucifer, the representative of egoistic forces, to keep all knowledge free of self love:

> Never from this hour will I
> Allow myself to be possessed by joy
> Such as is felt when thoughts grow ripe within.
> I'll steel my heart to serve as sacrifice
> So that my mind can always only think
> In such a way that through my thoughts I may
> Offer the fruits of Knowledge to the gods.

From the lectures of 1904 previously referred to it is plain that the sacrifice which the spirit-pupil Maria vows to undertake is similar to what is there described as the "sacrifice of the intellect."

In addition to the reference to the sacrament of Communion in spiritualized thinking, we also find references to the spiritualization of the sacrament of Baptism. In contrast to Spiritual Communion, which is an individual event taking place within the human being, the latter points to a spiritualizing of outward labor. A beginning can already be made to put this into practice in education and in lessons, if all children are looked at from the point of view that in their own personal ways they bring with them into the world the power of the Christ Spirit.[8] In another context comes the following remark: "What was previously enacted in the Mysteries as a symbol of the sacrament of Baptism should be carried out today in outer happenings and in outward deeds. Spiritualization of human labor, sacramentalization of outer happenings, that is the true Baptism."[9]

---

8. Dornach, November 27, 1916.
9. In notes from an Esoteric Class, Hamburg, November 28, 1910.

The Ritual-forms Created for the Various Groups

Ritual binds together those who unite in it.[1]

The extent to which ritual unites people in communities was thoroughly discussed in 1923 when, owing to the many new daughter-movements which had sprung up since the end of the First World War, and also the burning of the Goetheanum, a complete overhaul of the Anthroposophical Society became necessary. The problem of "community-forming" was particularly acute at that time, on the one hand because of the influx into the Society of younger members, which largely came from the "Wandervogel" movement, a youth movement struggling with the ideals of community, and on the other hand because of the founding of the Christian Community, a movement for religious renewal, which took place in the autumn of 1922, just prior to the Goetheanum fire. This movement had come into existence through the appeal made to Rudolf Steiner in 1920/21 by a group of young theologians, mostly students, who asked him for advice and help in their particular concern for a renewal of religious life. His reply was that his own task was to bring spiritual science into the world and he could not involve himself in founding a religion; if, however, they could carry out what they had in mind with a group of 30 or 40 like-minded people, that would be something of immense importance for humankind as a whole.[2] For he was convinced that for those people who were looking for a path to the spirit through the practice of religion, the renewal of Christian religious life was profoundly important. And, as requested, he gave his most energetic support to this young movement—not as its founder, certainly, but, as he said, as a "private person." In his lectures he gave the fundamental structure to fit "the needs of a future theology," and first and foremost he gave them "a valid and spiritually effective ritual

---

1. Dornach, March 3, 1923.
2. Emil bock in "Rudolf Steiner, Recollection by Some of His Pupils." *Golden Blade*, 1958.

full of substance;" for the establishment of healthy religious life must depend on the building up of a healthy social order, which, again, can only be given in the form of a ritual (Dornach, December 31, 1922 and March 3, 1923. *Man and the World of Stars*, [CW 219] and *Awakening to Community*, [CW 257].)

When, after the founding of the Christian Community, some uncertainty arose as to the relationship of the two movements, he felt obliged to speak about community-building and ritual work. Starting from the question as to whether the community-building as achieved in the founding of the Christian Community is the only kind there is at present, or whether there are other possibilities of achieving the same goal in the Anthroposophical Society, he described the two poles of community-building which were made possible through ritual work. Whereas the known pole of a religious service lies in the fact that beings and processes of the higher world are projected by words and ritual acts into the physical world, in the case of the other pole we are dealing with a "reversed ritual," which can be experienced by a group of Anthroposophists when, in striving together after supersensible knowledge, they raise themselves up into the spiritual world. When people meet together to experience through Anthroposophy what the spiritual world offers them, then "the experience within a group of people is different from that of an individual." If the Anthroposophical content is experienced in the right way a process of awakening to the other person's soul is brought about and the participants are raised up to the Community of Spirit: "When this kind of consciousness is present and groups of Anthroposophists are formed in this way, then something of an eminently community-building nature appears in this other pole of the cult—in what I might call the 'reversed ritual,' and out of this can grow this specifically Anthroposophical way of creating community" (Dornach, March 3, 1923).

This possible form of ritual experience, lacking outward ceremony, is obviously one of the ways in which the Cosmic-Ritual can be experienced. Nevertheless, if Rudolf Steiner had lived longer, he would have also created an outwardly practiced ritual as, so to speak, an effective help along the difficult pathway towards experiencing the Cosmic-Ritual through purely spiritual search. For to experience the Cosmic-Ritual as a spiritual-mystic union of the human spirit with the World-Spirit should always be the goal, but can, at any rate at the present day, seldom be achieved. That was once hinted at by Rudolf Steiner with the words:

> I call to mind one of the great mystics of the Alexandrian School, who confessed in his old age that he had rarely experienced a moment in his life in which his soul had reached a sufficient depth for the Spirit of Eternity to awaken within it, that mystical moment in which God could be experienced within the human breast. Those are midday moments when such things as this are experienced, when the sun of one's existence is at its zenith, and for those who are always at hand with their abstract ideas which lead them to say: "When people develop the right thoughts they will be led to the highest"—For them such "midday moments of life, which one must regard as moments of grace" are "not the hour in which they like to travel;"[3] for such theorists every moment should be a moment in which to solve world riddles (Heidelberg, January 21, 1909 [CW 109]).

The fact that Rudolf Steiner intended to recreate an Anthroposophical ritual-form in 1923, the year in which the Anthro-posophical Society was reconstituted, is vouched for by two statements made by him in the spring of that year. The one statement was made when he was describing the "reversed ritual" as a specifically Anthroposophical form of community-building. He added the following words: "many individuals are presently entering the Society, seeking Anthroposophy not just in the abstract but in a communal association that satisfies the yearning belonging to the age of the consciousness soul. It might be suggested that the Society too should adopt a ritual. It could do this, of course, but that would take it outside its proper sphere" (Dornach, March 3, 1923, *Awakening to Community* [CW 257]).

---

3. A reference to the words of the Will-'o-the-Wisps in Goethe's *The Green Snake and the Beautiful Lily*, the subject of the lecture.

The second statement was given as the answer to a question raised during a private conversation concerning a ritual for the Anthroposophical Movement. The questioner, René Maikowski, recorded the conversation as follows, and gave permission for its publication:

> I was a member of the committee of the Delegates' Meeting that took place in Stuttgart at the end of February 1923. After this meeting, at Rudolf Steiner's suggestion, the founding of the "Free Anthroposophical Society" took place. During the subsequent building up of the Society in this committee, as elsewhere in the Society, discussion often turned to the relationship between work in the Anthroposophical Society and that of the Christian Community. This was especially noticeable after Rudolf Steiner's lecture on December 30, 1922. A discussion arose in our group about our tasks and way of working. Some of us asserted that the work of the Christian Community was easier because there the spiritual substance is provided by a ritual that satisfies the needs of those who seek direct contact to the spirit, whereas we others rely mainly on lecturing activity for that purpose. And so some of us raised the question as to whether it would be possible to have a ritual for the Society. Opinions were divided. I turned to Rudolf Steiner with this question—it was in the spring of 1923—as I often accompanied him on his travels. To my surprise he reacted very positively to this question. He explained that a ritual had already existed before the war, but that in future it would have to take a different form. The ritual of the Christian Community did not come into question for this purpose. Then he characterized the difference in the basic structure of Anthroposophy and the Christian Community. The two movements represent a different approach and in part they were under the guidance of different Masters. A ritual activity in the Anthroposophical Movement must proceed from the same spiritual current as the School Services and represent a kind of continuation in form and content of what is given in the School Offering Service [*Opferfeier*]. And he intimated that he would return to this question, since he had been asked about it.

This new structuring of the Anthroposophical cognitive-ritual work was never put into practice however. After Rudolf Steiner's death, Marie Steiner tried to create a kind of substitute for it by the way she organized festivals at the Goetheanum, especially those of the seasons to which she gave an artistic-ritual character.

Retrospectively it can be seen that a variety of ritual texts have arisen from the requests and needs of different circles of people.

The first of these were the texts for the interreligious Cognitive Ritual as practiced in the Esoteric School from 1906 until the outbreak of the First World War in the summer of 1914.

Shortly before, or directly after the end of the war (1918) he was asked for a new formulation of the Church rituals. This plea came from a Swiss anthroposophical friend, Hugo Schuster, who had been so impressed by Rudolf Steiner's "Christ statue," that it induced him to become a priest. And in the summer of 1918, after having been ordained in the traditional Catholic faith—in which the rituals were already said in German—he received from Rudolf Steiner at the turn of the year 1918/19 a burial service and, during the course of the spring of 1919, a new version of the Mass.[4]

Other practicing or retired priests who were Anthroposophists received ritual texts on application. Pastor Wilhelm Ruhtenberg, who had become a teacher in the Free Waldorf School in Stuttgart, founded in 1919, received a baptism ritual and a marriage ritual in 1921. How this came about was recorded in the following way:

> Already in 1921 Pastor Ruhtenberg was often asked by Anthroposophical friends if he would marry them or baptize their children. Thereupon he asked Rudolf Steiner for a ritual of baptism. After having received it he felt that the black cassock with the white clerical band was not appropriate any more and he asked for a new vestment. Rudolf Steiner drew a picture of the desired object and told him what the colors ought to be. According to Ruhtenberg's report the marriage ceremony proceeded as follows: "When a bridegroom once came to me and

---

4. For details see Supplementary Notes, p. 507.

said he had asked Rudolf Steiner to perform a marriage ceremony for him, but the latter had sent him on to me, I did not
want to let the man down, so I performed the ceremony myself.
Afterwards I went to Dr. Steiner and said to him: "If you send
me someone for a marriage ceremony, will you please give me
a ritual for it." Some weeks later as I was attending a eurythmy
lesson with my class, the door opened, Dr. Steiner came
towards me, gave me a few sheets of paper and said: "Here is
the marriage ritual that I promised you." I sat down straight
away to study it with burning curiosity. After the lesson, in the
consulting room, I asked about the vestments for this service. I
still had the sketch of the baptismal vestments on me and Dr.
Steiner added the colors for the marriage ceremony. The cut of
the garments remained the same.[5]

Previously another teacher, Johannes Geyer, who had also been a
priest at one time, received a ritual of baptism for a child whom an
anthroposophical friend had asked him to christen.

So also for the Free-Christian religion lessons of the Waldorf
school, rituals were inaugurated after Rudolf Steiner had been
asked if he could arrange Sunday services for the pupils. The answer
was that this would then have to take the form of a ritual. In this way
the first Sunday Service ritual came about, even before New Year
1920. Upon receiving further requests he instituted the other three
services: the Christmas Service came into being at Christmas 1920;
in 1921 the Youth Service—as the equivalent of the Act of
Confirmation of the Church; and in the spring of 1923 the Offering
Service [*Opferfeier*] for the two top classes—as equivalent of the
Communion Service.

The Offering Service was instituted after Rudolf Steiner had been
informed during a conference with religion teachers on December
9, 1922, that a girl of the upper school had asked if the class could

---

5. From the biographical sketch "Wilhelm Ruhtenberg" in the collection of the
biographies of teachers of the Waldorf School, *Der Lehrerkreis um Rudolf Steiner*,
Stuttgart, 1977.

have a Sunday Service that went beyond the Youth Service. He accepted this suggestion with great seriousness and described it as having wide significance; he wished to give it further consideration. He did not want to introduce the Communion Service into the services of the Free Religion lessons, but something "of the nature of Communion" could be used. Some few months later, in March 1923, the text of the service was handed over and on Palm Sunday, March 25, 1923, the Offering Service for the pupils of the eleventh class and the teachers was held for the first time.[6]

To the wish expressed at the Teachers' Conference on November 16, 1921, to have a Sunday service only for teachers he indeed never responded later.

When, through the involvement of the Christian Community—founded in the autumn of 1922—in the school curriculum, the question arose as to the continued justification for the Free Christian religion lessons and the school services, Rudolf Steiner expressed the definite opinion that both kinds of religious instruction, the Free Christian and the Christian Community, possessed their own character and followed their own goals and both had full justification for the future. When some of the parents wanted their children to take part in both kinds of religious instruction he also acquiesced in this too, provided it did not overstrain the children themselves. (At that time the religion lessons given by the Christian Community were not held in the school, but on their own premises). The inner unchanging attitude of the greatest possible tolerance in religious matters is exemplified by the way he characterized the different aims of the two kinds of religious instruction: "The inner meaning of our Youth Service is that a person is regarded as a member of humankind as a whole, not a member of any one religious sect; the Christian Community, however, places a person into a particular religious community. And yet"—and that was repeatedly emphasised by him—"a discrepancy between the two as regards their inner content cannot

---

6. Maria Lehrs-Röschl in *Zur Religiösen Erziehung. Wortlaute Rudolf Steiners für Waldorfpädagogen*, Stuttgart, 1985. [Concerning religious education. Words of Rudolf Steiner to Waldorf teachers].

actually occur."[7] And when, from the side of the Christian Community, the ritual of the Youth Service had also been offered to them for their use (Confirmation Service) the question was asked if it should not be altered for their sacramental purposes, he replied in no uncertain terms that it was "educational" to use the same ritual "as the expression of different earthly connections."[8]

He expressed similar views with regard to the Offering Service. Maria Lehrs-Röschl records in what has been cited, how after the Service had first been performed, fellow teachers came to Rudolf Steiner with the wish to have it repeated for the teachers alone. Because the service holders tended to hold the opinion that the Service should only be performed for pupils with the participation of teachers and parents, they were asked to question Rudolf Steiner on this point: "I formulated my question in such a way that it was obvious that I thought it was not possible to hold the Offering Service for any other people than for pupils. But Rudolf Steiner looked at me with wide open eyes (I knew this gesture as an expression of surprised, slightly disapproving astonishment) and said: 'Why not? This Service can be held anywhere, wherever there are people who want it!'"

To the range of tasks to be undertaken by the Christian Community, apart from the Communion Service (The Act of Consecration of Man) and the earlier established rituals, which had already been given, other still missing ones were added bit by bit. The last one to be inaugurated was that for the Ordination of Arch High Priests [*Erzoberlenker*]. It was introduced not long before Rudolf Steiner's death.

The manifoldness of rituals thus devised is all the more remarkable owing to the fact that Rudolf Steiner once remarked himself that it is difficult to form a ritual: "You can see how difficult it is to initiate something of a ritual nature from the fact that for a very

---

7. See account of teachers' conferences in the *Free Waldorf School in Stuttgart 1919 -1924*, Vol. I (CW 300).

8. When asked the same question later he acceded to the desired changes. (Transmitted by Emil Bock, priest of the Christian Community).

long time everything of that kind was restricted to using what was traditional ... all forms of ritual that are extant today are actually very ancient, merely changed slightly in the one or other respect" (Stuttgart, June 14, 1921).

From this it follows that whoever undertakes to found a ritual, if it is to be a true image of what is happening in the spiritual world, must stand in close relationship to that world of the Spirit. We must also possess artistic ability, for ritual forms, as the images of spiritual events, are in no way to be compared with photographs, but are independent configurations produced by physical means. A supplementary explanation for this seems to have been provided by the following statement: "When we raise ourselves up to the next stage of existence, pictures appear to us, which we cannot now apply as we do our thoughts by asking: how do these pictures correspond to reality?—but things appear in pictures consisting of colors and shapes and we have to interpret through our imagination the beings that are thus presented symbolically" (Berlin, October, 26, 1908). That is illustrated concretely by the funeral rite and has the following remark appended to it: "It could be expressed in a more complicated way, but in its simpler form that which has to be won through inner struggle can be thus won" (Dornach, June 27, 1924, *Karmic Relationships, Vol. II*). The expression "*erobert*" [conquered] expresses once more how difficult it must be to initiate a ritual.

He explained the reason for simplicity—a striking characteristic of all his rituals—by saying that a complicated ritual would not satisfy the people of today and that he therefore had to make it extremely simple (Stuttgart, June 14, 1921). But it is just the simplicity that bears witness to artistically creative ability. Now art and ritual are closely connected in respect of their origin, as they both come from the same spiritual region: "During humankind's evolution ritual is evolved as the living picture of the spiritual world that reaches into the domain of artistic production. For art is also a product of the astral world—and ritual turns to beauty" (Paris, June 6, 1906). An interesting occurrence in this connection was recorded by Emil Bock: "When, early in 1923, I received from him the Burial Service for children, he was himself radiant with thankfulness for this special form of creativity, which was at the same time the highest art of receiving. Twice he came to me on that day—it was during a conference—with the words: 'Is not the text beautiful!'"[9]

Another characteristic feature results from the esoteric principle of continuity, which is a dominant theme of his:

May what is to come rest upon what has gone before;
May what has gone before carry what is to come
to strong existence in the present.[10]

Wherever possible he linked what he had recently investigated to the old tradition for the sake of the continuity of progress. Likewise in the creating of rituals. The necessity of taking past currents into account was once formulated by him in the following manner: "In order to preserve the continuity of human development it is still necessary today to link, as it were, to ritual and symbolism" (Dornach, December 20, 1918, [CW 186]). And as these rituals were preserved by tradition "something was preserved that can and will be wakened into life when human beings have discovered how to bring into all their deeds the power that streams from the Mystery of Golgotha" (Dornach, September 29, 1922, *Supersensible Influences in the History of Humankind* [CW 216]). The following words point to the current of the future, which is only beginning to manifest today: "It is only possible to arrive at symbols in our day by immersing ourselves lovingly in the universal secrets of existence; and it is actually only through Anthroposophy that a ritual or symbol can proceed" (Stuttgart, June 14, 1921). In this same sense we are told, in a lecture about different rituals, that rituals today have to include what modern spiritual-scientific training can reveal of the laws of universal spirituality and that in creating such a ritual "all we can expect is that we shall have to start right at the beginning again" (Dornach, September 11, 1923, "Lecture to Workmen on the Origin and Significance of Rituals").

---

9. From: "Rudolf Steiner. Recollections by Some of His Pupils." *Golden Blade,* 1958.
10. From: *Twelve Moods* (not included in *Verses and Meditations* [CW 40]).

The connection between elements coming from the past and those coming from the future as they are presented in the ritual now in use in the Movement for Religious Renewal (Christian Community) "takes humankind's historical evolution fully into account, and thus represents in many of its single details as well as in its overall aspects a carrying forward of the historical aspect. But its every aspect also bears the imprint of fresh revelations, which the spiritual world can only now begin to make to our higher consciousness" (Dornach, March 3, 1923, *Awakening to Community*, Lecture IX).[11] In a similar manner he expressed himself regarding the reformulation of the Catholic Mass for the Reverend Schuster who had asked him to "put the ritual text of the Roman Catholic Church into a form corresponding to what originally lay within it, not the strange translation which is widely extant today," and then "something new" could arise, even though it is only a matter of translation. He also said in this connection about the funeral service: "Of course one has to link up with the usual funeral rites. But through the fact that the usual ritual is properly translated and not just according to the dictionary, a different result is achieved" (Stuttgart, June 14, 1921).

The following statement also points to a characteristic feature of rituals: "One can only properly embody a single ritual from the spiritual world at any one time."[12] The question as to how the various ritual forms correspond with this single possible "ritual" could be answered by saying that the rituals given for the various circles—the Cognitive-Ritual of the Esoteric School, services for the Free Religion lessons of the Waldorf School, the Communion Service for the Christian Community—must be essentially the same in their deeper aspect. This appears to be confirmed by a statement by Emil

---

11. With this reference to historical development the four parts of the Mass are obviously alluded to—The Gospel Reading, Offertory, Transubstantiation, Communion—which represent "the path that the pupil of the heathen Mysteries had to take in undergoing initiation." (Dornach, January 11, 1919; Munich, November 4, 1906).

12. Carl Unger, "Zur Frage des Verhältnisses der Christengemeinschaft zur Anthroposophischen Gesellschaft" [Relationship of the Christian Community to the Anthroposophical Society], in *Writings II*, Stuttgart, 1964.

Bock, according to which the third of the School Services (*Opferfeier*) was an attempt to introduce an equivalent of the Act of Consecration of Man of the Christian Community, in so far as this could be carried out by lay persons, that is to say, by those who were not consecrated priests. Maria Lehrs-Röschl added to this in the previously quoted passage: "What constantly recurred in the evolution of Christianity as the urge and longing for lay-priesthood—but, to be sure, was constantly persecuted and finally also extirpated—has been re-sown by Rudolf Steiner [in the *Opferfeier*]." It is obvious from the foregoing that in Rudolf Steiner's eyes the Esoteric Cognitive-Ritual, the Free Religious Ritual of the Waldorf School and the Act of Consecration of Man of the Christian Community stood in no kind of contradiction to one another. On the one hand it was because, in religious matters as in all other things, the freedom of the individual was of paramount importance and true Christianity was that alone which allowed "complete religious freedom" (Zurich, October 9, 1918). On the other hand because it is only through the spread of ritual into all branches of life that the way to the high ideal of the consecration of the whole of life may be attained. The necessary prerequisite for that is that certain inner thoughts and feelings "shall interpenetrate and spiritualize our inner being, thoughts and feelings as fully consecrated as in the best sense of inner Christian development the Holy Communion has spiritualized the human soul and filled it with the Christ." When this becomes possible—and according to Rudolf Steiner it will become possible—we shall have progressed a stage further in evolution and thereby the "real proof will again be provided" that Christianity is greater than its external form (Karlsruhe, October 13, 1911, *From Jesus to Christ*, p. 124).

PART I

THE INTRODUCTION OF THE MISRAIM SERVICE INTO THE ESOTERIC SCHOOL

I have always respected what has arisen in the
course of history. In this is revealed the spirit
inherent in humankind's evolution. Therefore I
was in favor of linking whenever possible, the
new with what exists historically.

(*Autobiography*, Chapter 36)

Whoever goes his own road, as I do, must submit
to many a misunderstanding about himself.

(*Mysticism after Modernism*,
preface to First Edition, 1901)

PRELIMINARY REMARKS

HELLA WIESBERGER

Concerning the History of the Cognitive-Ritual Section

Just as the volume *From the History and Contents of the First Section of the Esoteric School 1904-1914* (CW 264) records the fact of and the reason why Rudolf Steiner began by linking the First Section of the Esoteric School to the already existing School of the Theosophical Society in order to preserve the historical continuity, so does the present volume record the reason for and the way in which the historical continuity of its Second and Third Section—the Cognitive-Ritual Working Group—is preserved through its link with the already existing connection working with ritual symbolism.

After it became known that this was concerned with the so-called "Egyptian Freemasonry,"[1] he was labelled a "Freemason" in a derogatory sense by some people. Rudolf Steiner himself expressed his opinion about this on two occasions, once shortly after he had formally joined the Freemasons, in a letter written on August 15, 1906, to A.W. Sellin, a Theosophist and Freemason,[2] and again in a note that he added one week before his death to Chapter 36 in his *Autobiography*. The attacks made on him after his death by those on the side of the National Socialist Movement were countered by Marie Steiner-von Sivers, the cofounder and administrator of the study group, with an article entitled: "Was Rudolf Steiner a Freemason?" All of these and other documents are collected together in chronological order in the first part of

---

1. See Supplementary Notes, p. 508.
2. See Supplementary Notes, p. 510.

the present volume; the only exception being the letter to Sellin, which, owing to its basically explanatory character, was placed at the beginning.

The form of the question that Marie Steiner-von Sivers gave to the title of her essay indicates a problem that is inherent in the subject. For this question can be answered both in the affirmative and in the negative. Affirmatively if we only consider the outward fact of the union and do not look at Rudolf Steiner's motivation for forming the link. Negatively if we consider that, in spite of the formal union, he never regarded himself as a Freemason in the usual term of the word. He had no connection with the ordinary Freemasonry (and Egyptian Masonry was regarded as irregular in any case) and was never considered to be a Freemason.

In order to elucidate this apparent contradiction and to explain the fact of this link to Freemasonry, just the question of the choice of Egyptian Masonry will be dealt with first.

Why the Connection Was Made to Egyptian Masonry

> We can look at the whole of modern civiliza-
> tion: it presents itself to us as a memory of
> Ancient Egypt ... This can be seen even in the
> principle of initiation.[3]

According to its legendary source Egyptian Freemasonry traces its origin back to the mythical First King of Egypt, Menes—Hebrew Misraim—the son of Ham, who was the son of the Biblical Noah.

---

3. Stuttgart, August 16, 1908, *Universe, Earth and Man* (CW 105), Chapter XI. The same thought is expressed in Rudolf Steiner's four Mystery Dramas in scenes 7 and 8 of the third play, *The Soul's Awakening*, in which the karmic connection of a group of modern pupils of spiritual science is traced back to their initiation in a mystery temple of ancient Egypt. See also: Dornach, December 27, 1918, *How Can Mankind Find the Christ Again?* Lecture III.

Menes occupied the Land of Egypt and gave it his name (Misraim, the ancient name of Egypt) and instituted the Mysteries of Isis and Osiris. At the beginning of the Christian era the Egyptian Priest-Sage Ormus, who was converted to Christianity by Saint Mark, united the Egyptian Mysteries with those of the New Covenant. Since that time they have been preserved as the Ancient Egyptian Freemasonry. In this sense they were described by those who brought the Misraim Rite from Italy to France at the beginning of the nineteenth century as "the root and origin of all Freemasonry rites."[4] According to Rudolf Steiner, King Misraim, after having conquered Egypt, was initiated into the then existing Egyptian Mysteries, which contained secrets from ancient Atlantis. A continuous tradition has existed since that time. Modern Freemasonry is only a continuation of what was initiated in Egypt at that time (Berlin, December 16, 1904, *The Temple Legend*, Lecture 9).

Along with the secrets of the ancient Mysteries goes the experience of the immortality of the human spirit[5] and esoteric Freemasonry also wished to awaken this experience. It is in this direction that the deeper meaning of Rudolf Steiner's words may be explained when he says (p. 69) that he linked up with the Memphis-Misraim-Order because the latter "presumed" to work in the direction of esoteric Freemasonry. In its manifesto of 1904 it asserts that it

4. Lennhoff/Posner, *International Dictionary of Freemasonry*, "Misraim-Rite." Compare also Rudolf Steiner's exposition, Berlin, December 16, 1911, on p. 98 of the present volume. Also, the Freemason Joseph Schauberg testifies to the correctness of the Egyptian origin of the Masonic symbols in his main work: *Vergleichendes Handbuch der Symbolik der Freimaurerei mit besonderer Rücksicht auf die Mythologien und Mysterien des Altertums*, Schaffhausen, 1861.

5. In this connection it is interesting to note that in Rudolf Steiner's opinion it is just *The Book of the Dead* that is an almost complete record of ancient Egyptian Mystery wisdom. This statement was transmitted by the Egyptologist Gregoire Kolpaktchy who translated *The Book of the Dead* at the instigation of Rudolf Steiner. Only a person holding the key to both the hieroglyphs and esoteric knowledge is able to make such a translation. (see: *Das Ægyptische Totenbuch*, translated and with a commentary by Kolpaktchy; published by Otto Wilhelm Barth, 1970—[see also *The Book of the Dead* translated into English by E.A. Wallis Budge, M.A., Assistant Curator of Oriental Antiquities at the British Museum].

is in possession of the practical means from the ancient Mysteries to acquire "proof of pure immortality" in this earthly life.[6]

When Rudolf Steiner, following the esoteric duty of preserving continuity, linked to this current, he did not for a moment contemplate working in it in the usual way. He was from the very beginning most decidedly of the opinion that people of the modern age should search for a new wisdom suited to their needs, which would have its source in the Mystery of Golgotha, and that a real knowledge of immortality can only be attained nowadays by a deep understanding of the Mystery of Golgotha (Berlin, May 6, 1909).

He characterized the need for this new wisdom in one of his descriptions of ancient Egyptian knowledge in the following way:

> Our age must give birth not merely to an ancient wisdom, but to a new wisdom, a wisdom that points not only to the past, but that must work prophetically—apocalyptically—into the future. In the Mysteries of past ages of civilization we see an ancient wisdom preserved, but our wisdom must be an apocalyptic wisdom, the seed for which must be sown in us. Once again we have need of a principle of initiation so that the primeval connection with the spiritual worlds may be renewed. The task of the Anthroposophical world movement is to supply this principle (Stuttgart, August 5, 1908, *Universe, Earth and Man* [CW 105]).

Another thing that is very illuminating is the findings of spiritual scientific research, which show that secret connections exist between what happened in the third post-Atlantean Cultural epoch, the Egypto-Chaldean epoch, and our own fifth post-Atlantean epoch.

Taking the whole of modern culture, we have to see in it a memory of ancient Egyptian culture; Egyptian thought is

---

6. See lecture given in Berlin, December 9, 1904, in which the manifesto of the Grand Orient of Memphis and Misraim Masonry is discussed in connection with the idea of immortality. (*The Temple Legend*, Lecture 8).

reflected in it from its beginning.... This can be seen even in the principle of initiation, and as modern life is to receive a principle of initiation in Rosicrucianism let us ask what it is? ... This wondrous harmony between the Egyptian remembrance in wisdom and the Christian impulse of power (*Universe, Earth and Man*, Chapter XI).

On another occasion Anthroposophy is directly alluded to as a new Isis-Wisdom of the new era. Even a new Isis legend is developed and in connection with it the suggestion is put forward that behind the wooden sculpture of "The Representative of Humanity between Lucifer and Ahriman," which was to have occupied the central position in the First Goetheanum and to have revealed to visitors through a work of art the central impulse of Anthroposophy, was another, invisible sculpture: the New Isis, the Isis of a new era (Dornach, January 6, 1918, *Ancient Myths*, Lecture III). Again, a deep connection was established between the Isis Mystery and the Grail Mystery, the latter being a Christianized revival of the Egyptian Mysteries, just as the Parzival figure acts as "a model for our spiritual movement" (Dornach, January 6, 1918; Berlin, January 6, 1914, not translated).

Another reason for this link to just the Egyptian Masonry is supplied by the results of spiritual investigation, which show us that the person of today is in the opposite position to the person of Egyptian times. For just as the spiritually-directed ancient Egyptian once prepared humankind for intellectual, brain-bound thinking of the intellect by preserving the human form by mummification, so must a person today acquire spirituality alongside intellectuality by a process analogous to mummification, namely through the use of the ancient ritual forms. These latter are analogous to Egyptian mummies because, in contradistinction to ancient times in which it was possible to attract real spiritual substance into ritualistic deeds, this is no longer the case either in the lodges or in the churches. In these ritualistic enactments today there is no more spiritual life than there was life in the Egyptian whose body had been mummified. Nevertheless, something was preserved in these mummified rites which can and will be awakened into life when people have discovered how to bring into all their deeds the power that streams from the Mystery of Golgotha (Dornach, September 29, 1922, *Supersensible Influences in the History of Humankind*, Lecture IV). These few results of spiritual investigation are sufficient to explain why Rudolf Steiner chose just Egyptian Masonry to elaborate his cognitive-ritual work.

The "Outer" Prehistory of the Cognitive-Ritual Section

> I want the step I have taken to be judged simply from the point of view of esoteric loyalty.[7]

The year 1902 was notable for three events connected with the Theosophical Society. Rudolf Steiner and Marie von Sivers took over the leadership of the nascent German Section of the Theosophical Society, founded in 1875 by H.P. Blavatsky among others.

Annie Besant, Blavatsky's successor in the leadership of the Esoteric School of Theosophy—although not President of the Theosophical Society at that time—was admitted to the so-called "mixed" Freemasonry Order. John Yarker,[8] honorary member of the Theosophical Society and General Grand Master of the Egyptian Freemasonry of the Order of Ancient Freemasons of the Memphis and Misraim Rite of Great Britain and Ireland presented Theodor Reuß,[9] Heinrich Klein and Franz Hartmann, who belonged to both the Freemasonry Order and the Theosophical Society in England, with a Deed for the founding of this teaching in Germany.

---

7. Letter to Sellin, August 15, 1906.
8. See Supplementary Notes, p. 510.
9. See Supplementary Notes, p. 511.

When it is stated in Rudolf Steiner's *Autobiography* that soon after the founding of the German Section in 1902, Rudolf Steiner and Marie von Sivers were offered the leadership of a society of the kind still in existence that preserves the ancient wisdom embodied in symbolism and religious ceremonies, this does not imply that the offer was made, as is generally supposed, by the chief representative of the German Memphis-Misraim-Society, Theodor Reuß, but, as Marie Steiner states in her essay "Was Rudolf Steiner a Freemason?" by a person who held the opinion about Rudolf Steiner that he understood more about spiritual matters than any Freemason. She added to this in private that it concerned a certain Czech. The fact that this person must have been connected with the Memphis-Misraim-Freemasonry can be inferred from the remark in the *Autobiography*: "I would have instituted a symbolic ritual without a historic connection had I not been approached by the above-mentioned society."

This offer may have been made around 1903/04, for since May 1904 a symbolic-ritual way of working had been prepared by a series of corresponding lectures. On September 15, 1904, Rudolf Steiner held a lecture in Hamburg, where he first became acquainted with the Freemason A.W. Sellin. He must have asked Sellin about the Memphis-Misraim-Order, as is evident from the report of December 12, 1904. But even before this report by Sellin appeared, Rudolf Steiner had already paid a visit to Reuß. And in his Berlin lecture, on December 9, 1904 (*The Temple Legend*, Lecture 8) in which he spoke about the multiple-degree and the Memphis-Misraim-Masonry, he quoted from its official organ, the *Oriflamme*, whereas Sellin was still enquiring about it. Rudolf Steiner's first conversation with Reuß must therefore have taken place between September 15 and December 9, 1904. The further conversations cannot be dated. On November 24, 1905, Rudolf Steiner and Marie von Sivers joined the Memphis-Misraim-Order. The discussions about the conditions under which the charter could be operated for the independent running of a study group dragged on, however, until the beginning of 1906. The contract was signed January 3, 1906.

The fact that Rudolf Steiner does not mention the name of Reuß in his *Autobiography*, but only the name of Yarker, is often interpreted by opponents to signify that he wished to cover up his connection to Reuß, because the latter soon afterwards got into disrepute in Freemasonry circles as an occultist. This, however, cannot be the real reason because, at the time his autobiography was written, it had long become publicly known that Reuß was the one who had issued Steiner's certificate. Much more likely was the fact that here too the motive of historical continuity was the decisive factor. As for Yarker, mentioned by Rudolf Steiner in his lecture of December 16, 1904, as a "significant person" and an "excellent Freemason," he was already at that time an authoritative representative of Egyptian Freemasonry in Europe and a central figure in the Theosophical Society. He was its honorary member, evidently on account of the fact that he had been crucially involved in its founding in the year 1875. As it is reported in the account by the Italian, Vincenzo Soro, in his *La Chiesa del Paracleta* (Todi: 1922, p. 334), a book in Rudolf Steiner's own library: "At the founding of the Theosophical Society the most celebrated heads of International Freemasonry participated, among whom John Yarker was especially prominent, the most intimate friend of Garibaldi and Mazzini."[10]

The Theosophical Society, which was of a decidedly Western trend to begin with, was to have become the pioneer for the necessary popularization of supersensible truths in modern times. Through the first great work of its founder, H.P. Blavatsky: *Isis Unveiled* (1877), an abundance of knowledge from ancient Western esotericism had been made public. For this Blavatsky was presented by Yarker with the highest adoption degree of Egyptian Freemasonry.[11] Both also

---

10. According to Robert Ambelain: *Cérémonies et rituels de la maçonnerie symbolique*, Paris, 1978, the Italian freedom-fighter Guiseppe Garibaldi (1802-1882) became the Grand Master of the Memphis-Misraim-Freemasonry in Italy in 1881, followed by Guiseppe Mazzini (1805-1872). For information about both these see Rudolf Steiner's lecture, Stuttgart, April 9, 1924, *Karmic Relationships, Volume VII*.

11. On November 24, 1877. Perhaps it was pure coincidence that Rudolf Steiner and Marie von Sivers joined the Misraim-current on the same day of the year, but in 1905.

conferred with each other in the inauguration of a ritual for the Theosophical Society.[12] This plan, however, was not realized at that time. When Annie Besant, Blavatsky's successor, started to work with the symbolic-ritual stream, this was within a different Masonic current.[13]

Rudolf Steiner had ample reason, therefore, to mention only the name of Yarker in his *Autobiography*, for it was Yarker who represented everything which was of decisive value to the promotion of Rudolf Steiner's intentions—not Reuß who, as merely the representative of the Freemasonry Order in Germany, represented something with which Rudolf Steiner could not work.[14]

The "Inner" Prehistory of the Cognitive-Ritual Section

It is no reward, but a heavy task.[15]

Confirmation of the fact that Rudolf Steiner acted out of the situation in which he was placed is provided by his letter to Marie von

---

12. Josephine Ransom, *A Short History of the Theosophical Society*, Adyar, 1938, p. 99 et seq.

13. See Supplementary Notes, p. 513.

14. Note by translator: Further reasons for Rudolf Steiner having linked to Freemasonry, not mentioned by Hella Wiesberger, were given by Dr. Walter Johannes Stein in lectures at Wynstones school near Gloucester in the nineteen-forties:

1) That Rudolf Steiner bought his membership certificate through John Yarker because the latter was impecunious and Rudolf Steiner wanted to help him financially.

2) That Rudolf Steiner, by becoming a member of a Freemasonry lodge had gained the right to be present at all meetings. He only used this right by his spiritual presence at meetings and never attended a lodge meeting physically.

15. Personal statement by Rudolf Steiner, recorded by Marie Steiner-von Sivers and Clara Walther.

Sivers on November 30, 1905, a few days after joining the Memphis-Misraim Order. From that we conclude that he did not act out of a personal sense of "doing good," but in conformity with the esoteric powers, that is to say with the spiritual world, and that—because "at present it seems valueless to all esoteric powers" to link his not-yet-formed work-group to this order—he is still unable to say if the thing can be carried out or not. This problem seems to have been solved for him during the last weeks of the year, for on January 2, 1906, the constitution of the group was given form when he lectured for the first time to a mixed audience of men and women on the theme of the "Royal Art in a new form;" and "although we can only look upon Freemasonry today as a caricature of the great Royal Art, we must nevertheless not lose heart in our endeavor to awaken its slumbering forces again, a task that is incumbent upon us and runs in a parallel direction to the Theosophical Movement." This statement receives further backing from a lecture about Freemasonry given a short while later in Bremen on April 9, 1906. According to that lecture there is an inner connection between Theosophy and Freemasonry in so far as Theosophy presents the more ideal and studious side of esoteric endeavor and the Masonic-Ritual the more practical side. But whereas in the Masonic world the ceremonies and effectiveness of the rituals are no longer understood, Theosophy is able to speak about the inner truth of these ceremonies and about the spirit that underlies the ceremonies and symbols.[16]

A further confirmation of the fact that Rudolf Steiner did not act arbitrarily follows from his orally transmitted statement that his task to save the Misraim-Service for posterity had grown for him out of his former esoteric investigations into the rainbow; "one has no reward but a heavy task."

Wherein the heaviness of the task lay, he seems not to have explained. It could, however, be thought to exist in connection with the important statement made in his preparatory lecture (for men

---

16. From telegram-style notes by Marie Steiner-von Sivers. See p. 145.

only) given in Berlin on October 23, 1905: "I have reserved to myself the achieving of a unification between those of Abel's race and those of the Cain race" [See *The Temple Legend*, p. 405, note 5 to Lecture XVII]. This intention—of overcoming through the Christ impulse the primordial polarization of humankind into two oppositely-striving main currents—did not lie only with his cognitive-ritual work, but with his whole endeavor.

The statement that his task arose out of his esoteric research into the rainbow is in a certain way borne out by the reference made to it in lectures given at the time that the Cognitive-Ritual Working Group was in preparation. It is there stated:

> The rainbow has a special significance in esoteric wisdom. You are aware of the rainbow which has appeared since the time of the Flood. We now find this symbol appearing again in northern mythology. [A rainbow leads over from Valhalla to the Earth.]
>
> That signifies the transition from Atlantean to post-Atlantean times. In Atlantean times the air was much denser and the water was much less dense than they are today; a rainbow could not have been formed at that time. Atlantis was actually a land of mists, a home of fog, Niflheim. In the North humankind evolved out of clouds of mist. Out of this region of fogs the water masses arose which engulfed and submerged the continent of Atlantis. There was no rainbow in Atlantis. Esoteric research has investigated what this explanation signifies (Berlin, May 5, 1905).

And in reply to a request for more information about Noah and the Flood, asked after a lecture given half a year later, he replied:

> The question of Noah belongs to what I have just been researching. You will not find anything in *Lucifer*[17] that I did

---

17. *Lucifer* is the magazine that was afterwards know as *Lucifer-Gnosis* and the article contained therein: "Aus der Akasha-Chronik" [From the Akasha Record] (See: *Cosmic Memory*, also called *Atlantis and Lemuria*).

not know at the time of writing the article. But now I know a little more. Now I am able to picture the climatic conditions clearly and vividly. I have understood something that I would have included in my account if I had known it at the time I wrote the article. I took the account of Noah to be allegorical at first. It was a picture to me of deep inner significance. Now I know, however, that the rainbow mentioned in the Bible corresponds with a true fact.

In ancient Atlantis other climatic conditions prevailed. The distribution of air and water was different ... , so that we find that in ancient Atlantis a rainbow could not have formed. Such conditions could only arise after Atlantis had become submerged and new continents had appeared. Now it is suggested [in the Bible] how the rainbow emerges out of the Flood (Berlin, October 22, 1905).

If one asks oneself what has the task of preserving the Misraim-Service to do with research into the rainbow, an answer will be provided if the characterization of the Misraim-Service as "the bringing about of a union of earth and heaven, of the visible and the invisible" (Berlin, December 16, 1911) is transformed into the picture of a bridge. Then the connection between rainbow-research and Misraim-Service will become clear. On the one hand the rainbow has always stood for a bridge between the visible and the invisible; on the other hand it was always Rudolf Steiner's intention to build such bridges in all walks of life.

How bridge-building in the realm of art should be put into practice in connection with the Misraim-Service is expressed in a letter he wrote to Marie von Sivers on November 25, 1905, in which he says concerning the union with the ancient Misraim current which had taken place the previous day: "It would now be the task to rescue masonic life from its externalized forms and to re-create it (...), to turn religious spirit into a form of sense-perceptible beauty."[18]

---

18. See letter on p. 84.

The first opportunity to do so came soon afterwards when at Whitsuntide 1907 the task of organizing the yearly Congress of the Federation of the European Sections of the Theosophical Society fell to the German Section, and by the use of Rudolf Steiner's models, sketches, and written contributions a harmonious scientific-artistic-religious experience could be conveyed. The rainbow too was included among Rudolf Steiner's sketches for the Apocalyptic Seals, and this appeared as a new element in contrast to its traditional portrayal. And with the performance of the *Sacred Drama of Eleusis*, which signifies a new birth of the dramatic art in the history of civilization, a link was forged, in however weak a form, to the essence of the ancient Mysteries.[19]

The latter statement receives a special nuance through the added information that the Misraim Rite is intended to be a renewal of the Eleusinian Mysteries.[20] The founder of these famous Mysteries, the Goddess Demeter, personified for the Greeks what Isis was for the Egyptians.

A few years after the German Section had hosted the Munich Congress at Whitsuntide 1907, Rudolf Steiner's first Mystery Drama was performed and work was begun on the construction of their own building. After an abundance of new artistic forms had been created within a short space of time these too, as also spiritual science itself, was characterized as a "synthesis between heavenly and earthly understanding,"[21] thus also, figuratively speaking, a bridge. Later he even used the word "bridge-building" himself. In describing how art is the best way of building a bridge between the invisible and the visible because it reveals what would otherwise remain hidden, he says, in retrospect of the twenty years he spent with Marie Steiner-von Sivers endeavoring to "channel the

19. See *Rosicrucianism Renewed: The Unity of Art, Science, and Religion. The Munich Theosophical Congress of 1907,* SteinerBooks, 2007 (CW 284). *(Bilder Okkulter Siegel und Säulen. Der Münchner Kongress, Pfingsten 1907 und Seine Auswirkungen).*

20. cf. Karl Heise in *Entente-Freimaurerei und Weltkrieg,* Basle, 1919.

21. Lecture, Dornach, September 20, 1916.

esoteric current into art," literally: "all that arose in this direction within the Anthroposophical Society proceeded from the impulse to build a bridge from the spiritual into the physical."[22]

If, therefore, the intention behind Anthroposophy as a science of the spirit and the artistic language of the form derived from it was to build a bridge from the invisible to the visible, the intention behind the endeavor to build a social life upon the basis of new insight had the same aim. This can be seen if one takes account of what is written into the constitution of the new Misraim Service.

Concerning the Constituting of the New Misraim Service

> What I have founded has no connection there-
> fore with what previously gave itself out to be the
> Memphis-Misraim Degree in Germany.[23]

The founding of the constitution took place quite apart from the transactions carried out with Reuß concerning the legal authorization of the completely independent leadership of the Working Group. If the negotiations would have come to nothing Rudolf Steiner would have instituted his Working Group even without regard to historical continuity. He had already begun the preparation for this a short while before the start of negotiations—namely directly after settling the outer affairs of the First Section of his Esoteric School with Annie Besant in London in mid-May 1904— through a series of lectures, which took place from May 23, 1904 until January 1906 (*The Temple Legend*), and a course of esoteric instruction, which was given in 31 lectures between September and November 1905 (*Foundations of Esotericism*).

---

22. Torquay, August 20, 1924, *True and False Paths,* Lecture 9.
23. Letter to Sellin.

There are no records concerning the time or manner in which Rudolf Steiner informed members of the German Section about his intention to found the cognitive-ritual way of working. Only from a letter of February 17, 1905, from a Leipzig member[24] can it be gathered that he had said "that he would try to introduce the esoteric teachings of Theosophy into Freemasonry in the near future," wherewith, of course, Freemasonry was alluded to as a "thing," not as an organization. He had already expressed in his Berlin lecture of December 16, 1904: "If you hear anything about the German Memphis-Misraim-Way, you must not think that this is of any importance for the future. It is merely a framework into which a good picture might be placed at some time." A further record has been preserved that informs us that at the end of his lecture to the Berlin Branch on October 16, 1905, he announced that he intended to speak about matters connected with Freemasonry at the General Meeting of the German Section fixed for October 22, and that therefore one should invite as many people as possible also from outlying districts. He then announced at the General Meeting that next day, according to an old tradition, which must be superseded by Theosophical ideology, he would speak to men and women separately about esoteric questions in connection with Freemasonry. Following that he spoke about the fundamental relationships of the Theosophical Society to esotericism, thus preparing the theme for the next day's lectures. On the following morning (October 23, 1905) a lecture, first to men and then to women, was held on the subject: "Freemasonry and the Evolution of Humanity."

Two days later, on October 26, 1905, in a public lecture, he spoke for the first time—not, it is true, in outer connection, but all the more so in inner connection with the intentions of the cognitive-ritual work—on the subject of the "main social rule of the future": that labor must on the one hand be freed from its commodity character by separating it from payment, and on the other hand must

---

24. Rudolf Jahn, Chairman of the Leipzig Branch between 1905 and 1908.

be sanctified by becoming the sacrifice of the individual for the good of all. In future, work must be carried out for the sake of others because they are in need of what we produce.[25]

The connection between the public acknowledgement of this "main social rule of the future" and the start of the cognitive-ritual work arises on the one hand from the significance of visual thinking for the social life and on the other hand out of the motive inherent in the cognitive-ritual work to stimulate selfless social activity out of one's own feeling of moral responsibility, as at one time the rules for moral behavior proceeded out of the Mysteries. Thus, in the sense of Goethe's words: "nothing is within, nothing without, for what is within, that is without," the constituting of the new Misraim Service and the simultaneous proclamation of the "main social rule of the future" prove to be the two poles of one and the same impulse. The aim of bridge-building is very evident here.

With the lecture, "The Royal Art in a New Form," held on January 2, 1906, for a mixed audience of men and women the constituting was brought to a close. On the next day there followed the written agreement with Reuß, whereby Rudolf Steiner became entitled to establish an independent working group. Marie von Sivers was authorized to admit women into the group, but from the very beginning both men and women had always enjoyed equal rights within Rudolf Steiner's group. The following illuminating remark was found in notes made by Marie von Sivers to a lecture about Freemasonry held in Bremen on April 9, 1906: "Because the Freemason wished to see his womenfolk banished to the family, he expelled them from the lodge. Something happened on the higher planes which made it necessary for women to be included in all cultural activities. The future meaning of Freemasonry lies in the cooperation between men and women. The excesses of the male

---

25. Lecture given in Berlin, October 26, 1905, "The Social Question and Theosophy," published in *Beiträge zur Steiner Gesamtausgabe*, No. 88. In the essay starting with the October number of *Lucifer-Gnosis*, the "main social rule" was first mentioned in the third installment, which only came out in September 1906.

culture have to be tempered by the esoteric powers of the female."[26]

From the beginning of 1906 onwards, wherever there were esoteric pupils of Rudolf Steiner, cognitive-ritual work was carried on. The first lodges to be inaugurated were in Berlin, Cologne, Leipzig, Munich and Stuttgart. After the admittance of the hundredth member at the end of May 1907, the leadership of the Misraim-Rite in Germany became vested in Rudolf Steiner, as had been agreed. From that time on he was the sole spiritual and legally historical representative of the Misraim-Service, until with the outbreak of the First World War in the summer of 1914 he declared the Rite dissolved. By that time about 600 members had been admitted.

The Cognitive-Ritual Work is Suspended Owing to the Outbreak of the First World War and the Opposition to Freemasonry Caused Thereby

> What was to have served humankind irrespective of race and differences of interest acquired a malevolent quality on account of the outbreak of the First World War and the opposition it aroused against Freemasonry.[27]

In the description of the Cognitive-Ritual Section that Rudolf Steiner gives in his *Autobiography* he states that it "fell asleep" at the outbreak

---

26. In an undated letter from Paula Moudra, a Bohemian authoress who had spoken to Rudolf Steiner in Prague in November 1907 about her admittance and was asked by him to present a written application, there occurs the following: "You pointed to an important happening in the astral world in November 1879, since women have now been accepted for inauguration. I consider it to be very significant that my approach to you and my application for admittance took place just in November 1907."

27. From Rudolf Steiner's foreword to Karl Heise's book: *Entente-Freimaurerei und der Weltkrieg*, Basle, 1919.

of war in the summer of 1914, because, although it was in no way a secret society, it could have been taken for such. Marie Steiner reports in her essay "Was Rudolf Steiner a Freemason?" that he regarded the whole thing as finished and to demonstrate this he tore up the relevant document.[28] This was evidently done because it had become plain to him, as a result of the war, that through certain western secret societies Freemasonry—originally a good and necessary institution serving all humankind equally—had been placed in the service of national egoism and the selfish interests of particular groups of people.[29]

It was to this misuse for political ends that he attributed and strongly condemned the catastrophic development which began with the First World War. This has been thoroughly explained by him in lectures given during the war years 1914/18.[30] He found it tremendously important at that time to discover all he could about its esoteric background, especially in order to be able to contribute towards a clear exposition of the question of who was to blame for starting the war. That is why he wrote a preface to the book *Entente-Freimaurerei und der Weltkrieg* by Karl Heise when asked by him to do so. However good or bad the book is, it was at any rate the first attempt to give documentary evidence of the tendencies that Rudolf Steiner had exposed.

The rigorous condemnation of the private political aims of certain Western secret societies was not directed of course against Freemasonry as such. This was confirmed, for instance, when, shortly after the end of the war, he advised a member of his quiescent Symbolic-Ritual Organization to join the Freemasons. That follows from his letter to Rudolf Steiner of February 25, 1919, in which,

---

28. Not to be confused with the Contract and the Brotherly Agreement as shown on p. 86 of the present volume.

29. See the note above.

30. See the seven-volume series of lectures: *Kosmische und Menschliche Geschichte.* [Cosmic and Human History]; *The Karma of Untruthfulness*, Parts 1 and 2, (CW 173 and 174); also *Middle Europe between East and West* (CW 174a); and *The Spiritual Background of the First World War* (CW 174b).

among other things, he writes: "On February 13, following your advice, I joined the Order of the Freemasons. Indeed, I joined the Unit of the Grand National Mother-Lodge in the State of Prussia called: 'To the Three Globes,' belonging to the St. John's Lodge 'From the Cliffs to the Sea.' It is the same lodge to which our friends A.W. Sellin and Kurt Walther belong, as also does Häckländer from Wandsbeck. I hope that in the course of time I shall be allowed to awaken an interest in the Anthroposophically-inclined esotericism in this group and to keep it alive. It was out of this motive that I took this step. May the restitution of the meetings in our own esoteric Brotherhood also soon take place!"[31]

Rudolf Steiner's tolerance towards Freemasonry was demonstrated some years later when in 1923 at the founding of the English Society the question arose as to whether the man put forward for the Chairmanship of the Society was eligible for the post, as he was a Freemason. Rudolf Steiner replied as follows:

(...) I always said, where it concerns coming to the Anthroposophical Movement from any other movement—in this case it was Freemasonry that was meant—It is really not a matter of what one is by virtue of belonging to another movement, the question is whether when one comes into the Anthroposophical Movement one is a good Anthroposophist. It really does not matter, therefore if, apart from this, one belongs, let us say, to a shoemakers' or a locksmiths' guild. I am not making a comparison, just stating the principle: the fact that a person belongs to a shoemakers' or a locksmiths' guild does not in any way interfere with being an Anthroposophist. If one is a good Anthroposophist that is what matters to the Anthroposophical Movement. Whether apart from that, one is

---

31. Johannes Geyer, at the time a pastor in Hamburg, and from 1919 on a teacher at the Free Waldorf School in Stuttgart. From 1912 onwards he belonged to Rudolf Steiner's Esoteric School. According to: "Der Lehrerkreis um Rudolf Steiner in der ersten Waldorfschule," Geyer gave many lectures in a Freemasonry context concerning the origin of Freemasonry symbols in the light of Rudolf Steiner's Anthroposophy and won great acclaim thereby.

a good or bad or indifferent Freemason is irrelevant to the Anthroposophical Society. (...) It would be a foolish conclusion to arrive at if eligibility of a person to become a member of the Anthroposophical Society were to be judged by whether or not he or she was a Freemason.

I said [earlier] that a number of just the oldest and most valuable members are Freemasons. I cannot imagine how an impediment to joining the Anthroposophical Society could arise out of any kind of Freemasonry. I cannot imagine it. I would say that the Anthroposophical Movement should be something on its own account. It would not be a creative world movement if it were not able to be creative out of its own procreative powers, would it! That is the crux of the matter, what the positive result is. How it appears when compared to the one or other thing is not important. If I buy myself a suit what matters is that it suits my taste, that it is what I choose. What has that to do with the opinion of someone else who comes and says: That suit is not the same as that worn by someone else. It really is quite irrelevant to think that one ought to put on another person's suit. One puts on one's own suit. One does not put on Freemasonry when one becomes an Anthroposophist. Thus it is quite impossible to hold such a view.

But there is, of course, more to it than that. There is, in my opinion—if you will excuse me for saying so—not always enough esteem paid to Anthroposophy by its members. There is a tendency nowadays to pay higher regard to what is older, what creates more stir, what assumes an air of mystery and so on, and to undervalue what is open and sincere according to the amount of sensation it arouses and its rather indistinct reputation. It is a kind of denigration of the Anthroposophical Movement when one says of it that it can be harmed by the fact that this or that member comes to it from one or the other movement. It would have to be terribly weak to be harmed by such things as that.[32]

---

32. London, September 2, 1923.

Why Rudolf Steiner Wished to Avoid the Term "Secret Society" for His Cognitive-Ritual Work

A secret society was not made through that.[33]

It was not so much the principle of secrecy in Rudolf Steiner's case, but rather of the basic difference between his method of symbolic-ritual activity and that of the so-called secret societies. He regarded it as his main task to make what is expressed in Symbols, Signs, Handclasp, and Word understandable by explanations corresponding to them gained through spiritual insight. But with the word "understandable" he did not mean "this symbol means this and that symbol means that," for in that case everything could be made to mean anything. No. Instruction must be so arranged that to begin with "one finds a solution to the secrets in the course of the development of Earth and humanity and allows the symbols to evolve out of that," that is to say, one must first have comprehended what can be grasped by the understanding; the content of Anthroposophy.

Over against that the mere gazing at symbols, as it is usually practiced in esoteric societies today, is an unauthorized extension of a practice that was fully justified in days gone by. For at that time human beings had a greater sensitivity of the etheric body at their disposal, by which means they were able to arrive at a corresponding inner experience.

To the person of the modern consciousness-soul age—for whom the sensitivity towards the etheric body has been largely replaced by an understanding connected to the physical brain—symbols, signs, handclasp, and word have necessarily become something external; they cannot be connected to the consciousness soul. In spite of that they have an effect upon the etheric body, that is to say upon the unconscious. To work directly upon the etheric without first engaging the consciousness is not permissible in our time, for the consequence of that would be:

---

33. *Autobiography*. See p. 100 of the present volume.

that one can make other people into ready tools for any kind of plan, if one so desires. That is obvious. For if you were to influence the etheric body of a person without him being aware of it, you would eliminate those forces that he would otherwise have in his understanding, that is if you do not provide his intellect with something such as spiritual science is to become. You eliminate that and turn such brotherhoods into a tool for those who want to carry out their own private plans, their own objectives. In that case you would be in a position to make use of such brotherhoods for any kind of political aims, or you could postulate the dogma: "Alcyone" is the outer physical vessel of Jesus Christ,[34] and those who have been conditioned in this way make themselves into instruments to carry that out into the world. One must then only be correspondingly insincere and dishonest and all sorts of things can be achieved by making tools in this way.

And now—it all follows from real insight, does it not!—whoever knows how the fifth post-Atlantean epoch differs from the fourth post-Atlantean epoch—and that is reiterated again and again in our circles—will know why a knowledge of spiritual science must first be present and then only can an introduction to Symbolism be given. Wherever a spiritual-scientific movement is honestly striven for, this course will naturally be held to. For whoever has got to know what, for instance, is contained in my *Theosophy* or *Outline of Esoteric*

---

34. Alcyone = the official name of Jeddu Krishnamurti (1895-1986) for whom the Order of the Star of the East was created by Annie Besant and C.W. Leadbeater in 1911. At a young age he was proclaimed as the intended bearer of the expected reborn Christ, the future World Teacher. The Order soon spread over the whole Theosophical world. Rudolf Steiner was the only one to vigorously reject this as occult nonsense. For that reason the German Section led by him was officially excluded from the Theosophical Society in 1913. Krishnamurti then disbanded the Order of the Star of the East in 1929 and publicly distanced himself from the role allotted to him. He also dropped his connection to the Theosophical Society because in his view every kind of organization is a hindrance to spiritual development.

Science and has tried to understand it, will never be harmed by any tradition or symbols (Berlin, April 4, 1916).

The hidden cause of the aversion to secret societies at the present day might lie in the instinctive, but justified feeling that it is not proper to employ ceremonial acts for personal ends. Rudolf Steiner always condemned this rigorously, but at the same time he always emphasized that this did not apply to all esoteric societies, but only to certain ones.

On the basis of what has just been stated and the fact that everything in his symbolic-ritual work was done for the good of all in general and to permeate the ritual symbols with consciousness—for that reason "Cognitive-Ritual"—it becomes understandable why, in spite of the obligation to observe secrecy, he did not wish his circle to be considered a secret society.

LETTERS AND DOCUMENTS

Rudolf Steiner to A.W. Sellin

Berlin W 30, August 15, 1906
Motzstraße 17

Dear Herr Director!

At last I am able to write my long-announced letter to you. In the first place I beg of you—I refer to one or two sentences in your last letter—*never* to assume that I can ever be *offended* by anything. Please delete that word from the dictionary of our correspondence.[1]

And now, without more ado, I shall come to the point. The doubt which you have voiced in connection with a section of my esoteric investigations rests on quite erroneous suppositions. And just as erroneous are the things which you have heard from others.

Let us speak quite plainly: recently I was obliged to embark on something in my esoteric work which, with certain assumptions, could be said to lie in the direction of occult Freemasonry. I would ask you now to accept my every word and every turn of phrase quite *exactly*. I do not use these turns of expression in a rigid or legal sense, but in order to describe *exactly* the *real* facts of the case.

Now there was in Germany a so-called "Memphis and Misraim Order," which *gave itself out* to work in that direction. This Order called itself a Freemasonry organization. And it *worked* "degrees" of which the first three corresponded to the recognized Freemasonry.[2] *My* esoteric endeavors have, to begin with, nothing whatever to do with this "recognized" Freemasonry. They cannot and do not wish

---

1. Sellin had asked for an explanation of the Misraim affairs (see his letter to Marie Steiner of April 9, 1925). The above mentioned letter from Sellin to Rudolf Steiner is not available.

2. The three St. John degrees. [See: *The Temple Legend*, Lecture 8, Note 11, p. 340: "The 'Blue Masonry' of Heckethorn is what Rudolf Steiner calls 'Johannesmaurerei' (St. John Masonry) and is usually known simply as Craft Masonry in England. This Order got its name St. John Masonry from the Charter of Cologne, 1535."]

to invade its territory. Freemasonry does not have the slightest reason to engage in these endeavors of mine in any way.

When I was about to start work in the aforesaid direction I was
obliged to introduce a ritual for certain happenings on a higher
plane for the people who were looking for such a thing. This ritual
can be nothing else than a *mirror image* of what is a fact on the higher
plane. This ritual is just the same as that which *occultism* has acknowledged for the last 2,300 years (see Hella Wiesberger's preliminary
remarks to part II, p. 127) and which was adapted for European
conditions by the Masters of Rosicrucianism. If in *this* ritual something is discovered that has been transmitted from the three St.
John degrees that only goes to prove that these St. John degrees
have accepted something from occultism. My source is only that of
esotericism and the "Masters."[3]

Now I had two ways open to me. Either to ignore completely the
so-called Order, or else to come to terms with it. The first would only
have been possible in a single instance: if the Order had rejected my
application. Under any other circumstances it would have been disloyal in the sense of certain *historical* concessions that esotericism
has to make.

I will tell you what I have now done, under the assumption that
you will not let it go any further.

The General Grand Master of the Order was a certain Theodor
Reuß. What the latter otherwise did has nothing to do with the present discussion. It could be anything whatsoever. What came into
consideration here is only the fact that he was the Grand Master of
the Order that gave itself out to work in the aforesaid direction. I
had to come to terms with *this* fact. For this purpose I had to visit the
aforementioned Theodor Reuß *whom I had never met before* and about
whose circumstances I had never been informed from any direction
whatever. It would, of course, have been easy for me to have made
enquiries about him. But it was of *no concern* to me.

---

3. See: *From the History and the Contents of the First Section of the Esoteric School 1904-
1914* (CW 264).

Then I said to Herr Reuß something like the following: I want to have *nothing*, nothing at all from your Order. But I will work along the same lines as this Order alleges that it works. What is important is that the Order recognizes on its own behalf, not for my sake, that I am working with the degrees which it lays claim to for itself. I make it a condition that the Order does not impart *anything* of its rituals to me. No one will be able to say that I have received anything from this Order. I want my step to be judged only from this point of view of esoteric loyalty. And nobody should have the right to interpret it otherwise.

Reuß replied rather abruptly that he could not do that, for it would put him in an impossible situation as regards his Order. At first I withdrew. What actually happened and will continue to do so, happened then and will go on happening whether with or without the aforesaid Order. After a few days Reuß summoned me to further discussions. He did not make any demands other than that I should recognize, *purely as a business proposition*, his right to receive a normal fee from all who liked to work in the direction which the Order looked upon as its own. All further arrangements concerned mere formalities. I established formally everything that had to be thus established without Herr Reuß ever having been present. On his part Herr Reuß recognized all that I did. I practically *ignored* the Order completely. Herr Reuß gave me the diplomas and rituals so that as he said, not to offend against the rules of the Order. That is to say, he brought them to my house. To have *bought* all these things would have been the greatest *folly*, even if for no other reason than that there was nothing contained in all that stuff that could not have been obtained for very little expense from any antiquarian dealer. The fact that Reuß simply received a fee from every member to which he is *legally* entitled is merely a loyal recognition of his entitlement, no matter what fault one might otherwise find in him.

What now takes place within the "lodges" that have been formed, can of course only be learned by someone who is a member.[4] I can

---

4. Sellin apparently only became a member later.

only say very little about it myself. But this is objectively quite enough. *In the first place* the name of Reuß is never mentioned in these lodges. *Secondly,* no one whom I have admitted can show a diploma issued by Reuß. *Thirdly,* nothing has ever taken place which in any way harms the loyalty due to Freemasonry. *Fourthly,* everyone has been informed about its relationship to Freemasonry. *Fifthly,* in conclusion, *only Theosophists* are included in our "lodges." If former members of the aforesaid Order wish to join us they must attest to the fact that they not only legally hold the degrees, having paid the fee, and the relevant diploma, but that they also have them "at heart."

What I have established, therefore, has nothing to do with what formerly pretended to hold "Memphis and Misraim degrees." And what goes on around the Order of Reuß and his associates is of absolutely no concern to me. There have even been naive people coming to visit me in order to bargain with me about what they know of Reuß, or even to "warn" me about him. But actually that does not affect me in the least. It also does not worry me that people who have formerly received "degrees" from Reuß feel they have been duped and are now angry about it. I understand their being angry; but it would be disloyal of me to get involved in any way in such matters.[5]

You see, esteemed Herr Doctor, how all is in order on my part. I have given you an answer because you asked me in a loyal fashion. What to do about people who try to blame me for things that have been said by those who know nothing about it, only the future can show.

✳

Today I have something to say about your exercises ...[6]

With hearty greetings

Your Dr. Rudolf Steiner

---

5. See in this connection the letter from Emil Adryánij, p. 92.

6. This part of the letter is contained in *From the History and Contents of the First Section of the Esoteric School 1904-1914* (CW 264).

Supplement to the above letter to A.W. Sellin

The above reproduced letter was given into Marie Steiner's care after Rudolf Steiner's death by the one who received it, A.W. Sellin. In the letter, which accompanied it, on April, 9, 1925, he writes:

> I am impelled to put at your disposal two letters of our dear departed one which may be of importance in future for the history of the Anthroposophical Society. At any rate, they will be better preserved in your keeping than in mine.[7]
>
> The first letter, written to me on August 15, 1906, concerns the history of the "Mystica Aeterna"[8] when it was first incepted and is the answer to the question I directed to the Doctor on this subject.[9]
>
> This question was all the more important to me, standing at that time amid the German Lodge activity, because Reuß had been so indiscreet as to publish, in the First Number of the fifth year's edition of his magazine, *Oriflamme*, the text of his permission granted for the founding of a Chapter and of a Grand Council for the Adoption Lodge under the name of "Mystica Aeterna" and to name Dr. Steiner as the Deputy Grand Master and you as the Grand Secretary of this new association.[10]
>
> This indiscretion of Reuß, who had sent the said number of his magazine to many of the Freemason lodges, caused me much annoyance later in the Freemasonry unions, which I only overcame gradually as a result of the explanation given in the enclosed letter from the Doctor.

---

7. The second letter is addressed to somebody else and concerns other matters.
8. The official name of the Cognitive-Ritual Working Group.
9. A written enquiry is not available; the question could have been an oral one.
10. c.f. p. 91.

A.W. Sellin to Rudolf Steiner

Three reports about Memphis-Misraim-Freemasonry

I

Hamburg, December 12, 1904[11]

Egyptian Freemasonry

The founder of the so-called Egyptian Masonry is thought to be Cagliostro.[12] According to his own assertion he became a member of the Order in London, but this has not been corroborated.

It has been supposed that the first idea of this way of teaching and the papers were given him by a certain George Coston.

Cagliostro attempted to found lodges in The Hague and in Russia, but without success. He finally succeeded on October 8, 1779, when his first lodge of the "Rite Égyptien" was established in Strassburg. It continued to exist until 1783.

In Lyons in October 1784, Cagliostro, along with 12 members of the local Freemasonry lodge, founded a mother lodge of his Egyptian Masonry, going by the name of "La sagesse triomphante" and on July 5, 1785, he founded a similar lodge in Paris.

At that time Cagliostro's reputation had risen to such an extent that the Freemasonry Convention held in Paris went to great lengths to engage his services as a teacher, even though he made it a condition that the Philalethes [= searchers after wisdom] were to burn all the books of the Freemasonry Archive. After this condition had been fulfilled he started to teach the Freemasons how to acquire the ability, by deeds and facts and also through sense impressions, to recognize to which science true Masonry offers symbols and points the way.

---

11. An accompanying letter to this report is not available.

12. See lecture: Berlin, December 16, 1904, *The Temple Legend*, Lecture 9, p. 95. Also: *Secret Societies* by C.W. Heckethorn, Volume I, Chapter XX.

On November 21, 1786, there followed the exposure of Cagliostro in London by the optician Mach, and therewith the collapse of his system of which he was the Supreme Head or Grand-Kophta.

His system admitted both men and women and consisted of a scale of 90 degrees and promised perfection through physical and moral rebirth to all who believed in it. (c.f. Goethe, *Neue Schriften*, 1792).

The Count Saint Germain stood in close contact with Cagliostro and introduced his system, probably in a changed form, at the courts of German princes (Ferdinand of Brunswick, Frederick August of Brunswick, Charles of Hessen, among others). Charles of Hessen, namely, who looked after Count St. Germain until his death, studied occultism with great devotion at the instigation of the latter. He was the author of *Explanation of the Zodiacal Stone in the Temple of Dendera*, which appeared in 1824 in Copenhagen.

"The Rite de Memphis," or as it called itself, "The Oriental Freemasonry Order of Memphis" is supposed, according to its own myth, to have come from Ormus or Ormuzd, a man converted to Christianity by St. Mark in 46 A.D. and those from an Essene school united under his leadership. The Rite is supposed to have been transferred to Edinburgh by Scottish Knights in 1150 and to be the predecessor of present day Freemasonry.

Nobody in Edinburgh is aware of this story, but on the other hand it is known that a certain Samual Honis from Cairo founded the first Grand Lodge for this kind of instruction in Paris in 1815 which, however, only lasted until 1816.

In 1838 a second attempt was made there to introduce this kind of instruction through the Osiris Lodge, but this also failed, as the Order was abolished by the police in 1843.

In 1848 the third attempt was made, and indeed the Order was then divided into 90 degrees of knowledge. The topmost degree (The Sanctuarium) is not meant to exert any influence over the management of the Order, but to be entirely esoteric.

In 1851 the Order was prohibited in France, and its headquarters was transferred to London. There it flourished better and produced daughter lodges in Geneva, Brussels, New York and Australia. Its 90 degrees were reduced to 30, and in this form an attempt was made to introduce it into Germany, but as a result of the opposition from the Masonic officials of the old Prussian grand lodges it did not succeed.

Its spread in other countries, such as England, Ireland, Scotland, Italy, Romania, Egypt, the East Indies, Canada, the U.S.A. and Australia was successful, especially since it had been fused with the "Rite de Misraïm."

The "Rite de Misraim" or "Rite Égyptien" was brought from Italy to France at the beginning of the nineteenth century by the Jewish merchant Michel Bédarride and developed there. The Order's legend avers that Misraim, a son of Ham, moved to Egypt, occupied it and called it after his name (Misraim, that is to say Egypt).

From him there spread to all lands and throughout all ages a very ancient doctrine, which was used, with some alterations, by the most varied religious and masonic societies at all schools of philosophy and mystical brotherhoods, namely the teaching about Isis and Osiris, Nature and her Creator.

The system is divided into four parts, of which the first is called the Symbolical, the second the Philosophical, the third the Mystical and the fourth the Hermetic-Cabalistical.

17 classes and 90 degrees are distinguishable, but are unevenly distributed. Those members who have attained the 87th-89th degrees are entrusted with the management of the first three degrees and the series up to the 77th degree. The Sovereign Prince of the 78th degree is the head of the fourth series and the 90th degree is held by the unknown "Souverain Grand Maître absolu puissant suprème de l'Ordre."

The bankruptcy of the founder of the French Order, Bédarride, did not hinder the spread of the latter, a fact that is attributed by Freemasonry literature—which otherwise has nothing but mockery and scorn for esoteric matters, namely for the honors conferred upon higher officials—to the exemplary administration of its charitable work.

The spread of the now amalgamated "Order of Memphis and Misraïm" is discussed in another place.

It has been represented in Hamburg for the last few years and appears in the address book as follows: A. and A. [Ancient and Accepted] Scotch (33°) and A. and P. [Ancient and Primitive] Rite of Memphis and Misraim (95°). Chapter, "Phoenix to the Truth" No. 3 in Tale[13] of Hamburg. Working Lodge every second Thursday in the month. Sym[bolic] (St. Joh[n]) Lodge "Phoenix to the Truth" in the O. [Orden?] Hamburg. Working Lodge every first, third and fourth Thursday in the month.

Work and jurisdiction of the Grand Orient and the Sovereign Sanctuary for Germany in Berlin. Friendship-Representative for America: Franz Held, Borgfelde, Henriettenallee 18. Enquiries to the First Secretary M. Lupschewitz, Dillstraße 4 or to the Treasurer A. Paasch, St. G. Steindamm 68/11.

The Order is not recognized by the Union of Grand Lodges in Germany, but it tries to convert individual Brothers of proximate ways of teaching, namely by the distribution of a periodical that contains almost exclusively the works of Dr. F. Hartmann. I will try to acquire this periodical.

A.W. Sellin

---

13. Tal is the name of Freemasonry officials.

II

Hamburg, 14 December 1904

Dear Herr Doctor!

Firstly I have ascertained the following facts about the Grand Lodge known to us. It was set up about two years ago in Berlin under the name of "Grand Orient of Scottish and Accepted 33° Rite and Sovereign Sanctuary of the Eagle and Pelican 95° of Memphis and Misraim" and has made known its constitution to the existing grand lodges of other systems, which have not responded to it.

From its official announcement to the masonic bodies of Germany the following can be learned:

> The new Grand Orient has been set up at the suggestion of German Freemasons belonging to lodges of this kind abroad.

> The Sovereign General Grand Master Brother John Yarker, 33°, 90°, 96° has provided Brother Dr. Franz Hartmann, 33°, 95° (admitted to the Union of the Washington Lodge No. 12, Orient Georgetown, America), Heinrich Klein, 33°, 95° (admitted to the Union of the Pilgrim Lodge No. 238 in the Orient, London) and Theodor Reuß 33°, 96° (admitted to the Union of the Pilgrim Lodge No. 238 in London) and those in union with the same Brothers, a Charter to constitute a Grand Orient and Sovereign Sanctuary of the Rite for the German Empire.

> The Supreme Spiritual Leader and Honorary Grand Master of the same is Brother Dr. Karl Kellner, 33°, 90°, 96° (admitted to the Union in the Lodge Humanitas in Vienna), Director of the Kellner-Partington Paper publishing factory of Hallein, Liverpool, Manchester, etc., and a member of the Royal Imperial Industrial Advisory Board of Vienna.

> Reuß can be reached in Berlin W. in the Columbia Office, Equitable-Palast, Leipzigerstraße 101/102.

The majority of the 33, respectively 95, degrees are to be looked upon as stages of knowledge which are worked on in writing and entail a study of the various religious and philosophical systems. Postal charges are not made.

In the higher degrees of this system according to a manifesto of the Grand Orient,[14] there are secrets that "have been handed down by word of mouth ... from the ancestors of all true Freemasons, 'the Wise Men of the East,' and will only be transmitted by us in like manner."

But, of course—as it says in the manifesto—the success of this practical instruction to unveil the secret, depends for its part entirely on the candidate himself.

Those Brr. [Brothers] who had discovered the secret guarded it as a precious, self-achieved possession, and in order not to be misunderstood or even made fun of by everyday folk, they concealed it through symbols, as we still do today.

Our higher degrees—with the help of these symbols—provide the Brother with the possibility of gaining a sure proof of human immortality. He needs to have this assurance of a life after death in order to be truly happy in this present life. Therefore also the Mysteries in the religions and centers of hidden wisdom have had this question as their highest and principle task. The Church does this as well, but it directs the candidate along the path of grace. Our Order, however, places it within the power of each individual seeker, by practical means, to unite consciously and voluntarily with the World Consciousness, with the ultimate forces of Creation.

The new Grand Orient publishes a periodical by Max Perl of Berlin under the name of the *Oriflamme*. Dr. Franz Hartmann contributes most of its articles. I only know the *Historical Edition of the Oriflamme* of 1904. The latter opens with the words: "Peace, Tolerance, Truth!" and reproaches Freemasons for their lack of knowledge as regards the development of the true essence of

---

14. This manifesto is published and discussed by Rudolf Steiner in a lecture given in Berlin, December 9, 1904, *The Temple Legend*, Lecture 8, p. 88 et seq.

Freemasonry. Particularly Findel, as a Masonic historian, is quite unreliable; what has been offered by way of examples to prove this statement are, however, not at all valid.

The editor rejects the idea of the derivation of Freemasonry from the old Craft Masonry and traces it back to the Knights Templar. But there is no recorded evidence for this statement, as it was strictly forbidden to make any written records of the meetings or about the association with Masonic or Rosicrucian bodies practicing in the tradition of the Templars. The proofs that existed about their association with the Knights Templar were only confided to initiates.

The correctness of this information is, of course, unverifiable and the maintaining of such trading in historical secrets in our time, which is so desirous of openness, is incomprehensible, to say the least.

Happily the origin of the Scottish 33° Rite, in so far as this can be traced in documents of Frederick the Great (Charleston System), has been described as a great lie perpetrated by the Order and the explanation is given that in this system, connected with the Memphis and Misraim Order, one is dealing with the legitimate system of the Cerneau Brothers.[15]

But because the new Order has a thoroughly Theosophical character about it, I shall give it my closest attention and even take up direct contact with its leaders.

Should I thereby get the conviction that it can be of use to the Theosophical Movement, the question can sometime be raised between us as to how this may be achieved.[16]

---

15. Sellin, whose own lodge then worked with the Cerneau Rite, is referring to the contrast between the two Scottish 33° systems (Cerneau and Charlston). Through the system devised around 1801/02 in Charleston (U.S.A.), the rituals originating from Cerneau (1763-1829) are supposed to have been altered by means of forged documents. In the *Historical Edition of the Oriflamme*, mentioned by Sellin, co-edited by Yarker, it tells us that with regard to the Scottish Rite one worked according to the legitimate Cerneau System.

16. Rudolf Steiner must have orally informed Sellin that he had meanwhile made contact with the Order himself. That would explain why the letter of August 15, 1906, takes no note of the fact of Sellin's endeavors in 1904. c.f. p. 48.

Enclosed herewith is my lodge lecture "Princely Brothers," which I would ask you to send back to me shortly, as it is part of a series of lectures which I may probably have to refer to.

With hearty greetings

Yours faithfully

A.W. Sellin

III

Hamburg, December 20, 1904

Dear Herr Doctor!

With reference to my letter of 14 inst. I am sending you herewith the last number of the *Oriflamme*, which contains an article by Franz Hartmann that might be of interest to you.

In the September number of 1903 of the *Oriflamme* I find the following strange contribution:

> In North America there are 50,000 women belonging to the Order of the Eastern Star, to which only wives, daughters and widows of Freemasons can belong. A so-called "mixed lodge" has been founded this year in London by the well-known Theosophist Annie Besant who was admitted to membership in Paris. It is a Parisian foundation.

The latter notice is clearly to be understood to mean that the "mixed lodge" founded by Annie Besant in London received its deeds of membership from Paris.[17]

Do you know anything about this?

_____

17. C.f. Supplementary Notes, p. 513.

"Mixed lodges" have only existed since 1893. At that time it was Maria Deraismes who admitted 16 women to the Freemasonry Union in Paris on March 14 and founded the Scottish Lodge "Le droit humain."

These "mixed lodges" are just as little recognized by our German Grand Lodges as the Memphis and Misraim Lodges and the Adoption Lodges, which are worked in the Order of the Eastern Star.

I should be very pleased if you would return the enclosed number, as also the two union notices and my lecture. I hope your time will allow you to vouchsafe me a few words in private about my inner progress when you visit in January.

With brotherly greetings and best wishes for the coming festival, from your highly appreciative and faithful colleague

A.W. Sellin

Receipt for Membership Fee for Rudolf Steiner and Marie von Sivers, Berlin, November 24, 1905, issued by Theodor Reuß, signed by Max Heilbronner.

Rudolf Steiner to Marie von Sivers in Berlin (extracts)[18]

I

Nuremberg, November 25, 1905

... You yourself saw yesterday[19] what little remains of the esoteric institutions of the past, which were once a physiognomic expression of higher worlds. In reality the three symbolic degrees of apprentice, journeyman, and master expressed the three stages in which human beings find themselves in the spirit, i.e., find their self within humanity. And the higher grades were meant to indicate the gradual growth through which the human being builds the temple of humankind. And in the same way that the existing human organism, i.e., the astral, etheric, and physical organism, is a microcosm of the past world, so the temple to be constructed by the Masons in wisdom, beauty, and strength is to be the macrocosmic image of an inner microcosmic wisdom, beauty, and strength of soul.

With materialism, humankind has lost the living awareness of these things and the outer Form has largely been passed to people who have no access to the inner life.

The task now should be to reclaim Masonic life from its externalized forms and give it a new birth; and, of course, this reborn life would have to create new forms as well. That should be our ideal: to create forms that express the inner life. For an era that cannot see forms, and in seeing create them, must of necessity cause the spirit to vanish into an abstraction without substance, and reality is subsequently forced to mirror this abstract spirit as aggregate matter devoid of spirit. If human beings are capable of comprehending forms, e.g., the birth of the soul from the etheric clouds in the Sistine Madonna, then spiritless matter will soon cease to exist for them. And because the masses need the medium of religion to

---

18. *Correspondence and Documents* (CW 262) pp. 68 and 75, translated by Christian and Ingrid von Arnim.

19. When they joined the Freemasons, November 24, 1905.

comprehend forms, which are spiritualized, future work must be directed toward developing spirit with an aesthetic form. But that requires a deepening of the content. Theosophy has to bring this deepening in the first instance. If human beings have no inkling that spirits live in fire, air, water and earth, neither will they have an art that reflects this wisdom in outer form....

II

Karlsruhe, November 30, 1905

... Let us deal with the Freemasonry matter steadily and without haste. Reuß is not a person on whom we can rely. We must be clear that caution is an urgent necessity. We are dealing with a "framework," not with greater reality. At the moment there is nothing behind the matter. The spiritual forces have withdrawn completely from it. All I can say just now is that I do not know yet whether or not one day I will be forced to say after all: that must not be done. Please therefore do not discuss anything with them except very provisionally.[20] If we should be forced at some time to say we cannot go along with that, then we do not want to be too deeply involved. Motives partly of a personal nature and partly of vanity are involved and the spiritual powers flee from both. Certainly, all the spiritual powers see no value in our doing such things at the moment. But I cannot say anything certain about it today either. If we notice that something is not right in the next talk with Reuß, then we can still take appropriate action. ...

---

20. "Them" might refer to those members who already knew about the intentions referred to here.

Contract between Theodor Reuß and Rudolf Steiner
Translated text of the handwritten original by Reuß, dated Berlin, January 3, 1906

GRAND-ORIENT OF THE ANCIENT AND ACCEPTED 33° SCOTTISH RITE

SOVEREIGN SANCTUARY OF THE ORDER OF ANCIENT FREEMASONS OF THE MEMPHIS AND MISRAIM RITE

Office of the
Grand-Master General   Berlin, S.W. 47, the....... 190 ...

Contract and Brotherly Agreement

The following contract and brotherly agreement between Theodor Reuß, Sovereign and Grand Master General ad vitam, 33°, 90°, 96° and Managing Director of the Order of the Ancient Templar Freemasons of the Scottish, Memphis and Misraïm Rite for the German Empire and Br[other] Dr. Rudolf Steiner, General Secretary of the Theosophical Society and President of the Mystic Temple and Chapter "Mystica Aeterna" 30°, 67°, 89° in Berlin, has been concluded and signed.

Herewith, upon compliance with the conditions here set down in this contract, Br. Dr. Steiner receives the right to admit, without previous consultation with Br. Theodor Reuß, an unspecified number of members of the Theosophical Society, or those not belonging thereto, into his Chapter and Mystic Temple "Mystica Aeterna" in Berlin in the Order of the Ancient Templar Freemasons of the Scottish Memphis and Misraim Rite for the German Empire and to perfect himself up to the 30° A. and A.

Br. Dr. Steiner engages, on the other hand, to pay a fee of forty Marks (40 Marks)[21] to Br. Theodor Reuß for every candidate he admits to the said Order; respectively, perfects in the Order's

---

21. The usual admission fee. According to a report in the *Vienna Freemasonry Newspaper* (1929, No. 7/8) a fee of 1,500 German marks is asked.

degrees. For this, when the candidate in question has attained to the 18th degree he receives a diploma of this degree from Theodor Reuß.[22] The fee is due to be paid to Theodor Reuß on the day of the candidate's admittance. The payment of this fee can be deferred by Theodor Reuß under certain circumstances. A candidate, however, only becomes a legitimate member of the said Order and can only claim a membership-diploma when the aforementioned fee has duly been paid to Br. Theodor Reuß. If the member wishes to receive further diplomas for other than the 18th degree, the issue of every further diploma will cost 10 Marks, which must be paid to Br. Theodor Reuß in advance. In respect of the use to which the fees paid to Theodor Reuß for himself or for his candidates and members is put, neither Br. Dr. Steiner nor the members admitted by him or belonging to his organization can exercise any control, that is to say they have no right to demand how the fees are used. Br. Dr. Steiner has no right to issue independent diplomas for the Order or for Theodor Reuß. Br. Theodor Reuß appoints Br. Dr. Steiner to be his Deputy General Grand Master and General Grand Secretary in the Sovereign Sanctuary during his absence from Berlin. This appointment takes effect on the day that Br. Dr. Steiner has admitted four candidates to the said Order and has founded his Chapter. Br. Dr. Steiner has, however, as Deputy General Grand Master, only the jurisdiction over the members he has himself admitted to the said Order. Over the latter, however, he has the exclusive jurisdiction up to 30° A. and A. and only when the latter rise above the 30° A. and A. do they fall under the jurisdiction of Br. Theodor Reuß. When Br. Dr. Steiner has paid to Br. Theodor Reuß the fee of forty Marks (40 M.) stipulated in this contract for the hundredth (100th) candidate will Br. Theodor Reuß appoint Br. Dr. Steiner to be the Practicing General Grand Master 33°, 90°, 96° for the German Empire with jurisdiction over all existing organizations of the Rite and Order for the German Empire. When the said number of one hundred candidates has

---

22. Such diplomas were never conferred.

been attained, the women admitted to the Order by Sister von Sivers and Br. Dr. Steiner can also be included. All printed rituals, catechisms, books, and lodge objects must be paid for separately by Br. Dr. Steiner.[23]

Br. Dr. Steiner is obliged to obtain all his Freemasonry vestments for his members from Fräulein Marta Gierloff at a fixed price. Br. Dr. Steiner must undertake not to admit or accept anyone into the Order who has been excluded, turned away or suspended from the Symbolic Grand Lodge in Leipzig or by Br. Theodor Reuß (S[anctum] S[anctuarium]). Furthermore Br. Dr. Steiner must undertake not to recognize or enter into relationship with any lodge or other Freemasonry ∴ organization or authority in Germany that has been dissolved or suspended by the S[anctum] S[anctuarium], otherwise Br. Theodor Reuß, or that has dissociated itself from him.

Br. Dr. Steiner immediately loses all rights and degrees in the Sanctum Sanctuarium and in the said Order if he acts contrary to the latter regulations. Br. Dr. Steiner will, of course, have the use of the official stamp and headed notepaper of the Order in the same way as Br. Reuß himself. As official stamp Br. Dr. Steiner will have the use of the stamp used on the present document.

Thus performed, read, accepted, and signed on January 3, 1906, and duly incorporated (that is, on the third of January nineteen hundred and six) in Berlin.

Groß-Lichterfelde

Theodor Reuß ∴ 33°, 90°, 96°.

Stamp   Stamp

---

23. c.f. p. 70 et seq.

Additional remark by Hella Wiesberger

Out of all the conditions of this contract the only thing that was of importance to Rudolf Steiner was the fact that he was legally entitled to admit members of his choice, from whom the regular fee was to be exacted, and that after admitting the hundredth member the Misraim Rite would be represented by him alone. c.f. his letter to A.W. Sellin of August 15, 1906. p. 69 of the present volume.

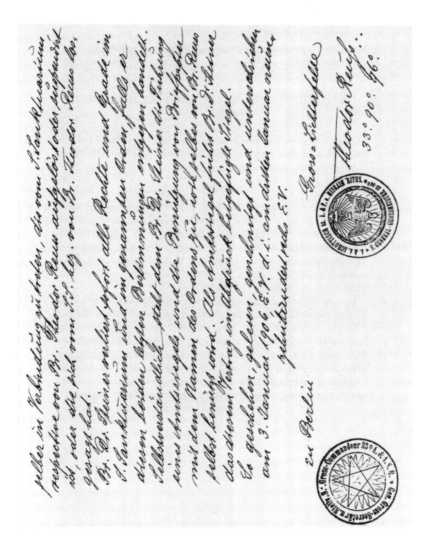

Concerning the admittance of women by Marie von Sivers

According to a handwritten, undated, and unsigned copy by Theodor Reuß

ANCIENT ORDER OF THE EGYPTIAN FREEMASONRY FOR WOMEN

Hon. President J.H. Princess Maria de Rohan,

Hon. Member (Mrs.) Dr. Maria v. Kellner,

General Grand Master Frau Colonel Alice Leighton Cleater,

General Secretary Fräulein Marie von Sivers.

Headquarters in Berlin

Since it has become known in Germany through the interesting Publication *Die Woche* [*The Week*], that in England the conservative motherland of modern Freemasonry, women are also admitted to Freemasonry Orders, the lively wish has shown itself in German Women's Circles to procure the same rights of admittance to Freemasonry for women in Germany as in England, France, Spain, America, India, etc.

Therefore it is herewith made known that ladies of standing and rank and of independent means can be admitted into a high-degree body of Adoption-Freemasonry, called the Ancient Order of Egyptian Freemasonry for Women, if they apply to Fräulein von Sivers, Motzstraße 17. Berlin W. This Freemasonry Women's Order awards the same degrees as its sister organizations in America, France, England, etc. Mme. H.P. Blavatsky, the founder of the modern Theosophical Movement in Europe, received the degrees of this Order on November 24, 1877. Applications must be accompanied by a stamped addressed envelope.[24]

---

24. Whether this rendering has been published or not could not be ascertained.

Announcement of the agreement of January 3, 1906 in *Oriflamme*[25]

CHAPTER AND GRAND-COUNCIL "MYSTICA AETERNA,"
partly in BERLIN

Permission has been given to Br. Dr. Steiner and the Brothers and Sisters associated with him to found a Chapter and Grand-Council of the Adoption Freemasonry under the name "Mystica Aeterna" in Berlin. Br. Dr. Steiner was appointed Deputy Grand Master with jurisdiction over

Theodor Reuß,	33°, 90°, 96°.
Henry Klein,	33°, 90°, 96°.
Max Heilbronner,	33°, 90°, 96°.
Paul Kirmiss,	33°, 90°, 96°.
Maximilian Dotzler,	33°, 90°, 96°.
Ernst Pfreundtner,	33°, 90°, 96°.
Dr. Lauer,	33°, 90°, 96°.
Andreas Ullmer,	33°, 90°, 96°.
Joseph Brucker,	33°, 90°, 96°.

the members admitted or to be admitted by him. Sister Marie von Sivers was appointed General Grand Secretary for the Adoption Lodges.

Berlin Easter 1906 incorporated.

---

25. Official organ of the Union of Ancient Freemasons of the Scottish Memphis and Misraim Rite, Grand Orient in Germany, Year 5, No. I, January-June, 1906.

Rudolf Steiner to Michael Bauer (excerpt)

Berlin, July 3, 1906

... Adriányj really does not need to get into a state because of Reuß, at least not as far as it concerns me.[26] I am just as little concerned about Reuß as I am about the others who have formed lodges with him. I do not have anything to do with any of them. I only had to remain loyal to Reuß. Furthermore it is very strange that people now attack Reuß so vehemently who formerly allowed him to bestow degrees on them for having done nothing at all—I am not, of course, referring to material things. But nobody should think of me as though I had anything to do with such trading in degrees ...

Excerpts from two letters to Rudolf Steiner from Emil Adriányj

I

Nuremberg, September 3, 1906

... I am very sorry that your time did not allow you to grant me a few moments of undisturbed attention on the occasions of your repeated visits to Nuremberg, which I asked Herrn Bauer to arrange for me. I would have liked to ask you for your unequivocal opinion about a certain matter which has often been linked with your name. I am personally very curious to know how you judge certain events which have caused great amazement in some circles. Likewise I can find no explanation for the fact that the leader of the Esoteric School of the Theosophical Society in Germany could

26. The Hungarian Emil Adriányj (*1865) lived in Nuremberg from the beginning of the century. Freemason, Theosophist and, shortly before falling out with Reuß, Grand Secretary of the Memphis-Misraim Order, later notable Masonic writer.

associate with similar people, whose names alone must be very compromising to the "Theosophical Society," as the Society has not been afraid to dismiss without further ado one of its oldest and, through his work, best known members for similar transgressions of black magic a short while ago ...[27]

II

Nuremberg, September 8, 1906

I acknowledge the receipt of your valued letter of the 4th inst. with my great thanks and take note of its contents with much pleasure.[28]

The fact that your name has always been linked to that of Reuß since the publication of No.1/6 of the *Oriflamme* and has also been discussed in the Freemasonry Press is because you are a member of the Order and its Sanctuary, as well as belonging to the "Mystica aeterna," according to the testimony of the *Oriflamme*. What critique the rest of the contents of the *Oriflamme* receive from these papers you may gather from the enclosed copy of a note in the *Lodge News* from Brunswick.[29]

I am sorry about this, already for the sake of the Theosophical Society, and would like to accept your explanation that you have nothing in common with Reuß, also to forward the Freemasonry papers when next there is something contained in them about Reuß.

It is not only a matter of your own prestige but also of the good name of persons who must mean more to you than the Orders created by Reuß, in which your name is used as reference.

As you were kind enough to hint at your concise views about the things that Reuß is accused of, so will I, with equal candor, give you

---

27. This refers to the so-called "Leadbeater case." See the volume: *From the History and Contents of the First Section of the Esoteric School 1904-1914* (CW 264). As also *The Elder Brother. A Biography of Charles Webster Leadbeater* by Gregory Tillet, London, 1982.

28. This letter of Steiner's is unfortunately not known.

29. This is not available.

my views—gained from older letters from Reuß, and from the latest explanations of Dotzler, as well as from a thorough study of the Cerneau- , Misraim- and Memphis-Rite—that Reuß's Order itself does not know anything at all about "exercises," nor does it possess any, or have any to award, here or abroad. The exercises that Reuß has confided to a select inner circle of pupils have been composed by him (allegedly after consultation with Dr. Kellner), or respectively in imitation of the T.S. [Theosophical Society], mixed together with the present "A. Pr. Rite" [Ancient Primitive Rite], whereby it was possible to proclaim it as the "conscious amalgamation with the original creative power."[30] Reuß's Order did not have an actual right to hand out esoteric "exercises": it would be hard to produce a hard and fast proof for things lying in that direction. At any rate it is my personal opinion that the T.S. does not need the help of Reuß in such exercises.[31] As the person in question had handed out his "exercises" without any kind of caution (as for instance that of Mme. Blavatsky in Volume III of *The Secret Doctrine*) and without the insistence of leading a moral life (the now included "address to the pupils of the occult degrees" was first devised by me in order to rectify this omission) and because his results manifest mainly on the astral, rather than on the devachanic [or mental] plane and through mediumistic-like appearances, so I came to the conclusion, soon after having received my first "exercises," that Reuß was either ignorant or a terribly irresponsible fellow. On top of that is the fact that in the case of many highly developed persons the exercises have *not had the slightest effect* even after months....

---

30. This is spoken of in the manifesto of the historical edition of the *United Scottish Memphis and Misraim Masonry*. See the text of this in Rudolf Steiner's lecture in Berlin, December 9, 1904. *The Temple Legend*, CW 93, p. 88 ff.

31. Adriányj does not seem to be aware of the fact that Rudolf Steiner did not need exercises from any other source.

Announcement by Theodor Reuß about the separation of the combined three
Rites (Scottish, Memphis, Misraim) into three separate bodies

In *Oriflamme*, fifth year No.2, July-December 1906

EDICT

of the Sovereign General Grand Master of the Combined Rites
of the Scottish, Memphis- and Misraim-Freemasonry
33° = 95°, in and for Germany

Z. R. D. A. B. A. W.![32]

Sovereign General Grand Council of the Ancient Rites

Deus meumque jus.—Exitus acta probat.—Spes mea in Deo est.

————————

Brotherly greetings on all points of the triangle!

We, Albert Karl Theodor Reuß, 33°, 90°, 96°, Sovereign General
Grand Master ad Vitam of the Order of the Combined Rites of the
Scottish, Memphis- and Misraim-Freemasonry in and for the
German Empire, Sovereign General Grand Commander, Absolute
Great Sovereign, Sovereign Pontif, Sovereign Master of the Order
of the Oriental Templar Freemasons, Magus Supremus Soc[iety]
Frat[ernity] R[ose] C[ross], S ∴ L ∴ 33°, Termaximus Regens I.O.
etc. etc. do hereby make known and to be understood that we feel
moved, by force of the powers and might of authority conferred
on and entrusted to us, to separate from one another the manner
of working and administration of the three Masonic Rites, which
are placed under our jurisdiction in Germany and German speaking countries, and to raise the three Rites to three independent
Masonic bodies.

————————

32. Zum Ruhme des allmächtigen Baumeisters aller Welten! [To the Glory of the
Almighty Architect of All Worlds].

From June 24, 1907, inc. the following will be under our supreme jurisdiction in Germany:

The Supreme Council of Scottish, Ancient and Accepted 33° Rite for the German Empire.

The General Grand Council (90°) of the Egyptian Rite of Misraim.

The Sovereign Sanctuary (95°) of the Ancient and Primitive Rite of Memphis.

For each single Rite we shall appoint a Serving General Grand Master with jurisdiction over the bodies under him. The single Grand Councils take up their own administrative rules, which may not contradict the general basic rules of the Rites. The Sovereign General Grand Master ad Vitam remains the final court of judicature in all matters of ritual and personal affairs. The Grand Officers of the individual Grand Councils are selected annually in private session by the collective Officers of the Chapter and Grand Councillors on the basis of a three quarters majority. The rights and duties of the Serving General Grand Master and all further decisions are laid down in the Constitution of September 8, 1906 inc.

Issued by our Sanctuary on this tenth day of September A.D. 1906 A.O. 788.

(L.S.)   *Theodor Reuß*, N.P.U. 33°, 90°, 96°.
                                    S[overeign] G[eneral] G[rand] M[aster]
                                    ad Vitam for the German Empire

Appointment of Rudolf Steiner to be General Grand Master of the Egyptian Rite of Memphis in Germany

Text from the original handwriting of Theodor Reuß, June 15, 1907

Memphis and Misraim Rite of Masonry
Order of Oriental Templars and Esoteric Rosicrucians
Z∴R∴D∴A∴B∴A∴W∴![33]

Brotherly greeting on all points of the triangle!
To whom it may concern!

In the carrying into effect of the regulations of the brotherly agreement of January 3, 1906 inc. and of the edict of September 10 A.D. 1906, A.O. 788, published in the *Oriflamme*, Volume 2, fifth year, 1906 inc. I hereby appoint by virtue of the rights and warrants of authority lent me by patent on September 24, 1902 inc.

S.E. Br∴Dr. Rudolf Steiner, 33°, 90°, 96°, in Berlin

to be independent

Serving General Grand Master
of the Supreme General Grand Council
of the Egyptian Rite (90°) of Misraim in Germany

as also of the Adoption Lodges of the Egyptian Freemasonry in Germany with the right and obligation to administer the Order according to the agreement of January 3, 1906 inc.

Issued by our Sanctuary on fifteenth June A.D. 1907, A.O. 789 London and Berlin.

Theodor Reuß, 33°, 90°, 96°,
Sovereign General Grand Master ad Vitam
Henry Klein 33°, 95°
General Grand Registrar

---

33. Zum Ruhme des allmächtigen Baumeisters aller Welten! [To the Glory of the Almighty Architect of All Worlds].

Rudolf Steiner on the Difference between Freemasonry and the Misraim-Service Celebrated in His Esoteric School

Notes from memory by a participant of the instruction class, Berlin, December 16, 1911

One might suppose that one is dealing here with an establishment of what is generally called "Freemasonry," but that is not the case. However secret Freemasonry may have been in former times it was nevertheless always something external. For as a matter of fact Freemasonry came into existence through a betrayal of the mysteries and that is why it comes about that many of the symbols one finds in Freemasonry are also to be found here. These symbols have found their way from the mystery schools into what, for the outer world, are secret societies, through pupils who were not sufficiently aware of their value and significance, but the esoteric societies, which are known under the general name of Freemasonry, have never been able to grasp or explain the real profundity of the symbols, because their very sanctity entails that they cannot properly be understood except in the Occult Temple.[34]

Up until now our esoteric current has borne the name of Freemasonry for the outer world because, from an esoteric point of view, one must always link to something already existing wherever possible, but from now on this name for our temple should no longer be used and our establishment should become known as "Misraim Service." We can shorten this if we like by using the initials "M.D." M[israim] D[ienst]. The designation "F.M." (Freemasonry) should now finally disappear and with that, for the outer world and

---

34. Supplementary to this remark in the lecture Cologne, December 27, 1907:

"You would be quite wrong if you were to misjudge the past with its profound wisdom of the occult schools, or in any way think of it as being superceded by our modern wisdom. Wherever the esoteric wisdom is expressed in signs and symbols it always appears in a form that has to be varified through direct spiritual perception of an initiate."

for all Freemasonry establishments, Freemasonry no longer exists in our movement. If somebody asks us if Freemasonry is also part of our movement we can truthfully say this is not the case. What is performed here is an esoteric service called Misraim-Service, which is as much as to say it is bringing about a union of the earthly with the heavenly, of the visible with the invisible.

Misraim-Service was already known in ancient Egypt and belonged to the most [practiced] esoteric service in the mystery schools. This same service will now be performed with the addition of further details and amendments that Mark practiced. The Mark here referred to is that pupil of Peter, one of the twelve Apostles, who wrote the St. Mark's Gospel when, as Bishop of Alexandria, he was staying in Egypt. Together with an Egyptian initiate he introduced new rules into the esoteric service (ritual) that we now know as Misraim-Service.

Notes from memory by a participant of the instruction class
Munich, August 30, 1911

Through Mark and Ormus, both pupils (disciples) of Christ since his Resurrection, the Mysteries and rituals were altered.

Notes from memory by a participant of the instruction class
Basle, September 25, 1912

What must be understood here is that this esoteric movement cannot be compared with any other movement in the world. The present day produces the situation that there are many occult or semi-occult currents, but one must be aware of the fact that this movement of ours cannot be placed in the same category as any others and that those who are accepted as its members are obliged to feel responsible for the task it lays upon them.[35]

---

35. The notes that follow on from here about the difficulties experienced at that time with the Theosophical Society are published in the volume: *From the History and Content of the First Section of the Esoteric School 1904-1914* (CW 264).

Rudolf Steiner on the History of the Cognitive-Ritual Section

From: *Rudolf Steiner: An Autobiography*
Translated by Rita Stebbing

Chapter XXXVI[36]

An activity was established within the Anthroposophical Society which, strictly speaking, does not belong within the framework of this account, as originally no connection with the public was intended. Yet I will describe it, as this too has been the cause of attacks levelled against me.

Some years after Marie von Sivers and I began our activity within the Theosophical Society, we were offered the leadership of a society of the kind still in existence which preserves the ancient wisdom embodied in symbolism and religious ceremonies. I had no intention whatever of working in the spirit of such a society. Everything Anthroposophy represents must spring from its own source of knowledge and truth. From this there could not be the slightest deviation. But I have always respected what has arisen in the course of history. In this is revealed the spirit inherent in humankind's evolution. Therefore I was in favor of linking whenever possible, the new with what exists historically. And so I accepted the certificate offered me by the above-mentioned society, which belonged to the stream represented by Yarker. It was an institution of Freemasonry of the so-called higher degrees. I took over nothing, absolutely nothing from this society except the merely formal right to carry on in historical succession my symbolic-ritualistic activity.

This activity was completely without dependence upon any tradition whatever. Though I was in possession of the formal certificate, nothing but that which symbolized anthroposophical knowledge was cultivated. It was instituted to meet a need arising among the

---

36. First published as the 68th installment in the periodical *Das Goetheanum*, No.12, March 22, 1925, one week before his death.

members. In addition to carrying further the ideas which clothed spiritual knowledge, there was a need for something that spoke directly to the heart and mind. Such needs I wished to meet. I would have instituted a symbolic ritual without a historic connection had I not been approached by the above-mentioned society.

But this is not to create a secret society. It was made quite clear to those who wished to participate that they were not joining an order, but that they would experience, as participants in a ceremony, a kind of illustration or demonstration of spiritual knowledge. And even if some of this took a form similar to a ceremony within existing orders on occasions when their members were accepted or promoted to higher grades, it was not a ceremony of an order. It was a visual, pictorial demonstration of the path the human soul follows when it ascends spiritually.

There was no question of doing or transmitting what was done and transmitted in any existant order; a proof of this is the fact that members of all kinds of orders participated in the ceremonial activities I arranged, and found the content completely different from what existed in their orders.[37]

One who took part in our activity for the first time came to see me immediately afterward. He had reached a high rank within a certain Order. His experience of what had just taken place made him wish to hand me his insignia of that Order. He felt that since he had now experienced a true spiritual content, he could no longer partake in something that remained a mere formality. But I was able to make him see the matter in a different light. Anthroposophy should tear no one out of his life connections. It should enrich those connections, not rob them of anything. So he remained with the Order to which he belonged, and continued to participate in our symbolic ceremonies.[38]

---

37. It always concerned those who were connected with Rudolf Steiner's spiritual science.

38. This can only refer to Herman Joachim (†1917 in Berlin, son of the famous violinist Joseph Joachim and godson of Herman Grimm), who held one of the highest leading positions in the Grand National Lodge of Freemasonry in Germany. See: obituary notice in *Unsere Toten* (CW 261).

It is understandable that misunderstandings arise when arrangements such as those described above become publicly known. There are many people to whom the external fact of belonging-to-something is more important than the content they receive. And many of the participants themselves spoke about the matter as if they belonged to an order. They were unable to discriminate that with us something was demonstrated free from the limitations of an order, which otherwise was given only within an order.

The fact is that in this sphere, too, we broke with old traditions. Everything was done as it must be done when spiritual reality is to be investigated directly and experienced in full consciousness.

When for the sake of historic continuity Marie von Sivers and I joined the Yarker institution, we signed certain certificates. This had no special significance in itself. But later it was deliberately used as a pretext for all kinds of slanders. Our signatures were a formality. The usual practice was maintained.[39] As we signed I made a point of saying that it was a mere formality, that what I wanted to institute would take over nothing from the Yarker institution.

Of course it is easy afterward to make the observation that it would have been more "intelligent" not to have made connections with something that provided opportunities for slanderers. But I may remark in all modesty that at the period of my life under consideration I still belonged to those who assume uprightness and not crookedness in the people with whom they deal. The ability of spiritual perception does not in the least alter one's trust in people. Spiritual perception should not be misused for the purpose of investigating the inner intentions of another, unless requested by the person himself or herself. Otherwise, to investigate the inner life of others is something forbidden for the spiritual investigator just as the unauthorized opening of a letter is something forbidden. Thus one's relation to others is the same as for someone who has no spiritual cognition. There is the difference, though, that one must assume people to be honorable till the opposite has

---

39. See Supplementary Remarks by Hella Wiesberger, p. 104.

been proved or else be distrustful of the whole world. In the latter case it becomes impossible to work in partnership with others, as this must be based on a foundation of mutual trust.

What was instituted within the Anthroposophical Society as ritual-symbolism with spirit-content proved to be a great help to many of the members. As was always the case in all spheres of Anthroposophical work, everything was done in full consciousness; there was no question of using unjustified magic, suggestive influences, or the like. The members received something that spoke, on the one hand, to their powers of thought, yet spoke also to their power of feeling so that they could enter the content in direct experience. And for many this was a help toward a deeper understanding. The possibility of continuing this activity ceased with the outbreak of the World War. Although there was no question of anything like a secret society, it was taken for such. This section within the Anthroposophical Movement was closed in the middle of 1914.

The fact that persons who had participated in this section—to which no one could raise any objection who considered the matter with good will and a sense of truth—became slanderous accusers, is an example of the abnormality in human behavior that can arise when people who are not inwardly sincere enter a movement that has genuine spiritual content. They expect things that will satisfy their trivial soul life and, as they naturally do not find this, they turn against what they themselves sought in the first place, though with unconscious insincerity.

An Anthroposophical Society must have a form that corresponds with the inner need of the members. An abstract program declaring that in the Anthroposophical Society this and that will be done cannot be instituted; the work must be based on reality. But the reality is nothing other than the inner needs of the members. The living content of Anthroposophy sprang from its own sources. It came before the contemporary world was created out of the spirit. Many who were inwardly drawn to Anthroposophy sought cooperation with others of like mind. Thus the Society received its configuration through the fact that some people sought primarily a religious, others a scientific and still others an artistic element. And what they were seeking they must also find.

Supplementary Remarks by Hella Wiesberger

The customary form signed by Rudolf Steiner and Marie von Sivers no longer exists in the original. The original form handed on by Reuß was destroyed, according to a lady who was an eye-witness. Because, however, there are copies extant, one such is included here, though unconfirmed as to its accuracy, in order not to be accused of having made a tendentious omission.

> Pledge and Obligation. I, the undersigned in my own hand of the present document, do solemnly undertake and faithfully promise to keep and follow the rules and customs of the Ancient and Primitive Rite of Memphis and Misraim O.T.O.,[40] to help to represent the Order according to my best endeavor, strictly to preserve the customary secrecy, to support and care for the maintenance of the Sovereign Section of the German Empire and unreservedly to recognize the Sovereign General Grand Master ad Vitam Dr. Theodor Reuß as the visible guardian of our ∴ secret, as also the supreme and final decisive authority in all ∴ matters. I further undertake to ensure that I will never allow anyone to hypnotize or mesmerize me or put me by any other means into such a passive state that any person, either profane or otherwise, or persons, beings or powers are able to influence me to lose control over my thoughts, will or actions so that the secrets entrusted to me may thereby be divulged through my fault or weakness. Should I ever break these my vows, then may my soul wander without rest through the immeasurable widths and depths of

---

40. Ordo Templis Orientis (Oriental Templar Order). To connect Rudolf Steiner with the subsequent aberrations of this Order is, for anyone who is acquainted with his life and work, undiscussable.

space and time for ever. Eternal Jehovah hear my words and help me to fulfil my vow.

Rudolf Steiner   Berlin, 11. 24. 05.

––––––––––––––

Marie Steiner Concerning the History of the Cognitive-Ritual Section

From a conversation with Kurt Englert-Faye, according to his diary notes Dornach, February 25, 1933

Interview with Frau Doctor Steiner. I asked her to give me the exact facts concerning Dr. Steiner's relationship to Freemasonry, as I needed to be clear about them in order to counter the statements made by Freemasons that Dr. Steiner had been a Freemason himself and then, when he had learned the secrets they held, had broken away from them in order to attack them.

She gave me the following explanation of this connection:

> Among other things dealt with by Rudolf Steiner in his lectures on different aspects of Anthroposophy he also described things which were contained in a certain way within the Freemasonry tradition, without him having taken them into account, but having arrived at them through his own spiritual investigation; for he only felt entitled to reveal facts which he had acquired through his own spiritual exertion. Now, among the many people who found their way little by little into the groups in the Society, were also some personalities who were members of Freemasonry lodges, some of them even possessing very high degrees. The latter recognized the competence with which Dr. Steiner spoke and the supremacy of his knowledge. They went to him and begged him, as their "Master," to renew the original impulse, which had been living in Freemasonry traditions, in conformity with present-day needs of consciousness.

This demand came to Dr. Steiner therefore from without, from the "outside" world, as a karmic task that had to be solved in like manner as formerly the commission to cooperate in the Weimar Goethe-Archive in the publication of Goethe's scientific writings within the framework of the great Weimar edition.[41] And in like manner as Dr. Steiner did not practice "Goethe-philology" in his studies of Goethe, but elaborated and extended the tendencies inherent in Goethe's ideas and thoughts in a manner conformable to the age, and renewed them according to the demands of consciousness, so also he took the essential kernel of the former Freemasonry impulses and allowed their formative forces to develop further according to the spiritual laws of our time. Wherever spiritual science came into play in association with something already existing it was never a question of simply taking over a tradition, but of realizing a spiritual succession. The initial phase of this renewal took place in this case, too, without disturbing the existing forms, just as this happened with the elevating of Goetheanism to spiritual science. Viewed externally Dr. Steiner worked in Weimar in the same surroundings and with the same means at his disposal as the Goethe-philologists; inwardly, however, something quite different was taking place. The latter were conserving, he was metamorphosing. Just as Rudolf Steiner was, as it were, scientifically legitimized for Weimar (in addition to his Dr. title), through the recommendation of Karl Julius Schröer, so was it also necessary to link to something already existing in the case of Freemasonry, as he himself often stated on later occasions.

That means, in this case, he acquired a charter, a right, the outer "historical" legitimization, in order to be able to be active in this field. (A process, in its way, comparable to the acquisition of a doctorate at some university or other of the present day, in order to share in all the rights that go along with it.)

The agent from whom the charter was bought was a man called Reuß. It was as a stroke of fate that the decadence of historical

---

41. See footnote p. 20.

Freemasonry should be represented by such a person as Reuß, who was at that time acknowledged by the institution as its fully recognized and competent head.[42] It was only later that Reuß was outlawed by the Freemasons as an imposter and charlatan.

The acquisition of the charter was the only point of contact between Dr. Steiner and the Society of Freemasons. Rudolf Steiner himself never became a Freemason and never received any directives from that quarter.

The fact that Freemasons sometimes describe the course of events somewhat differently does nothing to alter the facts of the case. It may be that the administrators of a "dead" knowledge, handed down from the past, are just as antagonized by Rudolf Steiner's spiritual independence and sovereignty as the administrators of Goethe's literary estate were antagonized by the further-developed Goetheanism of spiritual science, who afterwards made it their business to discredit the achievements of Dr. Steiner as editor of Goethe's scientific writings.

42. To be precise Reuß was only recognized as such by Yarker, not by Freemasonry in general.

Marie Steiner to C.S. Picht in Stuttgart, editor of the periodical *Anthroposophie*, in connection with the article: "Was Rudolf Steiner a Freemason?"
Dornach, March 11, 1934

... Are all Freemasons necessarily traitors? How does it stand then with Frederick the Great, Field-Marchal Blücher, Emperor William I, Emperor Frederick, and innumerable other German princes and generals? Must they all be pilloried together with the numberless others who are still alive, who belong to German Freemasonry circles?

Immediately on the outbreak of war [1914-1918] the first one to destroy the deed he had been given, which gave him the right to work independently was Rudolf Steiner himself. He declared that this work had been irrevocably dissolved. Of what had it consisted? In the interpretation of the symbols and some of the main features of the rituals by spiritual science. In order to do that in an honorable fashion he had to possess the right to do so. The right was conferred on him because some of the Freemasons thought they could gain an enrichment of their incomplete knowledge by this means. The man who bore the title of Grand Master, who had the right to confer such charters, was not a person with whom Dr. Steiner wished to have further dealings. So Rudolf Steiner's terms of agreement were for him to have no further connections of any kind, apart from the payment of the charges that were due. And that suited the gentleman very well.

What the slanderers wished to make out of it, however, as described in Rudolf Steiner's *Autobiography*, was that he belonged to such a society as those with political aims, or even those whose aim was to destroy Germany. It was a shameless, irresponsible lie. But what can one do in a world in which lies are so powerful, other than call them by their true names!

The only time Rudolf Steiner took part in a Masonic celebration was at the funeral service for Joachim,[43] and there was such a large

---

43. c.f. footnote p. 101.

military contingent and so many ladies present that it really did not suffice to provide the grounds for an accusation of internal machinations. (...)

Can one counter statements which are just snatched out of the air? A man called Herr Huber says in his book, that Herr Reuß was the inspirer of Rudolf Steiner.[44] If I should state that Mephistopheles was the inspirer of Herrn Huber, he would hardly be able to produce the necessary documents to prove to me that this is not the case. The probability is, however, that it may very well be the case to some extent, but never was there the slightest inspiration on the side of Herrn Reuß coming to Dr. Steiner.

Dr. Steiner had to acquire the outward authorization in order to save the spiritual contents expressed in time-honored symbols from total corruption, [brought about], shall we say, by Mephistopheles, who gains control over things through people who are under his influence and belong to Freemasonry societies. A person who understands these things also tries to protect them from the machinations of evil powers and makes many sacrifices on their behalf. Rudolf Steiner was the first to point to certain political aims harbored by some of the secret societies, of which the members of those societies, the Freemasons, for instance, were quite unaware.[45] For that reason objective clarity is necessary, but not fanatical, slanderous agitation, which conjures up ghosts and itself serves political ends.

Most of the German Freemasons are certainly ignorant of the hidden intentions of the few such circles and cannot believe that

---

44. Engelbert Huber: *Freemasonry. World Power Behind the Curtains*, Stuttgart, 1934. In this book it is maintained that Rudolf Steiner was commissioned by Theodor Reuß to compose a ritual for the Memphis-Misraim-Order in Germany. This is refuted by the documents in the present volume. The addition to this remark made by Rudolf Steiner in the lecture, Dornach, October 11, 1915: "It likewise happened that esoteric brotherhoods have made the one or other suggestions to me; and namely, when a quite respected esoteric society suggested that I should participate in promulgating a kind of esotericism that called itself Rosicrucian, I did not respond."

45. Note particularly the lectures held during the war years 1916/17, *Zeitgeschichtliche Betrachtungen* [Contemporary Considerations] (CW 173/174).

they exist. Their feelings would also turn against Dr. Steiner for having uttered some words of warning about them. So must "the one who knows" be exposed to the hate of all groups of this kind and allow the cry "crucify him," to resound over his head.

One also accuses the Freemasons of blasphemy and denial of Christ. Dr. Steiner's whole life's work served the task of making the Christ impulse more understandable to humankind, to revive it at a time when materialism seeks to smother it and atheism takes over. Therein lies the confutation of many assertions. But one has to take the trouble to go into such arguments.

The conclusive refutation of all the lies spoken about him by malevolent foes lies in a serious and conscientious study of Rudolf Steiner's works.

Marie Steiner
Three sketches for the essay "Was Rudolf Steiner a Freemason?"

I

It is very difficult to advance the statement that Rudolf Steiner had nothing to do with the Freemasonry Movement. Dr. Steiner says so himself on page 390 of his *Autobiography*.

The Freemasonry Movement itself is one that has split up into many organizations and has become decadent. It originally proceeded from those currents that still had a connection with the ancient mystery wisdom. The original stream has been diverted into many side-streams and channels. They have all progressed according to their own destinies and are in part a long way from their original goals of striving after knowledge.

It was Dr. Steiner's endeavor to rediscover the pure source of esoteric teachings, to present them to our inner vision in their historical sequence and to free them from the trash that has gradually accumulated over them, in order to show how, in spite of the trash and turbidity, the pure archetypal forces have continually sought out new channels in order to bestow upon humankind their enlivening and progressive influence. Rudolf Steiner places the Mystery of Golgotha at the center of the historical spiritual development of humanity with all the force that we know from his writings and lectures. All ancient mystery wisdom led towards this culminating point; all following wisdom, re-enlivened, rescued from oblivion and newly engendered by this force, strove to find the means and prepare the way through which the desire of all hearts could be gratified, not only in a religious sense but gradually making it possible for an understanding of the Christ impulse to be developed.

To this task Rudolf Steiner dedicated his life whole-heartedly. He worked creatively and inspiringly in all three domains—in religion, art and science—these three, which had once been a unity in the cultures emanating from the Mysteries. To all who came to him for advice and help in their search and striving in these three spheres he gave of himself without regard to the social background from which the seekers might have come. Many seriously striving Freemasons recognized with joy that in Rudolf Steiner's Anthroposophy a light was shed upon many things presented by their lodges in pictures and signs of a ritual taken from tradition. They began to understand better what these signs and symbols signified. There were others, too, who suffered greatly from the temptations into which some of the organizations had been led by their destiny. They looked around for help. From such an impulse as this arose the plea to Rudolf Steiner to try to build an organization free from all the accumulated rubbish of centuries in which the pure underlying principles of esoteric endeavor could be worked out. The way that came about arose out of the existing circumstances, which were just as unsatisfactory. When organizations get bogged down, it is the fault of those who work in them, especially those at the head. That was the case here to a rather frightening degree and Rudolf Steiner wanted to have nothing to do with societies under such leadership.

That was the condition imposed by Dr. Steiner when he set about forming a historically authenticated connection for which he undertook to pay fees in recompense for absolute freedom and independence in building up a work whose aim was to remove the veil from symbolic acts, which now have to be taken hold of in clear consciousness. What he constantly did through his Anthroposophy was to fulfil the obligations of knowledge imposed on present-day humanity, by gradually removing its mystical shrouds and creating a solid basis for the powers of understanding to grow from common sense to wisdom.

Through that he did what he considered to be his duty to humanity. For him it was a new burden, a sacrificial offering. But every sacrifice has also a positive effect in a spiritual sense by bestowing new sources of knowledge on those who willingly submit themselves to the burden. And perhaps Rudolf Steiner would not have been able to utter such profoundly truthful words of warning about the dangers of modern Freemasonry if he had not included this theme in his general studies of present-day social conditions, even though he treated it from a certain distance. It induced him to emphasize more rigorously and clearly than before that secret societies should no longer exist today and that they could not be tolerated at the present stage of humanity's development.

As with every science, so also spiritual science demands a gradual unfolding, a step by step development of the powers of understanding in order to lead to spiritual knowledge. In this sense one cannot expect the beginner to have an ability to grasp the higher stages of knowledge. These must gradually become accessible to his consciousness, just as the higher truths of mathematics are also a mystery to the novice.

Rudolf Steiner's work is something publicly offered to humankind, which leads to higher knowledge. It lies displayed before us in his writings, lectures, and artistic creations and has nothing to do with secret organizations, not even with Freemasonry. The explanations he gave for the time-honored signs and symbols have long been outdated by the results of his spiritual research, which he left behind him in innumerable works for the human consciousness and for the human "I," eager and roused to wakefulness.

II

Whoever takes the trouble to study Rudolf Steiner's works without prejudice will soon see that a knowledge of the spirit is revealed there that truly does not need to look for other sources than those available to one's own inner being. Knowledge that Rudolf Steiner gained from school and college was absorbed by him in fullest measure. His knowledge of the manifold circumstances of life and its social connections gave him an observant eye for things around him and for the many connections in which life had placed him. They came to meet him. It was not he who sought them. He did not need to seek them, for he was sought after because he had more to give than other people and he gave it with love, never out of a sense of superiority or reluctance. He did not reject what came to meet him, even if it was of little value, "he marks alone the goodness in others; he lets the evil work its ransom out, as cosmic justice in its course decides."[46] But he drew a sharp distinction where the working out of evil was concerned and did not let it break up the circles under his charge.

It is out of this attitude of soul that, on the one hand, his great forbearance and gentleness, his willingness to help and boundless sympathy and, on the other hand, his iron rejection of all persistently injurious elements is to be explained.

I am trying to indicate by this why it was that he did not immediately show the door to anyone of whose moral standard he did not approve, but, as far as he could, did not allow his influence to play a part in it. On the contrary, he tried by positive means to lead what had gone astray, or was threatening to go astray, back onto the right path. That was why he burdened himself with life in the Theosophical Society and why he did not decline to accept the offer to found, on the strength of his higher knowledge, an independent branch of High-Degree Masonry. The Grand Master of this order gave a very poor impression. One could not have anything more to

---

46. Words of the Grand Master in the 7th scene of the second Mystery Drama, *The Soul's Probation.*

do with him except pay the fees which were normally due in such circles. It was a short ceremony in which the deed of appointment was issued, which Rudolf Steiner tore up at the beginning of the war.

Perhaps this link, only performed on paper, enabled him to gain a clearer insight into the things that he then repeatedly alluded to in his lectures as a warning and to lead people's judgement into the right channels. Outwardly he never had any connection with any sort of order; he never attended any meeting or took part in any conference. Therefore it is an objective untruth when, in a book such as ... of Huber[47] and in inflammatory articles of a sordid kind, the connection of Rudolf Steiner to Freemasonry is used in a tendentious fashion. All the grand titles are recounted—Ah well; he never sought those! It is customary for Freemasons to adorn themselves with "most supreme," "most sovereign," "most illustrious," etc., that is part of the tradition and convention and is in itself droll, especially as in most cases this empty husk is all that remains. But just for that reason a serious-minded or knowledgeable person finds it necessary to rescue the kernel, which is being crushed and petrified by this husk. The kernel is all that concerned Rudolf Steiner. As a result he was completely indifferent to the titles that the various orders gave themselves. It did not matter to him if the order that had given him his certificate was a so-called derivate or upstart organization or not. He did not want to have anything to do with any organization. That was the strictly observed condition to which Herrn Reuß, with his many titles and decorations, submitted. Reuß, in conformity with his character, was treated by Dr. Steiner with reserve and was handled with kid gloves.

Rudolf Steiner knew in advance of others that the time of medieval, as well as modern masonry had run its course. He exposed the esoteric truths to the world because they were required by humanity and because their working in secret had led to bad results. But there is a power in time-honored symbols and one should not have to forfeit that because of outward signs of decadence. They can

---

47. Engelbert Huber: *Freimaurerei. Weltmacht Hinter den Kulissen* [Freemasonry. World Power Behind the Curtains], Stuttgart, 1934.

be rescued for humanity by art, for instance. That is what Rudolf Steiner did. In his Mystery Dramas, in the building of the Goetheanum, in many of the works of his pupils, this metamorphosis has become reality and has thus been of benefit to humankind. Therein lies the lasting value of these truths, which have to be saved from disintegration of the outward form. Continuity through change. In that lies the justification of Rudolf Steiner's way of working, which he encountered by way of duty.

The tendentiousness of the lies that were a part of this campaign of slander is plain for all to see. The Masons may have had a justified cause, from their point of view, to fight against Rudolf Steiner, and they did so with all their might. The turning of the tables—perhaps they also had a hand in it—is a skillful manoeuver that could have served some dark purpose. We need not fight shy of coming face to face with it.

<h1 style="text-align:center">III</h1>

If there is anyone who has understood and proclaimed, at the right moment, that the time for Freemasonry has now passed, it is Rudolf Steiner. It is not just his life's work—*Anthroposophy*—which proclaims it, nor is it only expressed in his "Mystery Dramas" (the representatives of the esoteric society hand over their insignia and retire),[48] but in the first days after the outbreak of war, Rudolf Steiner tears up the covenant, as a sign and to emphasize his opinion that the time is past in which Freemasonry can still be acknowledged. In order to have a clear conscience about such rejection, he felt it his duty to not avoid contact with it. And how short was the time of this contact— no sooner dismissed, than it showed up in all its vacuity. Such expressions as this are not aimed at the valued members who are numbered in their ranks, they ... [the text breaks off at this point].

48. See Rudolf Steiner's third Mystery Drama: *The Guardian of the Threshold*, Scene 10.

MARIE STEINER

Was Rudolf Steiner a Freemason?[49]

We are shown in the work of Rudolf Steiner that in olden times Mysteries existed for initiation, through which human souls were raised up to a participation in the life of the spirit. From them were derived the impulses out of which sprang the great civilizations of the past which are known to us. In them was practiced the secret knowledge, the science of the spirit, which was at the height of its development in those days and found its outward expression in the polytheistic religions. The counselors of kings and those great leaders of humankind who were chosen to be the innovators of new cultural achievements, came from these Mysteries. The wisdom that they acquired was the unifying bond amid the comings and goings and repercussions of nations. The fruits of every civilization were watched over and preserved for the progress of humankind and handed on from generation to generation. They formed a second current alongside that which flowed directly out of spiritual sources, but which faded in the consciousness of the majority of people to the same degree as the knowledge of the physical objects became more acute and comprehensive. The soul lost all memory of its origin. The time arrived when not only the single nations, but the whole of humankind would have succumbed to decadence if the Christ event had not taken place.

To point out the significance of the Christ event in the revivifying of humanity with all that it implied was the task to which Rudolf Steiner dedicated his life. For that he had to draw together all the wisdom that had been collected by humankind until that moment and to irradiate with his light every branch of this learning, both exoteric and arcane. To the arcane knowledge belong the ancient lost Mysteries: the dust that had settled over them had to

---

49. Published in *Anthroposophie. Zeitschrift für freies Geistesleben*, April-June, 1934, Stuttgart. Ed. C.S. Picht.

be cleared away, in a figurative sense, like the archaeologists who have to clear away the dust from ancient temple sites. But the most important thing to be saved was the living substance that still coursed through the Mysteries, resting on old tradition, but already falling ever more into rigidity and decay through their human exponents. Without revivification through the infusion of Christianity, without an understanding of this greatest of all mysteries, the ancient wisdom could only lead to abberation in the course of time.

Rudolf Steiner had a comprehensive insight into these connections, because of his philosophically-based and organically-developed spiritual science. That is the reason why he regarded it as his task at the present time, when approached by such circles as practiced the ancient esoteric knowledge—either from tradition or because of fresh stimulation—to make his knowledge available to them, not rejecting what they asked of him, but accepting it cautiously. He never sought contact with such circles, but wherever they approached him for elucidation or instruction, he did not refuse to provide them with it. That was a service to humanity on his part.

The efforts made by those who represented the Theosophical Society, who would like to have seen him in their midst, were initially rejected emphatically by him, for the Theosophical Society worked along one-sided Eastern lines and in many cases moved in a medium of dilettantism or psychic-phenominalism. But a basis for an understanding of true Christian esotericism was especially lacking. Only when German Theosophists wished to found an independent section under his leadership and consequently on the basis of Western Christian esotericism, did he feel it his duty to comply with their request.

When, after a number of years, the later President of the Theosophical Society, Annie Besant, tried to prevent this work for a living Christianity, did the separation from the Theosophical Society take place and the founding of the Anthroposophical Society was brought about. The details of these events are given by Rudolf Steiner in his *Autobiography*.

The other suggestion came from the direction fostered by Medieval Christian esotericism on the basis of ancient mystery knowledge. It laid value on its historical continuity stretching back to the times when esoteric knowledge was engendered in Egyptian temples. In their manifold ramifications, which developed over the course of centuries, the circles coming from the various mystical currents took what seemed spiritually appropriate and beneficial to them, especially the impulses of the Crusades, the "Bauhütten" unions [working-masons' clubs], etc. They survived under various names, such as Freemasonry Union, Illuminati Order, etc. As time went on, however, they began to lose their erstwhile knowledge and drift further and further from their original goals. They then succumbed to rationalism and often to atheism and their unions started to serve political, commercial or charitable ends. The disappointment of those who joined them to gain a knowledge of the spirit became ever greater. Ever more frequently those who were disappointed came to Rudolf Steiner to tell him that they only now understood, through his publicly given lectures on spiritual science what lay behind the symbols, which none of their members understood. Many deplored the fact that they were serving untruth because they repeated time-honored formulas that manifest a belief in a Divine Spirit, but at the same time they were completely skeptical about the content of what they professed. And one could encounter a great longing to experience something of the solemnity with which at one time the ancient rites had been connected. Freemasonry was revealed as a current that was obsolete and becoming submerged, whose outer organism was vulnerable to the powers of opposition, yes, had even fallen prey to them already.

But what had been preserved of the truth in these thousands of years old endeavors would and must continue to serve the rehabilitation of humanity in a changed form. That was the task that confronted Rudolf Steiner when it was suggested to him by those circles that he should found an independent organization on the strength of historically legal documentation. This suggestion was made to him by a spiritually aspiring person who had formed the opinion that Rudolf Steiner knew more about spiritual matters than all the others put together. The suggestion was then officially confirmed by someone who was more concerned with practical advantage and possessed a very indifferent attitude towards spiritual aspects. It was not Rudolf Steiner's task to pry into this person's past, nor was it his intention to maintain a relationship with him. Many of the officials, not only of esoteric societies, but also the dignitaries of the Church and other institutions often prove unworthy of their high office. The fact that the various Freemasonry orders—as it now appears from their writings—do not acknowledge each other, is something that they have in common with other human institutions, and it would take much time and pains, and also legal ingenuity, to sort it out. Rudolf Steiner, however, had to take into account something that is of decisive importance to everyone who represents spiritual truths—the historical connection to an ancient time-honored, (though in its form time-altered) spiritual current—in order to rescue it from decadence as far as he could. By accepting it he could preserve what truth it contained and waken it to new life in order for it to serve the progress of humankind in accordance with the forces of consciousness that now prevail. In terms appropriate to the consciousness soul the ancient symbols could be made to live again through the medium of art to inspire the whole of humanity.

Rudolf Steiner made one condition. He would implement the historically legal union, within the degrees appointed him to carry out the work independently—with that, however, their relationship should end. No further claim should be made on him either in respect of their cooperative activities or in human, social, or organizational matters. Nothing but an outward, non-obligatory formality should be practiced, no work at all done in conjunction with one another! The newly founded, completely independent circle, which had been recruited from those Theosophists who desired to approach this kind of Western esotericism in this way, were introduced to the ancient symbols, first of all in a graphically explicit manner and then more and more according to their inner nature, until they had been worked through by consciousness. In this way their connection with vague and mystical feeling was severed and artistic and scientific life was made available to them. *When war broke out in August 1914 Rudolf Steiner declared that the study group formed in this way under the name "Mystica Aeterna" had been annulled and as a sign thereof he tore up the relevant document.* The group never met again in this connection.*

With that is clearly stated the reason for the seeming contradiction that some people say Rudolf Steiner was a High-Degree Brother, whereas others state that he never belonged to the Brotherhood at all. Rudolf Steiner in fact never belonged to the Order of Freemasons. He was completely estranged from their company and was even strongly attacked by them, for since the beginning of his theosophical-anthroposophical activity he had revealed through his teachings what they regarded as the secrets that gave them their authority and respect. He laid bare esoteric knowledge because humanity was in need of it, and it is a requirement of the age we live in. He at the same time kindled an understanding for it. In order to bring new life into the ancient symbols in a proper fashion through a formally constituted work group attached to a historical current, he pledged himself by an outward contract and stood aside from any dealings with Freemasonry Brothers. Thus the word "High-Degree Brother," which his enemies liked to bandy about, since it was no longer possible for them to label him a "Jew," is actually misleading. Because Rudolf Steiner had never had any connection with any sort of Freemasonry order, but the name "Freemason" was to have made it look as though he had, a certain mood was thereby to have been created so that people would not try to come to terms with the spiritual science

---

* It must strike anyone who tries to arrive at the truth concerning Freemasonry literature that Rudolf Steiner is never mentioned therein (except in cases of outright rejection), and except for three isolated examples (out of a possible 200 publications) his writings do not appear in the great *Bibliography of Freemasonry Literature* by Wolfstieg, 4 Volumes 1911-1926, which encompasses the contents of all Freemasonry lodge libraries with 54,320 entries. Experts should also be aware of the fact that such titles as Misraim, Memphis, O.T.O. (Oriental Templar Order) [c.f. under "Egyptian Freemasonry" in individual notes], etc., referring to the documents in question, were for Rudolf Steiner just empty husks robbed of their content and long since reduced to mere names.

founded and developed by Rudolf Steiner. If they had done so the contrast to Freemasonry would have become immediately evident to them. From his knowledge of the fact that the present-day inclination of the human soul is such that one cannot inwardly accept the esoteric and that what is hidden must be brought to light, Rudolf Steiner made his spiritual science fully public.

Through that he made possible a true understanding of Christianity and showed the way and the method by which modern human beings can fulfill their life's tasks through a realization of spiritual facts. It will be of decisive importance for the destiny of the future how Rudolf Steiner's spiritual science, which is not restricted to secret circles nor practiced from the point of view of power politics but is available to all people, will be accepted in the consciousness of the present day.

Marie Steiner,
née v. Sivers

PART II

THE CONTENTS OF THE COGNITIVE-RITUAL SECTION

Ritual Texts

Explanations of the rituals, the symbolism of the things
employed therein, and of the Temple Legend and
the Golden Legend

The following two points must always be born in mind:

1. Every esoteric teaching is based on the correspondence between the macrocosm and the microcosm. For
that reason many of the teachings are connected with
the human physical body.

2. All rituals and ceremonies reflect:
   a) The cosmic history of humanity since Lemuria.
   b) Human development since before birth.
   c) The spiritual development of humanity considered as a descent into hell and an ascent to the
   mountains of God.

(From notes by participants, with no reference as to
date or place)

PRELIMINARY REMARKS

HELLA WIESBERGER

About the Meaning and the Spiritual Origin of the Cognitive-Ritual

> It is quite impossible to advance in one's progress towards higher worlds if one does not pass through the stages of imaginitive cognition.[1]

> The temple-motive in the case of both Goethe and Rudolf Steiner served as a vessel for the supersensible ritual, which Goethe brings to expression in the three kings and Rudolf Steiner causes to be spoken at the three altars.[2]

A decisive reason for any work with ritual symbols lies in the primary knowledge that events that take place in the higher world immediately bordering on the physical—the astral or imaginitive world—are the symbolic expression of astral facts, just as those things that can be observed in the physical world are the expression of physical facts. In this sense working with the symbolic ritual is to be regarded as a practical means towards getting to know the astral world. Rudolf Steiner expressly emphasized the fact that in no other way than by means of symbolic ideas can the way into the higher worlds be found. Literally: "The opinion often prevails in the various esoteric

---

1. *The Stages of Higher Knowledge* (CW 12).
2. E.A. Karl Stockmeyer, a member of the Cognitive-Ritual Circle, in his essay "Concerning the Unity of Temple and Ritual in Connection with the Goetheanum Building-Idea," found in *Rosicrucianism Renewed: The Unity of Art, Science, and Religion* (CW 284).

streams of today, that there can be an ascent into higher worlds by other means than by applying imaginitive and symbolical ideas. And there is a kind of fear, yes, even an aversion, to ascending into the astral worlds with the help of symbolic signs or other esoteric educative principles by people of the present day. If one were to ask: Are such attitudes of fear justified? one can answer: Yes and No. In a certain connection they are justified and in another connection they are not at all appropriate, because no one can truly rise to the spiritual worlds without passing through the astral world" (Cologne, December 29, 1907).

To the statement about the spiritual origin of the Cognitive-Ritual in the letter from August 15, 1906 (p. 70): "This ritual can be nothing else than a mirror image of what is a fact on the higher plane," there is an important addendum in lectures from the year 1924 in which this fact pertaining to the spiritual world is so described: "At the end of the 18th and beginning of the 19th century there hovers in the immediate neighborhood of the physical world of sense a great supersensible event, consisting of supersensible acts of ritual, an unfolding of mighty pictures of the spiritual life of beings of the universe, the beings of the hierarchies, in connection with the great ether-workings of the universe and the human workings upon Earth. I say 'in the immediate neighborhood,' meaning of course, adjoining this physical world in a qualitative, not in a spatial sense. It is interesting to see how at a most favorable moment a little miniature picture of this supersensible ritual and action flowed into Goethe's spirit. Transformed and changed in miniature we have this picture set down by Goethe in his fairy story of the *Green Snake and the Beautiful Lily....*" (Dornach, September 16, 1924, *Karmic Relationships, Vol. IV*). One of the themes most central to this fairy tale is that of the temple with the three kings, the representatives of Wisdom, Beauty and Power or Strength. It is also characterized by Rudolf Steiner as a path of initiation: the power of perception of the Golden King coming from the imaginitive faculty, that of the Silver King from objectivized feelings and that of the Bronze King springing from the will. (Berlin, October 24, 1908, *Goethe's Secret Revelation and the Riddle of Faust*). The three altars with their acolytes, both in the Cognitive-Ritual and the temple scenes of the Mystery Dramas, are in full accordance with that. And when in the letter of August 15, 1906, it is further stated that the ritual appropriate to European conditions, recognized by esotericists during the last 2,300 years[3] has been prepared by the "Rosicrucian Masters," the connection with the supersensible ritual becomes evident through the following words: "The Rosicrucians (said): 'shape the world in such a way that it contains wisdom, beauty, and strength, then will wisdom, beauty, and strength be mirrored in us. If you have used your time to this end then you will depart from this life taking with you the mirror-image of wisdom, beauty, and strength. Wisdom is the image of manas; beauty, piety, goodness, the image of buddhi; Strength is the image of atman ... It is not through idle contemplation that the human being progresses on Earth, but by incorporating wisdom, beauty and strength into the Earth'" (Berlin, October 24, 1905).

Goethe's "riddle of a fairy tale," as it has often been called, appeared at the end of the 18th century (1795). One century later, 1899, when the so-called Kali Yuga, the spiritually dark period, came to an end and once more a spiritually bright period was about to begin, Rudolf Steiner made the far-reaching decision, in the sense of the decisive words "The time is at hand!" in Goethe's fairy story, to give public expression to the esotericism that lived within him.[4] And in accordance with the esoteric principle of preserving continuity, he linked to the fairy tale of the *Green Snake and the Beautiful Lily*, the pictures of which had lived with him in his meditation for twenty years. On the 150th anniversary of Goethe's birth, on August 28, 1899, he published the essay, "Goethe's Secret Revelation," and one year later,

---

3. According to a statement by Günther Schubert, Rudolf Steiner once told him that all this refers to Melchizedek.

4. *The Story of My Life*, CW 28, Chapter 30. Marie Steiner made the following entry in a notebook (Archive No. 21): "When Rudolf Steiner first made his public appearance with the intention of removing the veil of esotericism, he took Goethe's fairy tale as his starting point and spoke about the altars of Wisdom, Beauty and Strength. He placed them in the temple of his Mystery Dramas and spoke to us once more and in greater depth about their significance. And again he placed them into our Esoteric School and let us approach again and again the various aspects of thinking, feeling and willing, which are an expression of these altars."

in the autumn of 1900, he carried the interpretation of Goethe's Apocalypse, begun therein, a stage further with a lecture to Berlin Theosophists and so became "completely esoteric."[5] Twenty years later, on the eve of the first gathering in the First Goetheanum, the so-called "First High School Course," he called this lecture, in retrospect of the development of the Anthroposophical Movement, its "Urzelle" [basic cell] (Dornach, September 25, 1920).

Through that it certainly may not merely be construed that the Anthroposophical Movement had its outward start with this lecture, but that, implicitly too, a start had been made in fulfilling the central demand of Goethe's fairy tale: to bring the Mysteries—that is the Temple—out of obscurity into the full light of day, to the attention of the public. For it is in this deeper sense that Anthroposophical spiritual science has been developed to act as a herald to humankind of the newly dawned Epoch of Light. And therefore, in the last year of his lecturing activity, there was uttered by Rudolf Steiner, in connection with his description of the Supersensible Ritual, those so preponderating words: "What is Anthroposophy in its reality? Yes, my dear friends, if you comprehend all the wonderful, majestic imaginations which were present as a Supersensible Ritual in the first half of the 19th century [and also at the end of the 18th century] and translate them into human concepts, that is Anthroposophy." (Dornach, July 8, 1924, *Karmic Relationships, Vol. III*).

Consequently there is a direct line from the perception of the Ritual in the supersensible world—which is certainly connected with the ancient ritual prepared by the Rosicrucian Masters—leading by way of Goethe's fairy tale to the translation of these images of the spiritual life into the scientific concepts of Anthroposophy and to the creation of the Cognitive-Ritual.

In this sense, according to Marie Steiner, the Cognitive-Ritual with its three altars was the sign and seal of Rudolf Steiner's activity, brought out of the depths of the Temple, in which it had stood since the time when the Mysteries first existed and handed over to

---

5. See note 4 on previous page by Marie Steiner.

humankind. (Marie Steiner's commemorative address on the first anniversary of Rudolf Steiner's death, see p. 502.)

Why the Cognitive-Ritual Was Practiced in Brotherly Union

> It is not just one person, plus a second and a third, but something quite different when people unite.[6]

In order to answer the question as to why Ritual-Symbolism was practiced in brotherly union, certain spiritual facts must be taken into account. One of these is to be found in the character of such unions, which Rudolf Steiner described as follows in the lecture "Brotherhood and the Struggle for Existence" given in Berlin on November 23, 1905, on the day before he became a member of Memphis-Misraim-Freemasonry:

> Union makes it possible for a higher being to express itself through the members. That is a general principle in the whole of life. Five people who come together having thoughts and feelings in harmony with one another, are more than 1 + 1 + 1 + 1 + 1, they are not just the sum of five, just as little as our body is the sum of its five senses. The living with one another and in one another signifies something very similar to the co-existence of the cells in the human body. A new higher being exists among the five, yes, even among two or three. "Where two or three are gathered together in My name, there am I in the midst of them."
>
> It is not the one and the other and the third, but something quite new which comes about through the union. But it only comes about when the one lives within the other, when the one does not produce one's forces merely out of the self, but also out

------

6. Lecture, Berlin, November 23, 1905.

of the others. That, however, is only present when a person lives unselfishly within the other person. Thus unions where human beings work together are the hidden places into which the higher spiritual beings descend in order to work through the individual members in the same way that the soul works through the members of the body.

This will not easily be believed in our materialistic civilization, but in the spiritual-scientific worldview it is not merely a figurative form of speech, but something eminently real. Hence the spiritual scientist does not speak in abstractions when he talks about the folk-spirit or the folk-soul, or the family-spirit, or the spirit of another community. This spirit that is at work in a community is not outwardly visible, but it is there all the same, and it exists through the brotherly love of the people who are active in the community. Just as the body possesses a soul, so does a guild or a brotherhood also have a soul and I repeat: it is not said in a figurative sense, but is to be taken quite literally.

Those who do work together in brotherhoods are magicians because they draw higher beings into their circle. One does not need to call upon the machinations of spiritualism if one is working together in a community in brotherly love. Higher beings are manifested therein. If we devote ourself to a brotherhood, this dedication, this merging into the whole confers power on our organism, giving us the strength of steel. When we then speak or act as a member of such an organization it is the spirit of the organization that acts or speaks through us, not the individual soul. It is the secret of the progress of future humanity to work through communities.

As one epoch hands over to the next and each epoch has its own task to perform, so does the Medieval epoch stand with regard to our own and our epoch to the one that will follow it. The Medieval brotherhoods acted directly in practical life through the founding of the useful arts. They only showed signs of leading a materialistic existence when the fruits of their labors had been reaped and when the basis of their consciousness— their brotherhood namely—had more or less disappeared, because the true feeling of unity within the community had given place to the state principle or to abstract spiritual life.

It is the duty of future generations to found brotherhoods once again, brotherhoods out of the spirit, out of the highest ideals of the soul. The life of humankind has brought the most diverse associations to maturity until now; it has caused a terrible fight for existence, which has now reached its high point. The spiritual-scientific view of the world strives to bring about the highest good for humankind through the principle of brotherhood. Thus you may see that the worldwide spiritual-scientific movement wishes to replace the struggle for existence by the principle of brotherhood. We must learn to lead a communal life. We should not imagine this or that person is able to achieve some goal or other on his or her own.

Perhaps you might wish to know, each one of you, how a struggle for existence and brotherly love are compatible with one another. That is very simple. We shall have to learn how to replace fighting with positive work, to exchange war for an ideal. But today that is all too little understood. People do not know which war is referred to, because all one talks about is fighting when one speaks about life. There is a social war, a war for peace, a war for the emancipation of women, a territorial war, and so on. Whichever way we turn we see struggles.

The spiritual-scientific view of the world strives to put positive work in the place of this struggle. Whoever is familiar with this outlook on life knows that fighting will not produce the right result in any sphere of life. Try to discover what, according to your experience and knowledge, is the best to be promoted in life without attacking your opponent. It may of course only be an ideal, as the spiritual-scientific principle has to be introduced into the life of the present day. People who unite with others to work for the good of all are those who build the foundation for a healthy development in the future.

The Theosophical [Anthroposophical] Society wants to set an example in this direction. It is not therefore a society based on propaganda like other societies, but is a brotherhood. One's own work in it is the outcome of that of every one of its members. That should be rightly understood. Those who are most effective are those who do not push their own opinions onto others, but take account of what they read in the eyes of their companions; those who search the thoughts and feelings of others and put themselves at the others' service. Those who never defend their own opinions in life are best able to work in such a circle of people. If we try to understand that our best forces spring from our union with others and that such a union must not be thought of as only an abstract idea, but as something to be applied first and foremost in a theosophical way in our every action and every moment of our lives, then we shall make progress. But we must not be impatient about our progress.

Another spiritual fact that is the basis of working together in a symbolic way is that when thought-forces are employed in a ritualistic fashion over a period of time, they become so enhanced that they change into outward reality. It is in this way that progress is made. Everything proceeds from within, not from without: "What at one time are thoughts and feelings become outer forms at a later time. The Individualities who guide the evolution of humankind have to implant into our minds the thought-forms that thousands of years later will turn into outer reality. There you can see the functioning of thought-forms, inspired by symbolical representations, ranging from a depiction of Noah's Ark and Solomon's Temple to the apocalyptical figures of Human Being, Lion, Bull and Eagle ... pictures that, if we ponder them ... will lead us to a participation in the world immediately bordering our own." This is expressed in a lecture given in Cologne on December 28, 1907, in which it is explained, by way of chief example, that the concepts of Noah's Ark and Solomon's Temple effect the remolding of the human frame.

By means of spiritual-scientific knowledge the following statement about Freemasonry also acquires clarity: "If you should ask me what is the essence of Freemasonry I should have to answer in abstract terms: it is a body whose members think the things that are going to be of benefit to the world several centuries before they become actuality"(Berlin, January 2, 1906)—some of them, however, have already come to pass.

If the general spiritual progress of humankind is helped by such brotherly symbolic-ritual cooperation, so also is the progress of the individual. That is attested to by the statement of Rudolf Steiner that a true consciousness of immortality is connected with the exercise of fraternity. The standard rule concerning the consciousness of immortality is expressed thus: Only that for which one does not strive merely on one's own account in order to gain full knowledge of the immortality of the spirit will contribute to the gaining of such knowledge (Berlin, December 23, 1904).

It is well known that the realization of ideals requires much patience. Rudolf Steiner explained this and comforted his hearers in an instruction lesson as follows:

Instruction Lesson, Berlin, October 28, 1911

Perhaps there may be some among you who feel oppressed by the fact that you are unable to convert what you have learned here into practical work, but are continually only absorbing spiritual teachings and now have to ask yourselves: Am I not a gourmet of spiritual delicacies? To that the Wise Masters of the East give us this answer: In absorbing spiritual teachings you do something that is of eternal value. The spiritual development of humanity could not progress by the activity of the "spirits of yore"—whether they be human beings who have lived in former times, or gods who have preceded us in earthly evolution—if there were no souls into which they could pour their teachings. It is as with the seed of a plant: so long as it is still in the blossom or the fruiting-body, it is valueless; only when it is placed into the earth is it able to sprout. Of much more importance for the evolution of the Earth are the people who take up into their souls works of art such as the *Sistine Madonna*, the drama of *Faust* and such like, than are the artists themselves.

If Raphael had only painted the *Sistine Madonna* and no one except he had seen it, then it would only have been of importance for him alone and not for eternity. Only when people allow works of art or other spiritual products to work upon them will something result which will outlast the Earth evolution and be taken up into the Jupiter condition. The one who creates is not the most important person. Of far more importance is the observer, the reader, and so forth. When artists or writers receive inspiration for their work out of the spiritual world, until the moment of conception it is of eternal importance to them. But the moment they set to work with pen or paintbrush they are only working for what is temporal, it is only of importance for them alone. Everything that is produced for the world comes under the sway of what is temporal. Only that which is stimulated within the human breast remains. The greater weight is therefore not where the intellect would expect it to be. The fact that the Evangelists wrote their Gospels was of importance to them, but it would not have meant anything for eternity if there had not been innumerable hearts upon which the Gospels could have worked. It is of far more value to read a classical work of antiquity and let it work upon you than to write an inferior book yourself.

Those who think that they must produce something for the world should wait until destiny calls them to carry out the one or other piece of work. And those who, for instance, have had a spiritual vision and ask themselves if they ought to divulge it to the world, they can apply the following rule in forming an opinion: If to divulge the vision were to be a source of pleasure to them then they certainly ought not to divulge it. Only what causes pain in the telling is of any value. Humorists who derive pleasure from their strokes of wit do not provide anything which is of significance for humanity; only those who have endured with pain the foibles of humankind and have transmuted them into humor, provide something of lasting value for history. Nothing but "devotion to the spiritual world" can produce fruitful results for work on Earth.

People may have accumulated treasure and feel the need to use it in the service of humanity, but without esoteric insight it will be impossible to know if the one or other philanthropic institution will presently lead either to the welfare or the downfall of humankind. People can engage in ever so many Samaritan works and make ever so many men and women happy, but it can be—and without the aforementioned devotion towards the spiritual world, it most probably will be—that, for example, great misfortune will befall the children of those men and women: that is, the next generation.

Here, in our lodge, because the members are present with their thoughts, more is done for the wellbeing of the world than in all philanthropic works. Physical values will be destroyed if one uses them for one's own ends; spiritual values will on the other hand be generated if they are taken up and used. Thus the one who creates is not at all the most important person. If one were to refer to the akasha record concerning the time of Raphael, Michelangelo and so on, and only give one's attention to these figures, one would not gain a true picture. Likewise, if in investigating Atlantean times by means of the akasha record, one were to only pay attention to what existed in the souls of the great leaders of the Mysteries—which, by the way, is very difficult to do—one would only get a correct vision by paying attention to what is awakened in the hearts and souls of those who were taught.

Whoever is able to write a fairly tolerable book, would accordingly also be able to grasp the contents of a good classical work from the past and would do far more good with it than by writing a mediocre book of his or her own.

Thus it is not for unauthorized pleasure when members are busily occupied with grasping what is offered to them here. Without the acceptance of the members nothing can be achieved for the future spiritual progress of humankind. Humanity would have to succumb to materialism, subsequent generations would then be ill in body and soul. The children who would be born to us would not find the thoughts in their spiritual surroundings that they need for their proper development if there were no circles of people to take up spiritual knowledge, even though it were not publicized. Materialism does so much harm, that it is impossible to do too much in this direction, to prevent it being exaggerated. Even if ten or a hundred times more study were to be undertaken than is actually the case, it still would not be too much to counterbalance the evil of materialism.

Concerning the Name of the Study Circle

It was a "Cognitive-Ritual."

For inner reasons Rudolf Steiner had no actual name for the study circle (c.f. p. 253). It was therefore abbreviated in one instance to "FM" (Freemasonry), in another to "ME" (Mystica Aeterna), later, at the express wish of Rudolf Steiner, to "MD" (Misraim-Dienst [Misraim-Service]) (see p. 98). For the present work the title "Cognitive-Ritual," which was later used by Rudolf Steiner, was chosen, because thereby its most essential feature was best expressed. It was in the year 1923, in response to a question by a priest of the Christian Community concerning the relationship of the Cognitive-Ritual to the earlier Esoteric Ritual, that he answered:

> The earlier Ritual was purely demonstrative. It was a Cognitive Ritual with degrees. The first degree brought knowledge of earthly humanity. It showed human development from Lemurian times until the present in imagination. The second degree demonstrated the connection to the spiritual world, the third revealed the secrets of the threshold of death, and so on. This Ritual was beyond time, interdenominational and interreligious; only one specific degree bore a Christian character. The use of this Ritual had to be abandoned because its demonstrative character could no longer be made clear to the outer world.[7]

Even before Rudolf Steiner had described the Ritual as a "Cognitive-Ritual" in his responses to questions, he had pointed to the importance that knowledge plays in rituals in a lecture given in Dornach, December 30, 1922, with the words: "For everything connected with Ritual must eventually disappear if the backbone of knowledge is lacking."

---

7. Lecture, Berlin, November 23, 1905.

The Preparation for Admittance

> To those who wished to participate it was made
> quite clear that they were not joining an order,
> but that they would experience, as participants in
> a ceremony, a kind of illustration or demonstra-
> tion of spiritual knowledge. And even if some of
> this took a form similar to a ceremony with exist-
> ing orders on occasions when their members
> were accepted or promoted to higher degrees, it
> was not a ceremony of an order. It was a visual,
> pictorial demonstration of the path the human
> soul follows when it ascends spiritually.[8]

An example of an application for membership occurs in a letter
from the leader of the work in Munich, Sophie Stinde, which
informs Rudolf Steiner on February 24, 1908, among other things:
"Countess H. wishes to become a member of the FM, but intended
to ask you beforehand in Stuttgart if she would be allowed to join
when you next come to Stuttgart, or if you would prefer her to wait
awhile. As she did not succeed in asking you herself in Stuttgart, I
suggested to her that I would ask you. As we have others seeking
admission it would be possible to admit her along with them, if you
do not find it too early for Countess H. Fräulein L. was here recently
and repeated that she and Dr. W. would like to be admitted in
March. Also Fäulein Kr. and Herr R. reconfirmed their wish (...).
We thought the plan of events could be as follows: Lodge on the
evening of the 17th. E.S. on the morning of the 18th. In the evening
the public lecture for men and women. Morning of the 19th FM
admissions. We would certainly have put the admissions before the
instruction, as we know that you prefer it that way, but because there
is a public lecture in the evening, we shall have to forgo it this time,
considering that the admissions will last a very long time."

---

8. *Rudolf Steiner, An Autobiography*, Rudolf Steiner Publications, New York, 1977,
p. 390. (See also *Autobiography: Chapters in the Course of My Life: 1861-1907*,
SteinerBooks, 2006)

According to how many candidates were to be admitted, the admissions often lasted for hours; the admission of single candidates was exceptional. Before the actual admissions a preparatory lesson was held, in which those to be admitted were instructed in their tasks and duties. Only two records exist of Dr. Steiner's conducting of such preparatory lessons (p. 151 et seq.). In exceptional cases such preparatory meetings were arranged in a festive style, as can be gathered from a letter by Rudolf Steiner to Sophie Stinde on June 10, 1908, in which it is stated: [CW 264] "St[ockmeyer]s can be admitted into the FM this time. It will not be possible to hold a short preparatory festival for the FM. St[ockmeyer] has the urgent wish to be admitted exactly on his 50th birthday. The admission can, of course, only be on Tuesday—the day after his birthday—but one could—perhaps without decorating the room—make the preliminary festival, with special arrangements, on Monday."

Concerning the Degrees

> Either one knows a truth, or one does not know it ...
> Therefore the democratic principle is not possible in matters concerning knowledge.[9]

Concerning the justification for working with degrees, it says in one of the lectures given at the time when the Study Circle was in preparation: "Truth is not something about which one can hold opinions. One either knows a truth, or one does not ... Just as little as one can discuss whether the angles of a triangle add up to so or so many degrees, higher truths are likewise indisputable. Therefore

---

9. Berlin, December 16, 1904.

the democratic principle is not possible in matters concerning knowledge" (Berlin, December 16, 1904).

In this sense the Cognitive-Ritual Circle was built up in degrees. A participant recorded this as follows: "It was an institution containing several degrees, to which those taking part were promoted according to how their souls were conditioned by their karma to the contents of these degrees. The promotion to a higher degree was in part carried out according to forms similar to those practiced in esoteric societies, for instance Freemasonry—but not in imitation of such orders, but, because they were the result of spiritual investigation … It is easy to see that, in rising to higher degrees, the esoteric impulse flowed ever more richly, and that during the course of nearly ten years of these practices—that is until the outbreak of war—the experience of these lessons signified something of immense depth for the development of the soul life of some of these participants."[10]

Altogether there were nine degrees, which were divided into three and six, whereby two sections or classes were formed that, with the so-called "ES," made up the three sections or classes of the Esoteric School as it existed from 1904 to 1914. In the three first degrees the ritual ceremony took precedence; in the six following ones, to which, according to reports, few people belonged, it mostly consisted of instruction. As to how far nine degrees are a realistic number for a true esoteric training nowadays was once explained as follows:

… Now it is very important to know that every esoteric brotherhood is founded on a basis of three grades or degrees. In the first degree—if symbols are correctly used (and by this I mean, of course, in accordance with what I have just said about our fifth post-Atlantean epoch) the souls progress so far that they come to a detailed inner experience of a wisdom that is independent of the ordinary sensory-physical knowledge. And in the first degree they must acquire a sufficient amount of such sense-free knowledge. All who are in the first degree today in this fifth

10. Adolf Arenson in *Rundbrief an die Mitglieder der Anthroposophischen Gesellschaft* [Circular letter to members of the Anthroposophical Society], October 1926.

cultural epoch ought to know approximately what is contained in my *Esoteric Science*. Everyone who is in the second degree ought to know—inwardly, actively know—the contents of my book: *How to Know Higher Worlds*. And whoever is in the third degree and has already received the significant symbols of Sign, Handclasp, and Word belonging to the third degree, will know what it means to live outside the body.—That would be the rule. That should be the goal to which one strives ...

But then there are people who reach the so-called high degrees—still higher degrees. That is a sphere with which a tremendous amount of vanity is connected, for there are brotherhoods in which one can attain to ninety or more than ninety degrees. Now just imagine what it must be like to be in possession of such a high degree of the Order! The so-called High-Degree Scottish Rite, which is built up on the three degrees, worked in the manner I have described to you, has thirty-three degrees, merely because of a mistake which arose out of a grotesque lack of knowledge. So there one has the three degrees, which, as you see, have deep significance. But on top of these three degrees another thirty follow. Now you can imagine; if with the third degree one acquires the ability to experience oneself from outside one's body, what sort of high being is one who has worked through another thirty degrees! But it all rests upon a grotesque misconception. In the esoteric sciences there is a different method of counting than by the decimal system: reading is not performed according to the decimal system, but by the system that accords with the particular numbers in question. That is, if one were to write 33, that actually signifies, according to the system of numbers in question: $3 \times 3 = 9$ ... It is only because people cannot read that they make it out to be 33 instead of 9.

Well, we shall disregard these vanities. There are still six degrees based on these three, which can be regarded as legitimate. And when these are worked they produce something of great significance. But at the present day they cannot actually be fully worked. It is quite impossible. They cannot be completed because humanity of the fifth cultural epoch has not yet progressed far enough to be able to complete all that has to be completed. For there has not been so much—I will not say "knowledge," but the practicing of knowledge—cultivated for it to have developed. That will only happen in the future (Berlin, April 4, 1916).

Symbolic Accessories

> As a matter of fact Freemasonry came into existence through a betrayal of the Mysteries and that is why it comes about that many of the symbols one finds in Freemasonry are also to be found here.[11]

The internal decoration of the lodge or temple has only been recorded for the first two degrees, but in essential features it may have been similar, at least for the third degree also: the walls were hung with black, which, in the final act of the Rosicrucian ending, were changed to bright red.[12] On the eastern wall was a square of blue material on which was a bright shining sun containing a central triangle. On the ceiling was a lamp on which, for the second degree, a letter "G" of gilded cardboard or metal was attached.[13] The floor was covered by a black and white checked carpet. At the borders of the large carpet stood three altars: on the east was the Altar of Wisdom (Master); on the south the Altar of Beauty (Second Warden); on the west, the Altar of Strength (First Warden).[14]

11. Instruction Class, Berlin, December 16, 1911. See p. 98.

12. The change from black to red was also introduced into the Easter scene of Goethe's *Faust*, produced by Rudolf Steiner and Marie Steiner.

13. It has been recorded that the letter "G" has been given various interpretations, such as "Gnosis," or "Geometry."

14. At the altar on the East Rudolf Steiner and Marie von Sivers always presided together, whereas at the other altars the role was changed.

Everyone who served at an altar carried a herold's mace, supposedly as in the Mystery Dramas. Beside each altar stood a large candlestick. On the front of each altar a plumb bob of gilded metal was attached. Furthermore, to every altar belonged a candle flame, matches, snuffers and extinguishers, and also a mallet and trowel. On the eastern altar was a chalice, the so-called "Holy of Holies:" on the southern altar a censer and dish with a set square; on the western altar two pairs of compasses, a plumb bob and a death's-head.

At the Altar of the East stood a cross with a crown of thorns, which, at the final act of the Rosicrucian ending, was exchanged for a wreath of red roses. Near to this stood a rather smaller altar with a Bible opened at the thirteenth chapter of the St. John's Gospel, on which lay a gilded metal triangle and a trowel interlocked with one another. On this altar the initial affirmation had to be sworn that one would not betray the secrets of the temple. This corresponded to an ancient tradition of esoteric practice.[15]

After having once more linked to the past, this policy was later abandoned, according to the reports of participants. It was Rudolf Steiner's opinion that modern human beings had to take more and more responsibility for their own moral behavior, also in esoteric life.

In the north, beyond the area of the great carpet, stood the two pillars Jachin and Boaz, also known as the Pillars of Hercules. The one on the left, (Jachin) was brick-red; on it lay a dressed cube-shaped stone (blue). The right hand pillar (Boaz) was dark blue; on it lay an undressed stone (red). Between the two pillars lay the carpet of symbols, called "the little carpet" in Elisabeth Vreede's sketch, used by Freemasonry lodges in general, (the so-called Tapis, Tableau). The participants had their places on the north and south sides of the lodge room.

For the third degree a fourth altar was portrayed in the north—just as in certain temple-scenes in the Mystery Dramas—where there was also a coffin.

---

15. c.f. p. 261.

The sketches of the arrangement for the first and second degrees and the sketches of details and explanations are the work of Dr. Elisabeth Vreede.

The Vestments

For this there are no authentic records that could be found. It has been reported that the apron (masonic apron, lambskin) was worn and that Rudolf Steiner wore an alb (the long, white priestly robe) over which a red cloak was put when the colors of the room were changed from black to red.

Concerning the symbolic significance of such vestments see the explanations given in the lecture to workmen on June 4, 1924, reported p. 287 of the present volume under the heading, "Concerning Sign, Handclasp, and Word."

Concerning the Rituals

> Everything portrayed in the contents of these rituals ... was completely without dependence on any tradition whatever. Though I was in possession of the formal certificate, nothing but what symbolized anthroposophical knowledge was cultivated.[16]

Everything available concerning the ritual texts has been presented in the second part of this volume. It has been recorded that in addition to this the one or other small ritual enactment took place: such for instance as the so-called "baptism by fire" of the

---

16. From: *Rudolf Steiner, An Autobiography.* See p. 100 of present volume.

fourth degree. The person in question received the name due from the spiritual world before a burning sulphur flame;[17] in individual cases marriage ceremonies were performed. But there are no texts available for such small ceremonies. Perhaps none existed, or respectively no such text was needed.

The rituals cannot be reconstructed in their entirety insofar as they do not consist merely in the spoken word, but to a large extent also in gestures, equipment, vestments and so on. But it is just about the latter that we possess insufficient information.

At the beginning of 1913, after several members had left the Cognitive-Ritual Study Group—when the separation from the Theosophical Society and founding of the Anthroposophical Society took place—and had evidently betrayed some of its secrets, Rudolf Steiner announced that it was therefore necessary to change the rituals. It is stated in the notes of an instruction lesson for members of all degrees given in Berlin, February 8, 1913: "Because of this betrayal it has become necessary to change our ritual in such a way that—while preserving the meaning in all main points—the rituals will have a different wording than that previously employed, so that they will not sound in unison with those of the others." Another participant recorded this in the following way: "We spoke about those who have deserted us. So that they cannot interfere by their thoughts in our present work it is necessary to change the ritual." There is no original documentation for this announced change. But a participant has nevertheless recorded how the words spoken at the three altars underwent a certain change (c.f. p. 181).

Ritual events only took place where adequate space was available, such, among others, as the anthroposophical centers in Berlin, Hanover, Cologne, Munich, Stuttgart, but also in other countries.[18]

---

17. There was a baptismal rite with water for the 2nd degree. See p. 225 of present volume.

18. From documents in the archive of the Trustees of Rudolf Steiner's Legacy it appears that there must have been translations of ritual texts (in part, at least) in English and French.

Explanations of the Cognitive-Ritual and the Symbolism of the Ritual Objects

> Theosophy is the inner truth of these cere-
> monies, it tells us what the ceremonies por-
> tray, and contains the spirit of these symbols
> and images.[19]

The instruction lessons in which the rituals and objects pertaining to them were explained and the results of general research on spiritual-scientific subjects were announced lay between the ritual opening and closing of the meeting. But there were also instruction lessons without any ritual; mostly for a single degree, sometimes for several and sometimes for all degrees together.

As it was forbidden to make notes during such sessions, it has to be taken into account that all recorded notes were written down from memory at a later time and are accordingly fragmentary or existing in cue-words only and that stylistically, as well as occasionally in their content, they do not always do justice to Rudolf Steiner's intention.

In the present documentation only those notes are included that refer directly to the Cognitive-Ritual and its symbolic accessories, as well as the Temple Legend and the Golden Legend. As this material is widely dispersed, selections were made from it and arranged under the pertinent sections in order to give a clearer survey. In some cases, where there are no explanations or instruction lessons to refer to, descriptions from other lectures, held at a later period, are used.[20] What has not been included are the notes from works on general spiritual-scientific subjects, because these, being derived from shorthand copies, exist in a more complete form and can be found in the already published volumes of the complete edition of Rudolf Steiner's works.

---

19. From notes by Marie Steiner of a lecture in Breman, April 9, 1906.

20. Information about symbolism in the history of civilization is given by Joseph Schauberger, referred to on p. 45.

The Temple Legend and the Golden Legend and How They Figure in the Rituals

> The Hiram nature is within all of us; we have to make it live in us anew.[21]

Legends as figurative representations of esoteric truths play an important role in all esoteric teachings, because they incorporate an immense number of concepts and act not only on the intellect, but also on the human feelings. In this sense great significance was attached to these two legends, because their pictures reflect what is considered an exemplary step forward along the esoteric path of the Hiram individuality.

The Temple Legend—of which it was once said that those who assimilate it take up into themselves something that will regulate their thinking (and much depends upon the regulation of the thinking)[22]—occurs twice in the ritual. The part that symbolically portrays humankind's evolution is used as meditational matter during the ceremony of admittance into the first degree; the end part of the legend, which describes Hiram's death and resurrection, is introduced as part of the ritual of promotion into the third degree. The legend was used in instruction lessons many times over. The existing notes are summed up in the section: "Explanations of the Temple Legend." The indications given there regarding the later incarnations of Hiram Abiff require amplification, as they only comprise a part of what can be called the Hiram research with regard to reincarnation. The supplementary material is added as an addendum to the section: "Explanations of the Temple Legend."

The Golden Legend—called the "second" Master Legend in a recorded note is portrayed symbolically in the two round pillars

---

21. See the section "Explanations of the Temple Legend," p. 379ff.
22. Berlin, May 15, 1905.

Jachin and Boaz. The text of this legend and the recorded explanations are to be found in the section "Sketches and Explanations of
the Ritual Objects."

PREPARATION FOR ADMITTANCE

Preparation Lessons

Notes of two lessons by Rudolf Steiner recorded by participants

I

(No location or date given. Presumably Munich 1906[1])

Theosophical knowledge has only been available to the public for a couple of decades, but so long as people were engaged in thinking, strove for highest aims and asked questions about the origin of the world and the goal of life, Theosophy has existed. But Theosophy has not always been presented to the world in the way it has been presented during the last thirty years or so. In earlier times it was cultivated in small and intimate circles of initiates belonging to occult or secret brotherhoods, whose members knew far more than could be openly revealed. The populace, humanity in general, was only to receive the fruits of the initiates' wisdom. The world did not recognize them for what they really were, but only recognized the effects of their work. One only knew: so and so is a cabinetmaker, the other a locksmith, another maybe a high state official. Such people were able to perform works in the world of such a kind as went unrecognized by the community at large. A word spoken by one of these initiates was inwardly of much greater significance than could be commonly appreciated.

What the world knows as the great ones of history were not the really great ones. The latter lived in seclusion. Such an occult initiate as that had a fleeting acquaintanceship with Rousseau, for instance. The words which the former spoke to Rousseau did not seem of much importance to him, but they worked in an esoteric way. When Rousseau became enlightened by them he published it in books; he himself was not an initiate, but the initiate stood behind him.

---

1. c.f. Lecture, Berlin, October 8, 1906.

Another example: How was it that Jacob Böhme, the poor cobbler, gained such wisdom? People who read his biography overlook some important things. In it is the following small anecdote: The little Jacob was standing as an apprentice in the workshop of his master, the teacher who was just then absent. It had been forbidden him to sell anything. He only had to mind the shop. A fascinating personality, who made a deep impression on the youngster, entered the shop and spoke only a few words. After he had left, Jacob heard his name being called three times from outside the shop: "Jacob, you are only small today, but one day you will be great. Mark that!"— This remained inextinguishably fixed in Jacob's mind.

Now and then someone spoke to a statesman; the words, seemingly of no importance, had a magical effect. It depends on it being the right words. Those are means by which initiates work. They supply the thoughts, they give the impulse. For example: someone receives a letter containing an appeal. The person who receives the letter is specially inclined to do something, but has to receive the impulse to do it. If the person could read it correctly, something strange could be deciphered from the letter, which apparently had nothing much in it. One had to leave out four words; in every fifth word the deeper meaning was concealed. They were the effective words.

Today one must discover other methods. The moment this secret was betrayed, the words lost their value. These were small elementary things pertaining to the secrets.

A German scholar who was initiated was Trithemius von Sponheim, the teacher of Agrippa von Nettesheim. In his works you find "Theosophy," if you leave off certain preceding and succeeding words in the sentence. That was necessary because only certain people were allowed to be initiated if they had received a completely adequate preparation: Knowledge must not be curiosity, but must be converted into deeds.

Theosophy is there to make practical advance in the world and to be active in the state and social life. Candidates for initiation had to submit to hard tests to see if they were worthy of initiation. Only those who stood the tests could be initiated step by step. This method has been abandoned now. The elementary instructions are taught publicly nowadays. That is only where the deeper wisdom begins. More and more of the divine wisdom will be imparted to the wider public, to the world at large. Theosophical wisdom is very ancient, only the method of preparation is new.

What we are about to hear is the body of knowledge common to all those who—not through speculation or theory, but by means of facts—create for themselves a picture of what it is like in the spiritual world.

All wisdom is derived from the spirit. In earlier times religion was the most effective means of acquiring it. The religions have been the dispensers of wisdom and knowledge for thousands of years. Now there are countless numbers of people seeking to know. It is through knowledge, not faith, that we want to proceed. Today there is discrepancy between science and religion, knowledge and belief. The real reason why Theosophy became necessary is the art of printing. With the popularization of material knowledge this discrepancy arose. That is where the initiates came in and bridged the gulf.

II

Cologne, May 7, 1912

The one who does not unite with the spiritual world is like a sleep-walker, who does all sorts of things in sleep by means of higher (semi-conscious) forces, without being aware of it. There are two friends. The one always feels fresh and strong and ready for work in the morning. The other is usually weak and exhausted. One day the strong one says to the weak one: "It is no wonder that you feel wretched in the morning, for at night you always get out of bed and work for several hours at your desk." And it was right. They found on investigation that the work which the weak one thought he still had to do lay finished on his desk.

In his subconscious state he was led by higher powers to perform the tasks for which he had felt incompetent in his waking life.

Something similar was performed for humankind by the religious confessions. Without people being aware of it they were led into the spiritual world and to spiritual knowledge by guiding powers. Certainly they did not attain to what was achieved in much earlier times in the hallowing of everyday things and actions. No stone was hewn without a definite rhythm, blow upon blow, and this rhythm was felt to be an echo of the Music of the Spheres.

Of that there exist only a few bare remnants today, as when in country places the corn is threshed [by hand] in rhythm. It all depends upon how you look at it. Let us take as an example children who are looking forward to Christmas. They have been told: In the night Father Christmas, or the Christmas Angel, will come in quietly and put the presents down. Then a child, spurred by a materialistic urge pretends to be asleep and spies how the parents—living people on the physical plane—lay the gifts down. The child's belief in the higher beings is disturbed. One can, however, look at it from the point of view of the parents. They might feel themselves to be the medium through which spiritual powers are working to shower gifts and blessings on the children.

Nowadays the world is bereft of the gods, and it is difficult to speak about divine guidance and rulership, one only has to think about those who built the Titanic and sailed in it.[2]

But, nevertheless, the higher powers have always been active on the physical plane in order to allow spiritual forces to flow into human life, especially into the Mysteries. One could go back to Atlantean times, but let us talk about the post-Atlantean Mysteries. Pupils were enlisted so that they could gradually be introduced into the secrets of the universe and human evolution. The pupils were prepared in such a way that they were exposed to fear and shock. As a result of this some of them became free, courageous and strong and gained a connection to the spiritual world in the incarnation they were then going through; the others, however, who were overcome by it, and proved to be too weak, felt: I am too weak at present to ascend to supersensible worlds, but, when I have passed through the gateway of death, I will receive some benefit from having made the attempt to gain access to those higher worlds. Later such great initiates as Ormus and the Gospel writer Mark incorporated the fruits of Christianity into the Mysteries of humankind; then the Culdees secretly introduced the spiritual truths into the Gothic cathedrals.[3] And ever and again there have been esoteric brotherhoods who, under various pseudonyms on Earth, guided humankind into the spiritual world. Such, for instance, was the Arthurian brotherhood to which Parzival belonged, which later worked under the name of the Rosicrucian brotherhood.

---

2. The English oceanliner Titanic had sunk with about 1,500 people on board after hitting an iceberg on its maiden voyage in the North Atlantic on April 15, 1912, shortly before this address was given. People had been so convinced of the invulnerability of this ship that no heed had been given to the iceberg warning.

3. Culdees = ascetic Irish [and Scottish] monks, to whose spiritual brotherhoods since the 8th century, great influence on Freemasonry, architecture and customs has been attributed. See Joseph Schauberg; *Vergleichends Handbuch der Symbolik der Freimaurerei mit Besonderer Rücksicht auf die Mythologie und Mysterien des Altertums.* [Comparative Handbook of the Symbolism of Freemasonry with Special Reference to the Mythology and Mysteries of Antiquity], Schaffhausen, 1861.

The knights of King Arthur's Round Table represented the young nature-forces, which then underwent a change in the knighthood of the Grail to gain conscious spiritual power. Through that we have the connection of the old esoteric knowledge to the new Christian knowledge. For we are told in the saga that a stone fell out of Lucifer's crown when he was thrown down from heaven and that this stone was remolded to form the Grail Cup, the Holy Vessel in which the blood of Christ was collected on Golgotha.[4]

One who was ripe for it was led by higher powers, as was Parzifal, to the decisive question that opened up the portal of initiation.

Today there is great opposition to such esoteric brotherhoods, particularly in pious Christian circles, which seek an ascent to higher worlds with the help of the Christ impulse. They fight against such brotherhoods as if they were fighting against Satan incarnate, because they say that through them, they would lose the Christ. It is not just bad will or an aversion on principle to the esoteric, but it stems from a dimly felt, but perfectly legitimate recognition, that only those shall find Christ in the spiritual world, who take with them the memory of Christ on the physical plane. For it is only on Earth that Christ can be comprehended and it is quite correct to say that those who enter the higher world without having established a feeling for and recognition of Christ can go astray.

There is hierarchy in our esoteric brotherhood, as in others too, and it is not a democracy, because no plebiscite can decide on truth. Only those gifted by spiritual powers with the one true knowledge can know what truth is. An idealization of human labor and human life, the light of wisdom and warmth of love, will be gained and all those will recognize the divine core in their brother and sister, who are striving for the same goal as themselves.

In the three lower grades everything that can be gained through knowledge of the higher beings and powers will be experienced symbolically. In the six higher grades one gains an intimate knowledge of the esoteric powers themselves.

---

4. For the connection of High-Degree Masonry to the saga of the Holy Grail, see the lecture in Berlin, January 2, 1906.

Formulas for the Pledge

Two handwritten notices by Rudolf Steiner

Notebook, Archive No. 611

I

I try to understand how I may develop through the Misraim Service and approach the sacred mystery, which demands respectful silence. I shall try to instruct my fellow human beings in the care of this kind of development through concern for the symbolic Sanctuarium and to understand the inner nature of human wisdom by preserving a sense for the degrees of truth.

I shall try to protect my selfhood from all influences that might reduce its fully conscious freedom and rob it, by means of hypnotism, suggestion, etc., at any stage of life, of the inner power of light and self-determination.

The soul can only find its goal and destination in the realm of duration, and direction and growth in the realm of time, when it strives in this way.

I perceive that such is the proclaimed teaching of those who I am told are the sages, who are said to hold the key to the hidden Mysteries.

II

I —— born in —— living at —— herewith pledge and promise to keep and follow the rules of the true and genuine Misraim-Service, to rigidly preserve the sacred mystery; to care for and intercede for the maintenance of the Sanctuarium as far as is within my power to do so and to recognize absolutely the General Grand Master as the highest decisive authority in all matters pertaining to the Misraim Service. I further promise and pledge that I shall not allow myself to have my freedom curtailed by hypnotism, suggestion or otherwise, in order that all which I encounter in life may find me in a state of wakefulness, so that no secrets of the great service can be betrayed to an outsider.

Should I ever break this solemn promise, then may my soul wander restlessly in space without aim or direction, and may it be without guidance during endless periods of time.

This I pledge to the Wise Masters of the East, who may fix their gaze upon my deeds.

Ritual Texts

Ritual Text for the Opening of the Lodge[1]

Text according to the original handwriting of Rudolf Steiner

Notebook, Archive No. 611, with a few comments by participants concerning the course of the ritual

Master (to the right of the altar in the East):
What is the Mason's first duty in the Lodge?

Acolyte (to the left of the altar in the East):
To see that the Lodge is covered.

(It has to be ascertained that the Lodge is covered, that is to say that no profane person, or brothers, or sisters of other grades are at the door and that the doors are carefully fastened).

The Lodge is covered.

Master: If the Lodge is covered according to regulation our work can begin.

Master: Mallet blow (three times):
May wisdom guide our building (lighting of candle).

Second Warden (South):

Mallet blow (three times):
May beauty adorn it (lighting of candle).

First Warden (West):
Mallet blow (three times):

May strength build it (lighting of candle).

Master: Brother (Sister) Second Warden, your regular place in the Lodge?

Answer: In the South.

––––––––––

1. This wording is applicable for the first, second and third degrees with slight alterations.

Master: Why are you stationed there?

Answer: To be the Sun at the meridian and to call the brothers and sisters to work, so that the Temple shall be built.

Master: Brother (Sister) First Warden, your regular place in the Lodge?

Answer: In the West.

Master: Why are you stationed there?

Answer: To be the Sun at its setting and to hand over the brothers and sisters to ordinary life after they have accomplished their work and have received strength and energy from the Lodge for their outward work.

Master: Where is the Master's place in the Lodge?

Acolyte: In the East.

Master: Why is the Master stationed there?

Acolyte: As the Sun rises in the East to lighten and to enliven the day, so has the venerable Master to lighten and enliven the inner work of the Lodge.

Speaking to the others:

The venerable Master will speak the prayer that will impress on your hearts the meaning of the Brotherhood. Stand up and listen to it in the sign of the ... degree:

Master: *Brothers (Sisters) of Ages Past,* may your creative activity become our wisdom; we take the compasses and plumb line of the heights from your hands; may your accomplished work be strength for our soul, be strength for our hands.

Brothers (Sisters) of the Present Time, since you are wiser than we, let your wisdom radiate into our souls, so that we become revealers of your thoughts of God.

Brothers (Sisters) of the Future, since you bear the building plan in your will, let your strength stream into our limbs, so that we may become the body for the great souls.

[With acknowledgement to Virginia Sease for the translation of these paragraphs].

Master: Mallet blow

The one on the left (acolyte):

> To you my Sisters and Brothers it is my task in the Order of the Misraim Service, to warn you to be attentive to the stroke of the sacred T (Tau)- sign. You received its sacred meaning at a significant moment, while blindfolded. From this you know that it tells you how the name of God resounds in your inmost being. The world's sublime mysteries include the sound of the T. What will for you be the teaching from the East will be established within you through the strength of the T. The spirit-word given you in the T shall become a part of your own being.
>
> You are urged by the Altar of the East to follow the path of the sacred T: take note of the word that will be spoken to you.

Master: T–stroke

Second Warden (South):

> To you my Sisters and Brothers, it is my task in the Order of the Misraim Service to call you to work. May what the builder of the Temple of Humanity calls "Beauty" inspire my message. You must work on the building whose stones are the hearts; whose connecting-parts are the well-considered thoughts; whose mortar is the power of the will. Survey the world that enlivens your hearts; whose seminal forces nourish your will. All of this is a beautiful expression of hidden spirit-beings. Take up into yourselves the forces of these beings and what lives within you will ray forth as "Beauty."
>
> You are urged by the Altar of the East to follow this path of Beauty: take note of the word that will be spoken to you.

Master: T–stroke

First Warden (West):

> To you my Sisters and Brothers, it is my task in the Order of the Misraim Service to release you from your labors. May what the builder of the Temple of Humanity calls "Strength," inspire my message. You should allow the work you have learned here to take effect when you have left the portal of this Temple to enter into outer life, from your hearts should flow into the rest of humankind what the heart can form into building stones of the Great Temple; in your thoughts should be active what can make the connecting parts of this building; from your will should flow what can become the mortar for the stones of this Temple. Do only that which comes from the sincerity of your hearts, to which you are led by the heedfulness of your thoughts, to which you have steeled your wills. Through that you will become the likeness of your archetype; and from you will come Strength that shapes the world.
>
> You are urged by the Altar of the East to follow this path of Strength: take note of the word that will be spoken to you.

Acolyte (East):

> Learn to be silent and power shall be yours.

Second Warden (South):

> Renounce power and volition shall be yours.

First Warden (West):

> Renounce volition and feeling shall be yours.

Master: Renounce feeling and knowledge shall be yours.

Instruction (Temple Legend).[2]

---

2. If occasion arises, the ritual of acceptance into the first degree, or promotion into the second degree, or advancement into the third degree might replace the instruction.

Ritual Text for the Closing of the Lodge [3]

The Lodge is closed in three ways:

1. According to the Masonic ending (the same wording, with corresponding changes, as with the lodge opening).

2. The Magical (Latin) ending.

3. With the Rosicrucian ending.

Master: Mallet blow (three times):
          May wisdom guide our building (extinguish candle).

Second Warden (South):
          Mallet blow (three times):
          May beauty adorn it (extinguish candle).

First Warden (West):
          Mallet blow (three times):
          May strength build it (extinguish candle).

Master: Brother (Sister) Second Warden, your regular place in the Lodge?

Answer: In the South.

Master: Why are you stationed there?

Answer: To be the Sun at the meridian and to call the brothers and sisters to work so that the Temple shall be built.

Master: Brother (Sister) First Warden, your regular place in the Lodge?

Answer: In the West.

Master: Why are you stationed there?

Answer: To be the Sun at its setting and to hand over the brothers and sisters to ordinary life after they have received

---

3. Can be used for the first, second and third degrees.

strength and energy from the Lodge for their outward work.

Master: Where is the Master's place in the Lodge?

Acolyte: In the East.

Master: Why is the Master stationed there?

Acolyte: As the Sun rises in the East to lighten and enliven the day, so has the venerable Master to lighten and enliven the inner work of the Lodge.

Speaking to the others:

The venerable Master will speak the prayer which will impress on your hearts the meaning of the Brotherhood, stand up and listen to it in the sign of the . . . degree.

Master: *Brothers (Sisters) of Ages Past,* may your creative activity become our wisdom; we take the compasses and plumb line of the heights from your hands; may your accomplished work be strength for our soul, be strength for our hands.

    Brothers (Sisters) of the Present Time, since you are wiser than we, let your wisdom radiate into our souls, so that we become revealers of your thoughts of God.

    Brothers (Sisters) of the Future, since you bear the building plan in your will, let your strength stream into our limbs, so that we may become the body for the great souls.

[With acknowledgement to Virginia Sease for the translation of these paragraphs].

Master: Mallet blow:

To one on the left (acolyte):

To you my Sisters and Brothers it is my task in the Order of the Misraim Service, to warn you to be attentive to the stroke of the sacred T (Tau)-sign. You received its sacred meaning at a significant moment, while blindfolded. From this you know that it tells you how the name of God resounds in your inmost being. The world's sublime mysteries include the sound of the T. What for you will be the teaching from the East, will be established within you through the strength of the T. The spirit-word given you in the T, shall become a part of your own being.

You are urged by the Altar of the East to follow the path of the sacred T: take note of the word that has been spoken to you.

Master: T–stroke

Second Warden (South):

To you my Sisters and Brothers, it is my task in the Order of the Misraim Service to call you to work. May what the builder of the Temple of Humanity calls 'Beauty' inspire my message. You must work on the building whose stones are the hearts, whose connecting parts are the well-considered thoughts, whose mortar is the power of the will. Survey the world which enlivens your hearts; whose wisdom instructs your thoughts; whose seminal forces nourish your will. All of this is a beautiful expression of the hidden spirit-beings. Take up into yourselves the forces of these beings and what lives within you will ray forth as "Beauty."

You are urged by the Altar of the East to follow this path of Beauty: take note of the word which has been spoken to you.

Master: T–stroke

First Warden (West):

To you my Sisters and Brothers, it is my task in the Order of the Misraim Service to release you from your labors. May what the builder of the Temple of Humanity calls "Strength" inspire my message. You should allow the work you have learned here to take effect when you have left the portal of this Temple to enter into outer life, from your hearts should flow into the rest of humankind what the heart can form into building stones of the Great Temple, in your thoughts should be active what can make the connecting-parts of this building; from your will should flow what can become the mortar for the stones of this Temple. Do only that which comes from the sincerity of your hearts, to which you are led by the heedfulness of your thoughts, to which you have steeled your wills. Through that you will become the likeness of your archetype, and from you will come Strength which shapes the world.

You are urged by the Altar of the East to follow this path of Strength: take note of the word which has been spoken to you.

Acolyte (East):
Learn to be silent and power shall be yours.

Second Warden (South):
Renounce power and volition shall be yours.

First Warden (West):
Renounce volition and feeling shall be yours.

Master: Renounce feeling and knowledge shall be yours.

The Magical Ending

According to the original handwriting of Rudolf Steiner. The remarks enclosed within round brackets have been added in accordance with notes from participants. [The Latin formula can also be found in the work of Eliphas Levi: *La Haute Magie*]

Salt

In isto sale sit sapientia et ab omni corruptione servet mentes nostras et corpora nostra, per Hochmael et in virtute Ruach-Hochmael,[4] recedant ab isto fantasmata hylae, ut sit sal coelestis, sal terrae et terra salis, ut nutrietur bos triturans et addat spei nostrae cornua tauri volantis. Amen.

Ashes

Revertatur cinis ad fontem aquarum viventium et fiat terra fructificans, et germinet arborem vitae per tria nomine, quae sunt Nezah, Hod et Jesod in principio et in fine per Alpha et Omega, qui sunt in spiritu Azoth! Amen.

While mixing water, salt and ashes

In sale sapientiae aeternae et in aqua regenerationis et in cinere germinante terram novam, omnia fiant per Elohim Gabriel, Raphael et Uriel in saecula et aeones. Amen.

(Ex Deo nascimur. In Christo morimur.

Per Spiritum sanctum reviviscimus.)

Exorcism of water

Fiat firmamentum in medio aquarum et separet aquas ab aquis, quae superius sicut quae inferius, et quae inferius sicut quae

---

4. Ruach = spirit, air; Hochma, Nezah, Hod, Jesod = Sephiroth of the Cabala. Azoth (according to Blavatsky: *Isis Unveiled*) = Alchemistic name for the "creative principle in nature (astral light)."

superius ad perpetranda miraculum unius. Sol ejus pater est, luna mater, et ventus hanc gestavit in utero suo, ascendit a terra ad coelum et rursus a coelo in terram descendit. Exorciso te, creatura aquae, ut sis mihi speculum Dei et vivi in operibus ejus et fons vitae et ablutio peccatorum. Amen.

[Translation of above Latin text into English by A.E. Waite from the French by Eliphas Levi: *Dogme et Rituel de la Haute Magic*—Waite's: *Transcendental Magic,* p. 230/1]

Over the Salt

May wisdom abide in this salt, and may it preserve our minds and bodies from all corruption, by Hochmael and in the virtue of Ruach Hochmael! May the phantoms of Hyle depart herefrom; that it may become a heavenly salt, salt of the earth and earth of salt; that it may feed the threshing ox, and strengthen our hope with the horns of the flying bull! Amen.

Over the Ash

May this ash return unto the fount of living waters; may it become a fertile earth; may it bring forth the Tree of Life, by the Three Flames which are Netsah, Hod and Jesod,[5] in the beginning and in the end, by Alpha and Omega, which are in the spirit of Azoth! Amen.

Mingling the Water, Salt and Ash

In the salt of eternal wisdom, in the water of regeneration, and in the ash whence the new earth springeth, be all things accomplished by Elohim, Gabriel, Raphael and Uriel, through the ages and aeons! Amen.

---

5. See footnote p. 169.

Exorcism of the Water

Let there be a firmament in the midst of the waters, and let it divide the waters from the waters; the things which are above are like unto things which are below, and things below are like unto things above, for the performance of the wonders of one thing. The sun is its father, the moon its mother, the wind hath carried it in the belly thereof. It ascendeth from earth to heaven, and again it descendeth from heaven to earth. I exorcise thee, creature of water, that thou mayest become unto men a mirror of the living God in His works, a fount of life and ablution of sins.

The Rosicrucian Ending[6]

Text according to the original handwriting of Rudolf Steiner

Notebook, Archive No. 6978

The stones are mute, I have placed and hidden the eternal creator-word in them; chaste and modest they hold it in the depths.

M.Pr. [Materia prima]

The plants live and grow; I let the eternal creator-word of the Sun's power stream into them; they carry it into the depths.

M.S. [Materia secunda]

The animals feel and will; I have livingly shaped the eternal creator-word in them; they mold it in the depths.

M.T. [Materia tertia]

Human beings think and act; I let the eternal creator-word suffer and rejoice in them; they shall carry it into the heights.[7]

S.T. [Spiritus tertius]

The soul knows and is devoted; I let the eternal creator-word of the Sun's power flow in it; it directs its flight into the heights of wisdom and piety.

S.S. [Spiritus secundus]

---

6. See also version p. 484 et seq., used in the Wachsmuth-Lerchernfeld Group 1923. [Facsimile].

7. At this moment the black curtains are changed to red.

The spirit releasing itself loves the universe; I speak in the spirit of my eternal creator-word, wakening and liberating the world in purity; it flows into the heights of the eternal light.

S.P. [Spiritus primus]

K. A. P. [Konx Aum Pax[8]]

---

8. According to the record of a participant.

Die Meine sind Meere: Ich fahre aus einige Schiffbruch u. bin gelegt eine unbeugsam; Klarlly und Hammete frielen hie es in die Tiefen.

M. Pr.

Die Pflanzen leben und welken; Ich fahre das einige Schöpfer war der Sonnenkraufe u. bei kleinen Lüften, die Tiefen es fürchte in die Tiefen.

M. S.

Die Tiere empfinden und wollen; Ich fahre das einige Schöpferwerk in ihrem Leben gefunden; die fernen es in dem Tiefen.

M. T.

Der Mensch denkt und handelt; Ich treffe die einige Schöpferwerk in ihm leiden und ich treten es in Licht es Tragen in die Höfen.

G. T.

Die Seele erkennt und gibt sich hin; ich lasse das ewige Schöpferwort der Sommerkraft in ihr heröniend sich erheben; sie leuchtet spiegelnd er die Hüsten der Weisheit und Frömmigkeit,

S. S.

Da sich leitet ich loisend die alles, zy ispreiche in So Phien- und ewige (Mödpherwort weckend und reifend in Reinzeit, die weelz, ruhig blöindt es in den Höfen des ewigen sichz

S. P.

K. A. P.

The Rosicrucian Ending, Old Style
Notebook, Archive No. 6977

The stones are mute—I have placed and hidden the eternal creator-word in them; chaste and modest they preserve it.

anaramaya

The plants live—I let the eternal creator-word of the Sun's power stream into them; they carry it downwards.

pranamaya

The animals feel—and will—I have livingly shaped the eternal creator-word in them; they mold it in the depths.

Human beings think and act—I let the eternal creator-word, springing up in them, suffer and rejoice; they enliven it in the depths.

manomaya

The soul knows and is devoted—I let the eternal creator-word flow upward in it; it directs its flight into the heights of wisdom and piety.

vijnanamaya

The spirit, releasing itself, loves everything—I speak my eternal creator-word in the spirit, wakening and liberating the world in purity; it flows quietly into the heights of the eternal light.

anandamaya

Atman

———

Explanation of Sanskrit names:
anaramaya [more likely annarasamaya], literally: created out of solid and liquid food.
pranamaya   literally   created out of living forces.
manomaya   "   created out of spirit.
vijnanamaya   "   created out of consciousness.
anandamaya   "   created out of joy.

Die Steine sind stumm — Ich habe das ewige Schöpferwort in sie gelegt
und verborgen; keusch und schamvoll verbergen sie es.

<u>annamaya</u>

Die Pflanzen leben — Ich habe das ewige Schöpferwort der Sonnenkraft
in ihren Strömen lassen; sie tragen es hinunter.

<u>pranamaya</u>

Die Thiere empfinden — und wollen — Ich habe das ewige Schöpferwort
in ihnen lebend gestaltet; sie formen es in den Tiefen.

Der Mensch denkt und handelt — Ich lasse das ewige Schöpferwort
in ihm sprechend sich freuen und leiden; er belebt es in
den Tiefen.   <u>manomaya</u>

Die Seele erkennt und gibt sich hin — Ich lasse das ewige Schöpferwort
in ihr sich strömend erheben; sie lenkt ihren Flug in
die Höhen der Weisheit und Frömmigkeit.

<u>vijnanamaya</u>

Der Geist lebt, sich lösend von sich, alles — Ich spreche im Geiste mein ewiges
Schöpferwort, weckend und erlösend in Reinheit die Welt; er strömt
ruhig in den Höhen des ewigen Lichtes.

<u>anandamaya</u>

Atman

The Rosicrucian Ending, An Outline
Notebook, Archive No. 6976

<u>Muteness</u> begins to speak

> I let my eternal creator-word whisper silently—I take it keeping it chaste and modest within my heart.

<u>Life and growth</u> become mute

> I let my eternal creator-word stream through them mutely; pure and unsullied they bear it upwards.

<u>Feeling and will</u> grow without personal desire

> I let my eternal creator-word dwell in them; it shall gleam through their transport sheath.

<u>Thinking and acting</u>, feeling and willing

> I let my eternal creator-word shine into them; they shall mold it into spirit matter.

<u>Knowing and devotion</u>, thinking and acting

> I let my eternal creator-word become God in them—they shall lead me into life.

I am - I - The creator-word rests in me,
lack of existence creates itself as a boundary.

A.U.M.

Stimmungsfülle wird sprechend — Ich lasse mein
ewiges Schöpferwort im Schweigen
rinnen — ich nehme ab, bewußtvoll
es Kräfte und sternenvoll in meinem
Herzen.

Leben und ~~Wachsen~~ umströmen — Ich lasse
mein ewiges Schöpferwort rinnen durch
sie strömen; jungfräulich tragen sie es
aufwärts.

Empfinden und Wollen wachsen wunschlos — Ich lasse
mein ewiges Schöpferwort in ihnen wohnen;
es soll leuchten durch ihre durchsichtige Hülle.

Denken und Handeln empfinden und wollen — Ich
lasse mein ewiges Schöpferwort in ihnen scheinen;
sie sollen es in Geistesstoff gestalten.

Erkennen und Hingabe denken und ~~handeln~~ — Ich
lasse mein ewiges Schöpferwort in ihnen
vergolten — sie sollen mich führen ins Leben.

Ich bin — ich — Das Schöpferwort ruht in mir;
die Wesenhaftigkeit schafft es sich als Grenze.

Stirn

The Rosicrucian Ending [9]

Text according to the original handwriting of Rudolf Steiner.
For the Wachsmuth-Lerchenfeld Group in 1923

Translation with acknowledgement to Virginia Sease

The stones are mute; I have placed and hidden the eternal creator-word in them; chaste and modest they hold it in the depths.

M.Pr. [Materia prima] Matter hardens itself.

The plants live and grow. I have placed the eternal creator-word in them; sprouting and thriving they carry it into the depths.

M.S. [Materia secunda] Matter opens itself to the spirit.

The animals feel and will. I have placed the eternal creator-word in them; shaping and molding it they hold it in the depths.

M.T. [Materia tertia] Matter shines in the light of the soul.

Human beings think and act; I have placed the eternal creator-word in them; they should fetch it from the depths.

S.T. [Spiritus tertius] The "I" finds itself in the world.

The soul knows and is devoted; I shall release my eternal creator-word from her, that she may carry it into the heights of purity and piety.

S.S. [Spiritus secundus] The "I" sacrifices itself to God.

The spirit releasing itself loves the universe; I speak in it my eternal creator-word, wakening and liberating the world in purity.

S.P. [Spiritus primus] The "I" works in God.

---

9. See facsimile copy of Dr. Steiner's handwriting from 1923, p. 485.

The Version of the Words Spoken at the Three Altars from 1913 Onwards

According to the report of a participant

East

To you, my Sisters and Brothers, it is my duty in the Service of Michael to warn you to be attentive to his sacred symbol. You received at a significant moment in earth existence its sacred meaning. From this you know that it tells you how the sublime name of God resounds in your inmost being. The world's sublime mysteries include the sound of the sacred symbol.

What for you has become the teaching of the East will establish Michael's strength within you.

What was given you as spirit-word in the sacred symbol, shall become the being of your own being.

The path of the sacred symbol was impressed upon your hearts by the Altar of the East; take note of the word which shall be spoken to you ...

South

To you, my Sisters and Brothers, it is my duty, in the Service of Michael, to call you to work. May what the builder of the Temple of Humanity calls Beauty inspire my message. You must work on the building whose stones are in your hearts, whose connecting parts are in your well-considered thoughts and whose mortar is to be seen in the power of the will. Survey the world which is around you, whose life moves your heart, whose wisdom trains your thoughts, whose solar energy nourishes your will. All of this is a beautiful expression of hidden spirit-beings. Take up into yourselves the forces of these beings and what lives within you will ray forth as Beauty. The path of this Beauty has been impressed upon your hearts by the Master from the Altar of the East; take note of the word which shall be spoken to you...

West

To you, my Sisters and Brothers, it is my duty in the Service of Michael to release you from your labors. May what the builder of the Temple of Humanity calls Strength inspire my message. You should allow the work you have learned here to take effect when you have left the portal of this Temple to enter into outward life. From your hearts should flow into the rest of humankind what the heart can form into building stones of the Great Temple. In your thoughts should be active what can make the connecting parts of this building. From your wills should flow what can become mortar for the building stones of this building. Do only that which comes from the sincerity of your hearts, to which you are led by the heedfulness of your thoughts, to which you have steeled your wills.

Through that you will become the likeness of your archetype and from you will come strength to shape the world.

The path of this strength has been impressed upon your hearts by the Grand Master from the Altar of the East; take note of the word which will then be spoken to you...

Ritual Text for Admission into the First Degree

Text according to original handwriting of Rudolf Steiner[10]

Notebook, Archive No. 612

All metal objects with a certain value in outer terms are removed from those seeking admission: jewellry, coins, etc. The candidate is thereby lifted out of his association with the physical world and its regulations. He must be freed from values other than those given him by his own inner being.

Then the candidate is led to the door accompanied by the usher. At the door he (she) is blindfolded. When the door is knocked upon by the usher (. . –)[11] the following dialogue takes place between the usher and the receptionist within:

Question: Who knocks so insistently at our door?

Answer: A free man (a free woman) who wishes to be admitted into the Mystical Temple of Wisdom, Beauty and Strength, in order to make sacrifice and to serve the spirit in company with the Elder Brothers of humankind.

Question: What is his (her) name?

Answer: Name.

Question: Who are his (her) sponsors?

Answer: Names of two sponsors.

Question: Have all conditions been fulfilled?

Answer: They have been fulfilled.

Receptionist: Enter!

---

10. The dots and dashes follow the original.

11. Dot dot dash (. . –) indicates the rhythm: short short long [anapaest].

The candidate is led by the usher in a spiral into the "Room of Self-Knowledge." Here he (she) is addressed in the following manner by an elderly mystic:

> Now we are in the right place. I come from the Universe, from the Dog-Star. I met this soul on my way here from the north. It has freed itself from its body. It has arrived at the portal of death. Listen now, thou soul, to the spirit which will and can lead thee to thy true human dignity. Since thou art no longer subject to the senses and to reason which draws its forces from the body, so thy gaze no longer lights upon the objects and occurrences through which the spirit—against whom I have had to struggle since Earth began—robs thee of thy freedom and would make thee a servant of his own being. In thy surroundings lives nothing created by him which thou wouldst have had to encounter if thou hadst looked around thee in thy sense body. Thus did my opponent infiltrate his being into thy soul; thou wast not thyself; in thine inner being thou wast filled with his being. Now thou canst draw out of thyself all that thou art able to experience, now that thou canst be the master, the exclusive master, in the world which grows out of thine inner being. Now thou wilt know thyself completely for the first time, thou wilt live in thy human dignity. Feel thyself therefore. Will to be thyself. If thou understandest thyself completely, thou canst not do otherwise than find thyself at home in the world into which I have led thee. So penetrate into this place in self-knowledge, where all about thee refrain from speaking about the creation of my opponent in thine own world. – – –

For a while everything is in complete silence. Silent peace reigns.... This peace is interrupted presently by loud knocking (. . –).

The mystic who had just spoken continues:

My opponent against whom I fight since Earth began, now approaches.

He would like to drive me from this place. He it is who wishes to make thy soul into a part of his being. If thou followest him thou wilt lose thy human dignity. Thou wilt become a slave of his being. Yet for the present I must yield to him. Do not succumb to him, thou soul!

The mystic who holds the Service at the Altar in the East, now begins to speak:

I have noticed about thee, oh thou soul, that the enticements of the spirit against whom I fight since Earth began, have made thee inclined to listen to him. It might be that he can induce thee to feel that thy human dignity would benefit from following him. I, the spirit from the East, now stand before thee. My opponent has now had to yield to me. Round about me stand the judges of the terrible judgement court of the dead. I ask them: What shall happen to the soul in whose depths I see an inclination towards the spirit who fights against me since Earth began?

The encircling mystics reply:

This soul must be consigned to Hell.

The serving mystic in the East:

Take this soul into Hell.

Thereupon the candidate is led in a spiralling circle into a room representing Hell. The sound of clanking chains is heard and the turning of a lock after the candidate has entered the room.

The mystic from the East now speaks:

Thou soul art now in the place where its desire can be realized. Thou art in thine own world. From now on thine eye shall never light upon a created being which is not derived from thine own soul. Thou shalt live wholly within thine own world and shalt be the sole sovereign therein. But know this, that for all eternity thou shalt live within thine isolated world. Nothing of all that has become dear and precious to thee in the world into which I have now led thee, shalt thou ever see again. For all eternity thou shalt learn nothing of beings whom thou hast loved, whom thou hast wished to help. They shall never hear anything more of thee. For the whole of the future thou shalt know only about thyself and so shalt thou also know the silence and loneliness which shall surround thee from all sides for evermore. And know this, that the more thou livest in thyself alone, the more terrible shall be thine existence. Thou shalt look into an endless empty future in which thou canst enjoy nothing but thine own self! This life with its view into the future will be more frightening the nearer thou approachest it. That is what thine inclination to my opponent has condemned thee to; the judges of my terrible judgement court of the dead have merely put into words the judgement with which thy soul has condemned itself. – – And yet, I am allowed, on account of the mercy which rays forth from the East, to parade before thee once more what thou hast experienced on Earth. Perhaps, when, armed with thine insight into all that my opponent has promised thee and what I have to inflict upon thee here and thou seest what has become of thee, thy soul will incline itself differently. Therefore I lead thee through thine earthly past and shall parade before thy soul what my messengers from the East have granted thee in thine earthly life in order that thou couldst become what thou now art. I have sent them forth, these wise messengers of mine; they may now bring to thine ear what they have accomplished in thee during thine earthly life.

The loud rattling of chains is heard once more and the lock (of Hell's gate) opening with a loud noise.

A mystic appointed for the purpose calls out:

Now shall the retrospect of thy life begin.

While the candidate is again led in a spiral course, the mystic thereto appointed who spoke the last words, says:

1. Humans pass through the whole of life in darkness; only knowledge of the spirit can release them out of darkness.

2. If the soul is only led by curiosity or the thirst for knowledge it will never find the spirit. For only such find the spirit who know that they do not belong to themselves but to the world and therefore feel it their duty to make themselves as perfect as possible as a part of the whole world. The *duty* to know the spirit; that shalt thou feel.

3. If thou art unable to penetrate so deeply into human souls that all earthly differences disappear before thy gaze and thou lookest upon all human beings as alike to one another, then thou wilt not attain to knowledge; for only one can gain knowledge who sees all human beings alike, free from the differences stamped upon them by the world submerged in darkness.

4. If the soul is not inclined to face its weaknesses and errors it will not find its way to spirit knowledge; for every unrecognized mistake is a hindrance on the way to knowledge.

After the candidate has heard these four sentences during the spiral pathway, a staircase is set up which he (she) must climb. Arriving at the top step, the candidate is allowed to fall down on the other side. During the time of this climbing and falling the following words are spoken by the mystics appointed thereto:

Thou hast sought to find light for thy soul along thy previous pathway, yet thou ascendest to the height of thy life's course in darkness. This ascent provides thee with a vivid perception of thy climb in the darkness. Thou canst only rightly attain to the height of life under the guidance of the light received from the spirit; without this thou art sure to fall down headlong, just as thou now fallest down.

After that the candidate is led to the two pillars, which stand at the entrance to the room which symbolizes ancient Atlantis. The candidate is placed before these pillars and the mystic thereto appointed speaks the words:

With the gaze of thy soul thou hast passed *backwards* through the incarnations through which thou hast lived since the Atlantean catastrophe. Thou hast now arrived at the epoch in which this catastrophe occurred. Thou art standing at the Pillars of Hercules which once led from east to north-west into the ancient land of Atlantis. Consider that thou hast had further former incarnations in this land of Atlantis. Thou hast lived these lives under quite different conditions from those later ones in post-Atlantean times. The land of Atlantis was so constituted that the ground was covered with thick mists. Within these constant mists thou hast lived in a quite different human form than later during post-Atlantis. In the latter the air had become free of the constant water vapors. Accordingly the whole perception and experience of humankind has changed. Post-Atlantis signifies the "trial by air" of humankind; the passing through the incarnations of the Atlantean epoch was its "trial by water." During the "trial by air" the messengers of the Good Spirits from the East let stream into thy soul the simple but profoundly significant rules of all existence of which thou art aware. These rules are the impluses which lead all souls to what is good, which the Sages from the East ever see before them inscribed in golden letters in the spirit-writing of the world; by this means they wished to lead thy soul to salvation. Yet the impulses which bring discord where there is harmony are introduced by my opponent into this process of salvation. Couldst thou now turn thy gaze unto the East, and should the reality of the spirit appear to thee, thou wouldst see my eagle in the radiant heights, which would bring to thee the wisdom of the East. And yet, beneath that thou wouldst see the vulture of my opponent, that has so influenced thy thinking that for thee wisdom had to become a destructive power that consumed the members of thy body in proportion to the amount of wisdom thou soughtest to obtain by means of earthly thinking.

If thou shouldst turn thy soul's gaze towards the South, thou wouldst see in the light from on high my angel, which would bestow upon thy feelings the revelation of beauty; my opponent, however, shows thee the owl, which mixes thy feeling for beauty with the powers that impress upon thee, when thy soul is outside the body in nightly sleep, the urge to rebel against beauty and turn its affections away from spiritual revelation. If thou wouldst turn thy soul's gaze towards the West, thou wouldst behold in the light from on high, my lion as the messenger, which could have bestowed upon thy soul the strength that emanates from out of the spirit and which would make thee strong, yet, under my lion wouldst thou see the black raven of my opponent, which implants into thy soul the urge to always mask the spiritual forces by physical strength.

Thus, as thy soul passed through its incarnations in post-Atlantis, it could never receive in an unmixed state what the wise messengers of the progressive World Spirits wished to give thee. It received it intermixed with the deleterious gifts of my opponent who fights against me since the Earth began.

After this the mystic who led the candidate into the "Room of Self-Knowledge" now enters while speaking the following:

> It is the time of the Atlantean catastrophe into which thou hast entered through the eye of the soul in retrospective insight. That is the time about which the spirit against which I have to battle since Earth began has not quite silenced me. Therefore I can now tell thy soul what it is that thou hast received from me during thy post-Atlantean incarnations. Without me thou wouldst never have gained the knowledge which thy thinking has acquired through the free observation of earthly creatures and earthly processes. For he who sets the direction for the system of the world which I oppose, wished to infiltrate into thy thoughts only his own wisdom; he wanted to inhabit thy thinking, feeling and willing. He wanted to live exclusively within thee; in thy life thou shouldst only portray him. Thy speech should only extol him. I have infiltrated thy speech so much with my being, that thou art able to express thine impulses of thinking, feeling and willing through it. I have persuaded my brother, who likewise attacks that other spirit since Earth began, that there can be preserved for thee on Earth in writing what, under the sole guidance of that other spirit could only live in the words which he had imbued and which would disappear with the disappearance of the word. So judge thou what has made thee what thou art become during the course of the post-Atlantean incarnations. Judge then what thou wouldst have been without speech that can express not only what is supersensible, but also, through me, what is sensible; consider what thou wouldst have been without writing. I am the bringer of earthly civilization, without me thou wouldst be the image of a divine spirit; yet no free, self-expressing earthly human being.

After this has been said, the other mystic who preceded the one who has just spoken, now approaches, speaking as follows:

I shall now lead thy soul through the Pillars of Hercules into the ancient land of Atlantis. In it thou shalt see in pictures of the soul, what thou hast experienced in thine Atlantean incarnations, but which thou hast completely forgotten, whilst thou wert acquiring the capacity to view the earthly conditions as has become possible for thee to do through the influence of my opponent. Only during post-Atlantean and in the final Atlantean times has his influence grown perceptibly. Before that my influence ruled in thy soul. At that time thou stoodst amid a life of watery mist closer to me than was afterwards the case. Thus thou wilt be able to judge, through that which entered thy life at that time, what he is to thee; and what the spirit I serve can become for thee—wisdom spoke, according to thy powers of comprehension of that time, out of all things and occurrences of the mist-soaked three kingdoms of nature. At present thy soul is only familiar with the articulated sense-filled speech issuing from the human mouth. The bubbling fountain, the rippling waves, the rustling leaves of the trees in the wood; they do not speak a sense-filled language. They did so, however, in ancient Atlantean times. And thy soul was able to commune with all beings in nature. At the time of the "trial by water" thy soul was still very close to the wisdom of the universe. And when the soul retreated into itself, when it withdrew its attention from all things which gave expression to their own being, then, too, when human beings retreated into the wilderness, where nothing spoke to them, there the soul was aware of a keynote or intermediate tone, which sounded through all things. When the soul became aware of this sound, then all the warmth of the world rulership flowed through it and the light of the world-creating powers flowed into it. The soul became filled with all-pervading wisdom. It said, in sensing what was there: "The Great Spirit is speaking." The soul became devout and reverential when it heard the "Great Spirit" murmuring within it.

Thus spake the Great Spirit . . . .; and, as in
an echo, worshipping and in reverence, the soul replied to
the Great Spirit . . . .; in this wise went the
dialogue between the soul and the Great Spirit in the
ancient Atlantean time: . . . .

Thy soul has forgotten this dialogue; I have reminded it
of it.

Now, however, thou art come by degrees in thy retrospective journey through life on Earth, to the place where
stands the spirit which the other spirit opposes since Earth
began. I have placed the Room of the Temple here on this
place, which is only attainable by the inner soul faculties.
When the bandage is removed from thine eyes thou wilt
be surrounded by pictures which will reveal to thy soul
what surrounded it on the occasion when it stepped for
the first time from the spiritual world into earthly incarnation. Thou wilt again be able to make a "choice." When
thy soul made its choice for the first time, it took the
intentions of my opponent into the impulses of its development. Through that the secrets of spirit-existence had
to be veiled from it.

The candidate is now led into the actual temple-room, which is
made completely dark at this moment.

The mystic who performs at the eastern Altar now utters the
pledge-like words, which are intended to make the soul aware of
its direction through space and time.

Then follow words that the soul must experience within itself in
order to learn what attitude it should take towards the first degree:

I pledge and promise to adhere to the spirit of the first
occult degree without insincerity, without faintness and
without double-meaning and to behave in like manner
towards all strangers with this degree. Should I act in a
manner not in accordance with what I here pledge, so

may that happen to my soul which I hereby state know-
ingly and in full consciousness, ...
. . . .
. . . .
. . . .[12]

The mystic serving at the eastern Altar continues:

> Thou soul, consider that thou hast left behind at the por-
> tal of this room everything that acquires its value from the
> outer world where I and my opponent both work. Here
> thou canst achieve nothing by these things, here thy soul
> can only do work if it avoids making use of such things.
> What here is of use to thee is expressed by the symbolic
> garment that my helpers will now place upon thee.

The candidate now has the symbolic garment of the first degree
laid upon him (her).

A light is now lit in the totally dark room. The one who stands
beside the mystic attending the Altar of the East receives this light
and places himself immediately in front of the candidate. Behind
him stands another mystic appointed for the purpose.

The mystic in the East speaks:

> What does the soul seek in this room?

The surrounding mystics answer in unison:

> The light of the spirit.

The mystic in the East speaks:

> The light of the spirit shall appear to this soul when it pen-
> etrates with the right attitude into all that will be said to it
> here.

---

12. See explanation on p. 261.

At this moment the mystic standing behind the candidate removes the bandage from the candidate's eyes; the light remains burning for only a few moments, then it is extinguished by the mystic who holds it.

The candidate is in the completely darkened room.

There follows immediately thereafter the opening ceremony with the lighting of the candles in East, South and West.[13] - - - -

After that follow the explanations and communications about the symbolic signs and words, which the candidate then learns to understand in the light of processes within the human etheric body, so that the candidate feels him (her) self to be a member of the first degree.

Then the candidate is led by two thereto appointed mystics before the Altar of the East. The mystic who serves in the East, mimes the . . . . sign; two mystics of higher grades join them; the latter make a cross above the forehead of the candidate with their sword-like symbols:

The mystic from the East speaks:

> In the n. o. t. W. M. o. t. E. [In the name of the Wise Masters of the East] and b. t. s. w. w. [by the strength with which] I serve them, I inscribe thy name into the book of the first degree of those who strive for the light of everlasting mysticism.

The candidate is led by the hereto appointed mystics to the place assigned to him (her).

---

13. Given on p. 161.

The ceremony is now interrupted and an instruction ceremony is inserted. While the latter is taking place an instructor among the mystics informs the candidate concerning:

    1. The symbolic legend of the evolution of humankind.[14]

    2. A symbol from the esoteric writing.[15]

After this instruction the proceedings are resumed, to close with the threefold symbolic ending which concludes every service of the first degree.

---

14. See p. 379.

15. A note by Marie Steiner reads thus: "I am now obliged to tell you about Symbol, Handclasp, and Word pertaining to the first degree. Symbol, Handclasp, and Word are not merely signs of recognition, they are not merely of deep symbolic significance, but exert a magical influence and have magical value. As an ancient Masonic maxim rightly says: He who trusts in Symbol, Handclasp, and Word shall have the Temple built for him; he by whom these are unrecognized will remain forever blind in life."

Ritual Text for Promotion into the Second Degree

Text according to Rudolf Steiner's handwriting

Notebook, Archive No. 613

The candidate is led by the mystic appointed thereto to the door leading to the "Room of Enlightenment." The mystic knocks (. . − . . − . . −).[16] Thereupon the following dialogue between the mystic standing without and the receptionist within takes place:

> Who is knocking?
>
> A member belonging to the first degree of this esoteric current, who wishes to be promoted to the second degree.
>
> What is the name?
>
> The name is given: Brother (Sister) − − − − − − −
>
> Have all conditions been fulfilled?
>
> They have been fulfilled (i.e., the Master has given dispensation).

Hereupon the door opens and the candidate is led before a brightly burning fire in the "Room of Enlightenment." A hereto appointed mystic [representing Lucifer] stands there too and speaks as follows:

> Gaze into this fire. As it appears to thee and is familiar to thee, have I made it. The Spirit of the East, against whom I battle since earth began, wished it to be otherwise. He wished to impress upon it only his own attributes from the elementary kingdom. There it would consume all passions, desires and urges that deviate in any way from the straight path of the natural order of things. As it would

---

16. According to a report of a participant this is performed for the first degree, twice for the second degree and three times for the third degree.

affect thy physical body, wert thou to put thy finger in its flame, so would it also work upon thy qualities of soul for evermore. That would have been the only reason for its existence if it had been directed according to that spirit's original plans. I, however, have taken it away from him. I have drawn it down from its elementary form into physical density; through that it has become a beneficial element in the physical culture of humankind, from which thou, oh soul, also benefitests. Consider what thou wouldst have become as a human being in the course of earthly civilization without fire. If thou understandest this, then thou wilt also know what I mean to thee and that thou must stand by me if thou wilt remain true to thy humanity and not lose it.

Consider this, that it was not wantonness in me that rebelled against the general order of things as they were preordained before my attack, but also a sacrifice, which I made for the sake of thy humanity. I have become the enemy of this regime for the sake of thy dignity and have taken upon myself all that my opponent accuses me of in respect of what I have done for thee.

After this the candidate is led before a second altar-like structure on which at first nothing is seen. The hereto allotted mystic speaks [as Ahriman] the following:

Consider, O soul, what the Spirit out of the East, against whom I fight since earth began, would and could have made of thee. He wished to implant his being into thy soul. He wished to fill thy soul completely with his being. I had to counteract that. As a result of my deed thy senses meet in thine earthly surroundings the manifold beings of the animal, plant and mineral kingdoms, meet the elements of air, water and earth densified by me, meet the physical corporeality of sun and moon and the splendor of the wide-ranging starry heavens. What meets thee in the physical world, in the manifoldness of Wisdom, Beauty and Strength, could not have been revealed to thee had I not intervened in the general order of things in the world. Under the sole rulership of my opponent thy environment would have been an eternal mirroring, in which thou wouldst have seen only thyself as a picture of his being. Wherever thou wouldst have turned thy gaze, upwards or downwards, right or left, forwards or backwards, only this alone wouldst thou have encountered.

At this moment a mirror is held in front of the candidate, in which is seen his (her) own countenance, at the same time the words are let fall:

Know thou thyself

Then the candidate is led into the "Room of the East." Here his (her) gaze is directed towards the East and the mystic who serves in the East says:

Just now my strong opponent stood before the eyes of thy soul; he is able to force himself upon the human soul when evolution is passing through an intermediate stage between one cycle and the next. The eye of thy soul was directed towards the beginning of thine earthly evolution, whilst thou wert being led in retrospect through thy past life during thine admission into the first degree. Thou wert able to recognize how thou descendedst for the first time out of spiritual heights and from a spiritual environment into an earthly incarnation. That was at an intermediate phase of development. My strong opponent addressed thine understanding. If thou allowest thine understanding to work upon it, his words must only appear to thee to be true. Thou canst not disprove them; and should I approach thee with arguments based on understanding alone, so could I too not invalidate what he said. For at the place where he stood and at the other place where thou now standest, the sole validity of intellectual argument ceases to exist. Thou canst only find the possibility of gaining the right concept if thou'rt able to understand what I shall now tell thee. Has my opponent spoken to thee? Has he convinced thee—now that he has rightly convinced thy soul?

Understand this: everything which has taken place here physically is only appearance. He stood before thee in physical picture form; in thy physical picture thou belongedst to him. And yet all this is just appearance. He did not speak to thee at all. He only spoke to that part of thy being which, since primeval beginning of the earth, he has gradually implanted into thy soul. He only spoke to that in thee which he himself is in thee.

He has only convinced himself in thee.

Consider this and thou shalt find the possibility of understanding me too, who will speak to that part of thy being which he is not.

And yet, his words are more congenial to thee than mine. He addresses that in thee which thou already art, which thou wilt fain look upon as thine own being; I have to speak to that in thee which thou wilt one day become; before thou art able to understand me I must demand from thee that thou learnest to know thyself through inner soul-strengthening, in that part of thy being which thou indeed art, but of which thou knowest nothing as yet. I must demand of thee that thou first of all workest upon thyself. So ascend to thyself with understanding and thou shalt find me within thyself.

The candidate is confronted by some stairs which he (she) must climb.[17] While the candidate is climbing them the mystic who serves in the East speaks the following words:

---

17. Compare with p. 431.

Form

Strength

Number

Harmony

Word

Thought

"I"

Seek within thyself for the power of these words in their sevenfold sequence and thou shalt find the key through inner soul-strengthening, which will point out the way to the second of the esoteric degrees.

Then the same mystic continues:

Consider, oh soul, that to have comprehended what has been said to thee here, means that thou wilt become endowed with new insight into the world and with an understanding, not only of the practical side of existence, but also of that which takes place when spirit meets with spirit. If thou understandest this manner of speaking thou canst progress from being a pupil of the spiritual world to becoming a fellow member of the spiritual world.

Next the opening ceremony is performed with the ritual for the first degree.

The candidate is then informed about Symbol, Handclasp, and Word in the sense of the inner mobility of the etheric body.

Then the symbolic garments of the second degree are adjusted.

Thereafter the Master in the East speaks:

> All who have become aware, from of old, of the significance of these degrees have pledged in their souls:
>
> I pledge and promise that, without insincerity, without faintness and without double-meaning, I shall guard the secrets of the second degree in my soul and conceal them from all strangers and those who have only attained to the first degree. Should I break my vow, so will I permit . . . .

Upon this the candidate is led towards the Altar of the East by two mystics appointed thereto. Two higher-degree mystics approach from left and right and cross their symbolic swords above the candidate's forehead.

The mystic from the East speaks:

> I.t.n.o.t.w.M.o.t.E.a.b.t.p. [In the name of the Wise Masters of the East and by the power] by which I serve them, I enter thee in the book of the second degree of those who strive for the light of everlasting mysticism.

The ceremony now changes to an instruction ceremony.

During this time a teaching mystic discourses on one of the ways—a legendary imaginative picture, for instance—in which, by its use in the soul's meditation, the path to the second degree becomes attainable.

Then follows the threefold ending of the service as a whole with the symbolism of the second degree.[18]

---

18. For the wording of the opening and closing ceremony see p. 161 et seq.

Ritual Text for Promotion into the Third Degree
Text according to the original handwriting of Rudolf Steiner

Notebook, Archive No. 6981–6987

1. Introduction

What characterizes the third degree, for anyone who has developed a feeling for such things, is that one's inner experiences, looked at from without, are comparable to what are normally the outer experiences of nature looked at from within the human being. From a point of view centered outside the human being what was formerly the outer world ceases to exist for the senses. It becomes an inner experience, as were previously thoughts, feelings and will impulses, and a quite new outer world arises. It is an outer world that appears like the thinking, feeling and willing of spiritual beings experienced within oneself, just as one previously experienced one's own thinking, feeling and willing within oneself. "I am," which was formerly only like a thought-point, becomes a rich inner experience in which organically co-operating spirit-beings develop their activity; this activity proceeds from a multiplicity and has as its goal a unity; and this unity is—the human being. One learns to know oneself from a view-point outside oneself. For that one must develop a feeling for how it is when the experiences one has are not one's experiences, but those that appear to be inserted into the continuous processes of nature. "Memento mori" contains the allusion to a switch in consciousness. Through this switch of consciousness a feeling arises in the soul of how it might be were the whole immediacy of its experience to be something belonging to the past, a memory. A different "present" now lives in the soul. And just as in ordinary life the consciousness sees itself as the subject and the outer world as object, so now a consciousness is experienced in which a new "present" becomes the subject and the ordinary life that belongs to the past becomes the object. This switch in the consciousness can be expressed schematically as follows:

The direction given to the soul towards the switch in consciousness can be expressed in words by the following sentences: [19]

1. Think of the end.
2. Think about death.
3. Consider that everything having a physical body is transitory.

These three sentences are actually incomprehensible for the ordinary consciousness I. [20] They can only make sense for the ordinary consciousness if the latter wishes to delude itself about its own experience.

1. To begin with, consciousness I [ordinary consciousness] cannot consider its own end. A thought such as this can only be grasped when the thought is "thoughtless." For a thought which is experienced, the demand: "Think of the end" is just as meaningless as: "Tear out thine eye so that thou canst hold it before thee and look at thine own eye."

2. "Think about death:" death shuts off thinking as far as consciousness I is concerned. The demand to shut it off is therefore as meaningless for this kind of consciousness as: "think about thyself without thinking." Consciousness I *can believe* it is thinking when it imagines that it has an object for its thoughts, even when it ceases to think.

3. "Consider that everything having a physical body is transitory:" For consciousness I that signifies "do not think." For consciousness I is unable to "think" without a physical body. With the thought about what is physical, thought itself ceases to exist.

19. See diagram on p. 205.
20. See consciousness I on p. 204.

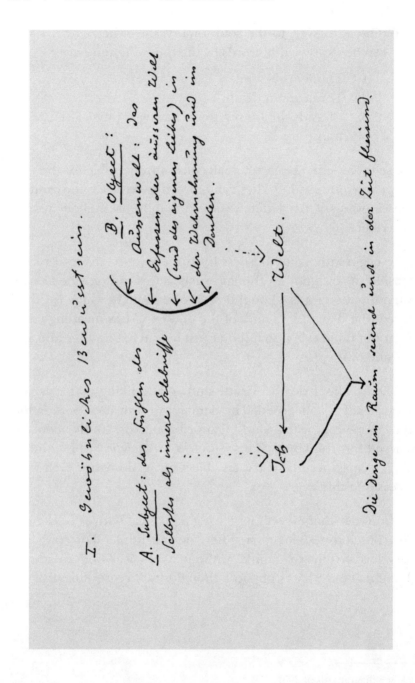

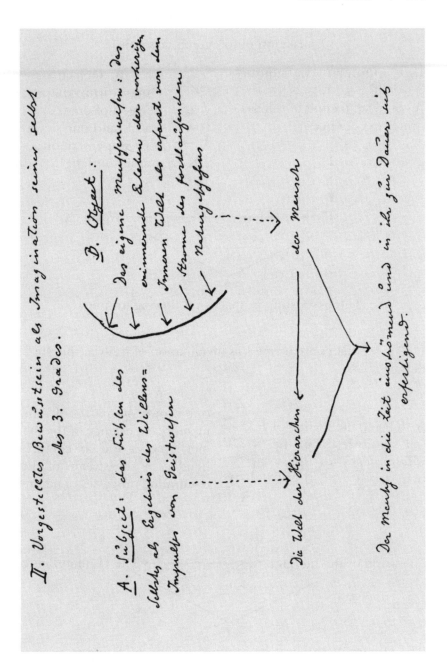

II. Vorgestelltes Bewußtsein als Imagination seiner selbst des 3. Grades.

A. Subject: das Fühlen des Selbst, als Ergebnis des Willens-Impulses von Geisteswesen

B. Object: Das eigene Neuschaffen: Das einmalige Erleben der vorherigen Inneren Welt als erfaßt von dem Strome der fortlaufenden Naturrhythmen

der Mensch

Die Welt der Hierarchien

Der Mensch in die Zeit einwöhnend und in ihr zur Dauer sich erübrigend.

(Translation of foregoing facsimile)

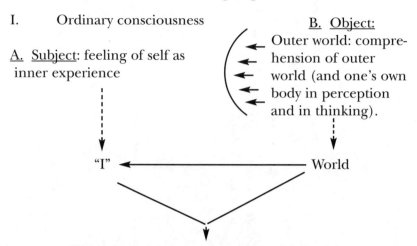

I.   Ordinary consciousness

A. Subject: feeling of self as
inner experience

B. Object:
Outer world: compre-
hension of outer
world (and one's own
body in perception
and in thinking).

"I" ← World

Things existing in space and flowing in time

II. Conceptual consciousness as imagination of itself in the third
degree

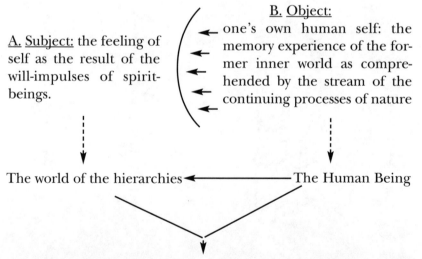

A. Subject: the feeling of
self as the result of the
will-impulses of spirit-
beings.

B. Object:
one's own human self: the
memory experience of the former inner world as comprehended by the stream of the
continuing processes of nature

The world of the hierarchies ← The Human Being

The Human Being flowing in time and consolidating to perma-
nence therein.

If, therefore, those who were clear-headed, heard these three demands, they would have to say: here something is being said which is an impossibility for my consciousness I. My ordinary consciousness has no possibility of understanding this. If, however, they have worked through their impressions from the second degree, then they will demand the following of their thinking: this kind of thinking would like every thought to be accompanied by an experience. It does not allow itself to think unless the thought can become an experience. It says to itself: "How shall I consider the end if I am unable to experience my thoughts, either as coming to an end or being thought. How shall I think about death, if I can only view death through thinking which dies? How can I think about the transitoriness of what is physical if I have to use my bodily nature to think with; that is to say: without my body thinking ceases?"

Those who have not made the experiences of the second degree may believe that they think the above sentences with consciousness I, for this consciousness is used to separating the thought from the essence of the thoughts. Thereby this kind of consciousness permits itself to have thoughts in which the essence of the thoughts are no longer experienced. Consciousness I, therefore is unaware of the inner experience that turns a thought into a non-thought by its very nature and thereby blows it away in infinitesimally small pieces into nothingness. But it has to be like that with consciousness I when, after having passed through the second degree, it hears the three sentences, which can only be thought without thinking by consciousness I, but cannot be thought livingly.

It is thus that a person stands at the end of consciousness I and has taken the full measure of this consciousness. Previously it had been a point from which rays seemed to spread in all directions, that is, it appeared that thinking stretched endlessly in all directions.

Now the thinking of consciousness I realizes that it is a circle complete in itself, which has to be broken through if an advance is to be made.

The above characterizes the soul-mood which should prevail when the content of the admission ceremony into the third degree is received.

The opening ceremony is carried out as for grade three.[21]

Then, the candidate is led through the door and is met by the words:

"Memento mori"

Then, the candidate is led further into the room, which has been partly darkened, so that the candidate cannot distinguish clearly what is in it, and hears:

"Think of the end"

Then:

"Think about death"

Then:

"Consider that everything belonging to thy body is transitory"

As the candidate hears these words, he (she) is led forwards in a curve and turned so as to be unable to see the coffin-like structure along-side which he (she) is being guided.

---

21. A note by a participant reads:
   3 knocks
   1. Who knocks?
   2. A Sister (Brother) of the second degree, who wishes to be admitted into the third degree.
   3. Have all conditions been met?
   4. The Grand-Master has given her (him) a dispensation.

While still at the door a pointed object is pressed against the candidate's breast (a copper rod with a point) and this warning is heard: "What happens next should not just be heard and understood by thee, but experienced in the depths of thy soul."

Now the candidate stands with his (her) back to the coffin, and cannot see it.

Now the server at the East speaks, whereas formerly the one who stands beside the server at the East had spoken.

The server at the East:

> "When Hiram Abiff had finished building his temple he thought that he would go inside to see that everything was in order. He did so. After his inspection he wanted to emerge into the fresh air. He tried to come out by the West door, but there stood one of the three conspirators. These three had conspired together because the Master had not conferred on them the Master-word or the Master's degree, for which he judged them not ripe enough. One of the conspirators in the West—(represented here by the server from the West)—gave the Master Hiram Abiff a blow on his left temple with a square, so that the blood flowed down from the wound over his shoulder.—(This action is carried out symbolically by the server from the West.)—The Master thereupon tried to go out by the South door, but there the second conspirator stood. He demanded—(as did also the first conspirator)—that the Master should give him the degree and the word, which the latter could not do. So the second conspirator lifted up a trowel and gave the Master a blow on the right temple, so that the latter's blood flowed down over his right shoulder. (This action is carried out symbolically by the server from the South.)—Thereupon the Master tried to escape into the open through the third doorway, but the same action took place with the third conspirator. The latter demanded the degree and the word, which the Master was not able to give.

Then the third conspirator gave the Master a blow on the forehead with a ruler, so that he collapsed. Yet, before he died—(the act was performed symbolically by the server in the East)—he was able to throw the golden triangle, upon which the ancient Master-word was depicted, into a deep well by the door, so that the word became lost. Then Master Hiram Abiff dies. Thou, thyself art Hiram Abiff. It is thy soul. Upon this the three conspirators took the corpse, carried it away and buried it in a solitary place, as now happens to thee"—

Next a symbolical interment takes place, represented by the server from the West, in a black cloak; the server from the South, in a red cloak; the server from the East, in a white cloak.

As the candidate lies in the coffin

a single bell-chime is sounded,[22]

upon which the following words are spoken (by the server from the East):

"The Master's soul makes its way backwards through the earthly periods in the land of spirit. It hears the Music of the Spheres. It hears it from the time when, in the course of its evolution the Earth separated from Sun and Moon and became a single heavenly body. The Master's soul was there at that time. At present thou hearest the chime; some day thou shalt hear it in its full reality. And thy soul goes further back in the course of evolution, to the time when Earth, Sun and Moon were still connected. Thy soul was present at that time.

(Three chimes are sounded.)

Thus thou hearest the Music of the Spheres. Thou shalt one day hear it again in reality.

And thy soul goes still further back in time to the period when the Earth was still Sun; when it was encircled by the

---

22. The beating of a gong (according to a participant).

planets, a planet among planets, which formed with them the seven—thou hearest this in the Music of the Spheres.

(Seven chimes are sounded.)

Thou shalt one day hear this again in reality.

And thy soul goes still further back in earthly evolution, to the time when the Earth was Saturn, surrounded by the twelve powers of the stars. It was the great midnight hour of existence, the point at which eternity proceeds into time.

(Twelve chimes are sounded.)

Thou hearest the great midnight hour of existence. Thou shalt one day hear it in reality."

After this has been said, the one who stands to the left of the server from the East commences thus:

"When Solomon's companions had noticed that Hiram Abiff was not present, they sent out twelve of their number to search for the Master. They found a freshly dug, grave mound in a lonely place, which they recognized on account of a cassia twig."[23]

(This twig is placed upon the coffin after burial.)

"They dug in search."

(At this point a procession is made around the coffin by those present).[24] During this time the helper of the server from the East says the following:

"Like Hiram thou shall be born again."

(Light appears now to the South where it was formerly dark.)

"Like Hiram thou shall be victor over death."

(It now becomes light towards the West.)

---

23. (Cassia = Acacia) is held to be a symbol of everlasting life.
24. In this connection see p. 214.

"Like Hiram, the light from the East shall illumine thee."
(It now becomes light towards the East.)
(The coffin is now opened. The server from the East takes
the candidate's hand.)

He speaks:

"With the Master's lion-grip I raise thee from thy grave."[25]

Then:

"I find thee in a state in which thy bones have come away
from thy body."

Then something is whispered into the candidate's ear: . . . . .

Thereupon the helper of the server in the East speaks:

"What thou hast here endured symbolically shall one day be
enacted before thy soul. Yet, thou shouldst seclude it in the
deepest part of thy memory. It should rise up again and again
in thy meditation. Not by brooding over this symbolic experience can it be effective within thy soul, but by renewing the
occurrence vividly in thy memory again and again. The image
will give thee the strength to find thy way, to see the things of
the world, thine own existence and the whole of life from that
point where not the body, but the spirit is stationed. Thou
hast felt the grip—the grip is repeated—thou hast heard the
word—(this is again whispered in the candidate's ear, a syllable at a time: the first syllable in the left ear—then the second
syllable in the right ear, by the other person—then the third
syllable again in the left ear by the former person—then the
whole of it from the latter to the former).

---

25. In the lecture of February 16, 1905, in Berlin it says of the lion symbol: "It is
the striving principle in the human being, which is at first exercised in isolation,
that is represented in alchemy by the lion. When freed from selfhood, from lust
and passion, it is able to unite with the lily [the spiritual]." See also the lecture in
Berlin, March 2, 1915.

Receive the symbol" (This is demonstrated.)—

By way of special warning the following is added:

"Do not understand with thy head this deeply significant image in which thou wert thyself involved and in which thou shalt often be involved in memory; understand it with the whole of thy being, so that it lives within thee; so that thou canst learn to know the feeling that arises when thou art completely one with it and livest and weavest in it for a time after it has been allowed to disappear from thy consciousness. Then, the result of the image will be that thou wilt experience how it is to know things both without and within thee and to know the whole of existence from the viewpoint of the spirit."

There then follows an address given by a teaching Brother or Sister, which is not an interpretation of what is portrayed in the admission ceremony, but which introduces thoughts that will lead the soul in a similar direction to what has been portrayed therein. The content of this talk is that the soul was already present within the essence of world evolution before the present solar system developed. That this Sun system has been created by high World-Powers for the further development of human beings. And it characterizes how the human being, as a spiritual being within the solar system, can feel united with Christ without any arrogance.

Then the service finishes with the ceremony of the third degree.

Notes by a Participant Concerning a Fourth Altar

After the chimes had sounded, there follows:

(To the Masters who were present):

   "Let us seek the grave of Hiram Abiff."

(A procession follows.)

   "Here is the grave of Hiram Abiff. I shall plant an acacia twig on this grave as a sign that thy higher self comes to life out of thy lower self, as this acacia twig springs out of this grave."[26]

(Upon this one of them says):

   "Memento mori! Think about death, think that all which is mortal in thee is not thee."

(Then speaks the General Grand-Master):

   "He shall be newly born, like once was Hiram Abiff."

(This is repeated by a Master standing at the North altar.)

(The General Grand-Master speaks):

   "Light shall shine upon him out of the East as it once shone upon Hiram Abiff."

(Again this is repeated by one of the Masters standing at the West altar.)

(The General Grand-Master speaks):

   "He shall be a victor over death as once was Hiram Abiff."

(Again this is repeated by a Master standing at the South altar.)

---

26. Acacia = Cassia (c.f. p. 211).

(Now the General Grand-Master approaches the coffin; the latter is opened and the General Grand-Master speaks):

"With the lion-grip of the Master I raise thee out of this grave."

(He lifts him out and speaks the Master-Word to him in a low voice):

"M . . b . . a . ." [Mach ben ach] the bones separate from the flesh —with the Master handgrip.

Notes and Parts of Ritual Texts

Notes about the Ritual for Admission to the First Degree
Entry in the notebook, Archive No. 611 (translation of the facsimile on following page)

Chl. Culd: – [= ? Culdee, member of monastic brotherhood in Ireland or Scotland in the 8th century]

Chamber of Contemplation:
Theme: In my Father's House are many mansions . . .
"Not I, but Christ in me – –"

Hell:

Journey through life: the wise Masters – based on St. John.

Atlantis: = *Ark* = *Temple.*

Lemuria: = The Word. The Sons of God. The Sons of God saw that the daughters of men were beautiful. [Genesis 6, 2]
    ================

Birds of the air: they sow not, etc.   [Matthew 6, 26]
    ========

Chr. Culd:—

Kammer des Nachdenkens:

Thema: In meines Vaters Hause sind viele Wohnungen

„Nicht ich, sondern Christus, der in mir ist—"

Hölle:

Gang durch das Leben: die weisen Meister— auf Johannes
gerichtet.

...Markus = Arche — Tempel.

Lemuria = Das Wort. Gottes Söhne. Die Söhne Gottes
fanden, daß die Töchter der Menschen
schön seien.

Vogel des Himmels; sie säumnisst etc. — — — —

Notes on the Admission Ritual for the First Degree

Entry in the notebook, Archive No. 612

Contemplation:	I feel myself
	Led away from life
	My senses extinguished
	Deprived of understanding activity
	Nothing surrounding me
	Myself in a void
	Loneliness
	Muteness
	Worthlessness
Lucifer:	Thou art within thyself
	Thou art master within thine own soul
	Thou canst be everything to thyself
	Learn to know thyself
	Feel thyself
	A world is thine.
	A world wholly spirit.
	A world full of worth.

J' as:[27]   *[Mallet] blow*

The expiation of this feeling:

        Prospect of an eternity of loneliness.

Forgiveness: Leading back to the world of misunderstood messengers – knowledge – through the incarnations: writing – two pillars. –

Atlantis: Speech.

        T.

Eagle: consuming the body – day consciousness

Owl: night – piercing – –

Raven: culture – dimming. –

---

27. Unclear what this stands for: Jehovas? Johannes?

Wording for "Chamber of Contemplation"
a) Text according to old typed copy

Thou sittest in the Chamber of Contemplation. This symbolic ritual should show thee at this moment how, in silence, without any outer stimulus, through repeated inner contemplation, thou shouldst recognise that a person must become a tightly enclosed personality with definite feelings, thoughts and will-impulses. Only through that is one able to find one's way as a citizen of our Earth-planet. Thou must be a tightly enclosed "I." In order for thee to become clear about this, and after mature consideration of the fact that thou wishest to be accepted into our company, the Brothers and Sisters gathered here allow thee a time of contemplation. Then, after hearing a loud mallet blow, if thy intention is still that of being admitted, thou should'st answer with a clear "Yes."

b) Text according to the original handwriting of Marie Steiner

Thou art sitting symbolically in the Chamber of Contemplation, as a sign that at this moment thou should'st direct a deep gaze inwards into the center of thy being. For one who sets out on the esoteric path must become clear that, in respect of feelings, emotions, opinions and will-impulses, everything must be evolved out of the deepest center of one's being. Only one who can find the sure support within oneself can become a citizen of our Earth-planet. Thereby the center of one's being becomes attached to the center of the Earth-planet and one discovers one's own evolution along with the mission of the Earth. In all functions of life strivers after esoteric knowledge have to derive their impulses from their own free perception, feeling and will-impulses. In order that this shall become clear to thee by means of a deep inward gaze and a reconsideration as to whether thou wishest to hold to thy former resolution of being admitted into this company, thou art sitting here in this Chamber of Contemplation. There will be a short period of complete silence, in which thou should'st think about these two things. After that a mallet blow will break the silence for a time and, if thou still persist in thy former intention, thou shalt answer my question with a clearly articulated "Yes."

Wording for "Hell"

Text according to original handwriting of Marie Steiner

Thou art sitting symbolically in Hell. This is for a sign that the forces of suffering, pain and evil project into life just as surely as do those of ideals, joy and goodness. Whoever treads the occult path must become aware of the fact that one has to face these forces of Hell just as impartially as one does the powers of Heaven. One can freely strive for good, only if one is also able to choose evil. In order to make thee aware of the fact that thy pathway also leads thee by way of the powers of Hell, this symbolical sitting in Hell is necessary.

Wording for the "Journey through Life"

Text according to original handwriting of Marie Steiner

This was the journey through life. You have been led symbolically along a path that you will later get to know in reality. We took our start from the place where you stood before you sought entrance into this community. It is the present time in which you are now living. From there you have retraced your steps through long periods of time, through times and races in which your soul, which now inhabits your body, was incarnated in other bodies of other ages, in other races. We are now living within the present race. It was preceded by the Greco-Roman, the Egypto-Babylonian-Assyrian race, the ancient Persian and the Indian race. Your soul was incarnated in all these races. And at present you are standing between two pillars, the Pillars of Hercules. If one had formerly passed between these from east to west, one would have entered the ancient land of Atlantis, which was swept away by the great flood, known in the sagas and myths of the various peoples as the "Deluge" or "The Flood." Your soul was also incarnated already in an Atlantean body. But you lived under quite different conditions, because the Earth surrounding you at that time was quite different from what it was like later. Rain and sunshine were not divided up in the air in the same way as after the flood, but the atmosphere was filled with thick and heavy mists. This brought it about that soul life has become quite different since the flood. Human beings comprehend the universal wisdom of the surrounding nature when the atmosphere is saturated with water, with the waters of wisdom. The bubbling of the spring, the rustling of the forest trees, the dashing of the waves, the rolling of thunder were not inarticulate sounds, but the wisdom-filled expression of a spiritual reality. Only after the floods had subsided and the air had become clear, were people obliged to hearken to the rules and regulations for their actions, the laws of social behavior from the lips of their fellow human beings. Rules and regulations first came into being in post-Atlantis. Everything that you experience here has a deep symbolic meaning. The fact that you have been led backwards through time, signifies that you have now symbolically retraced the stretch of time that your soul has actually gone in a forward direction through the aforementioned races and epochs. And you have been led blindfolded, because the majority of people have passed this time in darkness. But they have been led by more highly developed individualities, by the Wise Masters of the East. The great truths that have sounded in your ears during this symbolic journey shone before them as though written in letters of gold. The Wise Masters of the East guided humanity in the sense of these truths: human beings wander throughout life in darkness; only knowledge can lead them towards the light. Those who are only led to knowledge out of curiosity can never attain to it, for mere curiosity is never satisfied by knowledge. Whoever draws a distinction between one person and the next, cannot attain knowledge, for whoever would gain true knowledge must make no distinction between people. Those who are unable to face up to their own shortcomings and errors in full consciousness, cannot arrive at a knowledge of the world, for only those who recognize their own faults can attain to a knowledge of the spirit.

The Wise Masters of the East have guided humanity, have guided you, according to these golden maxims. At the start of your journey you were closer to God than you are at present, for humanity has descended from the spirit into material existence and every step you descended you will have to reascend; not, however, in darkness, but in the light of esoteric knowledge. Everything you met with on your way down, you will meet again on your way up, but in bright shining clarity in reverse order. So shall your ascent ensue under the influence of the truths you have heard from the Wise Masters of the East.

The journey through life proceeds through the two Pillars of Hercules into the ancient land of Atlantis.

You must now imagine that you are in the ancient land of Atlantis where your soul has been incarnated in an ancient Atlantean body. You have to imagine that you are surrounded on all sides by dense clouds of water vapor. The result of this is that everything about you speaks an articulate language, as is spoken later by human lips. Your soul at that time could understand the wisdom that issued from the bubbling fountains, the dashing waves, the rustling of the wind in the trees, and when your soul in the morning wished to know what it had to do, it did not have to consult the laws or commands from the lips of others, but it listened to the language of the elements and perceived their wise commandments. And when it wished to know about the great events of existence, it was informed about them by the rolling of the thunder. Everything in the world spoke in a clearly decipherable language. And when the soul grew perfectly quiet within, when it turned its attention away from the bubbling of the springs, the dashing of the waters and the rustling of the wind in the forest, then it heard a keynote or "in-between" note which sounded in all things in the world. The soul heard it when it grew inwardly perfectly quiet, or when it went forth into the solitude where nothing else was to be heard. On every hand it could be heard by the soul in ancient Atlantis—in the North, South, East and West. And when the soul heard it, it experienced it as the voice of the Great Spirit, which flowed through all things, the Great Spirit, which held sway in the waters of wisdom. And this was how the soul heard the sound of the Great Spirit: Tao—and then it became silent and reverential and gave back the sound to the Great Spirit with a prayer: Tao. Thus did the soul converse with the Great Spirit T T (more loudly) T T (more softly) and through that the soul experienced not only this sound—it felt in profound wisdom the shuddering of the world vibrating within it.

Sitting in the "Chamber of Contemplation" and in "Hell" is known symbolically as the earth-trial, because, in its present material existence, the soul must recognize itself as bound tightly to the center of the Earth. The succeeding journey through the clear air reminds one symbolically of humankind's trial by air, and here you are reminded symbolically of humankind's great trial by water in Atlantean times. All the religions and conceptions of life founded on esoteric wisdom have preserved the memory of this great trial by water undergone by humankind in the symbolism of baptism and the symbolical water-trial. And because humankind had to encounter once again in clear consciousness all the stages of its ascent, step by step, so do such beliefs and views of the world mirror the trial by water in a symbolic way during admission into this community. For humanity must be led once more along the esoteric path to become aware of the wisdom in the surrounding elements. This community is to lead you to a unity with the Community of Waters. That is why I have to practice upon you a symbolic act of baptism as a sign of acceptance into our Brotherhood.

I baptize you with the Water of Wisdom as a sign of your admission into our Brotherhood.

The journey through life proceeds further into the far distant past, into that region of the Earth in which your soul was incarnated when it had just descended from the lap of the Gods. At that time you were not yet surrounded by clouds of watery vapors, but the

Earth was enveloped in all its substance in warm and fiery vapor clouds. Your first body consisted of materials from the ancient Land of Fire, Schal-Male. And you were surrounded by fiery vapors and foggy masses. At that time, when your soul had just descended from the lap of God, it was not merely intimately bound up with the wisdom of the surrounding elements, but magically connected with the will of the elements. Its substance consisted of the same divine will from which the fiery element around it was derived. And your will acted magically upon these elements. When your will was gentle and the limbs you then possessed extended over the masses of flame, then the elements became calm. When, however, your will became wild, then the elements raged in wild tumult. And because the will of large sections of human beings became evil, it brought great regions of the Earth into tumultuous turbulance, and through the evil will of humanity itself Schal-Male perished. Only a portion of humankind escaped to Atlantis. This was the great trial by fire of humanity which you now encounter symbolically.

(Lights)

The journey through life has ended.

(seated on a chair)

You must also know that, by means of the esoteric path, you will be led upwards again into the lap of the Gods, whence you descended. This ascent has various conditions attached to it, which have to be met by the applicant. The latter must pay no regard to anything leading to promotion in the outer world—birth or heredity, blood relationships, rank or title, honors, wealth and possessions, all of which are worthless for the esoteric path. For all that derives from blood-ties, heredity, money, goods or possessions comes to an end at death ... The only thing that is eternal is what you strive to acquire through the power of your own soul—your humble soul, as it is called. For that reason you must think of yourself as naked and destitute of all that people strive for, when in the circle of your

Brothers and Sisters. Your only clothing must be the symbolic garments of a Mason, the deep significance of which will be revealed to you at a later time. The venerable Sister (Brother) will clothe the applicant in the symbolic vestment of the Mason.

Now for the first time you will be in the circle of your Brothers and Sisters with the power of sight. It is a sign that you wished consciously to undertake all the steps to the Divinity that you had descended during your previous earthly pilgrimage.

What do these ladies and gentlemen wish for

Light

——————   ——————   ——————

(Formulas   . . .   Prayer   etc.)

The general pledge

Now shalt thou lay the special pledge of the first degree of esoteric Masons here on the Altar of the East.

With the left knee on the step, the right knee bent at right angles, the hand on the sacred record of humankind, the open Gospel of John, speak after me the pledge of the first degree of Masonry : – – –

Notes on the Third Degree

Text according to original handwriting of Rudolf Steiner
Notebook, Archive No. 6969

Question: I have learned that reverence is the most important
                   virtue for the adornment of the Mason engaged in
                   building the Temple of Humanity. But I do not yet
                   know how to apply reverence. Therefore my ques-
                   tion today is: how many different kinds of reverence
                   are there, O Master?

Answer: · · · · · · · ·

2nd Question: How can I learn the first kind of reverence?

                   · · · · · · · · · · · · · · · · · · ·

3rd Question: How can I learn the second kind of reverence?

                   · · · · · · · · · · · · · · · · · · ·

4th Question: How can I learn the third kind of reverence?

5th   What have the Sisters and Brothers to do about such
                   talk as the "great teaching of the different kinds of
                   reverence" of the 3rd degree?

Fragments and Notes about the Rituals of the Higher Degrees

Notes about the Fourth Degree[28]

The realities of the macrocosm are the consonants

Various feelings

That which surrounds on all sides but one is: b

One should learn to feel how the different vowels that are within us, close themselves up outside of us. Learn to feel the vocalization of what is inside oneself and to adapt it in various ways to the outer world.

Vowels

Sun	i [ee]		|
Moon	a [ah]		V
Venus	e [eh]		⊙
Mercury	o [oh]		○
Mars	u [oo]		Fist
Jupiter	ö [oe]		(
Saturn	ü [iw]		Hands laid sharply one on the other

The vowels supply everything that one needs to know about the human being.

They supply the inner key to the macrocosm.

---

28. Original document not available. Text according to a handwritten copy by Berta Reebstein, Marie Steiner's secretary, in a notebook containing only copies of Rudolf Steiner's original texts.

Giving – bequeathing – warming   ☉

Receiving – mirroring   ☽

Resting within itself, suffering, melancholy   ♄

Powerful, leading, guiding   ♃

Passionate, compulsive, aggressive   ♂

Loving, mild, gentle   ♀

Mediating, conciliatory   ☿

———————

i – Striving towards the divine

ei – Holy awe of the divine

a – Supremacy of the divine

ä – Not quite so supreme

o – Embracing divinity

ö – Not wishing to be circumscribed

Notes about the Opening Ceremony for the Fourth Degree[29]

Text according to original handwriting of Rudolf Steiner
From "Grandmaster: Give me the sign"
From the original handwriting of Marie Steiner
Notebook, Archive No. 6970/71

IV. Degree

Question: How is this High Chapter prepared?

Answer: By seeing that the doors are carefully closed and that no profane people, apprentices, journeymen or Johannine Masters are present.

Command: This must be attended to.

Michael: With most respectful greetings notification is given that the Chapter has been covered on all sides.

Grand Master: As all is in order the Chapter may be opened.

Dialogue

Grand Master: Points with the dagger in the four directions.

Michael: The Grand Master has introduced the Chapter by calling on the 4.

Grand Master: Write the 4[30]

Earth	Water	Air	Fire
Gnomes	Undines	Sylphs	Salamanders

Grand Master: Give me the sign.

---

29. Nothing available concerning the opening ceremony.
30. For these symbols see footnote p. 312.

Michael: (Right thumb on forehead, right hand raised, face looking upwards).

Grand Master: Give me the sacred word.

Michael: Adonai.

Grand Master: Give me the password.

Michael: Cavaret.

Grand Master: What do you understand as a Knight of the High 4th degree?

Michael: To strip the cassia branch of its leaves.

Grand Master: What does that signify?

Michael: To reduce solid matter into fine particles.

Grand Master: What does the one pillar signify to you?

Michael: It signifies the Sun.

Grand Master: What does the other pillar signify?

Michael: It signifies the Moon.

Grand Master: Why is this?

Michael: Because Sun and Moon together form the cassia branch, i.e., they fit the finer material to the coarser.

Grand Master: What is now your salvation?

Michael: To obey the High Masters of pre-humanity.

Grand Master: What does this make you?

Michael: Frater latae observatiae.

Notes on the Admission Ritual for the Fifth Degree

Text according to the original handwriting of Rudolf Steiner
Notebook, Archive No. 6973

Rosy Cross or *"Knight of the Eagle and Pelican"*

Who knocks?

A Brother, Master, who wishes to be admitted to the company of the Knights of the Rose Croix.

Of what rank is he?

He is a Freemason.

(Talk about the meaning of the 18th degree)[31]

Where do you come from?

From Judea.

Which way did you come?

By way of Nazareth.

Of what tribe are you?

Of the tribe of Juda.

What are the signs?

I N R I[32]

---

31. This sentence in brackets is an insertion in Marie Steiner's handwriting. Near this page there is a note in her handwriting: "A Brother of the Red [Rosy?] Cross and of Babylon, who wishes to be accepted as a Knight of the Rosy Cross and admitted into the Order of the Eagle and the Pelican."

32. These initials may signify the Hermetic formula: "Igne natura renovatur integra [Through fire nature is completely restored]."

Notes about the Opening Ceremony for the Fifth Degree
Text according to original handwriting of Marie Steiner
Page of notes, Archive No. 6971/72

Royal Arch
Fifth Degree

Grand Master: My venerable Brothers. May our soul be filled with what the 6th day of Creation has made out of the 5th.

Your duty?

Michael: To see that the doors are closed on every side, the High Chapter is covered, no profane person, no Johannine Mason and no applicant Mason is present.

Grand Master: Carry out your duty.

Michael (does so):

The reverend Grand Master is notified by me that the High Chapter can function under the profoundest secrecy and with full coverage.

Grand Master: What is the aim for which we work?

Michael: We work for the four aims.

Grand Master: What are they?

Michael: Learn to keep quiet and power shall be yours.
Renounce power and the will shall be yours.
Renounce the will and feeling shall be yours.
Renounce feeling and knowledge shall be yours.

Grand Master: Where do you come to through these four?

Michael: To a knowledge of the seven.

Grand Master: Draw the seven.

Michael: (draws)[33]

| Salt | Sulphur | Mercury | Earth | Water | Air | Fire |

---

33. See footnote p. 312.

Grand Master: Wherein do you find the 7 realized?

Michael: In the 4.

Grand Master: Name the 4.

Michael: The astral, the animal, the vegetable and the mineral.

Grand Master: What holds the 4 together?

Michael: The lost word holds the 4 together.

Grand Master: How do you know the lost word?

Michael: In the sign.

Grand Master: Draw it.

Michael:

Grand Master: Give the sign of the Chapter.

Michael: (gives it)

Grand Master: What is the handclasp?

Michael: In the four.

Grand Master: The Sacred Word?

Michael: I am the I am. Jahv[e].

Grand Master: The password of the Chapter?

Michael: Resurrectus.

Grand Master: What is your task?

Michael: To form the Mercury-soul in the pure salt through the cleansing fire of the sulphur.

———————————

Fragments That Cannot Be Classified

Handwritten notes by Rudolf Steiner
Notebook, Archive No. 6974

Where do you come from?
From the Lodge of St. John.

What does one do in the L∴ of St. John?
One builds the Temple of Virtue there and digs dungeons for the Vices.

What do you bring from there?
Welfare, progress and benevolence to all humankind —
What do you intend to do here?
Conquer my passions, subject my will and make further progress.

Take your seat my Brother ∴ and be welcome in this place, where the beams of your lights will be received with consciousness.

———————————

Isolated texts by Rudolf Steiner in the handwriting of Marie Steiner-von Sivers

Wisdom should have guided you, as long as you were engaged in building this temple, for therein lies the earthly picture of the spiritual stream of life. *Water of light* is this wisdom, which will guide you now, for your soul is developing the seeds of wisdom.

Beauty should have enhanced your work, as long as you were engaged in building this temple, which is a picture of self-limiting creation of form: *dissolving salt* is now this beauty for you, for your soul dissolves the coverings of your spirit-germ.

Strength should have done the work for you, as long as you were engaged in building this temple, which is a picture of the creative powers of existence: *form-giving fire,* to which your body's ashes return, will be this strength for you in future, for your spirit will join the World-Spirits to create the Great Temple of Existence.

———————————

Brothers of Ages Past, your wisdom penetrated the waters of the elementary kingdom and gave to our Sister an earthly frame, so that she could reveal to the world what her soul had prematurely acquired under your wise guidance.

Brothers of the Present Time, our Sister sought to come under your wise guidance, so that on her part, your divine thoughts would be revealed.

Brothers of the Future, you wish to incorporate the soul of our Sister into the plan of your building, so that she shall flow onwards in your strength, in the body of your great soul.

———————————

And thou, Sister, who hast joined with us to strive for a sight of the heights of eternal light, whose forces are expended in another bodily state, allow these forces to stream into our work, join us in the work of the Sanctuarium of spiritual existence: our souls, however, are inseparably bound to thine.

One, United, Unity.

———————————

Prepared in silence, it comes to expression shrouded in inspiration from above.

———————————

To become the bearers of Wisdom is what the ⊕ [Rosicrucian] Masons vow to their God in the inner depths of their spirit. They glimpse a temple to this God in the human veil that shrouds their being. They dedicate themselves to the building of this temple. They do not allow themselves to harbor thoughts of which wisdom would be ashamed. Before their gaze stands the motto:

> My contemplation shall seek thee everywhere, Divine Spirit.

To be the servants of Beauty is what the ⊕ [Rosicrucian] Masons vow to their God in the inner depths of their spirit, for only in beauty's lap can Divine Life flourish in their soul. The ⊕ [Rosicrucian] Masons avoid an outer semblance that belies the inner reality. They seek the true embodiment of reality in outer semblance. They draw in with their breath the motto:

> My speech shall reveal thee, Divine Soul.

To make themselves the sheath for heroic courage is the vow of the ⊕ [Rosicrucian] Masons, for only through its fire can the Being of God ripen within their breast. The ⊕ [Rosicrucian] Masons seek to flee cowardice, which only weakens all that promotes health; they seek the courage that clears the pathway to all progress, with a sharp, double-edged, fiery sword. The motto pulsates in their heart:

> The beating of my heart shall give thee strength, Divine Will.

I

The Earth's surface supports me;

The Earth's air envelops me;

Around me I see the mountain rocks;

Around me the Earth's plant mantle blossoms.

Sensibility lives in the animal realm,

Which divides the fullness of my own being

As though into a thousand single beings.

I feel the strength to rise to ever new heights,

Only I, a human being, can make such an effort.

II

I, a human being, was born out of the ground of the Earth.

I was enlivened by Earth's atmosphere,

I was related to the mountains' rocks,

My existence is woven from the plants' mantle,

The animal kingdom supports my spirit's power;

Yet, how Earth, and rocks and life

Are combined in me into a miracle of harmony!

The Earth's ground will fall away from beneath my feet.

Air will become the bearer of death.

The rocks of the mountains will topple down,

The garment of plants will wither away,

The life of animals will be dazed.

But I shall bear the fruits of Earth existence

To a new World-Creation of the distant future.

To feel the immortal worth of this goal

Wisdom creates in all thinking,

Beauty conceives in every life breath,

Courage ripens in every pulse beat.

Ye Wise M.d.O. [Meister des Ostens = Masters of the East], we come before you in spirit with the purified wish that the heart's center may keep silence in expressing outer things and may burn with the fire of a new inwardness. Let the elementary fire be kindled in us, which shall fuse and unite the elements of the temple, which shall be the worthy Chariot of your Divine Being.[34]

The ancient temple shall give birth to the new one.

The three may enable a new chariot to arise out of our symbols. The Three may make Audhumla fecund.[35]

Thus speaks he who sits among the stars of wisdom:

The time shall come when human intelligence and the delight of the senses will become void and unreal. And fleshly strength will become sterile and the daughter of the brain shall be paralyzed. And what sense's thinking and sense's feeling have established among humankind will dry up and erode as the sea dries up in scorching heat. But the revelation of the stars of wisdom shall blossom. What has been changed into silver and what gold ye have saved up belongs to me—thus speaks he who sits among the stars of wisdom.

The revelation of the New Temple will be more radiant than the First, and the "I" will have found itself in the "I."

---

34. The "Chariot" may refer to Ezekiel's vision of the divine throne-chariot "Merkaba," with which a special esoteric teaching of Hebrew mysticism was connected.

35. Audhumla = the cow that was brought forth from the primeval frost in Nordic mythology. See lecture, Berlin, October 7, 1907.

The applicant before the gates: M.M.

Remember that you have to find your way in situations where you have never been before.

West = Ahriman: He wants to be *you.*

South = Lucifer: He wants to be *you.*

East = gold Δ

———————

Hand over to your sources

     1. 3. 7. 12.

———————

Water

In nomine Elohim et per spiritum aquarum viventium, sis mihi in signum lucis et sacramentum voluntaris.

Smoke

Per serpentum aneum sub quo cadunt serpentes ignei, sis mihi.

Breath

Per firmamentum et spiritum vocis, sis mihi.

Earth

In sale terrae et per virtutem vitae aeternae, sis mihi.

———————

242 *   "FREEMASONRY" AND RITUAL WORK

Sylphs

Spirit of Light, spirit of Wisdom, whose breath determines the form of all things—penetrate to us...

Undines

King of the Oceans, thou who hast the keys of heaven, we call to thee...

Salamanders

Immortal, eternal, uncreated Father of the World...

*

Invisible King, lead us to clarity...[36]

---

36. The beginning of the words associated with the gnomes in esoteric tradition. [British editor]

Handwritten note by Rudolf Steiner
Notebook, Archive No. 611

Green rises up from Mother Earth
With the glowing colors of the blossoms
The Sun-Spirit will envelop
What springs living from the Earth.

What sprouts from the Earth is a gown
What the Sun-Spirit weaves is a cloak
Living within it the soul is secreted
Powerfully the soul penetrates the Spirit.

You shall view the Spirit, oh Sisters, oh Brothers,
Only when you have become aware
Of what the Wise Ones from the East
Have made known to your inmost soul.

Receive the word of the Spirit.
Those who have served it since the world's beginning
Shall send down their strength to you
Through Wisdom, Beauty and Strength.

Meditation for the Second Degree
According to notes from a participant

If you approach me with true desire for knowledge
I shall be with you.
I am the germ and the source of your visible world,
I am the sum of the light in which your soul lives,
I am she who rules in space,
I am she who creates the cycles of time,
Fire, Air, Light, Water and Earth obey me.
Perceive me as the immaterial origin of all matter.

And as I have no husband on Earth, call me therefore "Maya."

Second Stage:
I am Isis
I am the daughter of Saturn
I am the sister of Osiris
I am the pupil of Hermes
The God Mercury
I am the mother of Horus
Who was born
With his head beneath Sirius.

Meditation for the Third Degree
According to the original handwriting of Rudolf Steiner
Participant's drawings bear the title "The 'I' speaks to the physical body"

From thee I was born	Y. Earth
I give thee my mortality	B. Water
The seed of eternity I receive from thee	M. Air
I fructify it with my warmth	Fire
May its light illumine thy end	Quinta essentia.

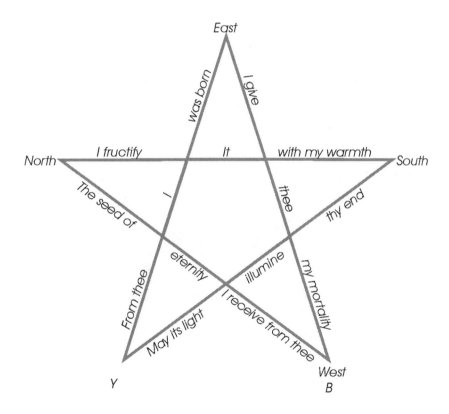

Note by a participant

1. = right foot to forehead, center between eyebrows
2. = forehead to left foot
3. = left foot to right hand
4. = right hand through heart to left hand
5. = left hand to right foot.

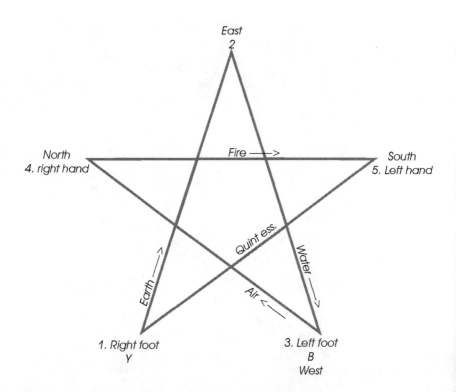

EXPLANATIONS OF THE RITUAL TEXTS

About the Three Words: "Wisdom – Beauty – Strength" (see p.161)

From a lecture, Berlin, January 2, 1906

If you wish to understand the civilization of the present day, you will find that it falls into three categories: that of Wisdom, that of Beauty and that of Strength. In these three words the whole extent of spiritual life is epitomized. They are therefore known as the three pillars of human culture. They are the same as the three kings of Goethe's fairy tale *The Green Snake and the Beautiful Lily*: the gold, the silver and the brazen kings. They are connected with the name "Royal Art," given to Freemasonry. Today these three spheres of culture have become separated. For the most part Wisdom is restricted within the realm of Science; Beauty is usually represented by what is called Art; and that which in Freemasonry parlance is called Strength is contained in the interconnected, organized social life within the state. The whole is summed up by the Freemason as the relationship of the will to these three realms: Wisdom, Beauty, Strength.

(...) When these ideals are talked about by those who really know about them, then something quite specific is alluded to; it is so specific that it bears the same relationship to the events of the coming centuries as the thought of an architect, designing a factory, bears to the finished building.

From a lecture, Bremen, April 9, 1906

Freemasonry is everything that comes about with the help of Wisdom, Beauty, and Strength. By this is signified the proper construction of the earthly temple, not just the temple within the human being. The work of building is performed both on the interior and on the exterior.

Freemasons are primarily concerned with advancing themselves so far that they become worthy collaborators in the building of humanity (and the Earth). The meaning of earthly life is to transform our Earth-planet. Human work will be involved on our Earth to an ever greater extent.

What will become of the Earth in future? It will be a building perfected by humankind. And it is the duty of every person to take part in the construction of this building. Three forces have to be built into this temple, otherwise chaos will ensue. The pillars that support the building are Wisdom, Beauty, and Strength.

Wisdom, when the spirit is ennobled; Beauty, when the feelings are enhanced; Strength, when the will is purified.

Therefore these three pillars are the basis for all activity.

From an instruction lesson, Hanover, Christmas 1911

Wisdom, Beauty, Strength really only exist in the spiritual world. Here below only their images exist. Whoever says the words Wisdom, Beauty, Strength, should be aware of the fact that they give utterance to a confession of faith. "I believe in an astral world," one says when one utters the word "Wisdom"; "I believe in a lower devachan," when one says the word "Beauty"; "I believe in a higher devachan," when one speaks the word "Strength." The mirror-picture of Wisdom here below is Truth, that of Beauty is Piety, and that of Strength is Virtue.

From an instruction lesson, Hanover, Christmas 1911. Notes in a different handwriting

In all mystery centers the pupils say the following as their tenet of faith: Wisdom – Beauty – Strength.

Concerning the Prayer "Brothers of Ages Past ... " (see p.162 et seq.)

From an instruction lesson, Munich, December 12, 1906

With our prayer "Brothers of Ages Past ..." we demonstrate that we link up with the Brothers of Ages Past, Brothers of the Present Time and the Brothers of the Future, the Mahatmas.

From an instruction lesson, Hanover, Christmas 1911

We should know and be aware of the fact that the powers of the Wise Masters of the East flow into us through the symbols that surround us within the walls of our Temple. When we look up to those who have guided the whole of human development since the beginning of world evolution, from Saturn, Sun, and Moon and through earthly evolution up until our present day, then we turn in prayer to seek help for our present evolution from those whom we call, "Brothers of Ages Past." And so we pray: "Brothers of Ages Past ...." When we look up to those who guide us spiritually today, we pray: "Brothers of the Present Time ...." And those who will be the leaders of humanity in the future, we address as "Brothers of the Future ...."

From an instruction lesson, Hanover, December 31, 1911

The Wise Masters of the East are beings belonging to the three higher worlds, who are active simultaneously in the past, present and future and whom we regard as being above us when we address them in our prayers.

From an instruction lesson, Munich, September 5, 1912

The first prayer is distinguished from all other endeavors of its kind based upon documents or on preserved wisdom. We do not depend upon anything of that sort; we only form connections to finished work, to work that has really been carried out.

Among other attacks we shall have to endure very soon is that people will seek to calumniate and cast suspicion on our esoteric movement, so that it will become necessary for us to know what we are joining. A community such as ours has its existence in the spiritual world, but its existence there is only justified insofar as there are souls who acknowledge it as the truth. And those who do not agree with what it stands for, have no need to affiliate themselves with it. We do not claim to be an order or Rosicrucian movement or anything of that kind. Our endeavor is to represent the truth in such a way that we do not claim it as our own possession, but seek to come into possession of the wisdom that has flowed out of creative activity.

There is wisdom there. There was a primordial store of human wisdom, such as is alluded to by the Grand Master in *The Guardian of the Threshold* [Scene 1.]. And Maria's attitude towards Thomasius in the second scene shows us how we should react, that is, how we should progress in esoteric life. It would have been much easier to have given instructions for all to follow, but at some time it had to be demonstrated in our Western movement, how people with the special gifts of a Thomasius, a Strader, a Capesius or a Maria had to follow the path of initiation.

"Compasses and yardstick" signifies: we shall adopt your customs.

Such prayers contain in words all that we need, as do likewise the Mystery Dramas. Every word therein stands in its proper place and is filled with esoteric significance. Nothing is uttered or included therein for any other reason than for its spiritual significance and force.

The opponents of spirituality, as for instance a Haeckel, bear spirituality deeply hidden within them, and their rage and anger is actually directed against themselves. Because, during their lifetime, they were unable to penetrate their subconscious soul life, their attitude towards the spirit is quite different after death and they can be quoted most easily, as for instance in spiritualistic seances.

Nietzsche is very interesting in this respect. He was unable to separate himself thoroughly from his material part. That is why he presented such a peculiar appearance to clairvoyant vision, already during his illness: the human being, Nietzsche, this unusual personality lying on the sofa and around him the aura.[1] The split personality comes to expression in such cases: while the consciousness remains materialistic, the subconscious is spiritual.

"Brothers of the Future:" we, too, are without a name, for Lucifer is the godparent who is present at the founding of every union or society.

From a lecture, Bremen, April 9, 1906

To be an apprentice means: catch up with what our Brothers of Ages Past have accomplished; to be a journeyman means: to be able to share the experiences of the Elder Brothers of Humanity; to be a Master means: to be allowed to co-operate in the building of the temple.

From a lecture, Berlin, January 29, 1906

As I have often said, it is not for nothing that the Theosophical Society was founded during the last third of the 19th century. The way in which it seeks the spiritual differs very greatly from that of other movements which likewise try to obtain proofs of our immortality. There is a great difference between the way the Theosophical Society searches for the eternal and the way that other streams orientated towards the spiritual seek it. Actually the

---

1. This refers to Rudolf Steiner's impression of him on the occasion of his being able to visit the sick Nietzsche. See Rudolf Steiner's *Autobiography*.

254 * "Freemasonry" and Ritual Work

Theosophical Movement is nothing other than the popular version of the esoteric brotherhoods which were secretly dispersed throughout the world during the last millennia. I have already mentioned the fact that the most prominent and largest brotherhood in Europe was founded in the 14th century as the Rosicrucian Brotherhood. This Rosicrucian Brotherhood is actually the source or origin of all other brotherhoods which are to be found in European culture. Esoteric knowledge was kept strictly secret in the brotherhoods. If I were to characterize what the members of these various brotherhoods wished to attain, I should have to say to you: those highly exalted teachings and works of wisdom which were cultivated in these esoteric brotherhoods, of which the Rosicrucian Brotherhood was the most exalted, enabled us to become conscious of the eternal core of our own being. They enabled us to discover our connection to the higher world, to the worlds which lie above us, and to obtain an insight into the guidance of our Elder Brothers, into the guidance of those who live among us and who have attained a level, which all of you will one day attain. We call them the Elder Brothers, because, anticipating the general development, they have reached this higher point of view in advance of the rest of humanity: that is to say, the certainty of their own eternal being, the awakening of the same, so that you will be able to look into eternity, just as ordinary human beings look into the sense world. In order to achieve this, you will have to emulate the Elder Brothers who live among us everywhere. These Elder Brothers, or Masters, the Great Leaders of Humanity, have themselves always been the chief leaders and supreme heads of the sublime esoteric wisdom, through which we are made aware of the eternal core of our being.

Concerning the Four Principles, "Learn to Keep Silence ..." (see p.164)

From an instruction lesson, Berlin, June 26, 1906[2]

The Freemasonry meetings are divided into those in which the rituals are fully employed and those which are concerned with instructions that underlie the whole of Freemasonry like a skeleton and teach things which every esotericist should inscribe deeply into his soul as the center-point of esoteric life.

One usually has quite false pictures of the way in which the esoteric world can be entered. There is an extensive literature on the subject, but of the really deep secrets nothing has been divulged; nothing of that is to be found therein. The most important things have never been made public. For that reason, after studying such books, one usually feels dissatisfied.

The really intimate details are given in the form of symbols. They are only of use to those who know how to convert them into living concepts. Most people spend their time of esoteric studies badly, because they think that it is possible to penetrate the esoteric world by means of outward magic.

There are times at which it is particularly dangerous to penetrate into the esoteric world by outward magic. This was the case in Atlantean times, during the time of its fourth sub-race, the original Turanians. That was where the actual black magic was developed. That was why the priests had to keep a part of the wisdom secret. The other is the time of our present epoch. We belong to the fifth sub-race of the [post-Atlantean] epoch. All outer expedients are predisposed to destroy humankind. It is therefore necessary for a number of people to become acquainted with the intimate paths that lead into the spiritual world.

If you are to become aware of the correct means of gaining access to the spiritual world, you must first of all become acquainted with

---

2. As Rudolf Steiner was continually traveling from the beginning of January onwards, it may well be the first instruction lesson with which we are here dealing. Whether or not the ritual took place on that occasion is not known. Additions enclosed between round brackets are variations according to different versions.

the obstacles. There are four principles which you have to learn in order to avoid the obstacles to entry into the spiritual world.

The first principle runs as follows:

Over that to which you have given expression in words, you no longer have any control from the depths of your soul.

Thus the best way of forfeiting strength is to talk a lot. That is why formerly one never spoke about esoteric forces in the brotherhoods. Those who talk about them a lot lose a part of the forces they are looking for. That is where the power of silence comes in. Those who chatter a lot must think about what they are doing.

Today the brotherhoods have surrendered that part of the forces which are contained in the teachings of Theosophy. Why is it that certain things can be divulged nowadays? Previous to 1879 that would not have been possible; something happened at that time which has made it possible.[3] Previous to 1879 it would have signified that the esoteric brotherhoods would have become corrupt if nothing else had happened. For that part which has been divulged they have also become corrupt. They must keep something back, which they do not yet divulge, something new, something more exalted.

Just imagine what a reserve of strength you accumulate through the things which you do not divulge. What you speak about must therefore signify a kind of resignation, a kind of sacrifice; for by the amount you impart to others, by so much do you saw away at the branch on which you sit. The mood must be very far removed from every kind of fanaticism or wish to chatter. As long as the wish to chatter predominates, it signifies a weakening of one's reserves of strength. Whoever takes the floor as a propagandistic agitator misses the target at which one is aiming.

---

3. In three separate texts it is given as "1879," in another it is "1875." "1879" could be the correct date, for "1875" is certainly the year of the founding of the Theosophical Society, but it is more likely that the event in the spiritual world is being referred to: the fall of the spirits of darkness (see book under this title).

The Theosophical Movement is discussed by us Freemasons quite objectively. It is the first of the agitative movements to make its appearance. If we take the doctrine, the concept of a doctrine, so much to heart that it does not just stick in our mind, but starts to simmer within us, it then stimulates our inner being. Whoever is not deeply stirred by such a book as *The Secret Doctrine* by H.P.B. [H.P. Blavatsky], or my book *Theosophy,* so that it works inwardly like fire, must read it again and continue reading it until it is completely mastered, even if it has to be read a hundred or more times.

So it is with the theosophical teachings, which—even though they are so necessary, because civilization will be unable to proceed without them, because civilization needs them—are also so dangerous when they are openly proclaimed in meetings, etc., where maturity and immaturity sit beside each other. But this danger has to be; civilization cannot proceed without demanding sacrifice. But one must be careful that one does not implant demons into the listeners' ears, and every sentence must be carefully weighed so that it does not become a fiery force.

Esotericists exist today and have always existed in the world. If someone had wished to approach them in former times, it would always have been by means of a "stroke of luck." But there is, of course, no such thing as luck. One used to travel for many weeks in order to meet and question such a person. That was a quite different situation from the one we have today, in which esoteric teachers appear among people or travel to meet them.

It was a part of one's strength to know: What you express in words you forfeit in strength. It is a question of turning one's speech into a sacrificial ritual; but then strength grows. There is nothing better for an esotericist than to get used to holding his peace on many occasions. Gossip and tittle-tattle and indulgence in loose talk produces demons and impure behavior on the astral plane. That can be observed by a clairvoyant person and from a higher perspective it is much worse than to behave immodestly on the physical plane.

Speech has become a means of destroying human progress. If you consider how much is read today for the purpose of self-satisfaction—

those countless productions of modern poets and poetesses—you can see how many destructive forces there are in the world. Today the greatest progress could be gained by reading and printing less.

The second principle is this, that one weakens the resolve insofar as one exercises power. Suppose that someone or other arrives on the scene with an important intention. He comes from an isolated part of the world, has no connection with anybody else and attempts to perform a deed in unfamiliar surroundings. He does not possess any power, but his resolve is tremendous. In a field of forces his original intention becomes paralyzed, because it is quickly blunted. From an esoteric point of view those who exercise the most power in the outside world are the ones who are most paralyzed in their inner resolve. That is why an esotericist prefers to travel the world with a thrice-knotted cord rather than be a king. Anyone who has acquired powerlessness would not want to exchange that lot with someone who rules over a great realm, for if one were to do anything except what benefits the realm, one would be doing something foolish. One who possesses a great fortune has to look after it and is hindered with regard to one's will. The power one exercises damages one's will.

A good example of what can be achieved in this way is the Englishman Oliphant.[4] He was a very, very rich man and threw away all he possessed; gave it to welfare foundations, etc., and emigrated in poverty to America, earning his living with his bare hands. After he had saved up something, he and his wife moved to Mount Carmel where they built a hut. There he began dictating to his wife and she recorded the most wonderful things you can read,[5] which were inspired from the spiritual world. Then his wife died. He tried to write himself, but that was only successful when he sat in the hut where he and his wife had lived.

---

4. Laurence Oliphant, 1829-1888. English diplomat, writer and journalist. Biography by Margaret Oliphant, *Memoir of the Life of Laurence Oliphant*, London, 1891.

5. The two works were written; *Sympneumata* (1885) and *Scientific Religion* (1888). See also the lecture given in London, August 24, 1924 in CW 240.

Here a strange spiritual phenomenon took place, which was the result of the abandonment of temporal power. One's resolve is weakened by outward power and one gains in inner resolve the less power one wields.

The third principle runs as follows: one loses as much inner life-force as the will one exerts. The will deadens the life force. To the extent that one exercises the will, the inner life forces are deadened, so that all we will is at the same time a hindrance for our inner life, for our spiritual development. Therefore we should restrict our will to that which the world demands of us, not will something out of an inner urge. One makes progress in esoteric life if one confines one's will to what is most necessary. The greatest benefit will accrue from the conscious suppression of the will, and that for no other reason than that one is able to suppress it. We have to learn, however, that in suppressing our will we do not neglect our duty.

The fourth principle is that the inner life deadens the thought through its feelings and perceptions. If you are prone to experiencing great pain and great joy by developing your inner life, so much the more will you deaden the purity of your thought. Whoever wishes to think objectively must exclude his inner life in the appropriate way. Every outburst of inner feeling deadens the purity of the thought.

If you wish to have purely spiritual thought then you must deaden your inner life. If you wish to preserve your inner life you must deaden the will. If you wish to strengthen your resolve then you must relinquish your power.

Those who wish to retain power must curb their talking. In order to have clairvoyant thoughts we must transcend joy and pain as a divine heavenly being. In order to gain command over our will impulses we must renounce power, and in order to be in control of power we must learn to be silent.

The first esoteric instruction received by the Freemason is to inwardly consider how to fulfil the four sentences:

1. Learn silence in order to gain power.

2. Learn to exert your will by renouncing power.

3. Learn to cultivate feeling by renouncing will-force.

4. Learn to think by renouncing feeling.

One should contemplate these sentences and the possibility of realizing them in one's own life.

These sentences are part of the understanding of the pentagram:

The five points correspond esoterically to what the human being will one day become, either by observing the foregoing rules or by the process of development. This pentagram will resemble a key to the esoteric world when it is put to use.

One need not dwell upon the above figure if one develops in the sense of the four sentences. When one has understood what is contained in the four sentences they will become a hieroglyph and be the equivalent of a key to the spiritual world.

When one has begun to exercise silence, a second hieroglyph that one begins to understand is the hexagram:

Concerning the Pledge-Formula (Vow) (see p.192)

An explanation for this from an instruction lesson has not been preserved; however, Rudolf Steiner traced the origin of this esoteric tradition in a lecture, Dornach, November 26, 1916:

People today know very little about the past. Above all they do not know why certain things have been handed down to us. They perhaps still know that they have been handed down, but they hardly know why. People know, for instance—for that can be read today in all kinds of exoteric books, namely also in Freemasonry books— that there were Mysteries in times past, and that the Mysteries were a secret arrangement, and that in these Mysteries—that is inherent in the word—there were things which could not be divulged, secrets also in the outer sense of the word. That is to say: Those who had access to the Mysteries were entrusted with certain things that they were not allowed to reveal to anyone, except to those who were members of the same order. It was a strict rule in those ancient times that the Mystery secrets were not to be betrayed. This rule states that it is one of the most punishable offences for someone to reveal an esoteric secret to an uninitiated person, but it is just as great an offence for an unauthorised person to hear one of the hidden secrets. This view, which was cultivated in the Mysteries, was adhered to in the most strict fashion when the Mysteries were practiced in the old way. Why was that? Why did it come about in this way?

I have often stressed the fact to you that humankind has changed during the course of earthly evolution and an important incision in this evolution came at the time when Christ passed through the Mystery of Golgotha. If one were to characterise a most important feature of this evolution, among other things which we have already mentioned, one would have to say: If we go back to the Greco-Roman time, namely if we go back beyond the fourth century B.C., to the fifth, sixth, seventh century B.C.—we can even remain within the Greco-Roman period, but we would discover more if we went back to the Egypto-Chaldean period, or even into the Persian Epoch—we would find on every hand that what was spoken by people of that time conveyed quite a different meaning for the rest of humankind, than say in the seventh or eighth century A.D. The word which one person spoke to another when the old atavistic faculties of clairvoyance were still active, had a quite different meaning then, than it has today, than it had later. At that time, if I may say so, the word, through its own inner strength, had a kind of suggestive value, for there lay within it much inherited divine-spiritual strength. When people spoke, the angel of the higher hierarchies always, as it were, spoke with them through their words.

From that you can imagine that what was communicated by means of words in those ancient times was something quite different from what it is today. We have no possibility of speaking like people spoke in ancient times, even if we were to know all those secrets, because we have to speak with words such as they have become through speech. The words are conventional signs. We can no longer go up to a person today and say, with the same force as a person of the third, fourth or fifth century B.C., "Your angel loves you." This caused a slight shudder in the person, in which there was a healing force. We cannot do that any longer. The old suggestive power of the words has been taken from them. In olden times a human socializing force flowed from one soul to another when people conversed together. Just as we breathe the same air as one another when we congregate in a room, so there lived in ancient times a shared spiritual force when people conversed. That has been lost during the course of human evolution. The word has become ever more debased.

If you look at that, if you consider it with spiritual understanding, then you will discover that there could be particular words and combinations of words, formulae, which have a much greater effect than other words used in everyday language. And such word-formulae, which exerted a far greater power than ordinary words, were handed down from the Mysteries. Now you can understand how it is that these secrets were not to be divulged, because, by knowing these formulae, a person was thereby entrusted with a mighty power over his fellow human beings, which should not be abused. It expressed a very real truth when the ancient Hebrew priest of the temple spoke that which is only called "Word" in ordinary life, but which contained a certain sequence of sounds which, when spoken correctly—because in those ancient times power resided in the sequence of sounds—to the people he was addressing, it actually happened that they were encompassed by another world, a spiritual world, but the spirituality was real.

So now you will understand, that it was not only a criminal offence to utter the Mystery formulas to an unauthorized person, thereby exerting unlawful power over him or her, but that it was also prohibited for an unauthorised person to listen to such words, and might thereby be put in danger of coming completely under the sway of such a person. These things are not so abstract as some people like to portray them today. They are real, concrete happenings and times have changed and it behoves us to be aware of the change of the times. Since the Mystery of Golgotha these words no longer have the same meaning, for you will agree, true freedom could not have arisen among people on Earth if these words had retained their former significance, for people would, so to speak, only have been the result of speech with regard to their soul. Words had to lose their inner power. But a different force had to enter world evolution, which, if used correctly, would eventually compensate human beings for what they formerly derived from words. Ancient people learned to think by means of words and there were no thoughts in ancient times except those that arose out of words. But the power of thought could only spring from words if the words were as I have described them. This power was no longer present in later times. But then came the Being that could restore the power of the thoughts, when they filled themselves with Him—that Being which said of Himself, "I am the Word"—and that Being is Christ. People must only find the way to bring the Christ to life in their soul.

Concerning Ashes, Salt, and Water (see p.169)

From an instruction lesson, Munich, December 12, 1906

Spirit descended to the Earth through a process of burning which deposited ash. Through the depositing of salt, wisdom came onto the Earth. Both must be washed once more by the waters of life.

From an instruction lesson, Berlin, February 1908, no exact date

It is important for us to gain an ever greater understanding of the formulas that are used in the lodge, so that we can follow the ceremonies to which they belong with more insight.

The ashes, the salt and the water have great significance. In early Atlantis the air was filled with water and the sun's rays could only be discerned vaguely through the thick mist. We were living in this mist outside the physical bodies—we, the spirits who have since entered into physical bodies. But at that time we were outside these bodies and controlled them [from outside].

Everything hard and firm on the Earth has crystallized out of this watery atmosphere. At that time water was not so dense as it is today and the air, by comparison, was much denser. But gradually the water subsided over the face of the Earth and left the atmosphere behind as air, whereas the water took on a thicker consistency. That is symbolized by salt in solution.

Salt is wisdom; from that evolved Ruach Hochmael.

At that time there were no bones in human bodies, but as the atmosphere gradually crystallized, the precipitated salt formed bones, where previously there had only been magnetic currents.

Death is quite rightly portrayed as a skeleton with a scythe. For bones represent the comparatively stable part of the human body, the part according to which the body of the next incarnation will be formed. The bones represent the future, whereas the soft parts represent the past, the past from which life ebbs away. The bones with their blood and lymph represent the future, because the "I" gains a foothold where the blood corpuscles are formed.

At the beginning of the Earth-period the Earth was filled exclusively with human beings. At that time the human being appeared first on the scene. While humans were evolving further, a few remained behind to form the animal kingdom. Among the latter were some which were incapable of further development and they formed the plant kingdom. And in the end some remained behind from the plant kingdom in order to form the mineral kingdom, as one sees in the formation of coal. What remained behind at that stage was engendered by crystallization. In order [for human beings] to develop further, their tools [or organs] had to remain liquid so that the dense, solidifying substances could be eliminated.

Concerning the Rosicrucian Maxim (see p.169)

We are presumably dealing here with a text by Rudolf Steiner, for which, however, the original is missing. The present text is from a handwritten document denoted as "F.M."

The human being is born out of God. Sublime spiritual beings formed the human body; they were cosmic forces, so the human being was built up out of the cosmos and grew out of the cosmos.

The first condition of development in which we can point to the influence of those cosmic forces, was the one which is called the ancient Saturn condition. It was then that these forces started to work in space and in time, so that ancient Saturn came into being in space and evolved in time. At that time there existed no solar system with planets, there existed only a body of warmth surrounded by the twelve signs of the zodiac, which poured their forces into this warmth-body as though from a periphery into a common center. Out of this center other powers worked from the opposite direction, but the inflowing forces were the stronger and hence the centripetal tendency of evolution. If one looks at the present-day minerals as they appear spiritually, the same effect can be observed there too, except that we are dealing in this case with solid matter. From all sides out of far distant spaces the spiritual forces work inwards towards a common point in space, and the stone or mineral appears at this point. From this central point forces work against the instreaming powers, but the latter are stronger. Thus arose the first embodiment of the present Earth as the sphere of warmth of ancient Saturn through the influence of the twelve starry constellations from the periphery towards the center. Because these forces working inwards towards the center, surpassed the other ones, a further densification and a kind of division took place. Several points were formed in the one central point during further development and so the whole planet consisted eventually of many such centers of power which arose through the effect of cosmic forces, or spiritual beings from the cosmos. In this central point itself spiritual beings were also at work, they enlivened it and worked on it in such a way that it could form the basis for what was later to become humankind. We were already endowed with the powers which, working on into the future, were able to supply us with the physical body in which we dwell today as self-conscious earthly human beings. We also acquired at that time the faculty that would enable us later to develop spirit human through our own efforts. On ancient Saturn at that time the nucleus was laid down for life on the physical and the spiritual planes and the human physical and spiritual center was established. When this development had proceeded to a certain stage, the spiritual powers ceased their activities, a kind of planetary night, or withdrawal, ensued and when the next day dawned, the Earth appeared again in its new embodiment as old Sun.

The development proceeded further. In connection with the former Saturn condition everything was repeated under quite different conditions. Then something new took place. The centers which had arisen in ancient Saturn appeared again in the old Sun condition. Owing to the still active centripetal forces, the old Sun, as a celestial body, was more compact than ancient Saturn. It had become more densified and was no longer so extended. As a physical center it did not need to disperse its forces so far into outer space, it was able to hold itself in more and retain something for itself as inner strength. It was able to display this in such a way that it could counter the influence from the zodiac with something which came from its own being in the light that it radiated into its surroundings. Just because of the densification with regard to what was physical, the possibility arose of giving away something of itself which was spiritually effective. So it was, too, with separate centers on the old Sun. Through their own strength they could ray forth something of themselves into their surroundings. A dispersal of their own being took place, which can be described as a growth in light. In our present development a similar power is active in the plant kingdom, only there it takes place within dense earthly substance. Just as the present-day plants grow from their seeds towards the sunlight, so did growth take place on the old Sun, an extension and advance in the light from the centers into the surroundings. Not only did the forces from the twelve constellations work down from the surroundings onto the old Sun, but the Sun itself sent back something in return in its outraying light. And there grew out of it the rudiments of those planets that we know today under quite different conditions in our present solar system. Just as the seven colors can be revealed in white light by deflecting the light beams, so did these planets become organized in their rudiments at that time as radiant points of light in the sunlight itself.

Once again spiritual beings worked in these centers and formed them in such a way that they became the basis for what one knows today as the life body or etheric body. Human beings were also endowed with the rudiments of what they will one day themselves acquire as life spirit. The principle of growth and extension was developed in both the physical and in the spiritual center of our being during the time of the Sun development. For just as the etheric body makes it possible for the physical body to grow, so with the life spirit is denoted what can be called the surroundings, the environment of the spiritual center of spirit human in which this is revealed.

The centripetal force which was active in ancient Saturn continued to work on in the old Sun condition. Through that came about the densification, so that the warmth sphere became a gas sphere. Through this force the living beings also divided up and became distinct from one another. But through the centrifugal force the Sun radiated forth and the living beings were enabled to forsake their set forms and to grow.

When the development had proceeded for a while, another pause for rest ensued, in which the cosmic powers withdrew their activity. Then the Earth stepped forth from its cosmic night in its new embodiment as old Moon and that which had taken place in the two previous stages of development was repeated under different conditions. The densification and contraction of the whole planetary body and of separate centers or living entities still continued, and thereby a stronger manifestation of inner forces became possible. The centripetal and centrifugal forces were both active and sought to come into harmony with one another. Through that a great oscillation came about. On the one hand the effect of the centripetal forces showed in the densification of the old Moon and in the ever-increasing emancipation of the separate centers from their surroundings. On the other hand the centrifugal force found expression in being able to reveal more and more of the spiritual forces from the center into the environment. These two forces worked in such a way that during the evolution of old Moon they came to a crisis. A kind of split took place. The part of old Moon in which the centrifugal forces were most active separated from the other part in which the centripetal forces remained more active. Thereby a planetary body evolved that chiefly radiated its forces outward and revealed itself to the outer world in its spiritual strength as a sun raying forth light, and another planetary body, the old Moon, which was exposed to further densification and on which the further development of those beings took place that were destined to become Earth-humans.

Through this contraction the bodies of these beings became ever denser and more independent and they acquired the possibility of manifesting stronger inner powers. That which worked upon them from outside was thereby enabled to echo within them and they could reply to it in a certain way. A sound then issued forth from the inner depths of these beings that was an echo of the sound which came to them from without. The old Moon had become a watery sphere through this further densification and the bodies of the living beings had become correspondingly denser as well. Light still shone forth from the Sun towards the Moon and those forces that strove for the spiritualization and refinement of matter were also contained therein. In the more refined part of old Moon, which had separated itself off as Sun, spiritual forces had also departed and left the courser body and rayed light and life into it. The courser body then rotated about this source of light as the old Moon. It was the same with the separate centerpoints on the old Moon. At the time of separation the part which was to continue to evolve spiritually, and above all to develop the centrifugal force, went away with the Sun, and the part which was to become more dense and develop the centripetal force within it stayed with the old Moon and densified to a watery condition. The bodies of the living beings were on the old Moon, and the spirit that enlivened them was outside on the Sun and rayed its light into them from there. There is something in the animal kingdom, as it appears in present earthly evolution, which corresponds with this operation, though it is adjusted to earth conditions. In an animal the physical body is animated by the real spirit, which does not dwell in the animal itself. There is a spiritual center, distinct from the forms of the animals out of which life streams down to them. On the present Earth a whole genus of animals is animated by the same spiritual entity in such a way that one can regard the entity as the center-point and the animals in the genus as the periphery, surrounding it and receiving its life from it. In this way the old Moon rotated around its Sun and was animated from this spiritual center. As a result of the fact that these spiritual forces had left the Moon and now worked on it from outside, as it circled around the Sun, movement was initiated in the Moon evolution, and this also applied to the separate centers. Spiritual beings adapted the latter so that, in embryo, they could develop what is today called the astral body. Within the human astral body the perceptions and feelings that are aroused in it by its surroundings are in continual movement. Through these perceptions and feelings we reply to the sound that comes to meet us from outside. An organ with which to gain spiritual understanding, a spiritual atunement to cosmic wisdom, was also implanted into humans during the Moon evolution, so that they felt at one with it. Just as we allow the stream of pulsating sensations to flow through our astral body, detain it within ourself and send out a force against it, in order to react consciously to it, so does the light of cosmic wisdom flow into our spirit self and it becomes possible for us to receive it and consciously to ray it back again. Because the old Moon split in half as a cosmic body to form two bodies mutually interacting, movement and also conscious sensations arose. The influences spread from one planetary body to the other. The influences of the Sun on the Moon were experienced there as forces coming from without, and it was the same with the Moon influences that spread to the Sun. At the place where the Sun and Moon influences met, a conscious experience was evoked. A kind of blockage occurred and a boundary was formed where the inflowing force met with the force flowing from the opposite direction. For every living entity on the Moon there was a limit to the field of experience in which it could consciously apprehend something. The possibility of projecting its forces further afield ceased at this point. Its own force was met by the instreaming forces. The living beings that later became human beings on Earth, possessed consciousness on the old Moon; they did not yet have self-consciousness, for they lived entirely in their surroundings. They had no experience of their own and could only let what was revealed to them from outside resound within them.

When the Moon evolution had reached a certain stage of maturity, the spiritual powers that had instigated it all withdrew. Sun and Moon forces neutralized each other; they gradually united once more and a period of rest began. Then the Earth emerged as a new heavenly body out of this planetary night. To begin with the former evolutionary conditions were repeated under new circumstances, the Earth underwent a period in which, as regards the physical, it was a body of warmth, as formerly on ancient Saturn. Then the separate centers gradually evolved again under the influence of the centripetal force. And then there came a period in which the Earth became a gas ball and the centrifugal force exerted its influence on it as it had done formerly on old Sun. The separate centers began to radiate outwards once more; that was the Sun condition on Earth. Afterwards came a repetition of the Moon condition on Earth. The Sun then separated from the other part of the cosmic body and left behind the Earth in which the Moon forces remained. Once again the forces seeking to become spiritualized departed with the Sun and from there they radiated light and life towards the planetary body, which continued to grow more dense. The planets also departed with the Sun, and only the Moon forces remained with the Earth. Some of the centers that were striving to become spiritualized also departed with the Sun and sent down their forces from there, while the coarser ones remained behind on the earth. Now a condition was reached in which there was a repetition of all that had happened on the old Moon. The Earth and the bodies of living entities became more and more dense. The centripetal forces were in the ascendancy. But then a new phase began, which came about through the fact that in Earth evolution not only the old Moon remained behind, as formerly during the old Moon evolution, but that a new force, the actual Earth force, was added. This Earth force acted in such a way that it formed a uniting force between Sun and Moon forces, which it was able to bring into harmony and balance with one another. When the densification progressed further, owing to it being only the Moon forces, which were connected with the earth, the earth force brought about a kind of balance by separating itself off from the Moon forces. The Earth left these forces with the Moon and remained on its own between the forces of Sun and Moon, between the impulse of spiritualization and the impulse of densification. It was influenced by both and carried both within it and held the balance through its own forces. A similar force is to be found in the modern human "I," for just as the Earth is the mediator between Sun forces and Moon forces, so does the human "I" form the connecting link between what is spiritual and what is material, so that both can unite in the human being. The Earth is also so placed in the universe that it is encircled by the Moon with its rigidifying forces and by the Sun from which it receives spirit light. The Earth is surrounded as though by a sheath by the Moon forces; the Sun forces come to it from a more distant center, situated far above this sheath. That is how the human "I" is embedded in its sheaths, but the spirit light streams towards it out of cosmic distances.

In the two forces, which worked upon each other during the Moon evolution, a third power showed itself, working vertically upon the other two. Through that something new came about in movement as a whole, which can be called self-movement. In Earth evolution the physical expression of that can be seen in the rotation of the Earth about its axis. On the old Moon a kind of consciousness was engendered through the blockage where the two forces met. Now, through their encounter with the third force, a double blockage is brought about that causes the general consciousness to be restricted and shut off, so that it is thrown back upon itself. Through that it becomes deepened to become self-consciousness, in which it comprehends itself and the seed of "I"-consciousness is laid down. The same forces influenced the bodies of the entities and thereby these entities all became more independent. They acquired their own movement, just as the Earth had acquired it, and just because of this movement further densification took place. The bodies became more restricted within themselves, so that an inner life of their own became possible. The further densification of the bodies was no longer brought about merely by the Moon forces, but through independent movement, through the Earth forces themselves, and these Earth forces represented the sum total of all that had taken place earlier in the three previous evolutionary stages and had become transformed in the fourth, the actual Earth stage.

Once again it was spiritual beings who brought self-awareness to humanity, by implanting in it during Earth evolution, the germ of "I"-consciousness, through which the human being was able to say "I." The physical center on Earth was inhabited by the human being and under the guidance of higher beings. This was gradually developed to become the human physical body as it appears today. The inner force, which was the foundation for "I"-consciousness, could only develop in a physical body, which, depending on itself alone, was distinct in form from its surroundings. Gradually the human physical body took shape in this way; but the foundation for the "I" was impressed on it at an earlier time. In the same way that the warmth-sphere of ancient Saturn densified to become the gas-sphere of the old Sun and then was able to ray out its own spiritual forces into the cosmic surroundings in the form of light, and as it later densified still further during the old Moon condition to become fluid, but on the other hand to reveal more inward forces to produce sounds and movements, so did a further densification take place during Earth evolution, which on the one hand produced hard earthly conditions, on the other led to a further revelation of inner forces manifesting as life, as individual inner life. On ancient Saturn everything was contained within a dark sea of warmth, on the old Sun everything shone in light, on the old Moon everything vibrated in sound and on Earth everything lived an individual inner life of its own.

When the repetition of earlier planetary evolutionary conditions took place, the Earth at first was in a fiery state; human beings lived in the element of fire and their physical body was also built up out of this element. Human beings at that time developed mainly their will and with it were able to influence the latter element. Already at that time the rudiments of "I"-consciousness were implanted into them. Later they hovered above the Earth in the element of air and their body also existed in a gaseous state. There came a time in which they lived amidst watery mist and their body was also adapted to this element of water. They mainly developed their feelings during that period and were thus able to influence the element of water. At that time the human "I" still did not live within the physical body. It was outside it, although connected to it. Only in the time known as post-Atlantis was the physical body far enough consolidated to accommodate the Earth element into itself, and it became possible for the human "I" to live within the physical body. Only then did the human being truly live upon the Earth. Only then was the human being able to develop thinking and influence things as well.

Thus proceeded the development of humankind to the stage we have reached today. We were engendered by the Godhead, woven into the web of life and all powers work towards our incorporation out of the great cosmos. For our sake the whole of the solar system was constituted, was transformed during the four phases that we call the incarnations of the Earth: ancient Saturn, old Sun, old Moon and the Earth itself. Numberless beings have made a sacrifice so that we might exist. We see some of these beings around us incorporated in the lower kingdoms of nature on Earth. Others we experience as powers working within us. There had to be beings that remained behind at the Saturn stage throughout all the three previous incarnations of the Earth planet including the present Earth. There had to be others that during the Earth evolution repeated the Sun stage and others that repeated the Moon stage, so that they might work and live in the mineral, plant and animal kingdoms on Earth. So there are beings that work within us as retarded beings from the old Moon, old Sun, and ancient Saturn. Just as little as we could live and exist on the physical Earth without the three lower kingdoms of nature, can we develop as a self-conscious "I"-being without these retarded powers or beings within us. We experience the effect of these beings that remained behind at the Moon stage in our astral body as inhibitory forces that express themselves through desires and passions of a lower kind, as they are also active in the animal kingdom. The beings that remained behind at the Sun stage work on the human etheric body as hindering forces, which bind us to habits and acquired modes of thought. In these effects something akin to the plant nature is present, for just as the plant always produces new leaves and goes on repeating the same until the astral brings about a change to the blossoms, so do the habits and accepted ways of thinking work on continually in the human being and something new has to be introduced through the power of the astral body, by means of feelings and emotions. The beings that remained behind at the Saturn stage and are active within us, pour their forces into the physical body as powers of hindrance, which bring about separation from the surroundings and a feeling of being alone and standing on one's own feet. Through that one is induced to regard oneself as an individual center-point and is inclined to act, think, and feel as though the surrounding world were only there for that purpose. There is a similarity here with the power working inwards towards the center in the mineral kingdom, by which physical matter is formed through densification, for this power also causes a concretization and exclusion in us by throwing us back onto ourselves. In the same way that these powers were active in former times on ancient Saturn, old Sun, and old Moon, so do they work inwardly in us today and are carried about by us as obstructive forces—but also as constructive forces, as the Earth bears them within herself.

When humans started to live within the physical body with "I"-consciousness in post-Atlantean times, from that moment onwards until our own day they have passed through various cultural epochs, in each of which they went through a kind of development. So, in the first of these, the ancient Indian epoch, work was mainly concentrated on the etheric body, in the second, the ancient Persian, on the sentient or astral body, in the third, the Egypto-Chaldean epoch on the sentient soul and in the fourth, the Greco-Roman epoch, on the intellectual soul. During this fourth cultural epoch, when human beings had sunk most deeply into matter, so that their eyes were completely closed to the spiritual world, something quite special occurred, which must be described as the greatest and most important event in the whole of earthly evolution.

When the Sun departed from the Earth and Moon, the powers intent on becoming more spiritual accompanied it and radiated their light and life from there onto the Earth. Through that, however, something was taken away from the Earth which originally belonged to it. The evolution of the Earth could advance to a certain stage without these powers, and especially because it received the rays of life and light from them. It was the same with regard to those entities that lived on Earth as human beings. They were able to develop an inner life of their own up to a certain degree, but they had also been deprived of something spiritual with the withdrawal of the Sun. When they had developed as far as they could as earthly beings; when, with the help of higher beings, they had developed their physical body to a stage where it could serve as a temple for the Divine-Spiritual, the Divine Being descended from above and inhabited this temple. The spiritual forces of the Sun united again with the Earth and therewith further spiritual development was made possible for humanity. Countless divine spiritual beings had sacrificed themselves in order for human beings to come into existence and evolve; many cosmic powers had helped to create humankind. Now the time had arrived in which the greatest sacrifice of all had to be made for humankind, in which the Godhead Himself, whose spiritual life was reflected in the Sun forces, descended to Earth to indwell a human body and allow His powers to stream down into the Earth. The Sun forces were bestowed upon the Earth and everything living on Earth had the stamp of the Spirit impressed upon it. From being self-aware human beings, we were then able to raise ourselves up to become self-aware spiritual beings. Our mortal "I" became an immortal seed living in the light of the Spiritual Sun.

Something similar to the way that the single human beings and humanity as a whole developed was enacted by the evolving Earth. After our physical birth we participate in the birth of our etheric and astral bodies; only then do we become independent of our surroundings and can develop further the "I." Then we develop our sentient soul; our intellectual soul, in which our "I" comes particularly to expression; and our consciousness soul, in which the "I" rises above itself to develop spirit self. Just at the time when human beings were evolving the intellectual soul in the Greco-Latin epoch, that soul-organ in which the "I" is particularly at home, the "I" received a new spiritual impulse through the fact that God descended to Earth and lived among humankind. Only then was humanity able to launch itself into a higher spiritual life. Earthly humankind was able to rise above itself and the human 'I" was given the opportunity to develop a divine "I."

An individual human being is at first born in respect of a physical body, later in respect of etheric and astral bodies, and only then receives the "I," so was the Earth first born out of the cosmos physically as ancient Saturn, then etherically as old Sun and astrally as old Moon, and only during the Earth evolution was the development of the "I" possible. So can ancient Saturn be thought of as an expression of the birth of the macrocosm or "cosmic humanity" on the physical plane, the Sun evolution as the birth of the macrocosmic etheric body, the Moon evolution as the birth of the macrocosmic astral body and the Earth evolution as the birth of the mighty, powerful macrocosmic "I." In the middle of this evolution the Higher "I" from the cosmos came down from spiritual spheres to unite with earthly development. The spirit of the cosmos descended into the World-"I."

Thus is cosmic evolution reflected in human beings and finds itself expressed in them. Only on Earth have we been born out of the cosmos as a self-conscious being and it is pre-ordained that we should learn to recognise the spiritual impulse that has been given to us, so that we may experience it inwardly and imitate what the World-Spirit has pre-lived on Earth.

Like plant blossoms opening to the sunlight, human beings opened themselves to the Spiritual-Sun long before these Sun forces had reunited with the Earth. They knew by that what a great event lay ahead in earthly evolution and how it was to take place through a mediator, rising from the ranks of humanity, who would surrender himself entirely to the light of the Sun, so that it might take complete possession of him. He would sacrifice his own being, so that the sublime Sun-Being might manifest through him on Earth. This knowledge was hidden as a seed, deep within humanity. And when the time had come, one of humankind grew like a living blossom towards the Sun-Spirit. It could receive the spiritual Sun forces into itself by sacrificing its three sheaths to that Great Spirit, so that He could descend into them and live in a human body on Earth. As a plant when it has been fertilized begins to die, so was this body dedicated to death when this event took place and when the blood flowed from the wounds of that body on Golgotha, the seed from that blossom sank into the Earth as a new impulse for spiritual life, which is to develop further in humankind. This impulse was implanted into every human being like a spiritual germ, which will unfold within when the soul is incited by new sensations and feelings to unfold a blossom to be fertilized by the sunlight of the Spirit. The same process takes place spiritually in the soul as takes place in the physical plant-form when the plant, with a kind of feeling of shame, withdraws into itself and starts to wither. This is how the human soul feels, full of shame for its own insufficiency, after it has been permeated by the light of the Spirit, and this feeling causes it to withdraw into its own inner being. When we have once experienced this Spirit Light in our soul, it illumines our inner self and we learn through that to see ourselves as we really are.

Then we follow the path that we otherwise tread when we abandon our bodily sheaths at death. We dive down into these sheaths and, as a personality, start to die. The human being dies as an individuality and gradually begins to live in the great Universal Being. Thus one can say: "In Christ I die." With the new spiritual impulse at first we rise into the astral body. We are confronted there by beings who act like those who have remained behind at the Moon stage. They express themselves through feelings, impulses and emotions of a baser sort. They stand at a level below that of "I"-development, because they belong to Moon evolution. Therefore they are not suffused with conscious "I"-force and are of an animal nature. Everything there like an outer world, which works in the human astral body as subconscious, unrestrained feelings and emotions. By facing our own inner world consciously we gain the strength to subdue these beings, to redeem them from within and gradually to transform them. If we descend still deeper into ourselves, into our etheric body, we find a world that we have built ourselves by the way we think in respect of all that we have collected from our surroundings in the way of traditions and habits. Beings who have remained behind at the Sun stage work there in the etheric body. They obstruct our development in respect of conscious, free and independent thinking. We will also eventually redeem these beings and transform them into wisdom-filled Beings of Light by means of the spiritual impulse which we received. If we then descend further, into our physical body, we encounter a whole world of forces that work there in our will as beings that remained behind at the Saturn stage. They strengthen our will as regards personal matters and direct it towards the center of our being. We are able to redeem these beings, too, through the Spiritual Light that streams into our inner depths from a center outside ourselves with which we feel intimately connected. Thus, at first, human beings experience themselves in their sheaths as the beings into which they have so far developed, but they view themselves from a new center, which has been created for them. They know that the development of those three bodily sheaths into which they have to descended belongs to earlier evolutionary stages of the Earth, and therefore they will of necessity also discover what has in particular to be developed during earthly evolution and has been established in their soul. It is this force that makes them into self-aware "I"-beings, so that they are able to descend in full consciousness into themselves. The plant seed gradually develops into the plant form and ripens to an independent existence within such a form. Human beings step in living existence through the gate of death when they make themselves independent of their bodily sheaths. Then they discover the spiritual germ within them which has been implanted in their soul by the Christ-impulse. The Christ-Light rays towards them out of their own being and, as the ripe seed sinking into the earth when the plant has died, this spiritual germ falls away from the personality and sinks into the great Universal Light. Then the Light, which has been united with the Earth since the event of Golgotha, shines forth from the interior of the Earth towards humankind. Then we are able to say: "I die in Christ, but I shall be born again to the universal existence." And we sense and experience the meaning of the words: "Those who loseth their life for my sake shall find it."

As humankind has been born out of the macrocosm as a microcosm, as a self-aware "I"-being, so will they gradually retrace their steps into the macrocosm by learning to live in it again with their "I"-consciousness. The spiritual powers have gradually withdrawn from humankind after having showered them with all their sacrificial offerings, so that they now must find their own path of spiritual ascent and learn to live once more consciously and voluntarily in the spiritual world.

The first experience humankind has of these spiritual beings is through their intimate connection with the great Earth-Mother, by whom they were engendered as individual beings, to whom they belonged, and with whom they were far more intimately connected in past ages of evolution. They experienced these past ages as the ancient Saturn, the old Sun and the old Moon evolutionary periods. They descended into their own inner self and experienced the beings who work there in their three sheaths; in their astral, their etheric and their physical bodies, and then they found the true center of their own being and the Christ-Light illumined them. They then also entered into those conditions of earthly evolution in which the three sheaths of the Earth were developed; the astral, etheric and physical bodies of planet Earth, and experienced there the spiritual beings that belong to this development and pour their forces into it. Then the human soul proceeds further and experiences that Spiritual Power which, during earthly evolution, entered into the Earth as the Christ-Light.

The whole cosmic development into which humankind themselves are woven, appears like a mighty tableau. Everything takes place around them and the whole of evolution lives and weaves within them. They feel themselves as a focal point in which all the beings and forces active in evolution meet together. The forces stream in and out of them and they themselves are the product of these forces. In these effects they find a firm center like an inner kernel around which everything is grouped and this center-point is the Christ-Being, the nucleus of macrocosmic and microcosmic evolution. Like a new center-point out of which everything flows and into which everything returns, the source of all life and of all evolution rays towards them as Divine Spirit, standing behind creation, which was active before created things existed. And as they feel themselves embedded as human beings within earthly evolution, so do they recognize themselves as spiritual beings in this divine source of all life. In the depths of the soul lives the Christ-power, within the self-aware spirit-germ of the "I"-forces. Beyond the bodily sheaths it exists as the Spirit of all things, the Holy Spirit, as a higher "I"-force that is the true and incorruptible center of all life.

When human beings recognize themselves thus as spiritual beings within the Universal Spirit, they can perceive the significance of the words of the Rosicrucian maxim: "I shall be reborn in the Holy Ghost," for as a new creation they stand confronting their former human self, a being who, to begin with, has to acquire the attributes and abilities they need for this spiritual existence, just as a child has to learn how to use its bodily organs in the physical world. And again, this spiritual being has to experience within itself the three spiritual forces that come to expression in cosmic evolution as feeling, thinking and willing; as love, wisdom and strength. For as the child at first learns how to stand and walk, so must human beings learn to find their direction and their route in the spiritual world. This can only be achieved through feeling, through a loving confrontation with all one meets. Then one must learn to recognize truth by understanding the wisdom of worlds as it resounds within oneself, by allowing the music of the spheres to sound within one and fathom its meaning, just as a child learns to understand speech. Then one gradually learns to recognize how truly to live in the spirit, by experiencing a center within oneself from which one's will-impulses and life-impulses radiate out, so that one can express oneself through speech and through one's whole being. That is why Jesus Christ speaks the words: "I am the Way, the Truth and the Life: no man cometh unto the Father but by me." No one can attain to the true spiritual source of all existence, to the Father, who has not developed these three forces in spirit and united them in the proper way.

The evolution of humankind is expressed in a symbol, the symbol of the black cross with the red roses, which belongs to a deeply significant Rosicrucian saying. One feels this symbol to be something that is alive, something that is interwoven and enlivened by the spiritual forces that have built up one's body as it has been formed by the Godhead. By that, however, one knows that it is possible for one to develop one's soul by exerting one's own powers. One knows that not only must one's blood become purified like the red sap of the rose, but that the black cross has to be transformed by purifying the nature of one's sheaths to grow beyond what is merely personal and by devoting oneself to something infinitely greater than oneself. Then one dies in Christ and the dark cross transforms in one's soul to a gleaming, shining cross. The red roses expand to an infinite circle when the soul penetrates ever further and further into the macrocosm until it feels as if it were itself this circle. In the all-encircling macrocosm one then experiences that one is in a new existence.

Then, in a mysterious way, the colors of the symbol are changed, the roses appear green and the cross white. The soul can only guess at the full meaning of this when it experiences the force that streams towards it. As though raying towards it from higher spiritual spheres, the soul sees and recognizes this holy symbol. It appears, strict and powerful, as a summons to constant work, so that someday the great ideal may be achieved, which is possible for everyone to realize when they are born again in the Holy Spirit.

———————

Concerning the Mantra "The Stones are Mute." (See p.172)

There are no explanations for this mantra in connection with the cognitive-ritual work. But in a lecture in Leipzig, October 13, 1906, the following statements were made, which refer to the content of the mantra:

I spoke to you earlier about the fact that powers are slumbering within every person that can be evolved to raise him or her to higher levels of existence. Just as the physical world can be perceived by means of physical organs, so can the supersensible world be perceived by means of supersensible organs. On that occasion the means were indicated—although only fragmentarily—by which a person can develop insight. Today we shall indicate certain methods used in intimate study that will lead over to our present theme.

At every step new instructions have to be followed. What is to be discussed today is not sufficient in itself, but it is all part of it. On the path of discipleship a direction is given, which states that a person should learn to cultivate a quite special relationship towards the spiritual world, a moral relationship. At the first step a person must realize that just as we are sensitive beings, so are the animals also sensitive beings. But as we each have an individual soul, so do the different animal species possess a group-soul. Thus all lions, all sharks, all frogs and so on have a soul in common. Put in another way: Whereas human beings have their soul within themselves, the souls of the animals—which, as it were, are the threads that link them together—stretch up into the astral world, where the group-souls are to be found. If one hurts another human being, that person alone feels the pain. But if one injures say, a lion, it is felt by the whole group-soul, which does not live on the physical plane, but on the astral plane.

The instruction consists of forming a relationship, a relationship in one's feelings towards the animal souls on the astral plane. There is an example for this: In some German districts the old Germanic peoples regarded the horse as an object of worship. They affixed a horse's skull to their houses as a symbol. The choice of such a symbol as this showed that the people had a quite special relationship to the horse. Where did that originate? The horse made its first appearance at a very definite moment. This animal appeared in the middle of the Atlantean epoch—of course, only gradually. This coincided with the development of intelligence. Though people did not realize it very clearly, they felt a connection with their horses comparable to the feelings between a lover and his loved one. The Arabs have even today a special connection with their horses. Some indications are to be found in mythology. It was thus that the intelligence of Odysseus invented a wooden horse. In this sense we will gain a perception of the group-souls of the different animals. When this is transferred into our consciousness, then the relationship to the astral plane starts to unfold.

In this way a moral attitude towards the plant world can develop. The esotericist does not only see the beauty of the plant, but perceives something akin to a smiling or a sad countenance. One gains a lot by this moral perception. If one cultivates such a moral relationship then one comes into relationship with the lower regions of devachan.

One can even acquire a fine perception for the lifeless mineral kingdom. The minerals have a group-soul on the devachan plane, just as the animals possess a group-soul on the astral plane. The souls of the minerals live in devachan. Therefore they are not available to us. As the fly, when it walks over our hand, is unaware that there is a soul within it, so have we no notion that stone's have souls.

If stones possess souls, then you will also be able to understand how a moral understanding of them can arise. A human or animal body has desires, passions, driving-impulses. The body of a plant no longer contains any passions, but it still has a driving force. The body of the stone has neither desires, nor driving-force, therefore it sets an ideal for us in that our impulses must become spiritualized. And in the far distant future of humankind that will be accomplished: we will possess bodies without desires and impulses. One day the human being will be like a diamond, no longer having inner impulses, but such things will then be outwardly under control.

The mineral already displays such chastity today, it is matter without desire. This desirelessness must already be cultivated by the esoteric pupil at the present time. In this sense the stone stands higher than animal, plant, or human beings. An ancient Rosicrucian saying states: I have placed and hidden the eternal creator word in the stones; chaste and modest they hold it in the depths of physical existence.

If one can raise such perception of the stones into spiritual experience, one will become clairvoyant in the highest regions of devachan.

Concerning Sign, Handclasp, and Word

The following detailed explanation answers a question about Freemasonry and its purpose in life, given in one of the lectures to the Goetheanum workmen. The answer Rudolf Steiner gave in a lecture in Dornach on the June 4, 1924, is here used as a preface to this subject (CW 353).

Present-day Freemasonry, one could say, is actually only a shadow of what it once was. I have already alluded here many times to the fact that in very ancient times of human evolution there were no schools as there are today, nor churches, nor art colleges as we know them, but that was all one thing. The ancient Mysteries, as they were called, consisted at the same time of education, art-training and religious instruction. Only later did they separate. So for our Central European districts, one could say, it only became like that in the eleventh or twelfth century; in earlier times the cloisters, I should like to say, were a token of former days. But in very ancient times it was the case that schools, churches and art colleges were one and the same thing. It was a fact that in the Mysteries all that went on there was taken much more seriously than it is today, for instance, in our schools and also in our churches.

It was at that time the case that one had to prepare oneself for a very long time before one was allowed to learn. Today the decisive factor as to whether one is allowed to study or not is a principle which is basically unconnected with learning. Today the deciding factor for the person who wants to learn is actually whether money is forthcoming or not, isn't it? That, of course, has nothing whatever to do with the person's abilities. But it was quite different in times gone by. At that time one sought throughout all humankind—one had much greater discrimination then than one has today—those who were the most gifted. Of course the thing came into decline in most cases, because people are so egoistic; but the principle was originally so that one chose the most gifted people. And they were only then entitled to be taught about spiritual matters, not simply through drill and outer training and by methods which are used today, but by inner spiritual education.

This spiritual education, however, is connected with the fact that one learns to develop some specific abilities during the time of preparation. You must only consider the fact that, when one takes something into one's hands in ordinary life, one only has a vague feeling of what one is handling; and the most one attains to nowadays is that people can sometimes distinguish one kind of material from another, that they are able to sense some kind of difference in what they feel. But people today have a very dulled sense of feeling—I mean in the purely physical sense—they can distinguish between warm and cold. At best there are people who develop a finer sense of touch if they are constrained to do so, as, for instance, blind people. There are also blind people who are able to feel the shape of letters by passing their hands over the paper. Every letter is slightly raised on the surface of the paper. If the sense of touch is finely attuned in the fingertips one is able to feel the letters. Those are the only people who learn to develop a more delicate sense of touch these days. Usually the sense of touch is not developed at all, but one can learn an enormous amount if one can acquire such a sensitive feeling especially in one's fingers and fingertips. Today one distinguishes heat and cold through other means than by the sense of touch. Yes, one can do that nowadays by reading a thermometer; by that means fine differences in temperature become visible. But the thermometer was only discovered in the course of time. Before that people only had their sense of touch. To begin with the sense of touch, especially in the fingers and the fingertips, was particularly developed in the preparatory instruction in the Mysteries. And so one learned to acquire a very acute sense of touch.

Who was it, whose delicate sense of touch was prepared in this way in the Mysteries? Well, other people had not such a fine sense of touch. Let us suppose that somewhere or other, in some other place, there was a Mystery center. People travelled about a lot in olden days; they travelled almost as far as we do today, and one can be astonished at the speed with which they got about. They had no railways; but they traveled because they were more nimble, because they could walk faster, became less tired, walked better, and so on.

And now such people met one another on their way. When two of them, with such a fine sense of touch, shook hands, they noticed this capacity in one another and one said about that: they recognize one another by their fine sensibility. That is what one calls the handclasp—the clasp with which one shook hands in olden times and noticed that the other person had this greater sensitivity.

Now, consider further this second thing: when one discovered that the other person had a greater sensitivity one pursued the matter further, for one learned something else. In olden times one did not do so much writing as one does today; one actually wrote only very seldom and those were the most sacred documents. Certainly there was also a kind of correspondence in antiquity; but this correspondence consisted mainly of signs. So many signs and symbols were created for a variety of purposes. It happened that people who did not belong to the Mysteries, who were not sages, as one called them, travelled only short distances, they did not go very far. But the scholars, the sages, travelled a lot. They had to know not only all languages, but also all dialects. It is of course difficult, if one is a North German, to learn the Swiss dialect. But for those who were in the Mysteries there were certain signs for the things which interested them, apart from the language they spoke. Let us say, for instance, that the usual gesture one uses to express one's feelings is developed further: I understand—; or: What you say to me is of no account—; or: We understand one another well—. One made the sign of the Cross in it. Thus there was a fully developed sign language, just among the wise old sages, and one put into such sign language all that one knew. So you can see: Everyone belonging to the High Schools of that time, to the Mysteries, had signs for everything. Let us say, for example, that they wished to preserve these signs, they first of all drew them. So did the drawn symbols originate.

It is interesting to note that there are still languages today that clearly demonstrate that they have originated from these symbols. This is shown for instance in Sanskrit, the ancient language of the Indian people. One is able to discern through this that everything has arisen out of wavy lines and straight ones. Crooked lines indicate dissatisfaction, antipathy; straight lines indicate sympathy.

Consider for a moment: someone knows that straight lines indicate sympathy and that crooked lines signify antipathy. And now I wish to tell that person something. I also have my sign for that. He wants to say something to me;—that might be all right to begin with, but later there may be difficulties. You see, here everything is still in good order; later he draws a snaky line; then things might go wrong. And so one had symbols for everything. With the one or other symbol those who belonged to the Mysteries came to an understanding with one another again. So that along with the handclasp one also had the sign.

One used to attach something quite special to words in earlier times. When one utters words nowadays one no longer actually has any idea what lies behind them. But one can still have a feeling for what is inherent in the sounds. You will easily perceive that when someone is in a particular situation in life and begins: A [ah]—then that has something to do with wonder. A—the letter A is wonder. Now you add to that the letter R: therein lies a "rolling forward," a "raying forth." A = wonder, R = raying forth.

Now we certainly know already what we have just said about the sunbeams. But even when the sunbeams are only apparent, when they are not what they seem to be, it will still appear as though they ray out. Now just imagine someone says to you: Up there is something that rays down to me on Earth, something that causes wonderment when it appears to me in the morning. He expresses his wonder with A, but the fact that it comes from above he expresses through R. Thus he expresses that with : RA. Yes, that is what the ancient Egyptian called his Sun-God: RA! In each of these letters there lies feeling and we have combined the letters to form words. There was widespread perception in that. That has long been forgotten. One gets an inkling of it through various things. Take for instance the sound I [ee]. It gives one a kind of slight enjoyment; one comes to terms with what one has experienced. I. That is why a giggle is expressed by "hee hee." That is a small pleasure. So every letter contains something specific. And there is a science by which one can invent words if one has an understanding of the sounds contained within them.

Now there is one thing you might say, gentlemen: Yes, if that is so, then there really ought to be only one language! Originally, in the very beginning, there was only one language; when one still had a sense for the sounds and for these letters, then there was only a single language. The languages then became differentiated when the people scattered. But originally they sensed that and the Mysteries gave proper instructions as to how one should develop this sense for sounds and letters and how to make them into words. Therefore the Mysteries had their own language. This language was universally spoken among people within the Mysteries. They did not speak with one another in dialect, but what was said was understood by all. When one of them said RA the other knew that it was the Sun which was meant. When one of them said E [eh], for instance—just feel what it is like: E, I start back in fear, it is not pleasant: E = I have a slight feeling of fear! Then, take the sound L: that is just as though something disappears into the air, like something that flows, and EL, well, that is as though something is dispersed which causes a slight uneasiness, something of which one is slightly afraid. Thus in Babylon EL signified God. Everything was named according to this principle. Or take what it says in the Bible: When one says: O—that gives a sudden involuntary feeling of wonder. In the case of A one has a pleasurable sensation, a feeling of wonder which one enjoys; O—one starts back. H or CH is the breath. So one can say: O = starting back in amazement; H = breath; I = one points to something and is pleased by it, it gives gentle pleasure = I. And M, that is: one would like to participate. You have the feeling when you say M: M—the breath is exhaled, one flows out after the breath; M therefore is a going forth. Now we shall put all that together: EL, as we have seen, is a spirit coming from the wind, EL; O = that is the yielding astonishment; H = the breath; that is thus the more refined spirit working in the breath; I is the slight feeling of pleasure; M = surrender. There you have the word ELOHIM with which the Bible starts; there are these sounds contained in it. One can therefore say: What are the Elohim? The Elohim are beings active in the wind, of whom one is slightly afraid and from whom one starts back with fright, but who give us pleasure through their breath and themselves take pleasure in us when we turn towards them in surrender: Elohim. And so it was originally possible to study what the words actually mean according to their sounds and letters. People have no feeling any more for how things actually are.

What is the plural of the word "Wagen" [cart, wagon] in the Swiss dialect? Is it "Wagen" here too, or is it "Wägen?" (answer : Wagen).[6] It is still "Wagen." Then the thing is already mixed up; the original would have been: "der Wagen, die Wägen!" We can form the plural in different ways. For instance, we have: "der Bruder, die Brüder" [brother, brothers]. But that is the same in Switzerland, isn't it? You do not say "die Bruder?" Well then, "der Bruder, die Brüder." Or let us say: "Das Holz, die Hölzer" [wood, pieces of wood]. One does not say, "die Holzer" here either, does one? You see, gentlemen, to form the plural the vowel becomes modified; i.e., a into ä [ae], u into ü [ew as in few], o into ö [as in œvre]. Why is that? You see, the mutation of the vowel means that the matter has become hazy! If I observe one brother he is quite distinct as a person; when I see several brothers the thing becomes indistinct, I then have to distinguish between one brother and the others, and if I am unable to do so, the thing becomes vague. One has to look at the one and the others. The process of becoming vague is always indicated by the mutation. Wherever there is a change of vowel sound in a word, something or other is not clear.

There is something in language by which the complete human being is made manifest, the whole person is there. And so people expressed how a meaning lay in the letters they inscribed, how the signs had a meaning. "A" was always astonishment. When the ancient Hebrew wrote [aleph], he then said to himself: Who has astonishment on Earth? The animals do not really show astonishment, only humans. Therefore he named the human being in general: "being astonished." When he wrote his [aleph], the Hebrew "A," this also signified the Human Being.

---

6. This answer is wrong; it is "Wäge" in Swiss-German, as Rudolf Steiner guessed.

And so it was that every letter signified at the same time an object or a being. All that was known to those who stood within the Mysteries. When, therefore, one of them was and met another with similar knowledge, they recognized each other through the word. So one may say: In ancient times it was so, that those who had learned something, those who knew a lot, recognized one another by handclasp, sign, and word. Yes, gentlemen, but there was something in that! The whole scholarship was summed up in symbol, handclasp, and word. For by cultivating a sense of touch one learned to distinguish objects. By being in possession of signs and symbols one had an imitation of all secrets of nature, and through the word one got to know the inner human being. So one might say: In the handclasp one had perception, in signs one had a revelation of nature, and through the word one experienced others with their inner astonishment or drawing back, enjoyment, and so on. One had nature and humankind and reproduced them in sign, handclasp, and word.

Now, in the course of human evolution there arose what, on the one hand, separated off as the university and later as the schools, and on the other hand as the churches and as art. None of these three understood any longer what it had been like originally and handclasp, sign, and word were completely lost. Only those understood who one day woke up to the fact: My goodness! Those old sages possessed a certain power through what they knew. We have a legitimate power when we know something that benefits our fellow human beings. If no one had known how to build an engine, no one would ever have had engines! So it is when someone knows something that will benefit humankind; that is a justified form of power. Later, however, people acquired power by merely copying what others did, by copying the outer symbol. Just as the one sign or other signified something in earlier times, and one forgot the meaning of it later, so did all that lose its meaning. And through copying the ancient Mysteries, all sorts of things developed which, I should say, is only an outer show. What did folk do? They did not possess any finely developed sense of touch, but they agreed upon a sign by which they could recognize one another. They shook hands in a particular way, whereby the one knew: This person belongs to that Society. Then they recognized each other by the handclasp. Then they made some sort of a sign. The sign and the handclasp were different according to whether one was in the first, second or third degree. By that means people recognized one another. But there was nothing more to it than a sign of recognition. And in the same way, for every degree there were certain words which they were able to speak in certain Freemasonry branches: Let us say, for instance, for the first degree they had, if you wish,—what is the word?—: Jachin. One knew that the person learned the word Jachin in the Freemasonry lodge, otherwise he would not be a member in the first degree. That was just a password. And in the same way he made the sign, and so on.

Now actually this kind of Freemasonry only developed after everything else about the Mysteries had been forgotten, and some of the old things that were no longer understood, were imitated. So that the parts of the ritual that Freemasonry has taken over are usually no longer understood by Freemasons; even sign, handclasp, and word are not understood by them, because they do not know anything of their meaning. They are unaware, for instance, of the fact that when they speak the word of the second degree: Boaz, that the B is the equivalent of a house; O, as I told you, is a restrained astonishment; A is pleasurable astonishment; S [sound of "z"] is the sign for the snake; with that has been expressed: We recognize the world as a large house built by the great World-Architect, a world about which one can be both anxiously and pleasurably astonished and in which there also exists evil, the snake. Yes, one knew something about that in olden times; one looked at nature in this way; one looked at people in this way. Today the people of certain Freemasonry branches possessing the second degree, pronounce the word "Boaz" quite unconsciously. In the same way, you see, if a person with the third degree placed a finger on the pulse of another person, that was actually in recognition of the fact that the other had a refined sense of touch. That was noticed by the way the finger was placed on the pulse. That later became the handclasp for the third degree. People today only know that if a person comes up to you and takes your hand in this way, then the person is a Freemason. So there is actually something ancient, grand and worthy of respect in these things, something in which all previous knowledge was embodied; that has now become a mere formality, something which does not mean anything anymore. So it is that the Freemasonry fellowship today retains such things as that; it retains ceremonies and has a ritual. That belongs to a time in which one portrayed everything through ritual and ceremony, so that it got through to people. Freemasonry still continues that practice. And so we can say that, in this inner respect, Freemasonry has no longer any meaning nowadays.

But in this way it has become very boring for some people to participate in what the Freemasonry societies instituted; for it actually degenerated into a kind of play-acting. It needed something to replenish it, to be poured back into it. And so it came about that Freemasonry became more or less politically motivated or engaged in the propagation of doctrines or religious enlightenment. The unenlightened Roman Catholic doctrines were administered from Rome. Those teachings which were at variance to Rome were diffused by the Freemasons. On that account Rome— the Roman liturgy—and Freemasonry became sworn enemies. That no longer has anything to do with what Freemasonry ritual, sign, handclasp, and word signify, but it is something that intruded. In France the Society was not called "Society," but the "Orient de France," because everything is derived from the East—"Grand Orient de France," that is the Great French Society of Freemasons—the other part of it: sign, handclasp and word, is only there to keep the people together, it is that by which they can recognize one another. The ritual gathering is that through which they meet one another on particular ceremonial occasions. In the same way others meet in church, so do the Freemasons come together for ceremonies derived from the ancient Mysteries. That holds them together.

It used to be a custom, especially in Italy, at times when secret political societies were inaugurated, that people gathered together amid ceremonies in which they recognized one another through signs and handshakes. Political societies and political unions have always had a link with this ancient Mystery wisdom. And it is a very strange thing today: If you go today into some Polish and Austrian districts you may find posters which have strange signs on them and letters which combine to form words. One does not immediately know what these placards denote, but such a placard as this, which is posted up everywhere in Polish and Austrian districts today, is the outward sign for a society founded on certain nationalistic lines by a youth organization. That is the same sort of thing. That kind of thing is very widespread and the people concerned know very well that the sign they use has a certain very powerful effect. There are groups, the German Folk-Group, for instance, that has an ancient Indian symbol: two intertwined snakes—or, if you like, a wheel which has been transformed into a swastika. Today those people have that as their emblem. And you will often hear that the swastika has been adopted again as the symbol of certain chauvinistic folk circles. That is done out of a tradition that the people of ancient times expressed their authority in this way. And so it always was on a grand scale in the Society of Freemasons. The Society of Freemasons actually exists for the purpose of uniting certain people, which it does through ceremonies, signs, handclasp, and word. And it also follows secret aims in that it keeps certain secrets among all those people who are linked together by the ceremonies, signs, handclasp, and word. Of course, secret aims can only be carried out when they are not known to everyone, and that is how the Freemasonry societies usually work when they follow political or cultural aims and such like.

But now there is one thing you could say, gentlemen. You see, those who are linked to the Freemasonry societies cannot be condemned on that account, for they often have the very best and noblest intentions: they just hold the view that the only way one can influence people for these aims is by means of such alliances, and for that reason most Freemasonry alliances also set themselves the task of promoting charities on a grand scale. It is good to practice charity and humanity. That is also something which is practiced on a large scale by these societies. Therefore it is no wonder that Freemasons are always able to point to the fact that a very great deal of very humanitarian and charitable work is endowed and founded by Freemasonry societies. One must only remind oneself that, at the present day, all such things are actually no longer appropriate. For what, to be sure, do we mainly reject in matters of this kind? We must reject differentiation. A spiritual aristocracy would soon arise as a result of that, and that should not be. And the democratic principle, which must come into its own more and more, is actually completely at odds with Freemasonry, just as much as is the closed priesthood. So one can say: It is a fact today that whoever can still understand what is contained in the first, second and third degrees in certain Freemasonry ceremonies—which Freemasons themselves often do not comprehend or recognize—often refer back to quite ancient wisdom; but that does not have such great significance. The thing of great significance is the fact that actually in many Freemasonry societies or alliances, many political or other charitable social endeavors are alive. But the Catholic Church and Freemasonry are at daggers drawn. That, however, only came about during the course of time.

Now it is very easy to misinterpret things. The following once happened: Freemasons wear particular garments for their ceremonies; they have an apron, for instance, out of lambskin, the lambskin apron. Some people have said: Freemasonry is only play-acting around the job of a mason, because masons wear leather aprons. But that is not true. The leather apron that they wear—which was originally always of lambskin, not having gradually evolved in that way—was there for the purpose of showing that a person belonging to such an order was not supposed to be a wild young blood on account of his passions; his sexual parts should be covered by his apron, and that was the sign for that. Thus it was something which expressed the human character by means of signs. And it is the same with very many symbols that are connected with garments.

There are also higher degrees in which vestments are worn that are very similar to those of a priest. Every single item has a meaning. For instance, I told you that, apart from a physical body, one also has an etheric body. And just as the priest wears a white shirt-like linen garment to express the etheric body, so do certain higher degree freemasons wear such a garment; and for the astral body—which is colored—one wears a toga, an over garment. That is what it expresses. And the cloak, connected with the helmet, expresses the power of the "I."

All these things lead back to ancient, very meaningful and important customs which have lost their significance today. If one is very attached to Freemasonry one should not take what I have said as something derogatory. I only wished to explain how it is. There can of course be such a thing as a Freemasonry order that is made up of exceptionally fine people, and so on. And at the present time something of that sort can be very important. Actually, what people usually learn when they become doctors or lawyers— Yes, that does not really touch their hearts! And that is why many lawyers and doctors become genuine Freemasons, so that they at least have the pomp and solemnity of the ancient ceremonies and something about which they do not have to think a lot. But that is at least something. Sign, handclasp, and word still point to the fact that human beings do not lead only a material existence.

From an instruction lesson, Berlin, December 16, 1911

Sign, handclasp, and word are not signs only to enable people to recognize one another, but they have a deep esoteric meaning.[7]

The sign, whereby one forms a right angle between the thumb and the flat of the hand, is connected with the fact that the hand is an organ of knowledge. It was already mentioned in the previous lecture cycle (cycle 41) that hands and feet are organs of knowledge, and even better ones than the brain.[8]

The physical brain is, as it were, crystallized from the etheric body, as ice is from water. One can sense an intimate connection existing between these two "brains," and how the physical brain is actually a kind of reflecting apparatus for what takes place in the etheric brain. One can experience that particularly when one exerts oneself to any great extent with things of the physical plane, or when one wants to call something to mind. It is always then—whether one knows it or not—the etheric body, which is sympathetically involved, but also particularly the physical brain, which lies like a block in the etheric brain and is prevented from keeping pace with the mobility of the latter. One then senses very clearly that it is not the etheric brain that tires—that could call up thoughts and memories ad infinitum—but the physical brain cannot keep pace with it and has the effect of a foreign body within the etheric body. Through that one feels the fatigue of the physical brain all the more. And though one could go on thinking with the etheric brain indefinitely, one would only make oneself ill thereby. The normal connection would be broken through and the physical part would become as though dead. It is impossible to

---

7. Sign and handclasp were different for each degree, but have not been authentically handed down. In notes from an instruction lesson in Munich, September 5, 1912, it has been recorded that on admittance to the first degree (1.°) it was also said that the sign for 1.° will in future be the expression for self-knowledge or for what is understood by the injunction: "know thyself!"—The word for 1.° was "Jachin," for 2.° "Boaz," for 3.° "Mach ben ach." On the subject of sign, handclasp and word see also: *Things of the Present and of the Past in the Spirit of Man; Flashlights on the Deeper Impulses of History* (CW 167) (typescript, lecture 4).

8. See: *Background to the Gospel of St. Mark,* lecture 7 (CW 124).

break the parallel connection between the physical and etheric brain to any great extent.

In our physical brain we have a very true impression of the functions and processes of the etheric brain. In the case of the etheric hands, the connection with the physical organs is different. Just as with the brain, the hands also express certain processes of the etheric body, but between the physical hands and their task and what corresponds to them in the etheric body, there is a much greater difference than between the physical head and the corresponding etheric part of the head. What the hands do has a much purer sense function, and what the etheric organs of the hands are able to do is very inadequately revealed and expressed by what the physical hands perform. These etheric hands are real spiritual organs of the elementary or etheric body. A much higher, more intuitive spiritual action is performed by the [etheric] organs of the hands, which are portrayed so inadequately by the physical hands. These etheric organs lead already into the supersensible world and can make observations in the same. Rather paradoxically one could say that the human brain is the most unsuitable organ for the perception of the world. The hands—seen etherically—are much more significant and skilful organs of perception than the brain. On the path of initiation one does not learn very much when one switches over from the use of the physical brain to the use of the etheric brain.

What the hands have to perform is connected with the petals of the lotus flower in the region of the heart, which sends out its forces from the heart into the hands in such a way that the etheric hands are transformed into organs of perception. Learning to understand these differences gives an idea of how one familiarizes oneself with initiation. To perceive how the physical brain fills up the etheric brain is not important. What is important is to perceive how quite different organs can be formed within the human being. What was at first established in the outer physical body, such as in the hands, was transformed from within to enable us to experience other things.

If we place the hands on the larynx so that the thumb of the right hand lies near to the ear and the flat of the hand lies below the chin at the height of the larynx, we thereby exclude the etheric currents from the head and form the rest of the body into an organ of perception.

That is how knowledge becomes spiritualized. If one stands up straight in this position, it helps one to absorb knowledge in a spiritual fashion. The larynx is connected with the thinking that humans developed during the old Moon evolution. Brain thinking is a product of Earth evolution and can only reach as far as the sense world, not into the spiritual world.

By the handshake, in which the thumb forms a right angle, we also perform something very significant. By that means, something of a most brutal nature, which occurs in the relationship between one and another person in our materialistic age, is excluded from taking place. We thereby refine the currents and so change our relationship to the outer world. If we touch a particular point on the back of the hand with a thumb bent in this way, the two currents connect with one another and a far-reaching beneficial influence can be exerted.

There are no primal causes in the sense world. These only exist in the supersensible world. On Earth there are only symbols. We should become familiar with these in our temple, so that we can apply them and learn to use them in a beneficial way. Ignorant anatomists of today think that the heart pumps the blood. But the blood is really driven by currents in the etheric body. The heart is only the sign that at that point there is a confluence of etheric currents. So, for instance, our muscles are a sign for the movement that arises in the astral body as sound. Without the muscles we should not be able to know anything about the movement, they reflect the movement. Our whole body is a reflecting apparatus in its every part.

The sacred word [JACHIN] is not pronounced, but spelled out, as it was explained during admittance. It is a word from the original tongue, and whoever exchanges it in thought with another person, is able to transmit healing forces from one person to another. If somebody is overcome by grief, or if we meet somebody who has to struggle against a violent feeling of discomfort or sickness, so one asks the question inwardly: Do you know the sacred word? One directs it towards the other person in one's thoughts, while one imagines that the other person gives the answer—of course, all by means of thought—in this way one exchanges the letters and the two syllables with the other person. With that the current from the one larynx passes over into the other one, and one is thereby able to influence people by that means in a good way, without interfering in their freedom.

The sign regulates the attitude of a person towards the outside world, the handclasp regulates the relationship of one person to another, and the word works therapeutically, bringing healing to one's fellow men and women.

From an instruction lesson, Berlin, February 6, 1913

What we do and think here as human beings, and the movements we make, are what the gods formerly did in order to bring about the creation of this our world. Spirit seeds for the future must be sown through the work and the ritual in our M.E. lodges. Magic is not something that can be carried out at random with the enactment of strange customs, but is something that prepares the way for the future of humankind and the world.

———————

Concerning the Seven Words of the Ritual for Promotion into the Second Degree (see p. 200)

From an instruction lesson, Christiania (Oslo), October 1913 (no exact date given)

The seven words:

Form	Strength	Number
Harmony	Word	Thought

"I"

should work in us like warmth and light do. We should meditate them separately as though we were absent from the body. In order to progress further you must really believe that the abilities that you possess can transcend what you are at present. You should trust in your soul, in your ability to progress. Human beings can do more than they do at present; they will evolve so far that they attain their goals.

*Concerning the Coffin Ceremony of the Ritual for Promotion
into the Third Degree (see p. 210 et seq.)*

From an instruction lesson, Cologne, May 12, 1913

Those who have taken part in the coffin ceremony of admission
into the third degree are unable to understand its meaning if they
regard the temple where we assemble as a place like any other
place on Earth and the symbols as though they were composed of
earthly objects. We should conceive of the temple as being something apart from the world, as for instance a vacuum produced in
a glass container when the air is drawn out of it from underneath
by a pump. Round about it there is air, but the air has been
extracted from the container. Or we could also say that it is as
though a piece of earth had been taken out and completely
removed from the remaining soil—meant symbolically, of course.
So, likewise is east, west and south meant spiritually. Everything
belonging to our temple is supersensible and the proceedings taking place therein must also be regarded as supersensible.

What is the meaning of the death we have to undergo when we
are admitted? When the Elohim decided at the beginning of
Earth evolution to create humankind, it was their intention to
create human beings according to their own image, so that every
part of human nature would express one of the Elohim. They
intended to mirror themselves in humankind. That, however, did
not occur on the Earth as we know it, but in a sphere, which we
now have to portray as surrounding the Earth like the ring
around Saturn. The Elohim worked upon this sphere from outer
space and saw themselves mirrored in the human beings whom
they had created. And human beings also looked down to a point
in the center of the sphere and saw themselves mirrored therein.
"That art thou," they could say to themselves. If Lucifer had not
interfered it would have remained like that for ever. Humankind
would have experienced eternal youth and the consciousness that
human beings had of themselves would have been the consciousness of what they saw on Earth as the "Thou art."

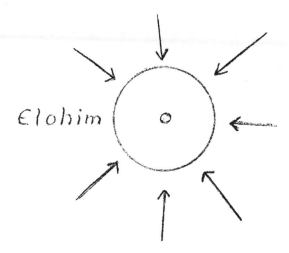

When Lucifer came with his activity, however, he also wished to be mirrored in humans and he accomplished this by penetrating into our inmost parts and raying out from there. Instead of the beauty and grandeur in which human beings had previously viewed themselves, ugliness and distortion now made their appearance. Like the serpent winding around the tree in the story of Paradise, so was the mirroring of Lucifer. In order to prevent humans from seeing themselves in Lucifer's ugliness, the Elohim squeezed the sphere together and cast human beings down onto the Earth.

The human being would have remained forever at the stage of a suckling babe, as humans were at that time, for even today the Elohim are still carrying out their formative work in the suckling child. Humans would have imbibed nourishment by sucking the substances of plants and animals, which at that time were quite different from what they are at present. In their consciousness, too, human beings would not have progressed beyond that of an infant.

In order for us to acquire self-consciousness, the Elohim introduced death into all earthly processes. Everything on earth is subject to death, and these forces now work in such a way that through the destruction they carry within themselves, they at the same time provide the strength to overcome destruction and thus to reach a higher condition. Our conception of death, as with almost everything on the physical plane, is the opposite of the true concept. It is only through death that we are enabled to return to that relationship with the gods and the divine world which we formerly enjoyed. Something in us has to die before we can find our right relationship again. The symbol of the coffin can only be understood when we conceive of it in this way.

We continually kill certain parts of our brain through our thinking. Thus there is a death process entailed in everything a person does after passing the age of the suckling child. The symbol of the coffin therefore signifies that we should be mindful of the fact that the whole of life is bound up with death. Thus our food is not a process of upbuilding for the body but a process of destruction, for nothing of the foodstuff is taken up into the body. The food contributes to the health of the body only when the forces of death have worked upon it to destroy it. If that does not happen our organism suffers. The whole of our nourishment serves the opposite purpose to that which science imagines. It serves to stimulate those forces that destroy the food, thereby building up the human being. It is similar with medicinal herbs. Only when they are capable of calling up the destructive forces of death, when they can destroy the remedy, do they work medicinally. And the reason why the chemical and metallic remedies work so strongly is because they bring about the destructive processes most quickly and easily.

And what would it have been like in the case of the Mystery of Golgotha if human beings had not descended to Earth to become acquainted with death? The Mystery of Golgotha would still have taken place, even upon Earth, and humankind would have observed it from their sphere, and what would have been destroyed there would have given human beings self-consciousness. They would no longer have said: "Thou art," but: "I am," and so would have attained self-consciousness in a supersensible fashion. Through the activity of Lucifer, the descent of Christ and the Mystery of Golgotha was delayed by a whole evolutionary period (from the fourth, Atlantean, to the fifth, post-Atlantean period) and it will therefore take us the same length of time until we can arrive at a true understanding of it (namely until the middle of the sixth age).

We know that, for about the last three decades, a new possibility has become available to humankind through the advent of Michael. Previously, since the fifteenth century, it had been the archangel Gabriel who had worked upon us, and indeed upon our brain, in such a way that we were enabled to form ideas about nature, which we could convert into science. Our intellect was led to form concepts about nature and people made laws about it which they held to be true laws of nature. Gabriel is the archangel who works upon the forces of propagation and upon the suckling child. His activity in the fifteenth and sixteenth centuries consisted in the fact that a part of these forces seized hold of the brain and built an organ into it through which the laws of nature could be taken up—it was not constructed from within, as one thinks, but received from without. Just as the infant howls and cries, so did humans cry out the laws of nature into the world with just as little awareness of their inner nature as the infant is conscious when it cries.

Then Gabriel was succeeded by Michael, and it is the latter's task to give us ideas about the supersensible in which truth and eternity are inherent. And Theosophy is the remedy which shall change our thinking so that we can find these ideas in ourselves and with them rise up once more above and beyond the Earth. The Michael forces are bound up with the forces of the Sun; they transform the organ in the brain in such a way that something akin to flashes of light occur in us, which reveal to us the depths that underlie the natural laws. This experience can come to us at any moment. The age in which we are now living is an age of expectancy. We should adopt the attitude of waiting for the higher concepts to come to us, to bring us knowledge of the eternal.

From the lecture in Stuttgart, June 14, 1921

Our temporal existence between birth and death is so constituted that we carry forces within us that continually kill us. These are the forces that make us solid and firm, that are involved in the building up of the skeleton and, in their morbid aspect, lead to sclerosis, gout, diabetes, and so forth. These are the forces that we have within us, which I should like to call the solidifying forces. That is the one thing. The other system of forces we have within us is the one that continually rejuvenates us. It is the power system that is especially typified when one succumbs to pleurisy, feverishness and everything that occurs together with a high temperature. From the anthroposophical point of view I have called the solidifying forces Ahrimanic and the forces leading to fever, which are warmth forces, I have called Luciferic. Both of these forces have to be kept in continual balance within the human being. If they are not kept in balance they lead in body, soul, and spirit to some kind of fatal extreme. If the feverish forces are not continually kept in check by the solidifying (salt-forming) forces [and vice versa], then one will inevitably develop sclerosis or get a temperature. If one develops only powers of understanding and has a leaning towards intellectuality one will fall prey to Ahriman. If one develops only the fiery element of desires and emotions, one will succumb to Lucifer. Thus one is always placed between two polarities and has to hold the balance.

But just think how difficult it is to hold the balance. The pendulum, which ought to be in balance, always tends to swing to one side or the other. There are three tendencies in us: the tendency towards balance, that towards warmth, and that towards solidification. We have to stay upright, so that we can typify humans symbolically as beings who have to continually struggle to maintain their upright position in the face of two forces which are always threatening our life.

The third degree of Freemasonry is portrayed as the threat to one's life by three traitorous powers, and by one's response to this threefold danger. This is symbolically represented by the applicant for initiation into the third degree being taught that one is in mortal danger at every moment of one's life and must raise oneself up. This is performed in different ways, the simplest of which is the following: the applicant is confronted by a man lying in a coffin with three murderers creeping up to kill him. The applicant thus experiences symbolically (in this guise) in a real ritual ceremony something important that is connected with life. So one really has to try to get acquainted with life, and then the symbols emerge from it as a result. Freemasonry has its shadowy side in the use of these symbols and in the performance of ritual ceremonies—up to the third degree in "blue" masonry and to many other things in "high-degree" masonry—and in the fact that these rituals are conceived out of age-old traditions, which are no longer understood. There is no longer any connection with their origins, which I shall make clear to you in a sketch. The people only look at the ceremonies, and that is the danger; they remain fixed in the ceremony and are not led deeper into it so that through it they could come to the spirit.

Concerning the Contents of the Fourth Degree

From an instruction lesson, Berlin, February 10, 1913

The human being is attached to selfhood in a 33-fold way. We have to overcome this selfhood through our "I." This selfhood of the human being is anchored in the 33 currents of the spinal cord. The seer observes how flowing currents emerge from the etheric and astral bodies, expressing themselves in the movements of the limbs, which are half held back in the organs of speech, in the larynx, where they form the sounds and then are rigidly detained in the head, brain, skull, and cerebral lobes. The brain: the symbols pertaining thereto in the lodge . . . [9]

Starting with the left hand : I   — an outward striving.

The sound I [ee]   — let the right eye wander.

Stretch = A [ah]   — let both eyes gaze into infinity.

Enclose = O [oh]   — look fixedly at a given point.

Cross over - E [eh]   — place right hand over the left, likewise cross the right foot over the left one in the same way that the optical nerves cross over in the human head.

Cupped hand = AO   — bend the body in a semi-circle.

Fist or grip tightly = U [oo]

---

9. The dots are like this in the notes.

You should not perform the movements, but check the same, pressing the limbs firmly against the body, but experiencing the movements as if you were carrying them out.

We ourselves are the lost word of creation

The sacred word is only used in the symbol

Where do we stand?

In the sign of the four.

Name the four:

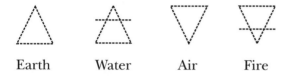

Earth   Water   Air   Fire

The four are also understood in the four sentences, which are always spoken in the lodge and which we know:

> Learn to be silent and power shall be yours.
>
> Renounce power and volition shall be yours.
>
> Renounce volition and feeling shall be yours.
>
> Renounce feeling and knowledge shall be yours.

The four complete the seven: Salt, Sulphur, Mercury.

Now the sacred word shall be separated again into the four: [10]

Earth	Water	Air	Fire
Gnomes	Undines	Sylphs	Salamanders

The one pillar is the Sun, the other the Moon; together they are the Earth.

---

10. The symbols reproduced here, in accordance with notes from participants, correspond to the handwritten symbols of Rudolf and Marie Steiner given on pp. 231 and 234. By comparison with the traditional Rosicrucian symbols, Earth-Water-Air-Fire, Earth has been exchanged with fire, water with air, air with water, fire with earth, but this may refer to a different esoteric aspect. Thus in notes from the Esoteric Class held in Munich, January 1, 1909 (published in CW 266) it is stated: "Earth and fire stand in esoteric relationship to one another, just as do air and water." Furthermore, in the Esoteric Class given in Berlin, February 12, 1908 (likewise published in CW 266) the symbols were used and explained in the traditional sense.

Why No Ritual Can Take Place between December 24 and January 6

From an instruction lesson, Hanover, Christmas 1911

The reason why no ceremony takes place in the gatherings of our esoteric brotherhoods during the days of the appearance of Christ, between December 24 and January 6, is that those we call the Wise Masters of the East retire during this time into their sanctuary in order to collect from there the forces that will then be bestowed by them in greater strength on the whole of humanity, as well as on our esoteric brotherhoods.

From an instruction lesson, Hanover, December 31, 1911

It has already been pointed out that in the days between December 24 and January 6, no esoteric meetings can take place in which a ritual is used. In the significant thirteen days that end with the spirit-birth of Christ, the Wise Masters of the East withdraw, in order to gather forces that they will let stream forth during the rest of the year onto humanity, and for us is the wisdom according to which we direct our striving.

Sketches and Explanations of the Ritual Objects

All preserved authentic instructions by Rudolf Steiner are reproduced in what follows. The sketch on the following page of arrangements in the Temple for the first and second degrees and the sketches on the following pages 320-327 are facsimile reproductions of drawings by Elisabeth Vreede of single objects according to Rudolf Steiner's instructions. On p. 328 is one of the sword symbols in its natural size, as it was used in admission ceremonies into the first degree. Pages 329 and 330 show sketches by Rudolf Steiner for a censer and the following page its completion.

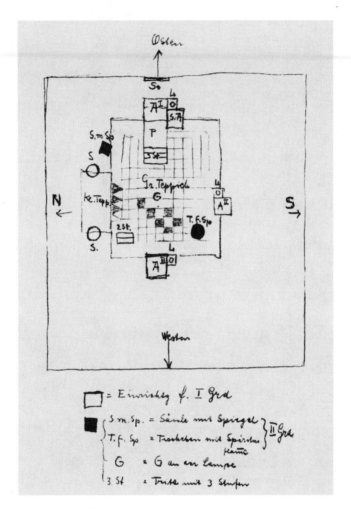

Layout of hall (temple) for the first and second degrees

(kl.Tepp. = Small carpet, Tapis; Gr. Teppich. = Large carpet;
S= Pillar AI, AII, AIII.= Altars I, II and III; So.= Sun.)

◻ = Arrangements for the first degree
     S.m.Sp.= Pillar with mirror
     T.f.Sp. = Small table with spirit   second degree
◼ = lamp
     G. = Letter G on the lamp
     [2 St. = 2 steps]
     3 St. = 3 steps

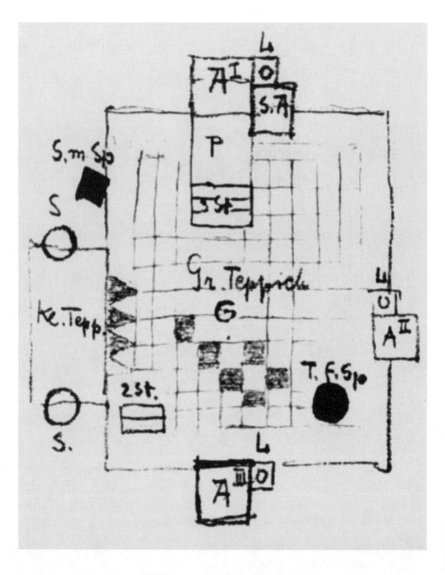

Enlarged detail of lodge layout

Sketches for Lodge Arrangements

Handwritten explanations of the sketches by Elisabeth Vreede (translated from Dutch)

<u>A.d.O.</u> [Altar of the East]

Cross with Crown of Thorns (sketch), in Catholic shops. The wreath [of Roses?] must hang in readiness on a nail within the altar. The Cross must be of a size which leaves room for the Holy of Holies (the Cup). Diameter of wreath 45 cm. Near the Holy of Holies: Mallet (see: "West").

<u>S.A.</u> Altar of the Pledge

Bible open at St. John Chapter XII / Upon it the triangle and trowel interlocked / (of tin, gilded) Drawing see "South" (trowel) / Form of the trowel exactly that belonging to an ordinary mason / Small candlestick. / Matches! / Snuffer in front of candle.

P = Small podium (P) in front of altar where Master stands.

S.   Sun above the altar: blue back- ground (more strongly ribbed material, sun of light yellowish-brown cloth. D as curtain decoration).

L = Candlestick (near every altar. See sketch at 'East').
In front of the Holy of Holies: a tray / with high rim. Can have an inner partition, but not necessary

On the altar a piece of felt. The rest will be attended to by Dr. Steiner.

<u>A.d.S.</u> [Altar of the South]

Censer, usual, from the Church. / Incense bowl, any kind, shape of no concern / square

<u>A.d.W.</u> [Altar of the West]

2 Compasses, rule, any size / Death's head (plaster cast). Pillars as desired. Dark blue and brick red /On the two pillars: a carved and an uncarved cube-shaped stone.

Large carpet (Like a chess board black/white). Of felt / width 1.80 / Length 3.10.

1° Padlock and chain. Stair with two steps.

II° Stair with three steps / Pillar with mirror.

From the ceiling: Lamp (the "ever-burning" lamp of the Church) / G made of cardboard or gilded tin-sheet.

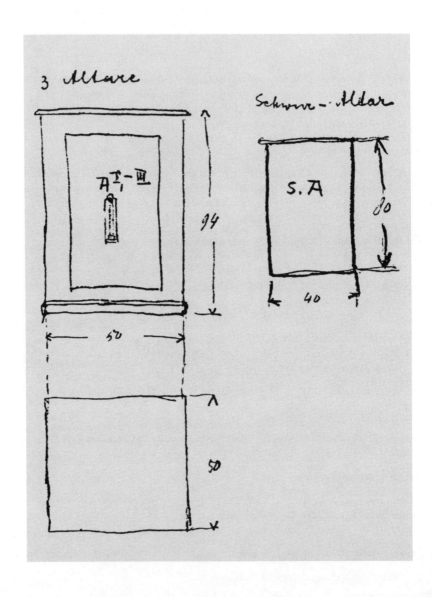

Altar measurements

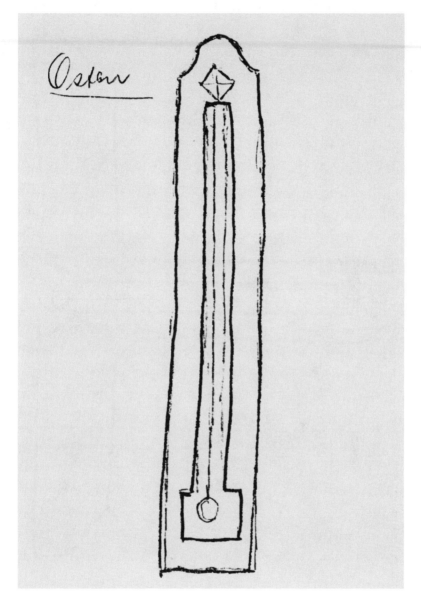

East

Plumb bob for the front of the altar. Height 18 cm.

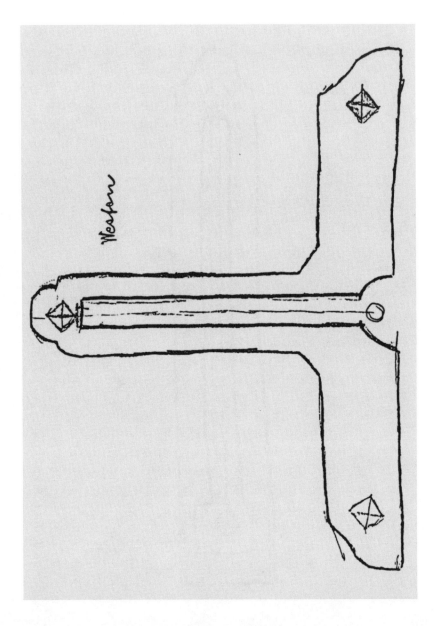

Weapon

Plumb bob for the altar of the West.

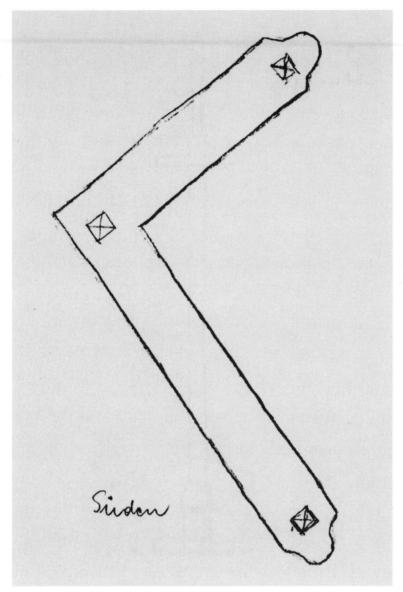

South

The Square (see p. 348)

Leuchter

1,35 m

The Candlestick (see p. 340)

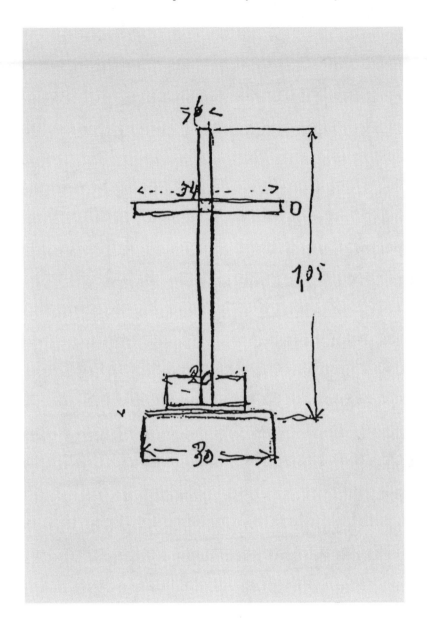

The Cross (see p. 348 et seq.)

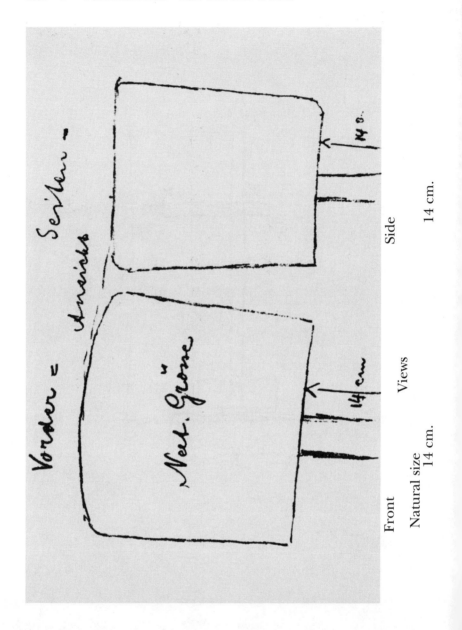

The Mallet (see p. 340 et seq.)

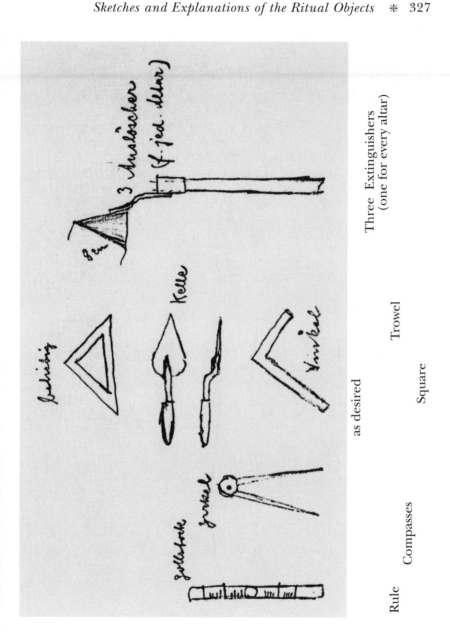

as desired

Three Extinguishers
(one for every altar)

Trowel

Square

Rule   Compasses

(For indications about the signification of these objects see p. 343)

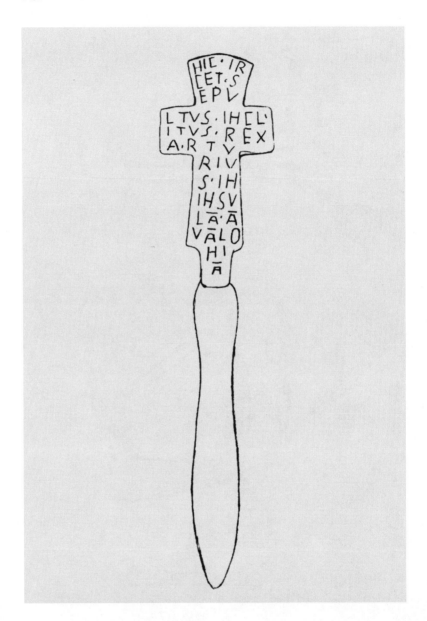

The Ritual Sword. Height 18 cm (see pp. 194 and 201)

Leaden cross excavated in the cemetery of Glastonbury Abbey c. 1191. Reproduced from: *Two Glastonbury Legends: King Arthur and St. Joseph of Arimathea* by J. Armitage Robinson. (Cambridge University Press, 1926). Inscription: "Here lies buried the illustrious King Arthur in the Island of Avalon."

Original drawing by Rudolf Steiner for a silver censer.

The planetary signs for Sun, Moon, Mars, and Venus are engraved on the foot. On the rim of the upper part are the stones belonging to the Zodiac. The vessel was probably made for the Cognitive-Ritual Section in England.

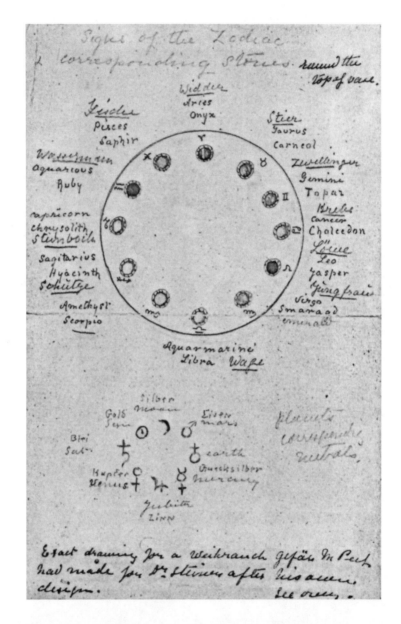

Copy in English of a drawing supplementing the foregoing one.

Silver censer. The cap is enameled blue.
On the bottom rim is engraved: "Rudolf Steiner 1911."
Work carried out by an unknown goldsmith. Height about 16 cm.

The Lodge or Temple Room

From an instruction lesson, Munich, December 12, 1906

Every object to be seen in the lodge has a meaning. Every word that is spoken, every ritual that is practiced, has a meaning that points to an event in world evolution. (. . .) The lodge itself is the world temple.

From an instruction lesson, Berlin, December 16, 1911

When we meet in an esoteric temple we should be aware of the fact that we are in a special place that shuts us off completely from the outside world. It is a sacred place, in which every object found therein has a special and esoteric meaning. (. . .) Every object existing in a whole and complete temple has not only a special meaning, but it has to be there in order to stimulate and make it possible for the stream of those beings whom we call the Masters of the East to be drawn towards our temple. The stream coming from these beings is then poured out over us and enables us to absorb those spiritual teachings which are entirely necessary for humanity's evolution. Without such an assimilation of teachings nothing could be achieved for the spiritual development of humanity. From this place what has been taken up must stream forth to the rest of humankind.

From the instruction lesson, Berlin, December 17, 1911

It has often been said that the symbols and rituals of our temple have not been created arbitrarily, but that they represent a deep connection with cosmic constellations and laws, which will only gradually be revealed to us. They will be handed down from century to century out of the Mysteries of the most ancient times, so that they can serve as the proper channel for the spiritual current that is showered upon us by the Wise Masters of the East. It is impossible therefore to explain or understand them in an exoteric way.

From an instruction lesson, Cologne, May 12, 1913

Everything connected with our temple is super-earthly and the arrangements in the same have to be regarded in like manner.

From an instruction lesson, Cassel, May 10, 1914

The temple is a mirror picture, both of humankind and of the world. All these connections are expressed therein.

From an instruction lesson, Basel, June 1, 1914

The temple should portray the sacrifice made by the spirits. There must be sacrifice, for without it there can be no development, no advance. We would like to sacrifice our intellect and offer it to Christ, so that He can arrange it in the wreath of pearls which He weaves from holy sacrifice, made by Him for the advancement of humankind.[1]

The Carpet
From an instruction lesson, Munich, December 12, 1906

The carpet is the plan of the universe. The squares are the fields formed by the black and white chequered rays. The chessboard and the game of chess are the remnants of ancient esoteric knowledge in secular life.

---

1. In the very fragmentary notes of this instruction lesson it was stated previously that "a single human ability has come to a very important stage in our time: i.e., human thinking. Infinitely much will depend for humankind upon how this faculty is used. We are faced with an ever greater danger of being deprived of our intellect by Ahriman, if we do not learn to make proper use of thinking." To the words "we would like to sacrifice our intellect" cf. introduction to this volume p. 23.

The Three Altars

From an instruction lesson, Munich, December 12, 1906

The position of the Master is in the East (Jupiter—wisdom). In the South stands glory, piety, beauty (Venus). In the West is Vulcan, strength.

From an instruction lesson, Cologne, May 12, 1913

East, West and South are to be understood in a spiritual sense in our temple.

From an instruction lesson, Cologne, May 10, 1914 [2]

The powers of understanding stream towards the Earth out of the East, and from there the Earth is penetrated by the sacred powers of intelligence. These are so to speak reproduced in the altar (of the East); there is the Earth's head. Let us turn towards the South from where the sacred heart-forces, the powers of love and devotion, stream towards the Earth. From the West there pours into the Earth the sacred will, which flows through the limbs, out of which deeds are performed.

If we visualize our temple during meditation we should remember that the altar in the East represents the head, the altar in the South the heart, and the altar in the West the limbs of the Earth, and we should feel how the intellectual powers from the East, the

---

2. The three altars also symbolize the three possible paths into the spiritual world. Compare this with the lecture given in Cologne, November 30, 1906 [The three paths of initiation]. It is also stated in *The Chemical Wedding of Christian Rosenkreutz, anno 1459* that four ways are available, but no mortal is allowed to attain his goal along the fourth path. When, according to the account of a participant, a fourth altar stood in the North for the ritual of promotion to the third degree, this must have been in the sense in which it occurs in Goethe's *Fairy Tale of the Green Snake and the Beautiful Lily,* and in Rudolf Steiner's first Mystery Play, *The Portal of Initiation,* in which in the underground temple, the fourth King standing in the North crumples together when the temple rises into the light of day.

forces of the heart and of love from the South and the will powers from the West flow together and meet in the middle of the temple. Then we shall turn towards these altars and beg that these forces may flow into us, stream through us and fill us with strength.

The Three Candles

From an instruction lesson, Berlin, December 16, 1911

The three lights that are now burning symbolize the three higher principles that lighten the darkness within our higher being. They also portray wisdom, beauty and strength, the words (names) of which are uttered as the candles are lit on the altars of the East, South and West. We shall find the light of wisdom if we always strive for truth in our thinking, if we learn to understand that a new kind of thinking must arise in us, and that in our thinking world-thoughts are living. We must become aware of the fact that "thinking takes place within us" and that what is thought within us is the revelation given to us by spiritual beings who wish to bring us wisdom. Living, weaving and actively moving wisdom flows towards us from the astral world and by letting our thinking be permeated by it we can glean the wisdom of those spiritual beings and acquire it for our souls.

Beauty flows into us when we acquire true piety. If our soul is able to open out in amazement and devotion to what is beautiful around us, then the beauty will become for us an expression of the spiritual beings which reveal their language and wish to make themselves known to us. Only profound and true piety can disclose true beauty. For you all know that in the spiritual (astral) world devils in the form of angels can reveal themselves under the mask of beauty. But you also know that this cannot come about unless our souls are filled with that inner purity which is associated with profound piety. Those beings which send down their beauty to us in truly lovely pictures and forms are to be found in lower devachan.

Strength flows down to us from higher devachan and will make us stronger in ourselves if we transform it into active virtue. True, active virtue ensues when we transform through our will power all the qualities springing from our lower nature, so that these forces become spiritual powers active in the world.

From an instruction lesson, Berlin, December 17, 1911

We behold the flames on the altars representing wisdom, beauty and strength. These are very profound symbols which we can also find again within us.

Where do we find wisdom in the human form? It is not to be found outwardly. It lies hidden in the human figure and in such a way that at this moment it is not compatible with the present stage of our development, so that our form does not make up a complete whole. Wisdom can be portrayed somewhat as follows:

It is different in the case of beauty, which comes to full expression in human hands when they are raised in an outstretched attitude so that the head is in the middle. The hands are the symbol of beauty and this is portrayed as follows:

The hand's mission in life is to be beautiful, not strong. The arm can be strong and muscular, but at its extremity it ends in the tendency towards beauty, which is exhibited in the human hand.

Strength resides in that which is the counterpart to the hands, that is the feet. No esotericist would see anything beautiful in the feet, and whoever would regard them as beautiful in ordinary life would only see a caricature of what is beautiful. Feet portray strength or power. They must be adapted to carry the whole of the human body. That is schematized thus:

So do we find in the figure of the human being these three important symbols which are called the three "World Mothers," as Goethe also calls them in his *Faust.*

From an instruction lesson, Hanover, December 31, 1911

Among the most important symbols to which our attention must first be directed, are the three candle-flames at the altars of the East, West and South. We should recognize in them symbols of wisdom, beauty and strength, but we should not take them to be symbols of earthly wisdom, earthly beauty or earthly strength.

Wisdom cannot be found on the physical plane. Anyone who takes part in esoteric life should undertake never to utter the word "wisdom" and imagine thereby that it is the earthly wisdom which we encounter, say, in outer science, or which one connects with scholarship in general. A scholar is not the same as a sage and a sage is not necessarily a scholar; he might even be a very naive person. A really wise man is someone who carries wisdom in his heart and who likewise speaks from his heart and has the experience: "I can see God at work in every flower petal." He is someone who feels God in the whole of creation and himself at one with creation and with God. One should consider, however, that this does not mean that one should be a pantheist. One must imagine a much more intimate relationship taking place in such a sage, an inexpressible feeling of being protected within the Godhead of the world, which then brings peace and bliss to his soul.

We must acquire such a wisdom as this. It must enter so strongly into our whole being, that it becomes impossible to imagine that we are not always and continually surrounded and nursed by the Spirit of the World, so that inner calm and certainly will never abandon us.

Such sensations and feelings will stream into us from the astral world, which consists of living, flowing, mobile wisdom and is the background and source of surrounding nature and permeates the whole of the physical world. It is from here that we must draw the strength to become wise. Wisdom cannot be found in the physical world.

Beauty, symbolized by the second flame, has also got nothing in common with worldly beauty, it has no connection with any worldly object. In order to get an inkling of what this beauty is like, we should turn our gaze towards the starry night sky and immerse ourselves so deeply into it with our inner gaze that we simultaneously feel that spiritual powers are at work in it. A deep inner piety should at the same time fill our being. Or, on the other hand, when we experience a sunset and perceive how the shining globe slowly sinks below the horizon in a deep crimson glow, so that the shadows become ever longer and longer and finally the landscape round about us becomes shrouded in darkness, then should a deep inner piety stream through our being and identify itself so strongly with the divine forces, that the inner sun will gleam and shine so brightly in our soul as it does for the esoteric pupil when the midnight sun shines into the dark Christmas days and the spiritual beings can be seen in their sublime beauty and in all their majesty. We should think in these terms when we speak about beauty and these thoughts should transform our concept of beauty.

Beauty is to be found in lower devachan. From there it rays out upon us from the heavenly beings in lovely pictures and forms. But on the same plane one also finds ugliness and, indeed, it is just in those things which on earth are often called "beautiful." Every untruth is seen there as ugliness. We can even find beautiful things in that world which, however, only rest upon illusion and hallucination. For instance, we find wonderful figures and forms there—even angelic forms—which have been created by black magicians, who have shrouded themselves with a veil in order to conceal their own selfish aims. A person can have advanced quite a long way in esoteric life and then in one particular life be occupied with the magical or black magical arts. Then, such a person can appear on the lower devachanic plane in such an angelic form, covered by a veil of beautiful garments. On this plane there is no absolute true beauty, but only genuine, intimate piety can reveal to us the real devachanic beauty.

The third flame symbolizes power, again, not the sort of power that we recognize as such in the physical world, but the strength from higher devachan that should flow into the physical world and develop there as "active virtue" in the human being. This is the virtue that constrains us to continually put a check on our own personality and combat our ambition, especially when it consists of showing off our gifts and abilities. This is the virtue that should make us aware of the fact that we rest in the Godhead and are only an insignificant part of real, true perfection, so that we truly feel that all vanity and pride is illusory and that it would only be great foolishness to wish to boast about anything.

Especially at the beginning of their esoteric career people often become arrogant or vain and proud. For instance, when they begin to notice small improvements in themselves they easily begin to imagine themselves superior to others. But that is not the way to attain to active virtue. Those also will not find their path who strive to impart knowledge or power to others by telling others what higher wisdom they have acquired, and if they then allow themselves to be venerated by those whom they have instructed. These vices are great hindrances that a person places in his or her own path. But also the others, the ones who show venerations in this way, lay these hindrances in the path of the esotericist. By opposing these vices in the physical world and by practicing "active virtue" and being continually on our guard against succumbing to them, the strength that is to be found in higher devachan in a host of high spiritual beings will flow into us as spiritual power and strengthen our inner being.

Higher devachan			Strength
Lower devachan		Beauty	
Astral world	Wisdom		
Physical world	Truth in thinking	True piety	Active virtue

The Three Candlesticks Beside the Altars

From an instruction lesson, Munich, December 12, 1906

The three candlesticks that stand here denote: Jupiter, Venus and Vulcan. "Angel," "Shining Being" are what the candlesticks are called in esoteric language. The angels are also called candlesticks in the Apocalypse.

The Mallet (TAO)

From an instruction lesson, Munich, December 12, 1906

The mallet represents the primeval sound of nature: Tao.

From an instruction lesson, Basle, September, 1912

T is not the name of God, but signifies God's presence.

From a lecture, Berlin, November 16, 1905

(. . .) If we look across to Asia what we first find are the remnants of a very ancient religion, which, according to our present views, can no longer be looked upon as a religion. We find this religion in the remarkable culture of China. I am not talking about the religion of Confucius, nor of that which later spread throughout India and China as Buddhism, but I wish to speak about the very ancient Chinese religion, the Tao-religion. That is the religion which refers us to Tao, a word which is translated as "aim" or "pathway." One obtains no clear idea of what this religion means, however, if one simply restricts oneself to the translation given here. The Tao expresses and, for millennia, has expressed to a large part of humanity the highest to which one can attain and to which one believes the whole world and the whole of humankind will one day aspire, the highest which one carries germinally within and which will one day develop out of one's innermost nature into a flower in full bloom. Tao is both a profound and secret basis of the soul and an exalted future condition. Tao is not only uttered in shy reverence by those who understand what it means, but it is also revered in thought. The Tao-religion is based on the principle of evolution and states: what surrounds me today is a stage which will be transcended. I must be clear about the fact that this development in which I am involved has an aim and I must develop myself towards a sublime goal. A force lives within me which goads me on towards the mighty aim of Tao. When I feel this mighty force in me and that all living things are working towards this goal, then this strength becomes a directing force that blows towards me in the wind, echoes to me from the stone, flashes before me in the lightning, rumbles towards me in the thunder, and sends me its light from the Sun. It manifests as growth in the plant and sensation and perception in the animal. It is the power that ever and again creates form upon form until it attains to that sublime goal through which I shall recognize myself as part of the whole of nature, flowing in and out of it with every breath, the symbol of the most exalted spirit, which I perceive as life. This power I experience as Tao. In this religion one never spoke about the otherworldly God, no one spoke about anything that was outside the universe, but about things through which a person acquires power for the progress of humanity.

Tao was most deeply experienced by humanity while it still was united with its divine origin, especially by the inhabitants of Atlantis. These ancestors of ours did not possess a very highly developed reasoning power and nothing of the intelligence of present-day people. Instead they possessed a more dream-like consciousness, a more instinctive and imaginative faculty and little calculative thought life. Imagine a dream life enhanced to become meaningful and not chaotic, and imagine a humanity from whose soul such pictures arise as reflect the sensations that are within their souls, which reflect everything from their surroundings. One has to imagine the soul world of these primeval ancestors as being quite different from that of today. People strive today to form thoughts and ideas of the surrounding world in as accurate a way as possible. In contrast to this, our primeval ancestors formed symbolical, pictorial notions, which appeared to them to be full of life. If you meet someone today, the first thing you do is to try and assess whether this is a good or bad person, a clever or a stupid person, and this is attempted in the driest possible way, just by observing outward appearance. That was never so where our ancestors were concerned. In their mind there arose a picture, not a cognizable concept. If an Atlantean man met an evil person, a picture arose in his mind that was dull and gloomy. The perception, however, did not become a concept. All the same, he attuned himself to this picture. And he became frightened when a picture arose within him having black, red or brown hues. If, however, a radiant beautiful picture appeared before him in a dream-like fashion, then he knew that he could have confidence in such a being. The truths did not yet present themselves to his understanding or intellect, but as inspiration. He felt as though the divine being working through these pictures was within himself. He spoke about the god who announced his presence in the rustling wind, in the rustling of the trees and in pictures of his inner soul life when he had the urge to look up to an exalted future for humanity. This he called Tao.

We modern people, who superseded our primeval ancestors, have a different connection to the spiritual world. We have lost the power of direct vision, which in one sense was duller and dimmer, and have instead reached the level of intellectual understanding, which is in some ways a higher, and in other ways a lower faculty. Through that, we stand at a higher level, for we possess a sharp and penetrating understanding; but we no longer experience the living connection with the divinely active, universal Tao-power. Through that, on the one hand, we have the world as it appears before our soul and on the other hand we have our power of understanding. The Atlanteans experienced the pictures that lived within them. We hear and see the outer world. These two things, outer and inner, confront one another, and we no longer feel a link between the two. That is the great significance of human evolution. Since the continents rose once again after having been inundated by the ocean floods, from that time onwards we have longed to rediscover the link between what we experience and perceive within ourselves and what presents itself to us from the sense-world without. This is the justification for the word "religare" = religion. Its sole meaning is that what was once connected and is now separated must be united again. World and "I" must be reunited. The various forms of the religious confessions are merely the means by which the great sages instruct humankind to rediscover this connection. The reason why they are so different is that, in the one or other form, it can be understood by people of every cultural level....

The Triangle

From a lecture, Stuttgart, June 14, 1921

If one considers the unique orientation of the human being in the universe, several important lines or directions come to our notice.

First there is the line that runs parallel to the earth's surface, the horizontal. Secondly, the direction that distinguishes us from the animal, due to the fact that our spine stands vertically upon the horizontal. With that you have created two structures; first the horizontal or level and secondly the right angle. When you become aware of the significance of the horizontal, essentially the creative principle of the animal nature, and the significance of the right angle for the posture we assume in the universe, then certain concepts, attached to what is horizontal and to the right angle, can become symbols.

The Freemasons, who wished to characterize the human being, have the right angle and the [spirit-] level among their symbols. And other symbols are also representations of the forces of the universe. The way in which they are copied from cosmic powers will occur to you from the following consideration:

Now you see, if we imagine this as the Earth: one moves over the Earth, shall we say, in this direction—I shall draw it radially—so is one in the vertical position, and the way in which one is linked to the center of the Earth is a triangle.

You again have the triangle as a symbol in Freemasonry ritual. Everything belonging to Freemasonry is primarily taken from the configuration of the human being. From that you can see how symbolism was evolved. It was, in essence, not arbitrarily conceived. Symbolism is only produced as a result of studying the reality. It is based in the universe and is to be found there somewhere. That is what ritual is.

The Triangle with the Eye[3]

From an instruction lesson, Berlin, October 2, 1910

It is through Ahriman that we are unable to see in any other way than we do today. For instance, we only see the exterior of a plant—the leaves, the cells, etc.,—and not the life force within it. Everything that is done in the lodge is intended to make it easier to pierce through the veil of Ahriman.

There is no place in the universe where powers that work within us are not present. Now, something strange must be said, which can only be said in a company such as this, where everything is taken in a sense of reverence: There is nothing that is so varied as the brain of individual human beings. One says that no two leaves on a tree are identical. But much more differentiated among themselves are the brains of human beings. Looked at clairvoyantly there are very many shining points in the etheric brain, and these are quite different in each person. If one could photograph these shining points—which, of course, is impossible as they are etheric—one would be able to recognize the starry heavens in such a picture, but without including the planets. The brain is like a half sphere. If one could get close enough, one would find for each person a different constellation of shining points reflected again somewhere in the starry heavens.

One's brain is the most distinguished part of our body. It is connected by spiritual forces with what you might call the uppermost regions of the cosmos. Lower down we approach the signs of the zodiac. These are connected with the twelve nerve strands of the sense organs. The higher the place from which the forces come, the more varied is their effect; the nearer to the earth their origin, the more similar is their effect. With the Sun it does not concern us whether it is fixed or moving; what matters to us is that it sends us its forces from the East, then from the South and then from the West: And we learned yesterday how it affects us when we spoke

---

3. C.f. p. 384.

about the altars; from the East, wisdom, which created us; from the South, beauty, in which everything is revealed; from the West, power, strength, with which we shall now continue to work during our lifetime.

All parts of our physical body are built up by the higher powers. One of the most wonderful parts is the human eye [the eye was drawn on the blackboard]. Atman, buddhi, manas have worked upon it. We should know that their power lies hidden in the eye. (These three powers are represented by the triangle). What can we do with our eyes? We can turn them to the right, to the left, up or down. We do that with our "I." The "I" works from without onto our eye. This is indicated by the rays that stream out from the triangle. But what do they light upon? Upon the veil that Ahriman has spread over everything, reproduced in the lines of the clouds. We had our astral body implanted into us on [old] Moon; behind that works Ahriman. So these lines of the clouds represent the astral body. Already on the [old] Sun work took place on the etheric body, so that the eye could some day develop into such a tool as it is. The further it is removed from the spiritual, the more dense is the body. The etheric body is denoted by the dense clouds. And also in [ancient] Saturn work was performed on the physical body in order that one day an eye like this could be created. The physical body is the densest and darkest part of the human being.

If one places this picture very frequently before the mind's eye, it will awaken one's soul forces. And in this drawing [eye with the triangle] so does the human eye actually appear. It is only a little different on account of the bony framework. The form is a little misshapen.

We must allow everything we receive from the lodge in the way of symbols and teachings to work upon our soul. We cannot do that, however, if we do not feel that we have become a changed person through admittance into the temple. We must encounter life differently. The picture of the triangle with the eye works upon us during the night, but so also do all the things which we see in the garish chaos around us, as for instance all the objects in a store, the hideous placards on a billboard, and so on. And if we allow all that to work upon us as before, so are the effects of the symbols simply eradicated.

If we absorb all the symbols and teachings with enthusiasm, so will the better side of us come to expression. If we then return to outer life and let the chaotic impressions storm into us as before, then doubt will arise within us. It will then seem to us as if it had been a blind belief in authority to which we adhered while we were in the temple, whereas it was really the best in us that felt that way—we only are not aware of it. Thus arise the conflicts that befall the one or other.

The socialite, for example, should not remain so in the same way as before. If, through social standing or from any other cause she has to be a society person all her life, she should continue to be so. She should not be so, however, in the same way, nor with the same feelings as before. If she has to join in small talk at a tea party, she should do so out of conviction of it being her duty. Theosophy should not estrange us from life, but make us more fitted thereto—should make us face life with other feelings.

I do not wish to give you a sermon, but the point I want to make is this: All of you should make it your duty, when engaging in small talk, etc., never to chat about Theosophy, either at table, or on other everyday occasions—for eating is also an everyday affair. To put it shortly; do not chatter everywhere about Theosophy wherever you happen to meet, because then it becomes tittle-tattle. If you wish to talk about Theosophy then only do so if you meet especially for that purpose. Theosophy should be a sacred thing, and that is how it should be treated, not as something by the way.

The ceremonies that have up till now been dealt with, apart from the two pillars, can be understood by those of the first degree. What follows now, the ending, is only to be understood after a long time.

The Right Angle

From an instruction lesson, Cologne, May 7, 1912

The inspirations from the spiritual world are conveyed through esoteric lectures and the inspirational means whereby to rise into the spiritual world are given in the M.E. [Mystica Aeterna].

The right angle, looked at from its more profound aspect, is such a means.

What the gods of old did in their lodges and from which all things of today have sprung, that must be enacted in our rooms for the creations of the future.

Compasses and Rule

See p. 252 for this.

The Cross (Rose-Cross) Beside the Altar in the East

From an instruction lesson, Munich, December 12, 1906

Let us look at the Rose-Cross: the wood of the cross is what is lifeless, the roses are the life that springs forth from it.

From an instruction lesson, Berlin, February 8, 1913[4]

If esotericists regularly carry out their exercises and engross themselves in contemplation of the Temple Legend, or the great cosmic pictures given in Theosophy or in Jakob Boehme's "Morgenröte" [sunrise] and the other symbols that are used in

---

4. c.f. the lecture in Pforzheim, March 7, 1014: "The Pre-earthly Deeds of Christ."

this temple, they might find that at a certain moment their brain appears not to function any more, as though their thinking had reached its limits. That is what esotericists should feel and experience within themselves. Ordinary people sometimes have the same kind of feeling, as though their brain would no longer serve them, but they do not experience the fact consciously. People actually sleep away the whole of their lives; they do not only sleep during the night time, but they also sleep through the most important events of the day, because they are entirely wrapped up in the impressions they receive through the senses. All those who, in important times like our own, have turned against everything that they could have achieved through a spiritual current—however intelligent they may have been in other ways—and refused to accept what is spiritual, who surrendered themselves completely to materialism, they have then, after their death, turned against the spiritual in just the same way and have developed a certain hate which they then directed as a force (or forces) back into the physical world. From the sixteenth century onwards it has really always been like that and those feelings of hate make themselves felt in the physical world and take effect therein. The worlds are not separate, they interpenetrate one another.

We also spoke of the fact that at the death of Jesus Christ on Golgotha his physical body penetrated the physical substances of the Earth; and from that, during the early post-Christian times for certain human beings the strength arose in them to endure martydom. At that time, too, Christ's etheric body was dissolved into the earth as etheric substance and through that it became possible for a few individuals to absorb this etheric substance into themselves and therewith to perform certain feats here on the Earth.

Christ's astral body, too, dispersed after a while into the Earth's astral substance (aura) and by that means human astral sheaths could become imbued with it to perform certain deeds on Earth. And now the "I"-substance of Christ can be imparted to humanity. For even though Jesus of Nazareth abandoned his three sheaths at the Baptism, a part of the "I"-substance nevertheless remained with the sheaths, so that this force, too, was inserted into the Earth.[5]

What is new and what will now gradually be communicated (revealed) to humanity, is a recollection or repetition of what St. Paul experienced at Damascus. He saw the etheric body of Christ. The reason why this will now become visible to us derives from the fact that a new Mystery of Golgotha has, as it were, taken place in the etheric world. That which took place here in the physical world at the Crucifixion as a result of the hatred of uncomprehending humanity, has now been repeated on the etheric level owing to the hatred of human beings who have entered the etheric world as materialists after death.

Let us visualize once more how, at the Mystery of Golgotha, a cross of dead wood was erected, on which the body of Christ hung. And then let us visualize the wood of that cross in the etheric world as green, sprouting and living wood which has been turned to charcoal by the flames of hatred and on which seven blossoming roses appear, representing Christ's sevenfold nature. There we have the picture of the second Mystery of Golgotha which has now taken place in the etheric world. And through this dying, this second death of Christ, we have gained the possibility of seeing the etheric body of Christ. The densification, the dead part of Christ's etheric body will be seen by human beings.

Notes by a different hand
From an instruction lesson, Berlin, February 8, 1913

The Rose-Cross is a symbol for the second death of Christ in the nineteenth century, for the death of the etheric body owing to the army of materialists. The result of this is that Christ can now be seen in the twentieth century as I have often described to you, namely in the etheric body.

---

5. C.f. the lectures on the principle of spiritual economy in connection with questions of reincarnation (CW 109).

Notes from an instruction lesson with no reference to place or date

Everything that surrounded the human being in Atlantis had a perceptible language. Wisdom (contained in the waters) rang with the sound Tao. In the German word "Tautropfen" [meaning "dewdrop" in English] the same meaning is expressed as by the word "Tao," designating what the water of wisdom revealed to humankind. The word dew [Tau] is "ros" in Latin and cross is "crux." Ros-crux means at the same time the sign Tao, the cross and the dew on the plants. This is the esoteric meaning of Rose-Cross.[6]

The Cosmic Cross and the Golden Triangle in the Cosmos and the Human Being

Text according to a copy with no indication of place or date, but with written comment in Rudolf Steiner's hand: "esotericist." It would appear to be a text by Rudolf Steiner of which the original is missing.

Four mighty exalted figures stand in space, each in one of the cardinal directions. They thus form the Cosmic Cross. They direct and lead world events and are the servants of the One who is the Life of the Sun. During each of the cosmic days one of them in turn is inspired by the Sun-Spirit. They are the primordial forces, which are mirrored as thinking, feeling and willing in the cosmos and within the human soul. One, which is the mightiest among them, contains within itself the forces of the other three. It is the most perfect and only through it can the others be seen and understood. It is the immediate servant of the great Sun-Spirit and directs the future towards the present. Its rays of light bring knowledge to the human soul. Its light shines out of the east like the announcement of a new day.

Each of these four figures directs one of the planetary stages of Earth evolution. The three, which are the primordial forces mirrored in thinking, feeling and willing, led the past planetary stages of Earth evolution, known as ancient Saturn, old Sun and old Moon.

---

6. C.f. the expanations on p. 266 et seq. and on p. 340ff, also the esoteric lesson in Munich, June 1, 1907, recorded in CW 264.

The fourth is the special leader during the stage of the Earth evolution itself. That is why it includes the forces of the other three, which repeat their activity on Earth, and brings them to a state of equilibrium by adding its own forces to theirs. On its right hand, towards the north, stands the one that is particularly connected with the Saturn evolution. Its light shines with a blue sheen, paler than that of the others. It is an exalted and austere figure, given the name Uriel. Towards the west stands the figure belonging to the Sun evolution. Its light rays out with a golden sheen. It is an exalted and powerful figure known by the name Raphael. Towards the south stands the one that is connected with the evolution of old Moon. It shines with a silvery white light. It is an exalted and loving figure known by the name Gabriel. The fourth one, which contains the forces of the others within it and joins its own forces to theirs, rays forth its light from the east with a rose-colored nuance and a golden sheen. It directs and leads the evolution of the Earth and thereby works on into the future. An exalted and victorious figure, which bears within it the capacities of the other three, it is called Michael. Thus stand the four mighty archangels and direct the events of the world. Each of them is connected with one of the four parts of the human being, for in each of the planetary conditions one of these four bodies was developed in its preparatory stage. The fourth figure directs the development of the human "I." It is most intimately connected with humankind and is the immediate servant of the mighty Sun-Spirit. It was just during Earth evolution that this mighty Being descended into earthly incarnation and united with the Earth for its further development. Three stages of planetary evolution have already taken place, the fourth is now in progress and there are three other stages to follow. During the latter the preparatory stages that were developed during the first three planetary ages will be perfected on a higher level. With the forces of our "I," which was bestowed upon us during Earth evolution under the influence of the mighty archangel Michael and the power of Christ, we will be in a position to develop higher organs during the three following planetary stages. We will be able to evolve three higher faculties, but we will develop them internally. Of the four parts of our organism developed in this way, three of them will be elevated to become a higher trinity. Outside of the human being in the cosmos, this higher trinity already exists, but we must gradually acquire it ourselves, so that it becomes an inner faculty in us.

Just as the four parts of our being are connected with the four archangels, by which their structure was first laid down, so there are cosmic powers connected with the three higher forces of human nature. The future planetary stages of evolution will be similarly guided and directed by lofty spiritual beings. They do not take up their positions in the four directions of space as do the archangels, which form the Cosmic Cross, as if they had emerged from a common center, but they are united in such a way that they form a triangle that shines with a golden light. In the "I am He who was, who is and who will be" they connect the three points in time: past, present and future, and weave them into a unity. They will pour their strength into the four, not by standing alongside them, but by being placed above them.

During Earth evolution the power of the Fourth joined the three that had preceded it and thereby the four will become endowed with higher powers. And the Fourth will become the mediator through which the activity of the higher trinity will be revealed. Through the Fourth they will be enabled to send their spirit-light, which is life, into the four, just as in the case of humankind, the fourth member, the "I," contains within it the force to form the three higher parts—spirit self, life spirit, and spirit human—and rouse them to activity.

At the turning-point of planetary evolution, during the fourth, or earthly stage, the first impulse was given for the powers of the higher trinity to work more deeply into the three following planetary states. The same power as that which lived in Jesus Christ on Earth and united with the Earth when the Word became flesh, will work further in a threefold way in the next three planetary conditions—in the fifth, sixth and seventh stages, which are known as the Jupiter, Venus and Vulcan conditions. The three higher members of the human being are connected with these three forces. Through the power of Christ the "I" was given the possibility of developing these members of our being on Earth in the future. By developing spirit self in the next planetary state, the Jupiter-condition, we will unite with those powers that manifest in the cosmos as the "Holy Spirit." We will participate in the Holy Spirit through our spirit self. In the following planetary state, the Venus-condition, by developing life spirit, we will unite with the powers that manifest cosmically as the "Son." By developing life spirit we will become the Son. And in the final planetary state, the Vulcan-condition, by developing the spirit human, we will unite with the cosmic powers, which are called the "Father." As spirit human we will become one with the Father. We will be in the Father and the Father will be in us.

In this way we will have developed the forces of the Golden Triangle. Then it will be revealed in us by the sounding of the divine Creator-Word, which has poured its forces into this triangle. This divine Word was the source of all things; it implanted its power and life into all things. It would gradually have been lost to humankind during world evolution, for we were ever less able to hear it sounding within ourselves and in the outer world. It seemed to have been split up into single syllables and letters and no one could immediately understand the connection of these letters to one another. It was impossible for anyone to construct a word out of these syllables, which was in itself a living, creative sound. The Golden Triangle, upon which the word was preserved, lay hidden in the deepest wells of existence. It was engraved thereon. It was unattainable for humans to begin with. Once, however, when the sounding of the Word seemed to have died away completely, when darkness was at its deepest, it was revealed once more to us and showed forth its power. Since then a resonance has remained within us like a memory of its sound. Through that it has become possible for us to find it again in ourselves and in the outside world. We become seekers of the Word when we start to develop our higher faculties and to construct the Golden Triangle within ourselves. And one day we will find it. And as we slowly build up the higher trinity within ourselves until it can be revealed as a unity, so will we learn to spell it out, syllable by syllable, until it resounds livingly within our own soul and we are able to grasp the divine Creator-Word.

The Two Pillars Jachin and Boaz, Otherwise Known as the "Pillars of Hercules" / the Golden Legend

The meaning of the two pillars was always explained in the "Golden" or "True-Cross" legend (first mentioned by Steiner in the lecture, Berlin, May 29, 1905). For that reason "The Golden Legend" and the explanations of it are included here.

The Golden Legend

Text according to the original handwriting of Rudolf Steiner

Notebook, Archive No. 6954

Adam had two sons

Cain = the independently striving human being

Abel = the one who relies on revelation

Abel fell by the hand of Cain. Abel's heritage devolved on Seth. Seth reached the gate of Paradise. There he was

not

denied entrance by the cherub with the flaming sword. This symbolizes that Seth was the ancestor of the initiated priesthood. The cherub then gave Seth three seeds (higher human = atman, buddhi, manas). After Adam's death Seth laid the three seeds in his mouth, following the instruction of the cherub. The tripartite bush, which sprang up from them had within it the writing of flame:

Ehjeh - ascher - Ehjeh (I am I)

Moses took from it the three-forked branch from which he made his rod.

David planted this rod in the earth on Mount Zion. Solomon took from it the wood out of which he made the entrance to the temple after this fashion:

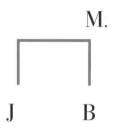

Only the pure might enter through it.

The Levites, through their lack of understanding, sunk these three pieces of wood into the pool of Bethesda.

At the time of Christ the Jews placed the wood as a beam across the brook Kedron.

Christ walked across it after the night of his arrest on the Mount of Olives.

And from it the Cross was made.

Text according to the original handwriting of Marie Steiner

Adam had two sons:

Cain, the representative of self-aware active humanity and Abel, the representative of that part of humanity which receives all its gifts as higher endowment and revelation.

Self-awareness must come about through guilt. Cain killed Abel. Seth inherits the gifts of Abel.

When Seth had re-entered Paradise after the twofold Fall of Humankind (the sins of Eve and Cain) he saw how

The Tree of the Knowledge of Good and Evil and the Tree of Life had united.

The Tree of the Knowledge of Good and Evil signifies human knowledge.

The Tree of Life signifies divinely revealed wisdom.

The cherub with the flaming sword gave Seth three seeds; in them were all the germs of the trees, which had united.

After Adam's death Seth placed the three seeds in his mouth, from which sprang a bush, in the midst of which was written "God's Name":

Ehjeh ascher Ehjeh = (I am I)

From this bush Moses fashioned his rod. This rod was continually in leaf and was later preserved in the Ark of the Covenant.

David planted the rod in the earth near Zion.

Solomon made:

three pillars

from its wood.

These pillars were set up at the entrance to the temple.

They are: Jachin, Boaz and M.

The Levites took the pillars and threw them into the pool of Bethesda.

At the time of Christ the pillars were removed from the pool and laid in the form of a bridge across the brook of Kedron.

Jesus crossed this bridge on his way to the Mount of Olives.

Then his Cross was made from it.

Explanations of the Golden Legend

As explanations of this subject from instruction lessons are only scanty, those remarks given at the Munich Conference in 1907 about the pillars erected there, will be dealt with first.
From a lecture, Munich, May 21, 1907

What is the meaning of the two pillars of the Rosicrucians? If we are to explain the meaning of the two pillars, which we have before us here, we must take our start from the Golden Legend. This is as follows:

When Seth, the son of Adam—who took the place of Abel—was sufficiently mature, he was vouchsafed a glimpse of Paradise. He was allowed to pass by the angel with the fiery sword and enter the place from which humankind had been banished. Seth saw something very special there. He saw how the two trees, that of life and that of knowledge, were entwined together. From the two entwined trees Seth received three seeds, which he took with him and placed in the mouth of his father Adam after his death. A mighty tree then grew out of the grave of Adam. This tree then appeared to people with psychic vision as though shining with a fiery glow; and this glowing light twined together for those who could see it, to form the letters J B, the initial letters of two words, which I am not allowed to pronounce here, but of which the meaning is: "I am He who was; I am He who is; I am He who will be." This tree divided into three branches. Seth took some wood from it, which was used in various ways during world evolution. A rod was made from it, which, according to legend, was the magical wand of Moses. It was the very same wood from which the beams of Solomon's temple were made. They remained there for as long as humankind could still understand the ancient secrets. Then the wood was thrown into a pool, from which at certain times lame and blind people could receive healing. After having been retrieved from there it was formed into the bridge across which Our Saviour trod as he went on his way towards the Cross. And, according to the legend, the wood of this tree, which had grown up out of Adam's mouth from the seeds planted therein from the entwined trees of life and of knowledge, was formed into the very Cross upon which Our Saviour hung.

This legend has a deeply symbolic meaning. Think for a moment of that transformation, which the pupil has to contemplate when taking the fourth step in the Rosicrucian training, the production of the Philosopher's Stone. We recollect that this entails a particular way of dealing with our red blood. Let us consider the significance of this red blood, not only on account of Goethe's allusion to it: "Blood is a very special fluid," but because esotericism of all ages has taught us this. As the red blood exists it is the result of breathing oxygen. We can only briefly allude to that. When we are referred in the legend and in the Bible to that very important moment of Seth's renewed entrance into Paradise, we must call to mind the reason for humankind's expulsion therefrom. Humankind was expelled from Paradise—our old condition of rest in the lap of the higher spiritual world— through what is hinted at in the Bible as the parallel physical accompaniment to our descent. Whoever wishes to understand the Bible must learn to take it literally. It is said: "God breathed into man's nostrils the breath of life, and man became a living soul." That which is pictured here as the breathing of the breath of life was a process stretching over millions of years. What does it mean?

There have been times during the creation of the human physical body in which humans did not possess lungs, so that the inhalation of oxygen could not then take place. There were times in which humans lived more or less in the liquid element and during which they had an organ something like air-bladders (waterwings), from which the lungs later developed. These former air-bladders were transformed into lungs, and we can follow their transformation. When we do so this process is revealed as what is described in the Bible as "God breathing into man's nostrils the breath of life" and "man becoming a living soul." With this inhaling of breath, the creation of red blood became possible for the first time. Our descent is therefore connected with the growth of the tree of the red blood within the human being.

Just imagine if a man were standing in front of you and you were only aware of the trickling of the red blood: you would have before you a living red tree. Of this the Christian esotericist says: It is the Tree of Knowledge. We have seized it for ourselves, we have eaten from the tree of the red blood. The setting up of the tree of the red blood, which is properly the Tree of Knowledge: that is sin. And God drove humankind out of Paradise, so that we should not also eat of the Tree of Life. We have another tree within us, which you can visualize just as easily as the former. But the latter has blue-red blood. This blood is a poisonous substance. The blue-red tree was planted in us at the same time as the other one. When we still rested in the lap of the gods, the Godhead within us was capable of interweaving what signified life and what signified knowledge—and in future times it will be possible for us, through our expanded consciousness, to change the blue-red blood into red blood, then the wellspring will be within us to change the tree of blue-red blood into a Tree of Life. Today it is a Tree of Death. In this picture lies a retrospective and a prophetic view of life!

You see that a tree of red blood and a tree of blue-red blood are intertwined in us. The red blood is the expression of the "I," it is the lower part of "I"-knowledge. The blue-red blood gives a picture of death. As a punishment the blue-red tree, as the Tree of Death, was added to the red Tree of Knowledge. In the distant future this Tree of Death will be transformed into the Tree of Life as it was originally. If you visualize the human being today, you will see that the whole of human life consists of interchange between these two trees.[7]

The fact that Seth was allowed to re-enter Paradise signifies that he was an initiate and could look back on the divine-spiritual condition in which the two trees were intertwined. And he laid three

---

7. A description of how the two pillars are connected with birth and death is to be found in the lecture given in Cassel, July 7, 1909. Also the paintings in the large cupola of the first Goetheanum (in the threefold motive "I - A - O" over the archway above the stage) point to this connection. c.f. the portfolio of twelve sketches for the paintings of the large cupola of the first Goetheanum and the book by Hilde Raske: *Das Farbenwort*.

seeds of the intertwined trees into Adam's mouth, from which a three-forked tree grew up. That means that the tree that grows out of the human being; manas, buddhi and atman, which comprises the higher members, is present within as embryo. So the legend indicates how already in our predisposition, that is in Adam, the divine Trinity exists, how it grows and develops and how, to begin with, it can only be seen by an initiate. Humanity has to follow its path of evolution. Everything that has taken place in human development that leads to initiation is further elaborated in the legend.

Through the knowledge that the tripartite tree resides within us, the tree of eternity that is expressed in the words: "I am He who was—I am He who is—I am He who will be!" we receive strength that carries us forward and puts the magical wand into our hand. That is the meaning of Moses' rod; that is why the wood of the tree that grew from the three seeds is taken to the temple; that is why the Cross is made from it, that sign of initiation which signifies the overcoming of the lower members of our being by the three higher ones.

This legend thus demonstrates how the initiate looks ahead to a future condition, in which the Tree of Knowledge—the tree of the red blood—and the Tree of Life—the tree of the blue-red blood— will twine around one another within us. Now those who wish to advance spiritually should engrave upon their heart what the two pillars—the red pillar on the one hand, indicating the pillar of the red blood, and the blue-red pillar, indicating the pillar of the blue-red blood—wish to say to us. Today they are separated from each other. Therefore the red pillar stands on the left in our hall today and the blue-red pillar stands on the right. They are there to indicate to us that we should transcend the present state of humankind and direct our steps to that point in which, through our extended consciousness, the pillars can intertwine in a way that one designates: J - B. The red pillar is denoted by "J" and the blue-red one by "B."

The inscriptions on the pillars will bring to your mind what is connected with each of them. The words on the red pillar are as follows:

In pure thought you will find	*Im reinen Gedanken findest du*
The self that can maintain itself.	*Das Selbst, das sich halten kann.*
If you transform the thoughts into a picture,	*Wandelst zum Bilde du den Gedanken,*
You will experience creative wisdom.	*Erlebst du die schaffende Weisheit.*

When one meditates this saying, through the power of one's thought one engrafts the column of one's blood with the power that leads to the goal—to the column of wisdom.

One engrafts the column of life with the power it needs when one gives oneself up to the thought that is inscribed on the other, the blue pillar:

If you condense feeling to become light,	*Verdichtest du das Gefühl zum Licht,*
You reveal the shaping power.	*Offenbarst du die formende Kraft.*
If you incorporate the will into an entity,	*Verdinglichst du den Willen zum Wesen,*
You will create in universal existence.	*So schaffst du im Weltensein.*

The one set of words concerns cognition, the other set refers to life. The shaping power reveals itself to begin with in the sense of the first saying; it only becomes "magical" in the sense of the second saying. To rise from the mere power of cognition to a magical effect lies in the change over from the power of the inscription on the first pillar to that of the inscription on the second.

So you see how that which these symbols, the two pillars, denote, hangs together with the ideals of the Rosicrucian pupil. In some esoteric societies these two pillars are erected. The esotericist will always attach the meaning to them that has properly been accorded them.[8]

---

8. In the lecture, Dornach, December 29, 1918, it is pointed out that the pillars in the present-day esoteric societies can no longer be erected in the proper fashion, and should also not be erected, because the proper setting can only be found when a true, inwardly experienced initiation takes place. In addition to that, one is not able to erect them as they should be erected in the case where a person through death or initiation leaves the body.

From the instruction lesson, Munich, December 12, 1906

The second master legend[9] speaks about Seth, the son of Adam, who was initiated into the priesthood. He was allowed to return to Paradise, where he took three seeds, which he placed in the mouth of his dead father, Adam and from which the living bush sprang up. The rod by which Moses performed his miracles was taken from the wood of this tree; it was the burning bush in which God appeared to Moses. Its wood was used to make the gateway into Solomon's temple, consisting of two pillars with the lintel thereon, which was thrown into the Pool of Bethesda, thereby giving it healing powers. This wood was laid across the Kedron brook over which Christ walked after his betrayal on the Mount of Olives. And from this beam the Cross of Christ was made.

The red blood and the blue blood signify the Pillar of Wisdom and the Pillar of Strength. It is upon these two pillars that the human being must be able to stand. The Tree of Life and the Tree of Knowledge stood in Paradise entwined into a single tree and the Tree of Life and the Tree of Knowledge will again unite into a single tree for the initiated and the wise of humankind; it had to be divided into two trees for the sake of human beings.

The inscription that appeared to Moses in the burning bush: Ejeh asher Ejeh! can be translated as: I am the I am; I was what I shall become!

Humankind has bought its knowledge with birth and death. The angel Gabriel is the one that guards the entrance to Paradise with the fiery sword.

---

9. Otherwise: Golden Legend. The first master legend is the Temple Legend.

Instruction lesson for the second degree, Berlin, December 1911. No exact date

J.   B.

This is how the angel appeared to Adam in Paradise under the fig tree. Adam looked upon this symbol as a picture of his angel and vowed never to deviate from the might recorded in J.B.

Adam always found strength and blessing when he visited the place where the vision could be seen.

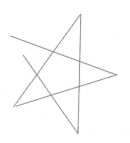

But during the Lemurian Epoch he nevertheless did what he had vowed not to do and deviated from the might of J.B. through Lucifer who brought temptation. And when Adam afterwards visited the place where the angel had appeared to him, he experienced horror there at his own being. In this symbol of the upside-down pentagram open at one side—that is reversed—it appeared to Adam as the angel threatening with the fiery sword. And Adam fled.

Report of a participant with no indication of place or date

Adam had two sons, Abel and Cain.
Abel signifies wisdom, Cain strength.

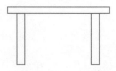

Cain killed Abel.

Another son was born to Adam: Seth.

Seth signifies piety, which connects wisdom with strength.

Adam died and Seth placed in his mouth three seeds. From these seeds three twigs sprouted from a single stem. This grew. The thorn bush in which God appeared to Moses grew from this stem. The two pillars of Solomon's temple were made from this wood. It came about, however, that there was no place for the third trunk which should have linked the other two. It did not fit anywhere. So they threw it into the Pool of Bethesda. When the Lord came He imbued the pool with strength and the beam appeared once more. It was hauled out and used as a bridge over the Kedron brook. The Lord crossed this bridge on his way to Golgotha. The Cross he carried had also been worked from this wood and he collapsed under the weight of it.

———————

The cross-beam that should unite wisdom and strength is the principle of piety, love and beauty. In pre-Christian times there was no place for that. When Jesus Christ appeared as the bearer of buddhi, his power was able to raise this beam out of the water—the astral plane—wherein it rested. A river was bridged by it (the path to the higher world). He walked across it on his path of sorrow when he offered himself up for humanity. That could only take place through love, refined and purified love; hence the pathway across this beam.

The Cross was also formed from this wood. Through his love for humanity he had to bear and suffer. But in him love and knowledge were combined. Through that his sacrifice was complete and everlasting and the three boughs of wisdom, beauty, and strength were united, because the place for beauty had been found. The three stems, which had separated like the three streams, will grow together again in the future, like three streams flowing together again and attaining their maximum effect in unity.

Seth reconciled the antagonistic brothers Abel and Cain.

The link between wisdom and strength is piety, or love, or beauty.

Concerning the meaning of the names of the pillars, see under the heading: "Sign, Handclasp, and Word." p. 287.

A historic aspect of the significance of the two pillars was given in lecture three of the cycle "Cosmic Being and Egohood" (CW 169), Berlin, June 20, 1916. in the words that follow:

It is really true that our passage through life can be compared to the Sun moving through the twelve constellations of the zodiac. On entering life our senses rise, as it were, at the one universal pillar and set at the other. We pass by these pillars when we go from the night aspect of the starry heavens into the day aspect. It was to that which these esoteric or symbolic societies wished to point when they called the pillar of birth, which one passes when one enters the life of the daytime, Jachin. Ultimately they were obliged to seek this pillar in the heavens. And those things that comprise our outer existence during our life between death and a new birth are the perceptions we receive from the sense of touch extended over the whole world, in which we do not ourselves do the touching, but in which we feel as if we were being touched from all sides by spiritual beings. Here on Earth it is we who do the touching. During the life between death and a new birth we live within the movement in such a way that we feel as though within us here a blood corpuscle or a muscle were to sense its own movement. In the macrocosm we feel that we are moving between death and a new birth, we experience ourselves in balance and feel as though we were a part of the whole of life. Here [on Earth] our life is enclosed within our skin; there, however, we experience ourselves as a part of the whole of life and in every situation as if we were holding ourselves in balance. Here [on Earth] it is the force of gravity and the constitution of our body that gives us our equilibrium, and we actually have no consciousness of it as a rule. We are aware at all times of our equilibrium in the life between death and a new birth. That is an immediate perception, the counterpart to the life of soul. Through Jachin one enters into earthly life and through Jachin one is reassured: "What is outside of you in the macrocosm now lives within you, you are now a microcosm, for that is the meaning of 'Jachin': the divine in you which is spread out over the world."

Boaz, the other pillar: Entry through death into the spiritual world. That which is summed up in the word Boaz signifies something like the following: "I shall find the strength which I formerly sought within myself, spread out over the whole of existence. I shall live within it." But one can only understand such things by immersing oneself in them with spiritual insight. In symbolical brotherhoods they are indicated symbolically. There will be further revelations to come during our fifth post-Atlantean epoch, so that it should not be entirely lost to humanity and so that in later times people can come along who will be able to understand again what has been preserved in the word.

But you see, everything that happens outwardly in our world is, after all, only a picture of what exists outside in the macrocosm. Just as our soul life is a microcosm in the sense I have indicated to you, so is the soul life of all humanity, as it were, formed from without by the macrocosm. And for our present age it is very important to have these two portrayals of the two pillars of which I have spoken to you, preserved in our history. These pillars give a one-sided picture of life, for life only exists in the equilibrium between the two. Life is not represented either by Jachin, which is only the transition from the spiritual into the bodily, or by Boaz, which is the transition from the bodily into the spirit. The balance is what matters. And that is what humankind finds so difficult to understand. We are always looking for the one side, for the extreme. We never seek the balance. That is why two pillars have been erected for our present epoch, but if we interpret our present age correctly, we should pass in-between the two pillars, imagining neither the one nor the other pillar to be, as it were, the power-base of human existence. One must pass—in between the two! We must really grasp what is present in reality, not brood in thoughtless existence in the way modern materialists brood. If you seek the Jachin pillar today, you have it present among you. The Jachin pillar is present in a very important man, no longer alive today, having died already but still present among us: it is there in Tolstoyism.

Consider that in Tolstoy a man appeared who, in principle, wished to deflect the whole of humankind away from outward life into inner life—I spoke about Tolstoy in the early years of our Anthroposophical Movement—who wished to refer solely to that which takes place within the human being. Thus Tolstoy did not perceive the spirit in its outward activity, a one-sidedness that struck me as being particularly characteristic when I spoke about him in one of the very first lectures that I gave here in one of the very first years. This lecture was shown to Tolstoy by someone who was friendly towards us. He understood the first two thirds of it, but the remaining third he could not understand, because it mentioned reincarnation and karma; he did not understand that. His one-sidedness consisted of the complete deadening of outer life. And how infinitely painful it was to experience how one-sided he was! Let us consider the tremendous contrast between the views of Tolstoy, which have dominated a great part of Russian intellectualism, and that which now emanates from there these days [Communism]. Oh, it is one of the most terrible contrasts you can imagine! That is one-sidedness.

The other one, the Boaz pillar, is also represented historically in our time. It, too, presents a one-sidedness. It is the search for spirituality in the physical world alone. It came to expression a few decades ago over in America where, I should like to say, the antithesis of Tolstoy appeared in Keely, whose ideal it was to construct a motor that was not powered by steam or electricity, but by the force that human beings engender in the sound waves of their

tone of voice and speech. Consider an engine that is so constructed that it can be set in motion by vibrations a person produces
by speaking or by soul activity generally. It was an ideal, but thank
God it was only an ideal at that time, for what would have happened in this war if the Keely ideal had been realized! If that
should ever come about, then one would see what happens when
vibrations synchronize to produce outward mechanical energy.
That is the other one-sidedness. That is the Boaz pillar. One has to
pass between the two pillars.

In the symbols that have been preserved to us a very great deal
lies hidden. In our time we are called upon to understand these
things and to penetrate to their meaning. The contrast that will
one day be experienced between all that is truly spiritual and that
which will accrue when the Keely motor will have become a reality
in the West, will be quite a different contrast to the one which
exists between Tolstoy's views and what will burst upon us from the
East. Oh, no more can be said about that! But it is necessary for us
to gradually immerse ourselves in the secrets of human evolution,
and to realize how in human wisdom there has been expressed for
thousands of years, symbolically or otherwise, what will one day
become reality at varying stages....

The Mirror[10]

From an instruction lesson with no indication of place or date

When a man sees himself reflected in a mirror he does not really
see himself, for what he sees is not really the human being. The
human being is spiritual when outside the physical being. What the
man sees are the spiritually reflected beams of light that fall upon
him from the spiritual world. The human being reflects the spirit-
light just as much as an object reflects the sunlight. What the man
sees of himself in the mirror is a reflection of his true self.

---

10. Is used in the ritual for promotion into the second degree.

Everything about us is a reflection of the spiritual world. In primeval times, before the so-called "Fall of Humanity," human beings did not look outwards as they do today. They looked inwards spiritually. This happened in the following way. They inhaled the substance that was all around them in their surroundings. This was spiritual substance. Then they had within them what was previously outside. This was then reflected inside. For example, where the eye later formed, was a tiny spirit-light, and so on. Inner knowledge was gained in this way. Outwardly they saw nothing. And that is how it was with all the later senses. That was the paradisal state. Humankind lost this paradisal state through Lucifer's influence when their eyes were opened towards the outside. For the first time, human beings saw themselves as physical beings from without, and they were ashamed of it in front of God in whom they had previously resided. It was as though their soul had become naked before God.

The Four Elementary Beings[11]
Munich, December 12, 1906

The four kinds of elementary beings that abound in space are called:

1. Gnomes, which live in the earth.
2. Undines, which are embodied in water.
3. Sylphs, which we have to think of as living in air and
4. Salamanders, which we have to think of as living in fire.

From an instruction lesson, Basel, September 24, 1912

It is self evident that if we have applied ourselves for a long time to our esoteric development by carrying out our exercises and meditations in a true spirit, we shall some day necessarily arrive at the point where we are vouchsafed a glimpse into the spiritual

11. It has not been recorded through which symbols these were expressed.

world. This moment will arrive at some time for all, who, in connection with their daily exercises, earnestly and devotedly allow everything that is here presented to them in ritual and symbols to work upon them. For the one person it arrives earlier, for the other later, but for everyone it will come sooner or later.

Between the sixteenth and nineteenth centuries it was very difficult to gain access to the spiritual world. One was not able during that time to get very much further than to certain imaginations, which indeed gave a feeling for existence in higher worlds, but could not provide any direct revelations about them. At the present time, however, since the last third of the nineteenth century, it has been even more difficult to acquire the necessary impetus to emerge from one's physical body and gain access to the spiritual world. Once one has managed to ascend in this way, then it is easier than before to have many spiritual experiences there.

During the course of the twentieth century humankind will begin to develop its slumbering organs, through which it will be revealed what is situated immediately above the physical sense world, what is manifested to us through nature. If, for example, one were by the sea or in some other place near to water, then one would look at the water and not merely describe it outwardly as a compound of hydrogen and oxygen, but would experience its nature as something quite different. One might recognize it as being a gigantic collection of elementary beings that interpenetrate and actually are the water. For water is the scene, the soul element belonging to these elementary beings. From that the word "element" is derived.

These elementary beings exist in water and also perish therein, namely if another element, "fire," arrives on the scene. Warmth causes a drying up process to take place and ensures that the water rises up in the form of steam or moisture or clouds. In this process someone who is clairvoyant can observe how the elementary beings are as though lamed and, so to speak, perish. But if the water becomes cooler again, and the rising vapors turn into heavy clouds from which lightning flashes, rain descends to the earth; then such a person can observe how these beings revive, yes, even come to life again. During the crippling and dying process caused by the heating and evaporation, the elementary beings scatter seeds, as it were, which sprout up again during the cooling and condensation of the water. The birth of innumerable elementary beings is entailed when the rain pours down onto the Earth, and we then feel the beneficial effect of these newly created beings.

The beneficial and vivifying effect of water on the human organism has been amply demonstrated by medical science during the last decades, but one has also to learn that when this force is applied too strongly or in the wrong way it can also cause damage. By using warm (hot) water the stupefying annulment of the elementary beings is aimed at. By using cold water the need for the life-stimulating force of all the newly forming beings is felt.

Still other things will be noted by somebody who has become clairvoyant. Such a person will see the clouds in a thunder storm, which to ordinary vision are black, threatening and pressed together, as gleaming brightly shining clouds. And when lightning flashes from the thunder clouds and the rain pours down, this person sees it as light streaming down to Earth. That is what an older humanity experienced as the draught of the Soma drink. They had a connection with the elementary world and for them light descended to earth with the rain.

A clairvoyant person could also see other elementary spirits, beings that stand at a different stage of development. These beings occupy the air that we inhale with every breath and that we exhale again as something dead when we have finished with it (without attaching any chemical ideas to it). For ordinary observation the inhaled air is the living air, and the exhaled air is the dead or death-bringing air. Looked at spiritually, however, the inhaling brings death to the elementary beings of the air and through exhalation they revive. So these beings permeate our whole organism, and they have helped to build it up from the very beginning.

Let us now pose the question: What is the particular evolutionary task of these elementary beings of the water and what is that of the elementary beings of the air? In long past epochs of earthly evolution, when the higher members of human beings stood in a quite different relationship to one another, these elementary beings also worked quite differently. At that time human beings did not possess what we call speech. The organs that make speech possible are enclosed within the breathing system. Human beings use speech in order to give expression to their soul, or also for conversation, but that is only the case during the age of materialism as we experience it today. In the age preceding our own age of materialism the organs of speech were at the same time organs of perception. Speech has come about because the elementary beings of water penetrated the embryonic organs (germ) of the larynx and slowly changed it into what it is today.

People at that time did not communicate by means of words as we do today, but as they still possessed clairvoyance, they looked into spiritual realms and beheld the world of the elements. They experienced the swirling elementary beings around them while they gave out sounds like our vowel-sounds A, I, U [ah - ee - oo] to express the inner pictures which they experienced within them. So they also expressed their sensations and feelings when, for instance, what they beheld aroused sympathy or antipathy in them. So, too, when they pronounced the word Tao, which sounded throughout the whole of nature; then they knew of the Great Spirit, the primal cause of all that exists.

This word, which, at the same time was spiritual perception, has been lost, since the breathing organs and the organs of speech have become more independent of each other than they were then.

[This copy ends here. What follows is an addition to another copy]

There is not only a breathing process taking place in the lungs, but there is one in the eyes, too, but in that case the eyes do not inhale and exhale air but warmth. When we see the color red, warmth is exhaled (red, orange, yellow). If a cold color such as blue, indigo or violet is perceived, then the eye inhales. What is the etheric basis for the eye (as air underlies the lungs physically), is warmth, and that is inhaled and exhaled. Basically every sense organ is an organ for breathing.

Higher beings that stand just above us have neither the same eyes, nor the same speech as we do. They direct warmth in a certain direction and at that place a gleam of color arises. Through that their being is expressed and in this fashion they communicate with one another. Those who have experienced colors thus in their living form experience pain when they then see fixed colors attached to physical objects. In the same way the whole physical world gives them pain to begin with. The pain only subsides when one learns to experience the colors morally. Then one experiences red as the punishment for egoism, blue as the reward for having overcome egoism. Then the colors begin to speak in a language which will also be the future language of humankind.

The nearer humanity approaches the Jupiter existence the more will language become perception; then the organs of breathing and speech will not be so separate as they are today. The process of seeing and the experiencing of warmth will also unite. It was necessary for the development of the independent "I" that these processes should remain separate for a time. If that had not been the case, then we would still have a perception of what was happening in our surroundings, but we would not have been able to attain self-awareness. In the future, humankind will begin to feel a connection between the spoken word and colors. One will experience green when matters of indifference are discussed; yellow will appear when one speaks egoistically; red will be present when egoism is being attacked.[12]

This coalescence of the organs is only attained when one understands the Mystery of Golgotha. That is the only thing that enables us to experience the whole of nature morally. If one then gazes up at the clouds and sees the lightning flashing from them, one will then be able to behold Christ in his etheric form. With the "clouds," that is to say with the elements, he will appear in spirit form. This vision will one day appear to every person, be it sooner

---

12. In notes by a different hand it is expressed thus: The red color will be experienced as a punishment for something bad, which should be overcome; yellow demonstrates selfishness, blue is something heavenly, which beckons us on.

or be it later—only the Father knows the day and the hour, as it says in the Gospel.[13]

The Book of Thoth (Tarot)[14]

From an instruction lesson, Munich, December 12, 1906

The Egyptian *Book of Thoth* consisted of 78 cards, which contained the world secrets. This was well known in the initiation rituals of Egypt. The names of the playing cards come from that—King, Knight, Keeper of the Tower, Commander-in-Chief are esoteric denotations.

From a lecture, Berlin, December 17, 1906

Those who were initiated in the Egyptian Mysteries were able to read

Þ

(the symbol for Tarot). They could also read the *Book of Thoth*, which comprised 78 cards, in which all world events were depicted from the beginning to end, from Alpha to Omega, which one could decipher if they were arranged in their proper order. The book contained pictures of life, leading to death and arising again to new life. Whoever could combine the correct numbers with the

---

13. In the same notes by a different hand the ending reads: "Holy service or eso-tericism eventually leads to vision. Only a few chosen people are called by Christ to have such vision, the others must earn it by meditation and holy service. The day and the hour is known to the Father alone for every individual, but for each the time will arrive. 'In the beginning was the Word and the Word was with God and the Word was God.'"

14. The way the cards were used has not been recorded.

correct pictures could read what was written. And this number-knowledge, this picture-knowledge had been taught from earliest times. It also still had a great influence in the Middle Ages, as for instance on Raymond Lully, but nowadays not much of it remains.

EXPLANATIONS OF THE TEMPLE LEGEND

The Temple Legend

"The symbolical part of the explanation of human evolution" as it was performed in the first degree.

Text according to the original handwriting of Rudolf Steiner

At the beginning of earthly evolution one of the spirits of light, or Elohim, descended from the Sun-kingdom to the earthly realm and united with Eve, the First Mother of all living things. From this union Cain was born, the first earthly man. After this another of the Elohim, Jahweh (Yahweh) or Jehovah, created Adam; and from the union of Adam and Eve ensued Abel, the step-brother of Cain. The inequality in the births of Cain and Abel (sexual and asexual descent) caused conflict between the two brothers and Cain slew Abel. Abel was engendered through sexual descent, Cain was deprived of life in the spiritual world through a moral transgression. In place of Abel, Jehovah gave the parents a substitute son, Seth. From Cain and Seth two types of human being were descended. The descendants of Seth were able to see into the spiritual world in special (dreamy) conditions of consciousness. The descendants of Cain had completely lost this faculty. They were constrained to regain their spiritual abilities during the course of generations by gradually developing their human earthly forces.

One of the descendants of Abel-Seth was Solomon the Wise. He had inherited the gift of dreamlike clairvoyance; he had received this natural ability to an extraordinary degree. Thus it came about that his wisdom was famed far and wide, so that it was recounted symbolically that he sat on a throne of gold and ivory (the symbols of wisdom).

The descendants of the race of Cain made it their business to elevate the human earthly forces to an ever greater extent during the course of time. One of these descendants was Lamech, the guardian of the "T-books," in which, as far as earthly forces permitted, the primeval wisdom was restored in such a form that it was incomprehensible to anyone who was not an initiate. Another descendant of Cain was Tubal-Cain, who developed the art of metalwork to a very high degree and could even make musical instruments out of metal. And, living at the same time as Solomon was Hiram Abiff or Adoniram, also a member of the race of Cain, who had progressed so far in his art that it almost gave him direct perception of the spiritual world and left only a thin veil for him to pierce by initiation.

Wise Solomon conceived the plan of a temple which was to express human evolution symbolically in parts of its form. Through dream-wisdom he was able to conceive the idea of this temple in all its detail, yet he lacked the knowledge of the earth-forces that he needed for the actual building work, which was attainable only by developing these forces in the manner of the people of the race of Cain. Solomon therefore joined together with Hiram Abiff. The latter then built the temple, which was a symbolical expression of humankind's evolution.

The fame of Solomon had spread to the Queen of Sheba, Balkis. The latter set out one day intending to marry him. All the splendor of Solomon's court was shown to her, as well as the mighty temple. Out of the ideas she had previously acquired she was unable to comprehend how an architect possessing only human powers could produce something like that. She had experienced only how the masters in charge of workmen were able to muster large enough crowds through atavistical-magical powers to construct their massive buildings. She demanded to see the exceptionally notable architect. When she was met by him, his eye at once made a profound impression on her. Then he was to show her how he controlled his workers by human agreement alone. He took his mallet, climbed onto a mound and at a sign from his mallet great crowds of workmen hurried towards him. The Queen of Sheba observed how human earthly powers could develop to such a significant degree.

Soon afterwards the Queen was walking with her nurse (here meant symbolically a person with prophetic powers) in front of the city gates. They met Hiram Abiff and at that same moment the Had-Had bird flew down from the sky onto the Queen's arm.

The prophetic nurse interpreted this as signifying that the Queen of Sheba was not destined for Solomon but for Hiram Abiff. From that moment on the Queen only considered how she could dissolve her engagement to Solomon. It is further told how the engagement ring was removed from the King's finger while he was intoxicated, so that the Queen could now consider herself as the appointed bride of Hiram Abiff. (The important thing about this feature of the legend is that the Queen of Sheba represents the ancient star wisdom, which up until that epoch was connected with the atavistic soul powers symbolized by Solomon. The esoteric legends express symbolically in female characters the wisdom that can be betrothed to the male part of the soul. At the time of Solomon the epoch had arrived in which wisdom should change from the old atavistic powers to the newly acquired earthly "I"-forces. The "ring" had always been the symbol for the "I." Solomon was always thought of as being in possession of a not-completely-human "I," but one which is only the reflection of the "higher I" of the angel in atavistic-dreamlike clairvoyant consciousness. The "intoxication" points to the fact that this "I" becomes lost again among the semi-conscious soul-forces through which it was acquired. Only Hiram owns a truly human "I.")

From this time onwards a great jealousy seizes hold of Solomon against his architect. For that reason it is easy for three treacherous journeymen to gain the King's ear for a deed by which they wish to destroy Hiram. They are his opponents, because they were perforce rejected by him when they asked to have the Master's degree and the Master-Word bestowed on them, a promotion of which they were unworthy.

These three treacherous journeymen next decide to spoil the work of Hiram Abiff, which was to be the crowning achievement of his work at Solomon's court. This was to have been the casting of the "molten sea"—an ingenious piece of work cast from the seven main metals: (lead, copper, tin, quicksilver, iron, silver, gold) in such proportions as to be perfectly transparent. The process had been completed except for the final touch to be carried out in front of the Queen of Sheba—and through which the still turbid substance was to be transformed into one of clear lucidity. The three treacherous journeymen mixed some wrong substance in the casting so that, instead of it becoming clear, sparks of fire shot out from it. Hiram Abiff tried to quench the fire with water. That did not succeed, however, and the flames burst out on all sides. The people who were gathered together scattered in all directions. But Hiram Abiff heard a voice coming from the flames and the glowing embers: "Throw yourself into the sea of flames, you are invulnerable." He threw himself into the flames and soon noticed that he was heading towards the center of the Earth. When he was halfway there he met his ancestor Tubal-Cain. The latter led him to the center of the Earth where his illustrious ancestor Cain was in the state he had been in before his sin. Hiram here received an explanation from Cain that the energetic development of human earthly forces would lead eventually to the height of initiation and that the initiation thus obtained during earthly evolution was to take the place of the vision of the Abel-Seth sons, which would henceforth cease. The encouragement which Hiram Abiff received from Cain was expressed symbolically by saying that Hiram received a new mallet from Cain, with which he returned to the earth's surface, touched the molten sea and was thereby enabled to bring about its complete transparency. (With the appropriate meditation this symbolism raises the inner nature of human earthly development to the level of imagination. The molten sea can pass for a symbol of what human beings would have become if the three treacherous powers—doubt, superstition, and illusion regarding one's personal self—had not usurped a place in the soul. Through these powers the earthly development of humankind encountered the unleashing of fire in Lemuria, which could not be extinguished by the watery evolvement of Atlantis. There rather takes place a development of human earthly forces so that the original state of soul is restored to what it was in Cain before the fratricide took place. The dreamlike soul powers of the Abel-Seth descendants are unable to prevail against the earthly powers, but the descendants of Cain, who have attained the genuine "I"-development can do so.)

Further notes about the Temple Legend

Text according to the original handwriting of Rudolf Steiner

[The first part is missing]

... From this time on Solomon became inflamed with jealousy towards his architect. That is why three treacherous apprentices who, in their vanity, had demanded the degree of master and the master-word from the architect, but were not allowed to receive it because of their immaturity, had found support in Solomon. They decided to have their revenge in the following way.

Hiram Abiff was to have performed what was intended to be the crowning success of his work at Solomon's court, the casting of the so-called brazen sea. It was to be a marvelous metal casting in which all the metals of the Earth were to be mixed in such proportions that an excellent harmonious whole would result. Everything had been prepared beforehand by Hiram Abiff in all detail. This was to have been performed at a special festival. The whole court was gathered together for the occasion, including the Queen of Sheba. The three treacherous apprentices added a wrong ingredient at the critical moment, and instead of the work proceeding to a successful conclusion, sparks flew out of the casting. Hiram Abiff tried to quench the flames by adding water, but terrible fiery masses issued from the casting. Everyone was quickly dispersed. Hiram Abiff, heard a voice coming out of the fire that said to him: "Do not be afraid, cast yourself into the flames, you are invulnerable." He flung himself into the sea of flames and soon noticed that his flight was taking him towards the center of the Earth. When he was halfway there he met Tubal-Cain, who led him to his ancestor Cain in the center of the Earth. Cain was in a state of innocence before he committed the sin. Cain gave Hiram Abiff a new T-symbol and told him that he would restore the casting with it when he returned to the surface of the Earth. Furthermore, a race of human beings would descend from him that would conquer the children of Adam and would reintroduce the fire-ritual and lead humankind back to the divine Creator-Word.

There is a deep meaning in this part of the legend too. Before humankind descended to Earth from the divine world, human beings had been in spiritual surroundings that they could discern. They were aware of the creative Word of God. They were incorporated into the metallic masses, which at that time were still fluid within the fire. Before this happened the three apprentices of doubt, superstition, and illusion of self could not harm them. Human beings could not doubt the existence of the spiritual world because it was all around them. They could not be misled into superstition, for they saw the spirit in its true likeness. Superstition, however, consists of seeing the spirit under a false guise. The illusion of the personal self could not befall them because they knew themselves to be a part of the general spirituality; they had not yet become separated from this general spirituality through imprisonment within the body. If the three treacherous apprentices had not clung to their heels, the human body would have been a pure harmonious composition of substances. The added ingredient caused them to forget the divine-spiritual Creator-Word. The casting was thereby spoiled. The journey of Hiram Abiff to the center of the Earth represents the advance of humankind along the esoteric path. Through that humankind regained possession of the T, the divine Creator-Word. Human nature (Cain) learned to know what it was like before the Fall of humanity and how to be creative in purity.

The following is another imagination:

The eye is the divine "Eye of Power" underlying all temporal things, including even the sevenfold nature of the human being.

One gains an idea of that if one calls to mind the words of Augustine:

"Human beings see things as they are,
They are as God sees them."[1]

Human seeing is passive, the things must be there for us to see
them. The seeing of God creates the things in the act of seeing
them. The enclosing triangle signifies:

Spirit Self (Manas)

Life Spirit (Buddhi)

Spirit Human (Atman)

The rays represent the "I"—the higher trinity shines through
the "I" into the lower members of human nature.

These are symbolized as follows:

1. through the illuminated part of the clouds: astral body.

2. through the unilluminated parts of the clouds: etheric body.

3. through the surrounding darkness: physical body.

The Temple Legend and this raying eye should constitute a per-
manent source of meditation for the ∴ [Freemasons]. They
should constantly call them to mind—gaze upon them as pictures
(imaginations) in the spirit. Then, if they have bestowed sufficient
energy and patience on them, they will become aware of the fact
that these pictures awaken powers and capacities within them that
had been asleep and by their arousal enable them to see into the
spiritual world. For we do not acquire supersensible organs of perception through tumultuous external means, but by such subtle
means as those here described, which are applied in constant
inward-looking soul activity.

———————

———————

1. *Confessions*: Book 13, Chapter 38 (beginning).

Adopt expressions for:
  right angle
  alter direction
  speak letters alternately

  _____

  sacred word
  password
  apron
  trowel and [cord?] for the trowel.

  _____

The Ebb and Flow of Macrocosmic and Microcosmic Energy

The following is probably a writing by Rudolf Steiner, of which, however, the original is lacking.

Text according to a typewritten copy

If we consider the nature of evolution, we find that wherever there is life—whether in the evolution of the Earth or of the individual—there are two great streams, symbolically expressed as a rising line and a falling line, manifesting in time and space and interchanging with one another. The forces themselves, which underlie these currents, are not observable, but project into them in such a way that the whole of evolution is enclosed between them. It passes between these two lines as through a doorway.

In every planetary evolutionary stage of the Earth, from its first embodiment as ancient Saturn onwards, these two forces have been active. There is a period in which the uprising forces are chiefly dominant, they induce a condition of waking-up and unfolding, until a point is reached in which the forces of falling-asleep and dying start to take over. At first there is always a period of blossoming and burgeoning that then reaches its culmination and is replaced by a period in which everything dissolves again and a dismantling of the whole begins. The same thing happens at every evolutionary stage of Earth: something new comes into blossom, unfolds to a certain point, decays, and finally dies away. Every earthly condition during a certain period of time is to be explained as a weaving and interplay of forces that come into flower and those that die away, those that belong to the rising and those that belong to the falling line—sunrise and sunset—and in between, the zenith at noon, where the two forces unite and become one.

Seen from one's horizon a person beholds the stars in the sky, rising in the east and climbing ever higher until they reach their highest point in the south. From then onwards they sink down until they set in the west. And though the stars disappear from one's sight in the west, one must nevertheless say to oneself: The real place of setting lies to the south and coincides with the zenith, just as the true place of rising is in the north and coincides with the nadir. The rising starts from the nadir. Through that a circular motion is described, which can be divided into two halves by a vertical line running south to north. In the part containing the eastern point the rising forces are active. In the part containing the western point the sinking forces are present. The eastern and western points cut the semicircle through the center. They are the two points in which, for our physical eye, vision of the forces begins and ends. They are one's horizon (see sketch p. 400).

The same rotation that is seen in the macrocosm can be found again in the circulation of the blood within the physical body. There the forces of blossoming and life are also at work in the red blood flowing from the heart. And then the forces of decay and death start to take over when the red blood is converted into blue. One could also divide the circulation of the blood into a rising semicircle and one in which the forces are ebbing.

And thus it is in human life. During the day one is active in the physical world of the senses, when one gives expression to one's impulses and uses up the forces that one acquired in sleep from the cosmos during the night. Just as the red blood flows from the heart after it has been refreshed by the oxygen which it takes in from the outer world through the lungs, so does one wake up in the morning with new forces. And just as the red blood relinquishes its life forces during its passage through the physical body and is gradually transformed into blue, dead blood, so does one give expression to one's forces in waking consciousness and is constrained to sink into the oblivion of sleep so that one may gather new forces from the surrounding macrocosm. Sleeping and waking are like inhalation and exhalation of the human self. During the night one inhales new forces, which one then exhales during the day.

The development of the human individuality in a physical incarnation on Earth is also subject to these two forces through the fact that up to about one's thirty-fifth year one develops the members of one's being out of oneself and thereby descends ever more deeply into the world of the physical senses. That is like an exhalation of one's being on the physical plane. Then follows the time when one does not acquire anything new and begins to withdraw more and more from the physical sense-world. One gradually dies as a physical human being and a drawing-in of one's being takes place. During the first half of life the activity of the upbuilding forces is so much in excess that there is always a surplus of life forces present and consequently a person grows in respect of the earthly self. In the second half, however, it is the dismantling forces that are prevalent and then there is always a residue that cannot be resuscitated, and the latter leads eventually to the decay and death of the physical body.

Long before one comes to Earth in a physical incarnation—appears on the horizon, as it were—one's being has been worked upon by divine spiritual forces from the macrocosm. The latter commenced their activity from a point lying at the deepest point below the horizon, at the nadir. As a microcosm one rises in the east, experiences one's zenith at about the thirty-fifth year in the south and sets in the west at one's death. But after that the divine spiritual forces continue to work from the cosmos for a long time on one's dissolution.

Thus the semicircle that lies between the eastern and western points and passes through the south belongs to the active, conscious life of the microcosm, and the semicircle that passes from west to east by way of the north belongs to the work of the macrocosmic forces on the microcosm. The former is therefore the light half for human beings on Earth, in which they are themselves active with wakeful day consciousness. During the dark second half everything works upon the subconscious self, because one has no individual consciousness while one is asleep. In both halves, in the light as well as the dark half, both the upbuilding and disintegrating forces are at work. Thus the whole circle is divided into four parts and two right angles are formed both in the microcosm as well as the macrocosm; in one of them the life-forces are active, as in the red blood, and in the other the death-forces are at work, as in the blue blood. Also in every cosmic revelation, in every planetary stage of the present earth, there is a period in which the upbuilding forces predominate and a period in which the disintegrating forces are prevalent. It is the exhalation and inhalation which is presented to our physical senses. Thus a rising and setting is seen here too.

So where the upbuilding forces first appear in evolution, there the disintegrating forces are simultaneously at work. In the same way, when the red blood leaves the heart the element of death takes over. Wherever life begins, the seed of death is planted within it, but it does not show itself until later. The starting point is at the same time the lowest point, just as the highest point is the start of decline. So it is in the human being and in the cosmos.

Because disintegrating forces have been active from the beginning, much falls prey to them before it has attained its highest point of development, before it has achieved what it set out to do. So something always remains unaccomplished that needs a new opportunity for it to develop further. When a new stage of development has been created, a certain culmination for it is also fixed, which is a continuation of the previous one, for even there an upbuilding process is continually at work up to a certain point. What was not achieved under the then prevailing conditions and remained behind, must be worked out further under quite new conditions. If this were not the case every stage of development would then stand apart by itself and, when it had passed, would bring no incentive for what was to follow. Now, however, through what remains behind, the seed has been laid for what occurs at one stage of development to lead over into the next. The stages of development lead on consecutively from one to the next.

In the development of human individuality this comes to expression in repeated earth lives. In such a case what has not been brought to the intended perfection in one life will be further developed in the next. From the beginning, forces that have been left behind from earlier incarnations live and weave in this way into the succeeding life. While the new is being developed, the old continues to live within it, adjusted to the changed conditions, because what is the normal level of achievement is different in every human incarnation. Like a dark force that opposes the new blossoming powers it adapts itself to the new incarnation. It is the same in the cosmos. It manifests in those beings that remain behind at every planetary stage of our present Earth. Because these forces intrude themselves into the normal course of evolution as something foreign to it, they form a counter pole lying outside it, an outer world over against what has developed normally during a certain period. And so evolution splits up into that which lives and blossoms within it and that which intrudes from earlier conditions and actually lies outside evolution and faces extinction.

Both are present during an evolutionary period from the beginning. During earthly evolution, which has as its task the introversion from macrocosm to microcosm in forming the human individuality, only what achieved its foreordained goal in every preceding planetary stage is part of the ascending line. What remains behind falls prey to the forces of disintegration, it does not become introverted to become a microcosm, but remains in the macrocosm. Thus, through the working of the two forces, an inner and an outer world are established from the beginning. There are thus Saturn beings still actively engaged at the Sun stage in developing the physical body without being able to achieve the goal of the Sun stage, which was the development of the etheric body alongside the physical. During the Moon condition, beings are active that only work on the physical and others that work on the etheric body, whereas the task in hand would be to develop the astral body. During the Earth condition beings are at work that are only engaged in forming the physical, others that work on the etheric and still others that work on the astral body, whereas the normal task is to develop the "I"-principle within the physical, etheric and astral sheaths. So there are retarded beings at every stage of development. For those beings who have developed their "I"-consciousness on Earth within the three sheaths, i.e., the human being, these retarded beings manifest themselves in the physical world of the senses in the surroundings. These retard beings are estranged from normal human development, and confront humans as something foreign. Their development has a different rhythm because it is projected into our present earthly evolution from earlier stages of existence. But it cannot quite keep pace with it and belongs to the descending line of evolution.

Just as these retarded forces express themselves physically on Earth as the outer world, so can one also recognize the activity of retarded forces in the spiritual sphere. There, too, the activity of the retarded beings interferes in the work of those beings that lead and guide the normal course of evolution for a certain period of time. It creates a counterweight and a basis for the activity of the more advanced beings, and in the same way that it would be impossible for physical human beings to live and develop without their earthly surroundings, so would it be impossible for the more advanced beings to carry out their work if the retarded beings with their forces did not oppose them and thereby form a counterbalance. Therefore, from the start, there must be beings that work especially in the upbuilding forces and those that manifest in the disintegrating forces. It is only between these two forces that evolution can proceed. And so there were beings that immersed themselves ever deeper into the human individuality and expressed themselves from within through the outward deeds of human individualities; they attained the set goal of earthly development, which was the creating of the "I"-consciousness within the three microcosmic sheaths. They then lived and expressed themselves through the active work of the "I"-force in the outer world. These spiritual beings work within the human "I" as it lives within its three sheaths and pours out its forces into the surrounding world. We sense them during our waking life, they are active while we are consciously aware in the light semicircle of existence. The powers of light and warmth that followed the normal course of evolution worked in humanity itself. They had turned inwards to become a microcosm, from which they rayed out into the surrounding world. But even in the light semicircle there is a part that belongs to the upbuilding forces and a part belonging to the disintegrating forces, an eastern and a western half. Those forces that radiate as light and warmth into the Earth from the Sun during the day are ones that have not accompanied the course of evolution in so far as it concerns the intensifying of the macrocosm. Already during the Moon stage when Sun and Moon separated, these forces had remained at the Sun stage; they did not accompany the further evolution of the old Moon. They remained in the macrocosm and did not deepen themselves to become a microcosm.

This was repeated during the earthly stage when the Sun again split off and radiated its light inwards from outside. The planetary body that we call Sun, as regards the microcosmic evolution, belongs to the retrograde line of development. The Sun forces that turned inwards to the microcosm belong to the ascending line. Everything that surrounds us in our environment, whether physical or spiritual is a part of the forces of decline, for it has only turned inwards to a certain extent. It then shares in evolution as part of the environment in which it can become constructive by working from outside into the microcosm. That which is transformed more and more into the microcosm and shares in the whole course of earthly evolution becomes part of the upbuilding forces. Through this a center-point is formed in the macrocosm, from which forces radiate into the surrounding world. They at first work in a retrograde way, for this center develops into a microcosm at the expense of its surroundings. It draws its nourishment out of its physical environment. There have to be macrocosmic beings in the spiritual world that pour new forces into it from outside as nourishment, so that it can develop further.

Those powers that did not participate in the normal course of evolution and that had not turned inwards to become a microcosm, act upon us during the night. They had not participated in the development of the "I" or the astral body, they were retarded in that respect and can therefore only work within the microcosm when the "I" and astral body have left it, that is during sleep. They had not dipped down into the microcosmic "I" and astral body, they had remained behind in the macrocosm. They could only introvert into a microcosm that consists of an etheric and physical principle. There they act like an outer world that has turned inwards to become a microcosm, analogous to substances and forces that are absorbed by us from the outer world to become our nourishment. Only subconscious action without "I"-consciousness can take place. For just as little as the beings that live in our physical surroundings have developed an individual "I"-consciousness, just as little have the macrocosmic beings developed a consciousness such as ours from our spiritual surroundings. These forces belong to the dark semicircle. Day and night the beings belonging to the ascending forces and those belonging to the descending forces alternate with one another in their work on the microcosm. During the day the ascending forces work within the "I"-consciousness, at night they are poured out into the macrocosm with the "I." During the night those forces work within the microcosm, which during the day are poured out into the macrocosm. When we are asleep the macrocosm awakens in us; when the microcosm awakes, the macrocosm in our environment sleeps.

A similar thing happened when the Moon separated from the Earth, as happened when Sun and Moon separated during the old Moon evolution and was repeated during earthly evolution. There, too, beings remain behind from the Moon evolution. They lapse into the retrograde line of development by not having achieved the goal of Earth evolution. That [part], however, which had followed the normal course of the Moon evolution and had attained the corresponding goal, could now take up the "I"-forces into itself and develop them further in the microcosm. The part, however, that remained behind at that time still had to develop astrality during Earth evolution. It had not turned inwards into itself and could only work into the microcosm as Moon forces from outside. The retarded beings from the Moon evolution were not able to penetrate into human "I"-forces, they worked in human day-consciousness only as far as the astral body. They cannot reach the goal of Earth evolution. They belong to the forces of the retrograde line. Their action in Earth evolution starts where the "I"-force begins to blossom. That came about in Lemurian times when the "I" turned inwards to the microcosm and the influence of the retarding forces from the Moon condition, the Luciferic beings, began to affect the astral body.

Alongside new evolutionary developments, prolongations from the previous condition also entered into the process. For a period of time, both developed beside each other. Then came the moment when the old had to die away, as the new continued to develop. The unfolding of those powers that have to develop during the Earth period and those that belong to a previous condition and have to proceed with their development under new conditions and therefore show a greater perfection than those which are just starting, is symbolically expressed in the Temple Legend. It is recounted therein that one of the Elohim descended [to Earth], married Eve, the Earth-Mother, and from this union Cain was born. He was the first earthly man. Another of the Elohim created Adam, and from the union of Adam with Eve Abel was born.

The Cain human being is the son of divine-spiritual forces, which worked into Earth evolution in such a way that a microcosm was produced in which the macrocosmic forces were portrayed. Cain belongs to those forces that attain a particular goal in earthly evolution by implanting the "I"-force in humanity and later developing it.

The Abel human being belongs to other macrocosmic powers, which were unable to implant the "I"-force into him so directly. The macrocosm acted in him by means of two human beings. Because Abel was not such a direct bearer of macrocosmic powers as Cain, the macrocosm acted in him by means of two human beings. This happened through sexuality. The Abel human being belongs to those powers that interpose themselves into earthly evolution from an earlier condition. In him work retrograde powers from the Moon evolution, which had not attained their goal at that time and therefore could not penetrate into the microcosm further than to the astral body. Only with the help of a human pair could they work creatively into earthly evolution. What they accomplished creatively had to be performed with the help of sexuality, because they were able to work with those powers that belonged to the Moon evolution. The principle of duality was active during the Moon stage in the form of two powers that worked creatively upon each other as Sun and Moon forces. It belonged to what had to be developed at that time. The retrograde powers, which also manifested in earthly evolution when the "I"-force was beginning to flourish in humanity, introduced these Moon forces into earthly evolution and implanted them into the microcosm in such a way that a duality arose within it, whereby either the Sun- or the Moon influence was uppermost in its physical or etheric body. In that way the two sexes came about.

The Cain human being, who belonged to the actual Earth evolution, did not need to be involved in sexuality. Just as the principle of duality prevailed during the old Moon evolution, so was a Trinity devised for the Earth evolution: Sun, Moon and Earth. Earthly humanity could embody the powers of both sexes within it, in the same way that the Earth carries within it both Sun- and Moon forces. Humankind could work creatively by means of that which is developed on the Earth, the force of the "I."

But in the Temple Legend it is further recorded that Cain became guilty through slaying his brother. He thereby got involved in the forces that worked in Abel, the retrograde forces from the Moon evolution. These forces could then take up residence in him. By causing death he became indebted to those forces that lead to death, the descending, disintegrating forces.

The Temple Legend further instructs us that Cain became a cultivator of the soil. Abel-Seth, the substitute son of Adam and Eve, became a herdsman. Those belonging to the Cain stream accompanied Earth evolution, cultivating that which bore fruit, and they worked their way up with the ascending evolutionary line. They have to work on Earth in the surrounding world with the forces that have become interiorized within them.

In those belonging to the Abel stream the cosmic forces did not work so intensely within them, but radiated into them more from outside. They received from the cosmos what the Cain human beings had to wrest from their surroundings through their own forces. They did not become cultivators of the soil because they were unable to work with earthly evolution as did those of the Cain stream. They became herdsmen, working upon the astral (animal) realm.

The streams of the Cain humanity and the Abel humanity continue to work on in earthly evolution. So the Temple Legend recounts further how there was once a time in which the famous King Solomon, a descendant of the Abel stream, and Hiram Abiff, his great architect from the Cain stream, were contemporaries.

King Solomon possessed wisdom that flowed into him from the spiritual world, the macrocosm. His architect constructed works of art out of his own initiative. His greatest work of art was to have been the building of a temple that would have contained everything that exists in the outside world. It was to have been a copy of the outer world. King Solomon was able to conceive the plan of this temple, but he could not erect such a building. As a member of the Abel humanity he was unable to deal with what was physical. The architect was able to build the temple because, as a member of the Cain stream, he had learned to work with earthly matter and to master it. The Cain human being could build the temple of the microcosm in which all the forces active in the outside world were transformed into microcosmic forces; one belonging to the Abel stream could only imagine the temple as a picture-image.

The architect's final great work of art was to have been the casting of the brazen sea. In this was to be mixed the seven earthly metals in such proportion that a transparent liquid would have been the result. In the seven metals (copper, tin, gold, lead, iron, quicksilver, and silver) the seven powers are at work that are an expression of the seven planets. Where the seven metals unite in a harmonious fashion they form a radiant unity that contains each ingredient, just as white light contains the seven colors of the spectrum.

Those of the Cain stream can act so harmoniously through their "I"-forces into these planetary powers, which are expressed in them as the seven members of their being (three higher and four lower), that together they constitute the human being who can see beyond the physical sense world into a spiritual world. That was to be the final great work of art.

From King Solomon's side something took place to hinder the casting. Three treacherous apprentices mixed something into the casting that destroyed it completely. Because at one time Cain had been guilty of slaying his brother Abel and had thereby absorbed into himself those forces that belong to the declining line, so could the demolishing forces now approach the Cain stream from the side of the Abel human beings, which proved disastrous for the work of building-up. It is further recounted how the architect was saved from the catastrophe that ensued and led through the fire to his illustrious ancestor, Cain, at the center of the Earth. There he received a new mallet and started his work all over again, which was then successful. The Cain human being was led by the power of the "I," expressed in blood and fire, through the blood of the generations to his great ancestor. There he gazed into the Spirit, which was revealed to him as the central point of earthly evolution, the World-"I" that had imbued him with His strength. Through that he acquired new strength to continue with his task.

Then a new period of work began for him, as the wisdom that had formerly flowed into the Abel current from the spiritual world now united with him. That is described in the Temple Legend as the betrothal of the great architect to the Queen of Sheba, who was previously pledged to marry King Solomon. From that time on those forces that work in the Abel current went into decline. They had reached their zenith in Earth evolution.

For every cycle of development a certain climax is determined; then the task of that period of development has been accomplished. This point can be described as the zenith or noontide. Until that point has been reached the forces are waxing and after it they wane. The noon point can be determined from the horizon. It is at the zenith that the forces that appear in the east reach their greatest expansion and until then work is done in a constructive manner. From then onwards the work of dismantling begins moving towards the west. Those forces, which impinge upon the new evolutionary conditions from past stages of development, are unable to attain the highest point, they are to be compared with those celestial bodies that have a short daytime arc and a long night arc. They have only a short stay in the light half of the circle and a longer one in the dark half. Their noontide height (compared with the horizon) is small. Their orbit lies only a little way above the horizon. So do they work chiefly in the dark half of the circle. During the evolution of Earth through its earlier planetary stages until the Earth evolution itself, macrocosmic forces gradually invert into the microcosm. Those forces that remained behind had not inverted sufficiently: they remained behind in the macrocosm while the microcosm was developing "I"-consciousness. That is why they could only work in the microcosm itself in the half of the circle that belongs to its subconscious life. Their work lies chiefly below the horizon. Beyond the horizon, in the conscious day-life of the microcosm, they could only work outside the microcosm. The lines formed by the horizon stretching from east to west and the fixed zenith standing perpendicularly upon it together form the symbolical figure of the Tao-sign. This is the mallet, which had been given for the building of a particular evolutionary period. With this mallet the temple of the microcosm was constructed out of the macrocosm, and work on this temple is continuing. Its strength is manifested in the light half of the circle; there, where the microcosm is able to work consciously with the introverted (personalized) forces, is where the mallet strikes.

During earthly evolution, when the divine spiritual forces of the macrocosm had inverted into the microcosm, the greatest deepening took place, when God Himself entered the microcosm. Then the culmination of Earth evolution had been achieved. From that time on the powers that work on the dissolution of the micro-cosm gradually begin to show themselves. The whole course of evo-lution has been reversed: from that point onwards the microcosm is expanding to the macrocosm. Up until that point everything in the microcosm that had kept pace with evolution had become inward. Now the microcosm must also take up into itself what had always remained behind, so that evolution can progress further. The divine-spiritual beings had gradually to withdraw from human-ity; so human beings could gradually take a hand in the affairs of the macrocosm. Instead of receiving they must start to give. They must volunteer out of themselves to approach those beings that have held themselves apart and remained behind so human beings could develop. Then humanity will be able to unite its conscious-ness with theirs.

Human beings had until then, when the culmination point was reached, to work upon the construction of the microcosm and to build into it all the forces from the macrocosm. In the light half of the circle they had to work in the microcosmic consciousness. Then, however, comes the time in which their task changes so radically that they must work out of the temple of the microcosm into the outer world, so that their forces flow out into the dark half of the cir-cle, where the macrocosmic forces work subconsciously within them. Then the darkness that surrounds them and what lives as sub-consciousness within them will become illumined with the light of understanding as a result of their work upon the temple of the microcosm. Their consciousness will extend over their surround-ings. Microcosm and macrocosm will join together and the light and dark semicircle will form a circle in which human beings can be consciously active when they experience themselves as a macrocosm within the microcosm. The upbuilding and dismantling forces, life and death, become one and change into one another. So will humankind stride consciously through the ascending and descend-ing lines of evolution, through the gateway that leads to the Divine Spirit Himself, Who is manifested in these powers.

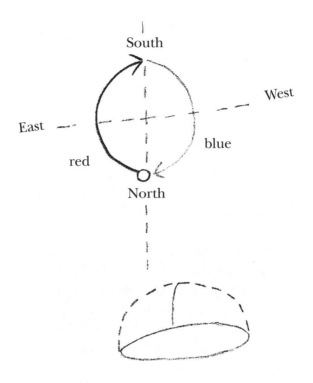

Meditational Instructions for the Beginning of the Temple Legend

Text according to a duplicated copy with the title: "On entering the first degree"

It is necessary to assimilate the Temple Legend as an impulse for gaining imaginative understanding. This legend is so arranged that by assimilating its pictures in our soul, a view of human evolution independently of the organ of knowledge can slowly be acquired through continual meditation. In the following the legend is presented so as to form the basis of the meditation when the noted effect is sought.

At the beginning of Earth's becoming one of the Spirits of Light, or Elohim, descended from spiritual heights and united himself with Eve, the Earth-Mother. From this union issued Cain, the first earthly man, who lived in such a way that his breathing consisted of inhaling and exhaling the substance of warmth.

Eve, the Earth-Mother, lived as a being, weaving in the element of air. The meditation must take account of how far

Air in conjunction with light produces the breath of warmth.

Then another of the Spirits of Light, Jahve, descended from spiritual heights and formed Adam out of the atomized elements of Earth (earth-dust). From the union of Adam with Eve issued Abel, the step-brother [half-brother] of Cain.

The meditation must address the question as to how far *the man of the earth-element in conjunction with the air being, Eve, produces Abel, whose material element is atomized water.*

There was a dispute between Cain, the human being of the fire and Abel, the human being of the water. And Cain killed Abel.

The being of the fire drew out of the planet Earth the human being of water.

Cain possessed a knowledge that originally penetrated into things as the element of fire; that was clairvoyant knowledge. Through having contact with Abel—the human being of the water—Cain's clairvoyance grew dark. From him springs the human beings of Earth, who have to work their way upwards from the darkness to the light by means of progressive development.

Jahve gave Seth to Adam and Eve as a substitute. Abel-Seth is henceforth the ancestor of the priestly race, which are certainly humans of Earth but that breathe in the element of air. Through the ᵎembodiment of Jahve the breathing of air was spiritualized in these ancestors of humanity to a primitive kind of clairvoyance. The divine secrets are revealed to them in dreams.

The contents of this evolution of humankind should be meditated by means of
the following esoteric characters:

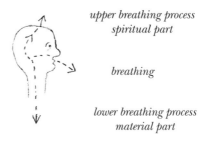

upper breathing process
spiritual part

breathing

lower breathing process
material part

The spiritualized breathing process,
which rises in the ascending stream of
breath into the space within the head,
becomes a conscious act of imaginative
knowledge in the forefathers.

In these diagrams all processes are
included, in Mystery form, according
to those that the two evolutionary
streams of humanity developed. The
apparatus for acquiring knowledge,
which belongs to the Sons of Cain and
is formed more from the element of
fire, absorbed the sense impressions
and elaborated them intellectually.
The organ of clairvoyance of the Sons
of Abel-Seth, formed more from the
element of water, was less adapted for
sense perception. Its apparatus for
acquiring knowledge expressed itself
through visions that could bring spiritual experiences into consciousness
without any direct sense impressions.

One gains an impression of these processes through the following diagram:

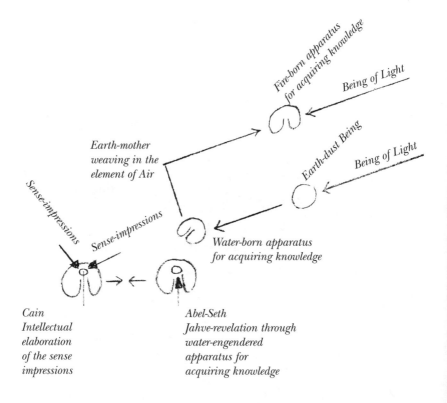

The primeval happenings, which have here been portrayed for imaginative perception, live on in our inner being. One is unable to fully explain them by means of abstract concepts, because the latter are too coarse and incomplete compared with the complexity of the real happenings. But through the way they are represented here they can be vividly brought to life in the soul. Then the pictures work on in the soul. And as the elements that provide the truth are contained within the soul, the pictures slowly awaken the living perception. By this means one attains a direct knowledge of what has taken place.

It is a good thing to take the given pictures as a basis for general discussion in our F.M. [Freemasonry] gatherings. One then gets familiar with the pictures in the group meetings. By this means every member can meditate the pictures in the intervening time before the next meeting. Then, when we next meet, the results of our meditations can be exchanged and discussed. By this means one gains a more exact and extensive insight into the content of the pictures. With this extension one again meditates during the interval before the following meeting. This process is continued. A satisfactory outcome will only be achieved after a longer period of meetings.

This is one of the ways—and a very sure one at that—by which one draws near to imaginative knowledge. One has attained this after the pictures have so identified with the inner mobility of the soul, that one perceives them as an inner element of life and knowledge within the soul.

One really ought to begin with this small part of the Temple Legend and thus start off the process of imaginative cognition. After that one can meditate the following esoteric diagram, which can provide the soul with an important basis of knowledge:

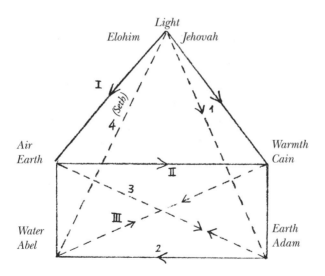

Another example of the text shows the sketch as follows:

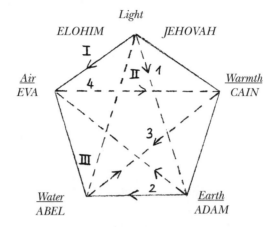

(Numbers and arrows not reliable)

Explanations of the Beginning [of the Temple Legend]

From an instruction lesson, Berlin, March 1908 (no exact date)

When it is said that one of the Elohim united with Eve, Eve must not be thought of as at all similar to a woman of today. Eve was a human being of the Polaric Race, someone quite different from modern humanity and much simpler. If we think of the warmth in the blood and dismiss from our mind all other considerations, if we just think of the blood-warmth, which pulses through every corner of our body from top to toe, and imagine it as pervading every single part of our body, excluding every thing else, then we get an inkling of how Eve appeared when she united with one of the Elohim. The Earth was dark at that time, but in the Second, or Hyperborean Epoch, the Sun-Spirits penetrated this dark Eve with light. The rays of the Sun did not only contain light but were also nourishment and the part of it that was not consumed as nourishment to sustain humanity, or Eve, was available for the purpose of procreation, and in this way Cain was engendered through the union of one of the Elohim with Eve.

During the Lemurian or Moon Epoch, one of the Elohim—Jahve—who was likewise a Sun-Spirit and had been appointed to the leadership of the Moon Evolution, created Adam. That is to say, he divided humanity into sexes, and when it is said that Adam married Eve, this signifies that the two sexes united for the purpose of procreation and Abel was born as the outcome of this union.

Thus, the Sun forces and the forces of reproduction, which were originally combined, had separated and produced two classes of human beings.

Cain and Abel attack one another continually within our own bodies—they even contend hourly, for Abel represents the arterial blood, which proceeds from the lungs and the heart, full of the life-giving spirit of the air, the pure, strength-giving oxygen. Cain, on the other hand, represents the venous blood, which is filled with poisonous carbon dioxide that produces death.

If that had been all, humankind would have ceased to exist at that time. But Abel continued to live on in Seth, who was the rejuvenated Abel, who received once again the living breath, the oxygen, into his lungs. For that reason, whenever Abel is killed, he is replaced by Seth.

When the Sun forces split up, the race of Abel-Seth became the bearer of divine wisdom and intuition whose descendants were priests and kings "through the Grace of God."

Seen physically they are negative or female (not necessarily physically female).

The members of the Cain race possess the force of procreation (not necessarily sexual) instead of intuitive wisdom. They are positive, male (not necessarily physically male) and are the world-workers, scientific researchers, and so on. This will perhaps be made more comprehensible by the following diagram:

Sons of God ...[2] physically feminine, etherically masculine, possessing intuition: Abel

The power of the Sun contains nourishment, intuition and procreative forces	blue	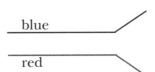
	red	

Daughters of Man ... [3] physically male, etherically female, possess forces of reproduction: Cain.

In Atlantean times an attempt was made to unite these two classes of human beings, but that led to black magic of the worst kind. That is referred to in the Bible: "The Sons of God saw the daughters of men that they were fair; and they took them wives of all that they chose" [Genesis, 6.2.].

The arrival of the Queen of Sheba is the attempt of the present day [to unite the two classes]. Science, represented by Hiram, can now unite with the wisdom of soul, which is symbolized by the Queen of Sheba. The wet nurse is the prophet who foretells the future. The bird Had-Had is the spirit of intelligence that descends to the soul [the Queen of Sheba] and turns her away from the revelation, represented by Solomon, to self-acquired knowledge, which finds expression in Hiram.

The Temple is a picture of Earth evolution. Solomon resembles a mirror that reflects cosmic wisdom without any exertion on his own part. Hiram, on the other hand, sees the picture and elaborates it. He is not able to create directly out of the divine source of inspiration; he epitomizes material know-how that is able to put into practice what Solomon can only visualize.

For that reason Balkis, the soul, is not satisfied and ends her relationship with Solomon when she realizes Hiram's beauty, by retrieving the ring from Solomon's hand while he is intoxicated.

---

2. The row of dots is reproduced thus in the original.
3. As note 2 above.

The fact that Hiram wields the Tau-mallet in order to call the workmen together at the request of Balkis, expresses symbolically how all great world achievements have been brought about, after working for many years like ants to attain a particular goal: it was the power of mass suggestion. This power was exercised in such a way that the workers assembled through their own free will. It would not be right to make use of such a force today, but at that time people were not so individualized [as they are today] and when temples were to be built to serve humankind's needs, priests were justified in using these methods to achieve their ends. The Crusades and the army of Joan of Arc are other examples of such mass suggestion. Sometimes fanatics who are rather unbalanced tend very much in this direction.

When Hiram threw himself into the fire, he met Tubal-Cain on his way, who led him to the center of the Earth (where the plant that represents the "I" grows: Cain was a cultivator of the soil), and there they find Cain in his state of innocence. Cain gives Hiram a new mallet and a new word.

Extracts from notes of various participants (lacking further details)

When the preparation for Earth-evolution had progressed so far that human souls could be incorporated into it, the Sun had already departed and rayed down upon the Earth, which was a fireball surrounded by an atmosphere or aura of warmth. In the globe of the Earth the human physical and etheric body grew up from it like a plant and, as the Sun shone upon the warmth atmosphere, the warmth penetrated the physical and etheric bodies and built from them the astral body, which is the soul. This radiation by the Beings of the Sun upon human forms introduced the forces of wisdom of these Sun Beings into human beings, which became the higher "I," the innate divine wisdom, that makes a human being into a spiritually perceptive being. This must all be seen as the effects or deeds of Divine Beings. The Sun Beings, or Elohim, sent their rays down to Earth through the mediation of the Archangels and introduced currents into the human form that, on the one hand, penetrated the warmth aura to bring light, which became the human brain in which intellect and spirituality could be revealed, and at the same time, currents that became human blood; thereby the universal warmth became inner warmth. The first of these currents also represents the active power of the Archangels, the second is the passive power. The current that formed the brain out of light was Cain, the man of the fire-earth; the accompanying current, which introduced the blood into the human being, is Abel, who was born of Adam. The watery substance was the blood. That is the fluid human.

Thus in Cain we have a being possessing all the faculties that enable him to progress to a universal wisdom by means of an understanding that functions in the dark; in Abel we have a being that has taken up the watery element, the blood, along with the light and has thereby gained a different kind of contact with the spiritual beings, the passive side of the light.

It is indicated in the Genesis cycle[4] how, at a particular moment in earthly evolution, forces from the center of the fiery Earth globe radiate out into the cosmos and are reflected back from there into the center. Through that the warmth atmosphere is created; it is a kind of intermediate substance that exerts resistance. While the inhalation and exhalation is in progress, resistance comes about in the warmth atmosphere and the Sun Beings can no longer send their rays to the Earth through this layer as they did at the beginning. While the beings that grew up in earthly matter were being endowed with the pure fire of wisdom, which became the first beginnings of the brain development, the fire was later dimmed by the resistance and came to the earthly beings in the form of air, which brought about a different configuration of the brain. We therefore find Eve, the Earth Mother—who, since the birth of Cain, consists more of atomized material—in association with Adam, the darkened current of the Sun Beings, from which Earth Beings formed Abel, the breather of air. Through the

---

4. *Genesis, Secrets of the Bible Story of Creation* (CW 122).

general densification through air, Cain also experiences resistance, the direct contact with fire-breathing grows dimmer, which is personified by the slaying of Abel by Cain. Cain is now cut off from the Gods of Fire, but has received into himself the faculty of evolving the inner fire of wisdom out of himself by means of understanding, which he is able to convert into wisdom.

What is meant by "the dust of the Earth," out of which Adam was created? The whole of evolution is densification, a working towards form during a particular epoch. So also, the preparation for the earthly condition is a working towards creating form, towards densification, the joining together of spiritual forces.

When Eve, the Earth-Mother, had been created by the activity of the Thrones and Elohim, the first modeling of Cain took place. Then the active part of this process aroused the element of fire and the passive part caused the densification towards matter, the element of air. Put in other, simpler words: Matter, which they would henceforth influence, had become denser by being worked upon the first time; it is more physical, but is imbued with an efficient spirit. Out of this more intense cooperation Adam is born, and the product of the Adam and Eve interaction is Abel, the watery, or airy being. The encounter between the fiery and the airy element caused conflict and resistance. The fiery element is dimmed and absorbs something of the dark elements into itself.

Already in the characters of Cain and Abel two definite directions had become visible: Cain was a cultivator who wrested his produce with effort from the earth; Abel was a shepherd who received without effort what was supplied him by his herds. As a result these two directions were clearly stamped upon the descendants of these two brothers, so that humanity was divided in two directions, the Cainites and the Abel-Sethites. The former were those who raised themselves up by their own effort, the artists in all fields of human endeavor. The latter received their wisdom as a gift. From them are descended the priest-kings initiated "by the Grace of God."

The fratricide also signifies that the blue blood slew the red blood.

――――――――

From the Seth-Abel current came Solomon, the wise King Solomon, who received his wisdom from higher inspiration. He was able to visualize the plan of the temple, but was unable to carry out the building of the temple through his own powers. For that he had to employ Hiram-Abiff from the race of Cain. Solomon wanted to construct a temple in such a way that every part of it should represent a piece of human evolution. A copy of this temple is our own temple. The two pillars, for instance, represent the Pillars of Hercules in the Straits of Gibraltar, through which the peoples of the Earth passed as they travelled from east to west. Hiram Abiff built this temple.

――――――――

Personal notes by Rudolf Steiner for a female participant. Dated Stuttgart, February 21, 1912

Solomon knew three secrets: those of the two Pillars of Hercules, of the trinity of wisdom, beauty and strength and the secret of light and darkness.

――――――――

The Hiram nature is in each one of us; we must bring it to resurrection within us.

――――――――

Explanations of the Brazen Sea

Instruction lesson without reference to place or date.

The brazen sea is the pure, unclouded human nature. The three traitorous apprentices are: doubt, superstition and self-illusion. Through incarnation into the physical world we come into a position of doubting our spiritual reality and acquiring false concepts. That is superstition, for instance the concept of being an isolated being and not a part of the great whole, the illusion of personal selfhood. These three traitorous apprentices destroy the originally pure human nature. From that springs the fire of passions.

From an instruction lesson, Cologne, December 22, 1907

If the brazen sea had become a reality it would have transformed the Earth into a clear, transparent planet. The three apprentices hindered the casting. Doubt, superstition and belief in a personal ego have dimmed the casting. There are three points in the human etheric body—heart, spleen, and back—which are particularly important. The one in the back is the microcosmic brazen sea. In a person who still has doubt, superstition and belief in the personal ego, this point is dimmed and clouded like smoky quartz. It is our task to transform it into a clear, shining crystal.

Cain, at the center of the Earth, still possesses the pure, divine power of the Elohim. Hiram Abiff descends to him and receives the original creative word written on the Golden Triangle.

Place and date of the following is not known. It is from a copy made by Mathilde Scholl, Landin, August 31, 1906

The brazen sea could not be made by Hiram Abiff until humanity had completely passed through the fire of passions, until it had immersed itself fully in the earthly fire. Until then the brazen sea would not congeal. It would have to remain tempestuous, for if one were to make it rigid it would burst. When passion becomes might it is a destructive principle that leads to universal ruin. But after Hiram Abiff had dived into the fire, into the glowing mass of the brazen sea and had emerged again bringing with him the Golden Triangle—the higher principles of wisdom, beauty and power (manas, buddhi, atman)—he was able to complete the work of the brazen sea. The brazen sea is the fusion of the lower and higher principles of physical existence during the Mineral

Round. It could be fully restored after complete immersion in the mineral world, in the consolidation of what is physical.

The brazen sea is the rigidification of the astral. As the astral was before the consolidation of the physical took place, it might not become solid. But by passing through the consolidated physical substance the astral became so purified that it could emerge refined and only then might it become consolidated itself. Only then can the word inscribed on the Golden Triangle be discovered. For only when the astrality has become purified can the word arise anew as the etheric body in its new form, which expresses the Christ-principle.

The education of humankind is an education towards freedom. In order for the "I" to live in human beings and to make us into individuals, it had to appropriate a part of all the earthly forces. That is why the development of "I"-ness was necessary from the middle of the Lemurian race onwards. Until we humans developed our "I" we had no individual kama [personal astrality], all astrality was cosmic. After the division into the two sexes, kama descended into individuals; the superfluous kama was discharged into the Moon. Then kama developed in the single human being. The more humankind became physically established on Earth, the more concentrated was the kama of the individual, for we confronted the outside world ever more and more, while the "I" learned to discriminate between the outside world and the self. Finally we forgot that we were part of the rest of the world and we therefore confronted the outer world as our enemy—(Cain kills his brother Abel). From that time onwards we wanted to have everything for ourselves alone, to appropriate everything to ourselves, because we experienced the great difference between what we were ourselves and what did not belong to us, but belonged to the outside world. Through that the power of kama was raised to its highest peak.

While we were becoming ever more impetuous in our greed for possession, we had, on the other hand, to learn that we could not possess everything. We had to learn to renounce many things. We had to learn that, in the way we wanted it—outwardly—we could never appropriate everything to ourselves, and it was shown to us, through death, that, though we could seemingly get much into our possession, we would again have to relinquish it all when death snatched us away from the physical world. Thus we learned resignation. Thus we had to learn to discriminate between the temporal and the enduring through many lives. We had to learn that all outer possessions are ephemeral. Next we searched for what was imperishable; we found it in higher worlds. In this way we learned to direct our longing towards what is enduring. We learned to renounce outward possessions. We now start to build ourselves up inwardly. But as long as there are still any longings for private possessions, we are unable to complete this work of inner construction.

In the beginning the force of kama was driven to its greatest extremity by our entering into mineral consolidation, but then—just by having passed through this objective mineral world—it was refined once more and appeared again as selfless love for humankind. So did cosmic warmth turn into individual warmth, into individual strength. This consists at first of piety. Piety introduces order into the chaos of the passions. It turns them into harmony and beauty. Piety was the missing lintel of Solomon's Temple, which was to have united the two pillars. It had first to be discovered before the temple could be built. Only after humanity had acquired piety, devotion to what was higher, could it be perfected. Devotion to what is higher could only be learned by passing through the stage of "I"-consciousness and consolidation within the physical world. Piety also enables us to discover the Master Word which leads us to perfection. After having brought the astral body into harmony by means of piety, we will have obtained the Master Word, which is wisdom, with which we can transform the etheric body into something eternal, into the sounding word that is productive.

Humanity was given the pillars Boaz (strength, physical body) and Jachin (wisdom, etheric body) and in addition the means whereby to attain its own perfection (astral body—kama—fire).

We had to learn how to work with fire: outwardly in nature, with the physical fire, and inwardly in ourselves, with the fire of the soul (kama). Outwardly we had to work upon the mineral world with the help of physical fire, to harmonize it and create works of art from it. In the soul we first of all had to develop individual consciousness through the force of kama and then acquire inner harmony, piety, enthusiasm (residing in God). We had to dive down completely into longing and desire and then emerge from it again like Hiram Abiff, bringing with him the Golden Triangle, which denotes the higher powers. Only then, after having converted our passions into piety and outwardly our soul-fire into beauty, would we be able to unite the pillars Jachin and Boaz. That is to say, we could raise ourselves up to wisdom and strength—buddhi and atman—because we had worked upon our kama spiritually. We would attaine wisdom by purifying our kama through piety. Through that kama is transformed, on the one hand, into pure love of humanity and, on the other hand—by imbuing manas, (intellectual power), with this refined kama—it becomes enthusiasm. Thus is kama irradiated by manas and the warmth of kama penetrates the spiritual.

The lintel, laid across the two pillars, thus leads, on the one hand, to higher wisdom (buddhi) by way of piety, love, Christ, and on the other hand to creative force (atman), by way of knowledge, enthusiasm, Lucifer. This is how the two pillars of the temple are united.

The transformation of the mineral kingdom into an outward temple goes hand in hand with the transformation of the turbulent astral body to become a harmonious love of humankind. That is how the brazen sea is outwardly and inwardly constructed. The mineral world ultimately becomes the expression of human love. Inwardly love, outwardly beauty: that is then the picture of what the world will be like.

The following was added to the foregoing under the heading: "supplement"

The three apprentices of Hiram Abiff are the three lower principles; Hiram Abiff represents the "I." These three have to serve him but they may not become Masters. They destroy the brazen sea. To begin with the three lower principles are a hindrance for the human being in building the higher self, in the development of the "I" to become free. Hiram Abiff dives down into the interior of the Earth by plunging into the sea of fire. He dives through the kamic fire down into the physical. There he is endowed with the three higher principles: the Golden Triangle. But when he emerges once more he is attacked by the three apprentices and killed. That represents the battle which rages between the three lower principles and the higher principles within the human being. The "I" is the East, by which the higher principles enter. (They rise in the human being like the Sun). The three apprentices come from the three other directions of space.

Before he dies Hiram Abiff inscribes the Master Word upon the Golden Triangle and submerges it in a deep well. Through that he points to the time in which we will have so purified the astral body that the brazen sea sets hard, that the desires are set at rest and the physical and astral bodies then form the solid ground upon which we will be able to stand during our further progress. In the days of Hiram Abiff, directly after the emergence of the "I" with its self-awareness, at the time of the objectivization of the outside world, the Golden Triangle could not be erected above the brazen sea. That could only come about after the astral body had undergone complete purification.

The Initiation of the Hiram Abiff Individuality through Jesus Christ

I

From an instruction lesson, Berlin, April 15, 1908

Starting from the Gospel according to St. John, Chapter 11.

The festival of Easter does not only have its date fixed according to the beginning of spring. There is a much more profound reason for that. In ancient times humankind shared a group, or racial "I."

In the consciousness of the initiates (Moses, Hermes, Buddha, Krishna, Zarathustra) the consciousness of the whole race was mirrored. At the time of initiation the etheric bodies of these leaders were outside their physical bodies and observed the nature of the whole race. This they then established in the laws that they gave their people when they returned to their physical bodies. By that they became responsible for the transgressions that were perpetrated against the law and they were obliged to reincarnate into their nation until the folk-karma of that people had been expiated. That was the case for all initiates before the time of Christ when they received their revelations from within during the time of the initiation sleep. Solomon, who was of the Abel-Seth line, underwent this kind of initiation.[5] In the case of these old initiates the group-soul of the nation united with their etheric bodies during the ceremony. It continued to live on in them afterwards, too. Thus they had to pass through many incarnations.

Those who were not initiates in remote times and who also did not belong to a race that received its inspiration from such initiates—who lived in scattered groups and had to collect their wisdom themselves from the physical world—were the Sons of Cain. Such a one as these was Hiram Abiff who gathered his knowledge from life in the physical world and raised it and enhanced it to become wisdom. He gave expression to his wisdom in the building of the temple. It was not the God within him that gave him his wisdom, as was the case with the Sons of Abel-Seth, but knowledge wrested from physical existence. The Abel-Seth initiates were under the influence of Jehovah. Higher knowledge was given to them during dimmed consciousness under the influence of the Moon divinity (Jahve).

Hiram Abiff came at that time to the borderline of initiation, but his actual initiation came later. For that purpose the Spirit-Sun had to appear on Earth. He descended into physical incarnation in Christ. Only Christ could initiate Hiram Abiff. The clear [spiritual]

---

5. Concerning Solomon as an initiate see the lecture, Berlin, February 8, 1910.

sun had to shine upon him during his initiation. That was Lazarus, who was called John after he had been brought to life again. He was initiated by Jesus Christ. What Hiram Abiff had acquired through his life on the physical plane had to remain. Not the life of the group, but that of every single incarnation was now of importance. Every single incarnation was to add a page to the Book of Life, a page, the content of which would be taken up into the spiritual world as something that would remain and could not disappear, which would remain throughout all eternity. That was what Hiram Abiff stood for.

Importance was not attached to an inner experience, inspired by the nature of the race, but to a single incarnation that was of importance for all future times.

Before this initiation of Hiram Abiff took place through Jesus Christ, the Spiritual Sun, the spring Sun had to appear and the old principle [of initiation] had to withdraw. First of all the Sun had to shine upon the full Moon, before the day of Resurrection could ensue. Christ brought the new principle in place of the old Jehovah principle, that is why He was hated by the Pharisees, who belonged to the old principle. And when they realised that He belonged to the new, that He brought the new initiation, they attempted to kill Him, after Lazarus had been raised to life again ("for this man doeth many miracles").

In Jesus Christ the soul of the whole of humankind was united in the Jesus-bodies. Christ incarnated only once in the flesh. He will come again, but not in the flesh, and only when humankind is able to recognise Him in His etheric body.[6]

Note: The folk-spirit that united with Moses at his initiation, and then dwelt in him, was Michael.

---

6. See the full account of this in: *The True Nature of the Second Coming* (CW 118), Karlsruhe, January 25, 1910.

II

From an instruction lesson, Berlin, April 15, 1908
(Notes by a different writer)

1. The raising of Lazarus.

2. Why did the Pharisees want to take Christ and kill Him?

3. Why does the Easter festival fall on the first Sunday after the full Moon following the Spring Equinox, March 21?

The raising of Lazarus signifies a kind of climax of the St. John's Gospel. An initiation is described there—but a quite special, quite unique initiation. The initiations which until then had taken place in the fastnesses of the mystery centers in pre-Christian times, were of quite a different order. In those pre-Christian times there were very high initiates and also lesser ones. The greatest initiates: Moses, Hermes, Zoroaster—also Buddha and Krishna—who were at the same time lawgivers of their nations, had undergone initiation in such a way that the etheric body was lifted out of the physical body during the space of three and a half days, and during that time the candidate for initiation experienced the spiritual world in the etheric body.

The mutuality of love had previously been founded on the common blood tie: people of the same stock loved one another. The ego of the nation or tribe ran through many generations, the individual did not count. Each one looked up to the ancestor of the race—the Jew, for instance, to his progenitor Abraham. One felt oneself united to him as a Jew. One said: "I am nothing—I and Father Abraham are one." This solidarity passed like a bar of light from the single member of the race to the ancestor. The initiate beheld these bars of light, he beheld the whole race as though submerged in his spiritual essence, which found expression in the peculiarities of the people and rayed out from their ancestor. All that was clearly seen by him as he lay in death-like sleep. Yes, even more; the group-soul of his people incarnated in him. He now became the group-soul of his people. So Moses was united with Michael at his initiation. The laws that such an initiate as this afterwards gave to his people had been conceived out of the soul-properties of the nation itself. And by formulating and fixing these laws, the initiate simultaneously became responsible for them. He was obliged to incarnate again and again within this, his people. And the sins of the people against these laws were his sins. He was karmically connected with them. The sins of the nation lay in his karma. The great initiates who took on these tasks were fully and completely aware of this fact.

All these old initiates belonged to the Abel-Seth line. That is to say, they received their inspiration from above. The revelation came to them from the Moon forces. It was the forces of Jahve that they received. And it was not in the clear light of day, but in darkness that they received them. Their etheric body received these Jahve forces from the spiritual world while their physical body lay as if in a death-sleep.

But that would begin to change. The people of the Cain current, those who had worked themselves up with the labor of their hands, had progressed so far that they could raise the science they had achieved for themselves to wisdom: that means, they could receive initiation. Their physical body had stamped its impressions into their etheric body. Through their own effort they had purified, purged and ennobled their physical and astral bodies. The children of Cain were distributed around the world, and Hiram Abiff is mentioned as the first of these universally scattered offspring of Cain who had worked himself up in this way. Hiram Abiff, the lone recluse, was faced with initiation. He received it in his next life. On that occasion he was called "Lazarus"—For Lazarus had been Hiram Abiff in his previous incarnation.

And this initiation of Lazarus was different from all previous ones. Until then the candidates for initiation had received the Jahve-moon forces, that is to say the forces that are connected with birth and propagation, and every person had received the forces of the nation to which they belonged. But now the forces of the Moon were to cease their activity. Now the time had arrived in which humankind was to receive the all-embracing power of the Sun, the Christ-power, which belongs to the whole of humankind. This power of all humanity was to initiate Lazarus. The Moon forces were to be overcome by the more universal forces of the Sun, which shines for all humankind. No longer should the blood, which runs through the ancestors, be of sole account. From this point onwards what every single person achieves in their soul shall count. Every single human being during their incarnation shall be of value, the single incarnations shall become dedicated to a striving after sanctification, spiritualization, quite apart from whatever name a person might have. That is the deepest meaning of Christianity.

From this time onwards every incarnation must be like a page upon which the everlasting values of humanity are inscribed by the struggling, striving human soul. And, at the end of such an incarnation, a page of this kind shall be inserted in the Book of Eternity, which shall encompass within it the ever higher values, ever deeper significance, ever greater enrichment of every human individuality. These are the fruits of existence that every single person should gain for their individuality by working for it in continual endeavor, and then lay these fruits in the lap of all humankind so that they may blend with the progress of the whole of humanity.

Christ is the mighty divine individuality who appeared once in the flesh of Jesus of Nazareth, who once set us the example of an incarnation to which all searching, striving human souls can aspire as to the great model and ideal of individual endeavor. Only once did Christ appear in the flesh! But He will appear again on Earth! He will appear in a spiritual body and those people who have become sufficiently spiritualized through their soul-strivings, will be able to recognize Him in His spiritual body and be able to live with Him.

This Christ, the high Sun-Spirit, initiated Lazarus, the reincarnated Hiram Abiff.

That, however, signified a radical break with previous initiation practices. That was thoroughly recognized by the Pharisees, who were also initiates, and it filled them with fear and dread. They certainly knew what was taking place there; but they also saw that, from then on, if the new practices were to succeed, it would mean the end of their power. From that time onwards they strove to render this bearer of the new principle of initiation impotent, and it was they who then ultimately made it possible for Christ to be put to death.

It is said of Lazarus that he was the disciple whom Jesus loved. And later it is told to us that John was the one who lay on Christ's breast. A profound mystery of soul development lies hidden in these two statements, which we find in the Gospel of St. John.

Now we can also understand why it is that the celebration of Easter takes place every year at the time when the spring Sun at the equinox is opposite the full Moon. It is to become the vanquisher of the Moon forces. Christ, the Sun God, vanquishes the Moon God! That is why, when the Sun has regained its full strength in spring, the Moon must look it full in the face, before it is overcome. Thus Easter is a festival to remind us of the fact that from the death-sleep of matter that human soul arises, which, looking up to the Christ-Sun, living in its light, striving in its love, is able to receive new life, the life of resurrection.

III

Instruction lesson, with no mention of place and date,
under the heading: "The human being's mission on Earth"

When a person begins to question who he really is and how he is able to feel as he does inwardly, it must begin to dawn on him that he feels himself to be an "I"-being and that everything he experiences in the way of joy and pain, everything that drives him to act, is centered around the middle-point of his being and that it is from there that he receives his true impulses. The human being is separate from other beings and differs from them in the feeling of self-hood; and yet it is just because of this "I" that a person is able consciously to make contact with the outside world. Regarding the physical body, which visibly portrays what we experience inwardly as our self-sufficiency and independence from the outside world, it is plain that the heart is the actual center of our being. The heart enlivens the other organs by sending the vivifying blood into the minutest parts of the physical body.

Just as the "I" is the inner center from which all impulses flow out into the world to reveal a person's character and to which all impressions flow back from the outer world to be taken up and worked upon, so does the enlivening blood flow out from the heart through the whole of the body and return to its center. The heart is like an expression of the "I"-activity within the physical body.

There are in both the human "I" and in the physical heart two kinds of activity: the one that sends out its forces towards the outside, and the one that collects them again and transforms them inwardly. For in the same way that the returning venous blood is changed again into the red, life-giving blood with the help of the breathing and by means of the lungs, so must the experiences that are taken up by the "I" from the outer world pass through the feelings and experiences of the astral body and thereby become a stimulus for new activity. The human heart does its work at a particular pace: there is a short pause, a short space of time between the heartbeats. The human "I" likewise needs a certain breathing space between the upsurge of the impulse to act and the digesting of the impressions that the outside world makes upon it as a result. This pace is different in every human being according to the individual's disposition and level of development.

If, however, one wishes to gradually acquire a knowledge of one's own capacities, one must try to understand the pace which is appropriate to oneself, to listen to one's own heartbeat and to get to know oneself and one's inner life. One must be able to observe one's own being as if it did not belong to us. One must learn to regard it as a thing apart. Only then will one be able to gradually descend into it. As one formerly sent out one's impulses into the surrounding world, so must one now transform those forces and, instead of sending them out, must direct them inwards. In this way what was one's inner world will become the outer world.

What one first discovers on entering the three sheaths of one's own inner world is described in a beautiful way in the Temple Legend, handed down to us from ancient times. In this legend the whole course of Earth-evolution is symbolically portrayed in the building of the temple—the human body—and the development of the human "I."

In this legend it is recounted how the great architect, Hiram Abiff, wished to enter the temple once more in order to look at his work. When he wished to leave the temple again he was met at the first door by the first of the three treacherous apprentices, who gave him a blow on his left temple, so that the blood flowed down to his shoulder. Then the Master turned towards the other door and he was met by the second of the treacherous apprentices who dealt him a blow on his right temple, so that the blood flowed down. Then the Master turned to the last of the doors and was met by the third malicious apprentice who gave him a blow on his forehead, so that he fell down dead.

When the human "I" descends into its three sheaths, it first meets the astral body. It experiences this astral body as it really is. As though by a blow the "I" becomes aware of itself and recognizes itself in this astral sheath. There one encounters doubt about everything, including oneself. One is attacked by doubt. That is the first of the treacherous apprentices.

Next one meets with the etheric body, into which one descends. And again one learns to know oneself as one is in this body, one is made aware of it as if by a blow. There one encounters superstition: all beliefs and all opinions that have been acquired by education. That is the second of the treacherous apprentices.

Then one descends into the physical body and becomes acquainted with the illusion of the personal self. That is the third of the treacherous apprentices. When one is met by the latter one is deprived, as though by a blow, of the possibility of experiencing oneself within, as separate from the outside world and from one's surroundings. One gets to know illusion and truth and ascends out of one's narrow limits. No longer enclosed within the three sheaths one steps freely out of oneself into the surroundings and recognizes oneself as a microcosm within the macrocosm.

If the human being is portrayed symbolically as the pentagram, it must be looked on as containing the three lower kingdoms of Earth. The mineral kingdom has only a physical body on the Earth. It can be symbolized by a line: \ The plant kingdom has a second principle in addition, an etheric body. This can be indicated by two lines that touch one another:╳ The animal kingdom possesses still another principle, the astral body. That can be indicated by three lines: ⋝.

The etheric body contains the principle of growth. It would continue leaf after leaf according to its plant-nature if it did not come to the end of that through the astral forces, coming from above and calling forth the blossom. The etheric principle, which would cause continual growth in the plants, has become partly transformed in the animals so that its forces work more inwardly as a receiver of the astral body. The straight line of the etheric is terminated and deflected by a new line, which symbolically indicates the astral principle, and this new line deflects the physical principle in the opposite direction. For that reason the physical form, which is portrayed by a vertical line in the plants, is bent the other way and has become horizontal in the animals. The animal can thus be symbolically indicated by three lines: with the human being the "I" is added to the three lines. One can depict this "I" symbolically as a dot over the three lines ⋛ , which pours its strength into the etheric body and the physical body by two lines that pass through the astral, acting on the one side through light and on the other through warmth. Through the activity of the "I" the human form is again raised into the vertical, and in this way the symbol of the pentagram has been evolved.

If one is oneself the pentagram and lives completely within it, one will not be able to see oneself as such. One will only be able to consciously survey that part of one's being that is beneath one's "I," above which one has grown. Those are the three lines that depict the symbol of the animal. For that reason one sees only the part of one's anatomy that lies in front and below the shoulders.

If, however, one would really know oneself as an "I," one must emerge out of oneself in order to get to know the upper part of the pentagram. One must create a new center of orientation lying outside the pentagram; one must be able to adopt a super-human standpoint lying outside the "I," which is nevertheless a center of consciousness.

It is further recounted in the Temple Legend that the Master receives the first blow on the left temple, the second blow on the right temple, so that the blood runs down onto both shoulders, and the third blow on the forehead. After which physical death ensues. With that is indicated just the upper part of the pentagram. With physical death one emerges out of one's personal self and experiences oneself in the macrocosm. We are told in the Temple Legend that the Master's corpse is buried by the three apprentices and that the Master himself, newly born into the cosmos, experiences the evolutionary conditions of the Earth as old Moon, as the Sun with the seven planets, and as Saturn with the twelve signs of the zodiac. When one has emerged from the three sheaths and has experienced oneself rejuvenated in the cosmos, the first thing one perceives is the Being of the Great Mother, the Earth-Mother, from which one has sprung, and one experiences earlier stages of evolution in which one was more dependent and more intimately bound up with the Earth. One experiences this as Moon condition, Sun condition and Saturn condition.

What the great architect, Hiram Abiff, could not experience at that time, however—because, as the Temple Legend says, he lived on Earth before the Christ event—was the light and warmth of the Christ-Being in the Earth's aura. For this Being had not united Himself with the Earth at that time. He could be seen in the Sun, as once Zarathustra beheld Him as Ahura Mazdao, the great Aura, as the cosmic Heart, when it was revealed to him that this Sun-Being would one day descend to Earth and dwell in a human body. Zarathustra's own great mission was revealed to him; that of working throughout many incarnations and in many different ways to prepare a human body capable of bearing the Sun-Spirit within it. He was to adjust the individual pace of his own "I" to synchronise with the higher "I" of humankind. The tone and rhythm of his heartbeat was to fit in with the tone and rhythm of the great Cosmic Heart, so that the sublime Sun-Being could inhabit a human body.

When the great architect, Hiram Abiff, was living on Earth, this tremendous event had not yet taken place. But the individuality of Hiram Abiff lived on and was reborn on earth at the time when the Christ-Being, the Great Sun-Spirit, was living in Jesus of Nazareth. At one time the great architect, Hiram Abiff, was led to his ancestor to receive the new mallet, in order to continue his work. He was led to him through the fire. The human "I" at that time had to raise itself up to its ancestors through the blood of the generations, in order to attain higher wisdom. Afterward, however, since the great Sun-Spirit had descended to Earth and lived in the body of Jesus of Nazareth, it was Jesus Christ Himself who laid the new seed of life into the heart of the reborn Hiram Abiff. It was He Himself who reawakened him to spiritual life, and he was born again in the disciple whom the Lord loved. The human "I" was revived and raised to higher existence by the divine "I." Thereafter this disciple could become the writer of the Gospel that takes its start from the human and divine "I." And the development of this human "I" throughout the post-Atlantean cultural epochs and on into the future, until the end of Earth-evolution, was revealed to him in the way it is described in the Apocalypse. And it is written in his Gospel, how, with the last words that sound from the Cross, Jesus Christ hands over this disciple to His mother, who was not His natural mother. As son He gives the human "I," which He has enlivened with His own forces, to the Earth-Mother, for her to look after and care for. As mother He gives the Earth to this "I" so that the son may give his forces to the Mother. The human "I" is to become the redeemer of the Earth, to raise the Earth to spiritual realms, in full consciousness of the fact that without this Earth, it will be unable to develop into what it ought to become.

With the event of Golgotha, when the blood flowed from the wounds of the Great Redeemer, when the Cosmic Heart's blood penetrated the Earth and its forces poured down as far as its center, the Earth became illumined from within and light rayed outward into the surroundings. The opportunity was then given to every single human individuality to experience this light within the self. When the Earth became the body of the Great Sun-Spirit, through having been impregnated with His spirit-powers, all the beings on Earth were equally endowed with these forces. The seed was planted for the reunion of Sun and Earth. The physical body of Jesus of Nazareth was the mediator through which the powers of the cosmos were united with the Earth aura. And when the blood flowed from this body on Golgotha the Earth was taken up again into the Sun power. Since then this Christ power streams from its center into the surroundings; and from the Sun, Christ's power streams into the Earth. One is able to experience this power, this light, within oneself as a human being, when one knows oneself to be a part of the Earth which, as Christ's physical body, is infused with His Being. Then the white light streams towards one from within oneself, as it streams out from the center of the Earth.

One can also experience the power and light of Christ in such a way that, approaching one from without, it shines on one and imbues one with a higher existence. It then surrounds and penetrates one in the same way as, streaming in from the Sun, it enlivens the Earth. Then one feels oneself united in spirit with this Sun-force, one feels as though one's heart were growing together with the Great Heart of the cosmos. One realizes one's true self as a higher being, living within the Spiritual Sun, as closely knit to it as an earthly human feels connected to the Earth itself. And just as the Sun forces illuminate and enliven the Earth, so does the higher being illuminate and enliven an earthly human with its forces.

In the temple of the human body is the Holy of Holies. Many people live in the temple without knowing anything about it. But those who have an inkling of it receive from it the power to purify themselves to such an extent that they can enter into this holiest place. Therein is the Holy Vessel that has been prepared throughout the ages as a fit container for the blood and life of Christ when the time for it arrives. When one has entered therein, one has found the way to the Holy of Holies in the great Temple of the Earth. Therein, too, many are living on Earth without knowing anything about it, but when one discovers oneself within one's innermost sanctuary, one will be allowed to enter in and there discover the Holy Grail. The vessel will appear as though cut in wonderful shining crystal, and is formed into symbols and letters, until one gradually senses the sacred contents and it gleams in golden radiance. One enters the Mystery Center of one's own heart and a divine being emerges from this place and unites itself with the God outside, with the Being of Christ. It lives in the spiritual light which shines into the vessel and thereby sanctifies it.

Because the human being lives as a two-fold being, one is able to pour the Sun-force into the Earth and act as a connecting link between Sun and Earth. As the enlivening blood flows from the center of life, the heart, and surges through the whole physical organism, even into the bony system, which can be interpreted as being—through its outward consolidation and rigidity within the organism—as the very antithesis of the living, ever-active heart, so must every human individuality become a channel for the blood, flowing from the cosmic life-center, which permeates the rigidified Earth with life. The Earth can be thought of as a cosmic bony-system. It would have become totally ossified and desiccated if the Cosmic Heart had not poured into it, by means of a human body, its life-giving blood and thereby resuscitated it.

Once the great Sun-Spirit lived in a human body, in advance of the rest of humanity, a life which every human being should emulate. Through Him that has been made possible. It is the mission of every single human being and of the whole of humanity to fill themselves with the Christ-Spirit and to recognize themselves as a center living in this Spirit, through which spiritual light, spiritual strength and spiritual warmth can flow into the Earth, thereby redeeming it and raising it aloft into spiritual realms.

IV

Authentically preserved statements

Lazarus, the favorite disciple, initiated by Christ Himself, the later author of St. John's Gospel, is the reincarnated Hiram Abiff.

Adam-Eve	Cain
Abel-Seth	Lamech
	Hiram Abiff
Solomon	Lazarus-John[7]

The individuality that reincarnated as Hiram Abiff and Lazarus-John was newly initiated in the 13th and 14th century and bears the name Christian Rosenkreutz since that time.[8]

V

From an instruction lesson, Berlin, February 10, 1913, for the third degree

The Legend and the seven-runged ladder[9] and other given things should be kept in mind by each one of us during the day, then one

---

7. Note by Rudolf Steiner for Helene Röchling as addendum to the Temple Legend.

8. Information from Rudolf Steiner imparted by Marie Steiner in a cognitive-ritual context. See appendix, pp. 443 et seq.

9. The so-called "Jacob's ladder." Schauberg says (*Vergleichendes Handbuch der Symbolik der Freimaurerei* ... Vol. II. [Comparative Handbook of Freemasonry]): "The Persian symbol at the heavenly portal of the seven planetary spheres which the soul passes through at death is a staircase or ladder leading to seven different doors. (...) According to Origines a similar symbol was used by the Egyptians to represent the descent of the heavenly souls in the Milky Way, through the seven planetary spheres, by a ladder stretching from heaven to earth, with seven rungs, each with a doorway. (...) The ladder which Jacob saw in the well-known dream, which likewise stretched from Earth to heaven, was presumably the Egyptian ladder which led the human soul from heaven to Earth and from there back to heaven, which also did not only have three rungs," as is generally the case.

will perceive—when things that are performed here are carried out correctly—that the proper forces play in.

During the following night the person can then draw near to Hiram Abiff or Adoniram, Lazarus, whom the Lord Himself initiated. To this is given the meditation: "I am not on the Earth only for my own sake, but in order to become a likeness of my archetypal self."

This endeavor is a duty, it is not egoism. These things are recorded in the first scenes of *The Soul's Probation* and *The Guardian of the Threshold*—as in the Mystery Dramas in general a very great deal of meditative material is given.

You should not forget that you are being relied upon by the spiritual powers in the leadership of humanity.

Every person is a citizen of the spiritual world; you, however, should be so consciously! You are always in the spiritual world during the night and associate there with beings of the other world and pass judgements. A person might suddenly become aware of this on waking, or otherwise during the day, and realize: "I must learn to make myself into a revealer of the heavenly prototype of myself."

Meditate on death; that is of great importance.

APPENDIX

Hella Wiesberger

Rudolf Steiner's Research into the Hiram-John Individuality

The information about the reincarnation of Hiram Abiff as Lazarus-John and Christian Rosenkreutz in the section "Explanations of the Temple Legend" requires some additional remarks, because it only contains a portion of what one can call Rudolf Steiner's research into the Hiram, respectively John, individuality on the ground of reincarnation. For this refers not only to the individuality of Lazarus-John, the Evangelist and writer of the Apocalypse, but equally well to John the Baptist and likewise the mysterious union of the two.

This research into reincarnation, which encompasses equally both the John figures, occupies an outstanding position in the work of Rudolf Steiner, because it appears like Alpha and Omega at the beginning and the end of his spiritual-scientific lecturing activity and above and beyond that, like a red thread running through the whole of his work (Marie Steiner).

The first results of his research are to be found at the beginning of his spiritual-scientific lecturing activity (1901/02) in connection with the triple defence of Christianity as a mystical fact and as the central event of human evolution in his lecture cycle "From Buddha to Christ"; in the avant-garde literary circle "Die Kommenden" in Berlin; in his series of lectures in the circle of the Berlin Theosophists about the Egyptian and Greek Mysteries and Christianity; and in his book *Christianity as Mystical Fact.* All these three accounts culminate in the interpretation of the St. John Gospel, starting with the raising of Lazarus as an initiation carried out by Jesus Christ and with an assertion that the awakened Lazarus was the writer of St. John's Gospel. The lecture cycle "From Buddha to Christ," of which there are no copies, ends, according to Rudolf Steiner's statement in his lecture given in Dornach, June 11, 1923, with this motive; in the copies of the series of lectures given to Theosophists, it is dated March 15, 1902. In the book *Christianity as Mystical Fact* it is not directly stated that Lazarus is the author of the Gospel of St. John, but it is evident from the whole context.[1]

Immediately after commencing his defense of Christianity, Rudolf Steiner also began to introduce into European spiritual life his teaching about reincarnation and karma, because on that depends all spiritual-scientific investigation.[2] This applies especially to his teachings about history, as history is created by reincarnating human souls who carry over the results of their life in one epoch into their lives in other epochs. And because this also applies to the spiritual leaders of humankind, their active impulses at different periods form an essential chapter in the widely spread subject of history and reincarnation. A large space therein is devoted to the two John figures.

The first announcements of earlier lives of these two Christian leader-figures was made by Rudolf Steiner in 1904, beginning with John the Baptist. In the public lecture in Berlin about Christianity and reincarnation on January 4, 1904, he states that reincarnation was always taught in the Mysteries, also about Christ, who, as it says in the Gospels, pointed out to his intimate pupils that John the Baptist was the reincarnated prophet Elijah. Further statements followed at the turn of the year 1908/09. The background out of which he arrived at this statement was described by Marie Steiner in a memorial essay after Rudolf Steiner's death, which runs as follows:

> It was at the time when Rudolf Steiner encouraged me to continue ever further with my recitation. I had tried at that time to wrestle my way through to Novalis. I informed him of the fact that I would not find it easy and that I had not yet found the key to Novalis. He advised me to immerse myself into the mood

---

1. Rudolf Steiner pointed to this in his last address given on September 28, 1924. In the lecture on July 25, 1904, it was said that according to the akasha record the awakened Lazarus was the writer of St. John's Gospel, who is the same as the disciple whom the Lord loved and who stood beneath the Cross.

2. See *Reincarnation and Karma* (CW 135).

of the Holy Nuns. The nuns did not help me. Quite the reverse.
I did not know what to do with them. Then all of a sudden it
became clear: Raphael's figures surrounded me. The Child
shone in the arms of its mother with its world-penetrating eyes.
"I see thee, in a thousand forms, Mary, lovingly expressed ..."
All around, sounding world-ocean, and color harmonies. I said
to Rudolf Steiner: The nuns did not do the trick, but another
person helped me: Raphael. Novalis is quite transparent to me
now.—A radiance spread over Rudolf Steiner's gentle features.
A few days later he revealed to us the mystery of Novalis-
Raphael-John-Elijah for the first time.[3]

This "few days later" cannot be exactly dated.[4] The first certain
date has been handed down in a description from memory of a
Novalis celebration that took place in Munich on January 6, 1909,
of which it is said: "I saw and heard Marie von Sivers recite for the
first time, verses by Novalis beneath the Christmas tree in the
room of the Munich Branch, surrounded by colored reproductions of Raphael's paintings. It was at the turn of the year 1908/09.
The whole room was decked out in rose-red satin, a rose-cross—at
that time still having 12 red roses—hung in the center above the
speaker's desk, from which we had just heard Rudolf Steiner speak
about that being who incarnated as Elijah, John the Baptist,
Raphael, and Novalis."[5]

It must have been the occasion of a very solemn event. Likewise,
half a year later, during the lecture cycle "The Gospel of St. John

---

3. From: "On the Eve of Michaelmas" in *What is happening in the Anthroposophical
Society. Announcements for its members.* Year 2, 1925.

4. "The Songs of Mary" by Novalis were recited by Marie Steiner for the first time
at the Christmas celebration in the Berlin Branch on December 22, 1908. Thus
this "few days later" could have been the lecture on December 28, 1908, in which
this theme was introduced, which was described as a highlight of spiritual science, but on which occasion Rudolf Steiner had not allowed notes to be made.
The fact that it is unlikely that just in Berlin, the main center of activity at that
time, it would not have been spoken about, strengthens the argument in its favor.
For in the Berlin lectures this series of incarnations was mentioned much later
and as if already known.

5. Max Gümbel-Seiling in *Memorial for Marie Steiner-von Sivers.* Stuttgart, 1949.

in relationship to the other three Gospels," a Novalis Matinée was again celebrated (Cassel, July 4, 1909). From it, too, there only remains the later-noted memoirs of a participant: "After a musical introduction, Rudolf Steiner announced that Marie von Sivers was going to recite some poems by Novalis. Marie von Sivers spoke with deep empathy in her own developed way of speaking. Afterwards Rudolf Steiner began his lecture, in which he told us of the incarnations of Elijah-John the Baptist-Raphael-Novalis as the sequence of lives of the same individuality.... Rudolf Steiner spoke afterwards about the mood of this recitation in an unusually warm, intense, even solemn way. The lecture had an utterly sacred character.... And so at the end of the lecture—of which the sole content was this sequence of repeated earth-lives—there lay a deep emotion among his audience and many an eye glistened with tears—more restrained by the men, but uncontrolled by the women."[6]

That the process of reincarnation is, however, not so simple as one usually imagines, as has already been pointed out:

> Everyone, including Theosophists, usually accept the mystery of reincarnation in far too simple a way. We must not suppose that a soul incarnated in its three bodies today simply incorporated in a previous incarnation and then in an earlier one and that this always proceeded according to the same plan. The hidden things connected with this are far more complicated. (...) It is often not possible to bring some historic figure into line with such a scheme, and the work has to be gone about in a much more complicated way if we are to understand it (Leipzig, September 12, 1908).

That was an announcement, so to speak, of what was going to be started from the end of 1908 onwards as a more advanced chapter of the teaching about reincarnation. Illustrations were given from

---

6. From notes by memory from Rudolf Toepell for the executorship of Rudolf Steiner's estate (Nachlaßverwaltung).

concrete examples of historical personalities to show that, conditional on the law of spiritual economy for the preservation of what was of spiritual value for the future, not only the human "I," but also other members of the human being can reincarnate, even in other individualities. The descriptions of such "penetration"-incarnations in the case of great spiritual teachers, the highest of whom are the so-called Bodhisattvas, comprise one of the main subjects of the years 1909-1914.[7]

Among the figures thus portrayed we find John the Baptist time and again. Especially in the lecture cycle "The Gospel of St. Mark" (September, 1912), not only is a broad space allotted to him, but also a life previous to the Elijah incarnation is alluded to. Since that time five spiritually historic incarnations of his are known: Pinehas (during the time of Moses), Elijah, John the Baptist, Raphael, Novalis. It is all the more surprising, therefore, that a year later, in the lectures about the fifth Gospel (1913/14), this remark about John the Baptist is made: "I am not saying this now as part of the Fifth Gospel"—whereby is meant the results of the akashic research into personalities from the Gospels—"for in connection with the Fifth Gospel research has not yet reached as far as John the Baptist; but I say it out of a knowledge which can be acquired in a different way" (Berlin, January 13, 1914). On the grounds of all the investigation which had been made up till then about the Baptist, this remark can only refer to research into "penetration"-incarnations, as they had already been investigated and recorded in the case of other Gospel personalities. A reason for the fact that this research into John the Baptist only occurred years later is given by the answer that Rudolf Steiner gave during the war years, 1914-1918, when he was asked in connection with the Fifth Gospel if this theme could be taken further. He said then, that as a

---

7. See: *Das Prinzip der spirituellen Ökonomie im Zusammenhang mit Wiederverkörperungsfragen* (CW 109); *The Gospel of St. Luke* (CW 114); *Das esoterische Christentum und die geistige Führung der Menscheit* (CW 130). [*Esoteric Christianity and the Spiritual Guidance of Humankind*—not translated in one volume]; *The Gospel of St. Mark*, (CW 139); *The Fifth Gospel* (CW 148).

result of the war, the spiritual atmosphere was much too turbulent for such research; and when the war ended, he was asked this question again, the answer was that other tasks were then more urgent.[8] That later, however, the possibility must have presented itself, is shown by Rudolf Steiner's "Last Address" on September 28, 1924.

In the course of the years from 1904 onwards, there were also five spiritually historical important incarnations given for the other John figure, Lazarus-John: Hiram Abiff, Lazarus-John, Christian Rosenkreutz in the thirteenth and fourteenth centuries, and the Count of St. Germain in the eighteenth century.[9] In the Berlin lecture of November 4, 1904, it was explained that the Count of St. Germain was a reincarnation of Christian Rosenkreutz and the connection with Hiram Abiff is evident from the context of the whole lecture, though it was not directly stated. The reincarnation of Hiram as Lazarus-John was first given in a cognitive-ritual working connection at Easter, 1908; in the two lectures on September 27 and 28, 1911; in Neuchâtel the two incarnations of Christian Rosenkreutz in the thirteenth and fourteenth centuries were described. The only thing that cannot be exactly dated is the first mention of the connection between Lazarus-John and Christian Rosenkreutz from the point of view of reincarnation, as this was recorded verbally without reference to an exact date.[10]

At Easter 1908, even before mention had been made of a cognitive-ritual work-connection of Lazarus as the reincarnated Hiram Abiff, the Lazarus-John research had been documented in a very special way. This consisted of displaying the Lazarus-John initiation experience through the esoteric seals and pillars of the Apocalypse at the Munich Conference at Whitsuntide 1907. It also formed the

8. Friedrich Rittelmeyer in *Rudolf Steiner Enters My Life*.

9. This name was also given to other people, however, "so that not all which is told about the Count of St. Germain can be attributed to the real Christian Rosenkreutz" (Neuchâtel, September 27, 1911).

10. Stated personally by Marie Steiner to Günther Schubert and by the latter to the editor, Hella Wiesberger. Later in the year 1923 Rudolf Steiner spoke about it again to a small group, c.f. M. Kirschner-Bockholt in *Was in der Anthroposophischen Gesellschaft vorgeht*, 1963.

fundamental element of the new building plans. In addition to that it was made known in pictures and words that the authoritative course of instruction for Western humanity was the Christian-Rosicrucian way founded by Christian Rosenkreutz.[11] In the lecture during the Congress and the subsequent lectures of 1907, Rudolf Steiner constantly refers to this course of instruction and to its founder, Christian Rosenkreutz, the great spiritual leader of the West. In one place it is said: "... he has always lived among us and is still with us today as our leader in spiritual life" (Munich, June 1, 1907, esoteric lesson, in CW 264).

The spiritual connection revealed during the Munich Congress, between the individuality of Lazarus-John and the new building plans, was seen again some years later, also in connection with the new building plans, in Rudolf Steiner's intention to introduce a new way of working together, which in the way it is presented, is directly attributable to the individuality we have known "since earliest times in the West, as Christian Rosenkreutz" (Berlin, December 15, 1911, in CW 264). This founding-attempt was solemnly announced shortly beforehand on a cognitive-ritual occasion in Stuttgart on November 27, 1911. As nothing else besides this fact has been preserved, it can only be supposed that at that time—it was shortly after the two lectures about the life and work of Christian Rosenkreutz in the thirteenth and fourteenth centuries (September, 1911)—the incarnation connections of Lazarus-John and Christian Rosenkreutz had been announced for the first time.[12]

---

11. *Rosicrucianism Renewed: The Unity of Art, Science, and Religion. The Theosophical Congress of Whitsun 1907* (CW 284).

12. A certain confirmation of this assumption can be seen in the triptych "Grail" by the artist Anna May, which was painted, according to a statement by Marie Steiner, after the lectures in Neuchâtel. In the middle section it shows the Golgotha scene with Joseph of Arimathea who collects the blood of Christ; on the left side panel are the figures from the Temple Legend; King Solomon, the Queen of Sheba and Hiram Abiff; on the right panel is the initiation of Christian Rosenkreutz in the 13th century, described by Rudolf Steiner for the first time in Neuchâtel. Rudolf Steiner also gave Anna May certain instructions about it. See Margarete Hauschka in *Das Goetheanum* 1975 No. 24, with a black and white reproduction of the painting.

To what extent the individuality of John the Baptist can also be seen in connection with the building scheme can be judged by the following procedures. When the founding ceremony for the building, which was originally to have been built in Munich, was planned to take place on May 16, 1912, Rudolf Steiner spoke repeatedly during his journey there about the already known four incarnations: Elijah, John the Baptist, Raphael, Novalis; and finally, in Munich, and indeed, on the very day that the founding ceremony was to have taken place. As a result of difficulties caused by the authorities, it was not carried out there after all. In place of it, however, that which underlies the idea of the building— the plan to create a modern, that is to say public, Mystery Temple— was artistically-dramatically created that summer with the first great scenes of the Mystery Drama, *The Guardian of the Threshold*. This scene takes place in the antechamber of the rooms of a Mystic League and many of its members have been invited to be informed of the fact that, through a recently published scientific work, the necessary conditions have now been created for many people not previously admitted to the Sanctuary—because not initiated into its secrets—to now attend. The Grand Master of the Mystic League accounts for this fact in a speech about the continuity of humankind's spiritual leadership, which, following a stage instruction by Rudolf Steiner, takes place in front of the portraits of Elijah, John the Baptist, Raphael and Novalis, hung at the back of the stage. His speech begins with the words:

> In that same Spirit's Name, which is revealed
> To souls within our sacred shrine, we come
> To those who until now might never hear
> The word that here doth secretly sound forth ...

And when, eight years later, in autumn 1920, the building on the Dornach hill near Basel had meanwhile been erected and was in use, Rudolf Steiner reconstructed this same speech into the first person singular, which is a very uncommon form for him to use, and gave it to Marie Steiner to recite from the organ gallery into the two cupola-rooms on the occasion of the first event to take place therein:

> In that same Spirit's Name, which is revealed
> To souls within our place of striving do I come
> To those who now are eager to accept
> The word that here resounds within their souls ...

Through the text, which was included in the artistic program from *The Chemical Wedding of Christian Rosenkreutz anno 1459,* another John individuality, Lazarus-John, was also included in this first event taking place in the building.

Then, when Rudolf Steiner ceased his spiritual-scientific lecturing activity in September 1924 (it was exactly four years after the first performance had taken place in the new building in September 1920), the significance of his studies of John came once more vividly to expression. For when, on Sunday, September 28, 1924, the eve of St. Michael's Day, he recovered sufficiently from his serious illness to address the members who were present, what was his concern? The two John individualities! In a deeply moving way he spoke about the four incarnations: Elijah, John, Raphael and Novalis, in order then to lead on to the results of his new John research—the mysterious connection between the two at the time of the raising of Lazarus. However, his strength did not allow him to explain the results of his new investigation. It was only touched on through the fact that he did not refer, as he had always previously done, to John the Baptist, but to Lazarus-John as the reincarnated Elijah. As this could not be further elaborated it made it difficult for his audience to understand him. Some friends, who were able to ask him about it recorded what he said as follows:

> At the awakening of Lazarus, the Spiritual Being, John the Baptist, who since his death had been the overshadowing Spirit of the disciples, penetrated from above into Lazarus as far as the Consciousness-Soul; the being of Lazarus himself,

from below, intermingled with the Spiritual Being of John the Baptist from above. After the awakening of Lazarus, this Being is Lazarus-John, the disciple whom the Lord loved." And as further explanation it is recorded: "Lazarus could only develop fully out of the earth-forces at this time as far as the Intellectual- or Mind-Soul; the Mystery of Golgotha took place during the fourth post-Atlantean period and at that time the Intellectual- or Mind-Soul was being developed. Therefore another cosmic Being had to lend him the forces from the Consciousness-Soul upwards: Manas, Buddhi, and Atman. Through that a human being confronted Christ who extended from the depths of earth into the highest heaven and who bore the physical body in perfection throughout all its members into the spiritual bodies of Manas, Buddhi, and Atman, as they will one day be developed by all humankind in a far distant future.[13]

Concerning the still unanswered question as to how the union of the two individualities can be understood in the light of succeeding incarnations, Marie Steiner gives the following explanation:

We are ever and again led to it [the Novalis-Raphael-John-Elijah secret] from the most varied angles. The last, most difficult riddle, because it is intercepted by the line of another's individuality, was given to us on Michaelmas Eve—and then was broken off. Rudolf Steiner did not say all he wanted to say. He gave us the first part of the mystery of Lazarus—at that time he not only said to me, but later wrote it on the cover of the first copy: Do not give it to anyone until I have given the second half. One nevertheless got it out of him, as

---

13. See: *The Last Address* of September 28,1924, printed as a separate volume, with further explanations in the preface by Alfred Heidenreich.

There is in German the study by Adolf Arenson: *Elias-Johannes-Lazarus* contained in *Ergebnisse aus dem Studium der Geisteswissenschaft Rudolf Steiners*, Freiburg im Breisgau, 1980, as also the article by M. Kirschner-Bockholt in *Was in der Anthroposophischen Gesellschaft vorgeht. Nachrichten für deren Mitglieder*, 1963, Nos. 48 and 49.

with so many other things. Now he will never give the second half. It will be left to our powers of judgement to distinguish between the incarnation and incorporation secrets, the line of interception of individualities. He ended with what had run like a red thread through all his revelations of wisdom, with the mystery of Novalis, Raphael and John.[14]

With that Rudolf Steiner's research into the Hiram-John connection and the mystery of the merging of the two Johns, indicated in his last address, becomes a spiritual legacy that calls upon us to strive continually for an explanation. It is moreover a question, the solving of which is of particular importance for the future. This has been preserved as one of the last utterances of Rudolf Steiner's life.[15]

Now, indeed, a fully valid answer to the question asked by Marie Steiner about being able to distinguish between the secrets of incarnation and those of incorporation will have to be left to future spiritual investigation. Nevertheless, from the results of research as they are presented here, some light can be shed on the question as to the meaning attached to the merging of the two John individualities. If one brings together the statements made by Rudolf Steiner on various occasions, it becomes apparent that a decisive factor of this explanation will lie in the importance of the Mystery of Golgotha as the "conquest over death by the life of the spirit" (Berlin, October 23, 1908). What is to be understood by that follows from the basic explanation of the relationship between individuality and personality.

> One easily confuses the concepts individuality and personality nowadays. The individuality is that which is eternal and persists from one life to the next. Personality is that which a person brings to a single life on earth for its improvement. If we wish to study the individuality we must look at the

---

14. See footnote on p. 435.

15. Handed on by Count Ludwig Polzer-Hoditz from a conversation with Rudolf Steiner on March 3, 1925.

human soul. If we wish to study the personality we have to look at how the innermost part of our being expresses itself. The innermost part of our being is incarnated into a race and into a profession. All of that determines the inner configuration and makes it personal. In the case of those who are at a lower stage of development, one will notice little of the work upon their inner being. The mode of expression, the kind of gestures and so on conform to those of their race. Those, however, who produce their mode of expression and gestures out of their inner being are more advanced. The more the inner being of a person is able to work on the exterior the more developed he or she becomes. One could say that the individuality thereby comes to expression within the personality. Those who have their own gestures, their own physiognomy and even have an original character in their way of doing things and in their environment, possess a decided personality. Is that all lost for posterity at death? No, it is not. Christianity knows quite exactly that this is not the case. What is understood by the resurrection of the flesh or the personality is nothing else than the preservation of what is personal throughout all following incarnations. What we have won as a personality remains in our possession, because it is incorporated into our individuality and is carried forward by it into the following incarnations. If we have made something of our body that is of original character, so will this body and the force that has worked upon it be resurrected. Just so much as we have worked upon ourselves, and what we have made of ourselves, is preserved (Berlin, March 15, 1906).

The real consciousness of immortality is connected therefore with the personalization of the individuality, the higher spiritual members of the human being. And the fact that this process signifies at the same time the Christianization of the human being is pointed to in the following short commentary to a passage out of the so-called Egyptian Gospel:

There is an ancient writing in which the highest ideal for the development of the "I," Jesus Christ, is characterised by saying: When the two become one, when the exterior becomes like the interior, then man has attained to Christ-likeness within himself. That is the meaning of a certain passage in the Egyptian Gospel (Munich, December 4, 1909).

The meaning of what is within and what is without, of individuality and personality, is made even clearer by the interpretation which Rudolf Steiner gives in his lecture in Berlin on May 6, 1909, to the provençal saga of Flor and Blanchflor. This saga stands in close connection with the Hiram-John research, because it relates that the soul renowned as Flor reincarnates in the thirteenth and fourteenth centuries as the founder of Rosicrucianism, the Mystery School which has as its task the cultivation of the new Christ-secret appropriate to the present day. This saga tells the story of a human pair, born on the same day, at the same hour, in the same house, brought up together and united in love from the very beginning. Separated through the ignorance of others, Flor goes in search of Blanchflor. After difficult and life-threatening dangers they are ultimately reunited until their death which takes place on the same day.

Rudolf Steiner interprets these scenes in the following way: Flor signifies the flower with the red petals, or the rose, Blanchflor is the flower with the white petals, or the lily. Flor, or the rose, is "the symbol for the human soul, which has taken up into itself the personality or "I"-impulse. This allows the spirit to work from its individuality which has brought the "I"-impulse down into the red blood. But in the lily one perceives the symbol of the soul, which can only remain spiritual insofar as the "I" remains outside it and only approaches as far as the border. Thus rose and lily are two opposites. Rose has self-awareness completely within it, lily has it outside itself. But the merging of the soul that is within and the soul that works from without and enlivens the world as the World-Spirit, was present. The story of Flor and Blanchflor expresses the discovery of the World-Soul, the World-"I," by the human soul, the human "I." (...) In the uniting of the Lily-soul and the Rose-soul was envisaged that which can unite with the Mystery of Golgotha" (Berlin, May 6, 1909).

When it is said that the uniting of the soul that is within and the soul that enlivens the world from without as the World-Spirit "was present," it is surely the uniting of the Christ-principle as the highest spiritual principle with the personality, the earthly body of Jesus of Nazareth, that is referred to. For only through the fact that these two have fully united as far as the physical, could earthly death truly be conquered.

In how far the contrast of the Rose-soul and Lily-soul can be applied to the two John individualities is shown by the fact that Hiram-Lazarus is always characterized as the representative of the forces of personality, whereas the Elijah-soul is often described as such a highly spiritual being that he can only be loosely connected with his earthly vessels, as was also the case with John the Baptist.[16] If the uniting of the Rose-soul and Lily-soul can lead to union with the Mystery of Golgotha, so may we conclude—in view of the merging of the two John souls at the raising of Lazarus by Jesus Christ—that the disciple whom the Lord loved has become the being to whom the Christ-secret of the overcoming of death has become attached and to whom it is still attached, as is expressed in the words that refer to Christian Rosenkreutz: "With this individuality and its activity since the thirteenth century"—by having experienced a further initiation—"we connect all that includes for us the continuation of the impulse given by the appearance of Jesus Christ on Earth and through the accomplishment of the Mystery of Golgotha" (Berlin, December 22, 1912).

A further aspect follows from this if we combine the words from the Egyptian Gospel: "When the two become one and the exterior becomes the interior" with the second half of the saying: "and the male becomes like the female, so that there is neither masculine

---

16. See the lecture in Berlin, December 14, 1911 and *The Gospel of St. Mark* (CW 139).

nor feminine." This latter word points to the fact that there will be no more death when sexuality ceases, for death and sexuality are mutually dependent on one another. Hiram Abiff already was promised in the Temple Legend that a son would be born to him, who, even though he would not see him himself, would give rise to a new race of human beings, which, according to Rudolf Steiner, would not know death, because propagation would come about by means of speech and the word connected with the heart and not by means of death-bringing sexuality (Berlin, October 23, 1905). Thus, according to the lecture in Cologne on December 2, 1905, the perfecting of the human race will come about through the raising of the forces of propagation from the womb to the heart, and the "soul-power of John" will be the force that will raise "streams of spiritual love" to ray forth from the loving heart. This is hinted at in the Gospel when it describes the scene at the Last Supper in which the disciple whom the Lord loved, who knew the secret of evolution, raised himself from the lap of Christ to His breast.

Against this background all the documents that recount the initiation experiences of the Hiram-Lazarus-John individuality in the various incarnations (*The Temple Legend, The Gospel of St. John, The Saga of Flor and Blanchflor, The Chemical Wedding of Christian Rosenkreutz anno 1459*), and also the cosmic deed of Christian Rosenkreutz at the beginning of the seventeenth century,—by which it was to have been made possible to overcome the polarity of Cain and Abel, both in the single human being as well as in humankind in general[17]—point to the central Christian secret of the conquest of death.

Rudolf Steiner himself also saw the goal of his activity along these lines. That shines out in a saying of his at the founding of the cognitive-ritual working group, when he said that the significance of the Theosophical, respectively the Anthroposophical Movement lay in the fact that neither purely male, nor purely female, but

---

17. See: *Das esoterische Christentum und die geistige Führung der Menschheit* (CW 130) (not translated as a single volume).

supersexual wisdom was to be prepared therein on a spiritual level, which would later take place on the physical plane: "Die Wiedervereinigung der Geschlechter" [the reunification of the sexes] (Berlin, October 23, 1905). With that not only the fully equal cooperation between men and women, which has everywhere been put into practice by him, even in ritual matters, but also the words he spoke during the same lecture: "I have reserved for myself the task of uniting the members of Abel's race with those of Cain," receives a very special meaning in the context of practical application. And through that again it becomes understandable why the Hiram-John research stands like Alpha and Omega at the beginning and end of his spiritual-scientific lecturing activity and runs through the intervening years like a red thread through the whole of his life's work.

PART III

DOCUMENTS OF A NEW BEGINNING
AFTER THE FIRST WORLD WAR

As this armed combat (of the First World War) is one to which nothing in previous history is comparable, so will it be followed by a spiritual struggle to which likewise nothing in history is comparable.... One will see that the whole of the world will take part in this spiritual battle and that East and West will confront one another in spirit and soul as never before seen in history. (Stuttgart, June 15, 1919)

PRELIMINARY REMARKS

HELLA WIESBERGER

From the New Beginnings after the First World War
until the Refounding of the Esoteric School as the
"Free High School for Spiritual Science"

The First World War had become a fiery symbol to Rudolf Steiner
that for a fruitful continuation of the general, as of the esoteric
social life, quite new forms would have to be devised. He must
have been under a lot more pressure with regard to the refounding of his esoteric activity than he had been before the war,
because of the necessarily contradictory endeavors on the one
hand to preserve continuity in adherence to previously held principles, on the other hand to conform to the needs of the new age,
that is, to introduce the democratic principle, or openness, into
the esoteric work. That is made plain by the two following statements. Whereas the one (lecture in Dornach, December 20,
1918—i.e., immediately after the war ended) ran as follows: "In
order to maintain the continuity of human evolution at the present day, it is necessary to link up with ritual and symbolism," the
other one (which was given in response to a question by one of the
workmen at the Goetheanum regarding Freemasonry) was as follows: "At the present day all such things are actually no longer
appropriate. For what should we chiefly reject in this connection?
We have to reject its isolationism. Through that a spiritual aristocracy would soon develop, which should not be. And the democratic principle, which must gain more and more influence, is at
variance with the Freemasonry confederacy, just as it is with the
priesthood" (Dornach, June 4, 1924).

At the time this last remark was made Rudolf Steiner had already undertaken the remodelling of the Society and the Esoteric School, by which he wanted publicly to merge into a higher synthesis the antithesis between the old hierarchical way of working and of the modern demand for democracy. The steps that he made in this direction between the end of the war and his death were somewhat as follows.

When he was asked on several occasions in late autumn 1918, immediately after the war ended, to restart the esoteric instruction, he at first flatly refused. For one reason because of the often occurring inappropriate attitude, and surely for another, because the new and appropriate forms had not yet been worked out. But when, one year later, at the end of 1919, he was again asked in the school in Stuttgart, if a religious service could be arranged on Sundays for the pupils of the Free-Religion lessons, he answered that it would in that case have to be in the form of a ritual, and he added: If this ritual could be given it would thereby be the first linking-up again with the esotericism which was interrupted by the war,[1]—apparently insofar as it again related to a non-ecclesiastical ritual.

Soon after this ritual, this "Sunday Service," had been inaugurated and had taken place for the first time (February 1, 1920)[2]— this remark was recorded from the Teachers' Conference in Stuttgart on November 16, 1921: "A ritual is the most esoteric event one can think of"—Rudolf Steiner took up the esoteric work again within the Anthroposophical Society. First of all this took place in Dornach with two esoteric lessons on February 9 and 17, 1920. It was not continued, although it had been intended, because once again several members had acted improperly. That is why, in the Teachers' Conference on November 16, 1921, in which he had again been asked about the esoteric lessons, he answered that it would be very difficult to arrange them and that he had had to drop them because everything to do with esotericism had been "shamefully abused."

---

1. Told by one of the two first religion teachers, Herbert Hahn.
2. See: *Conferences with the Teachers of the Free Waldorf School in Stuttgart 1919-1924*, Vol. I (Introduction) (CW 300a–c).

Esotericism was a painful chapter in the Anthroposophical Movement.[3] Nevertheless, shortly afterwards he took an esoteric lesson in Norway on December 4, 1921, where for the first time since the outbreak of war in the summer of 1914, lectures could once more be held. In addition to that a gathering of members of the cognitive-ritual section took place, in which—although two or three new members were accepted—the circle was solemnly pronounced closed (p. 464), just as this had happened immediately after the outbreak of war in the summer of 1914. Through that, however, the "old" was not dead—as he explained in Christiania [Oslo]—but would arise again in a metamorphosed shape. During the course of 1922 two esoteric lessons also took place in England (London), one of them during his stay in April and the other one during his stay in November. Shortly before that, in October, young Anthroposophists who were involved in the Pedagogical Youth Course[4] in Stuttgart, approached Rudolf Steiner with the request for esoteric instruction for the strengthening and deepening of their community. From that arose the so-called Esoteric Youth Circle, and they, too, received esoteric classes. In the course of 1923 until the beginning of 1924 the following esoteric classes took place: In Christiania in May 1923; in Dornach on May 27, October 23, and January 3, 1924, for the circle called by Rudolf Steiner the Wachsmuth-Lerchenfeld-Group after its founders; in Stuttgart on July 13 and December 30, 1923, for the Esoteric Youth Group; in Vienna on September 30, 1923, for a small circle gathered together at the request of Polzer-Hoditz.

From the notes that have been preserved of these classes only those which have a recognizable bearing, in respect of their content, on the earlier cognitive-ritual esotericism, have been included in this volume. This comprises the two in Christiania and the three in Dornach for the classes of the Wachsmuth-Lerchenfeld-Group.[5]

---

3. See: *Conferences with the Teachers of the Free Waldorf School in Stuttgart 1919-1924*, Vol. II (Introduction) (CW 300a–c).

4. See *Becoming Michael's Companions* (CW 217).

5. The other notes that have been preserved are intended for inclusion in a separate volume.

The esoteric, and particularly the cognitive-ritual way of working, which had necessarily undergone a metamorphosis as a result of the changed conditions of the times, as was indicated in Christiania in December 1921 on the occasion of the ceremonial closing of the circle, is addressed by Rudolf Steiner in the lecture given on December 20, 1918, in Dornach immediately after the war ended. Already at that time it was stated that the passage of time necessitated that a renewal of many things must take place. For from now on, and becoming more and more obvious as time progresses, new revelations break through the veil of events into the soul and spiritual horizon of humanity. As these new revelations are the expression of a new creative principle resting on the spirits of personality, the stamp of the personality-impulse will become more and more decisive for the future. In connection therewith the fundamental difference between the old and the new revelation has been explained and the symbolism and ritual, through which one formerly communicated has been characterized. This old symbolism has had no essential part to play in Anthroposophically orientated spiritual science. If symbols are referred to, it is only in the sense of "borrowed symbolism," in order to exemplify the one or other thing or to prove the correspondence of "that which has been newly discovered, which is of use to new humanity, and that which is antiquated and belongs to the past" (Dornach, December 20, 1918—"In the Changed Conditions of the Times").

The wording of this lecture, in which Anthroposophical spiritual science is emphatically described as belonging to the new revelation, is apparently partly due to the request of various friends that he should take up the esoteric, and particularly the cognitive-ritual work again.

There are some of you, who know that in our circles too we have by no means hesitated to set forth the life of symbolism and ritual that has remained from olden times. But we have always done so in a very different spirit. Generally the greatest value is attached, in an antiquated spirit, to the symbolism and ritual itself. To maintain the continuity of human evolution, it is still necessary to establish a connection, as it were, with symbolism and ritual. But in our circles symbolism and ritual have never been presented in any other way than as something that should lead us to the spiritual reality itself and to its immediate incorporation into the living value of our time. Hence it is just in Anthroposophical spiritual science that we find the explanation of many, nay, in fact of all the principles of ritual and symbolism from the past. We show how humankind received by other paths a Wisdom that in our time is antiquated and out of date. This Wisdom brought us, in a certain sense, into an unfree condition. Today we must set out on new paths of Wisdom.... It is immensely important, my dear friends, to bear this in mind. To be able to be, in the deepest sense of the word, a human being who identifies with that which the new Revelations of the Heavens are wanting from the Earth—this is the thing that matters.

That is why in future it will be no good to conceive of everyday life as a miserable, profane existence and then retire to the Church, or to the Masonic Temple and leave these two worlds entirely separate from one another.

Since then Rudolf Steiner must have pondered how the esoteric work should receive an up-to-date form, so that the outmoded principle of secrecy could be replaced by something else (Dornach, December 20, 1918). Marie Steiner reports how at that time he often pondered over the form that the new should take, so that it should encompass something binding and solid to overcome mediocrity and yet be compatible with the freedom of all. "He was not of the opinion that one could practice esotericism as in former times, in deep isolation and with strictly binding vows. These things were not compatible with the feeling of freedom of the individual. The soul had to appear before its own higher "I" and recognize the obligation of respectful silence that is due towards this "I" and to the spiritual world."[6]

---

6. Marie Steiner in *Erinnerungsworte* [words of remembrance] printed with the first edition of the lectures about the karmic connections of the Anthroposophical Movement, Dornach, 1926; reprinted in *Nachrichten der Rudolf Steiner Nachlaßverwaltung* [News from the executors of Rudolf Steiner's Estate] No. 23, Christmas, 1958.

These considerations, arising from the changed conditions of the times, the tragic loss of the Goetheanum Building through the fire on New Year's Eve 1922, and the necessary but so difficult reorganization of the Society, bring to a head the decision at the refounding of the Society at Christmas 1923, not only to reconstitute it on a completely public basis, but also to give the Esoteric School a form compatible with the new consciousness of the time. As the "Free High School for Spiritual Science" it was to be built up in three classes and with several scientific and artistic sections and be incorporated in the Statutes of the Society as the "Centerpoint" of its activity, to which every member had the right to apply for admission after having been a member of the Society for a certain length of time. Rudolf Steiner characterized in many articles how he wanted this new Esoteric School to be understood as "Free High School for Spiritual Science." He said that this High School would not be like the usual high schools and therefore would not try to compete with them in any way whatsoever, nor be a substitute for them. But one should be able to find in the Esoteric School what the ordinary high school could not provide, the esoteric deepening for which the soul strove in its search for knowledge. For those who were searching for a path into the spiritual world in a general human way, there was a general section. For those who were looking for an esoteric deepening in a particular scientific, artistic, or other direction, other sections would try to show the way. Thus all seeking human beings can find what they are looking for at the "High School at the Goetheanum" according to their special needs. The High School was not to be a purely scientific institution but a purely human one, that also fully covers the esoteric needs of both the scientists and the artists. Rudolf Steiner said that he himself would see to it that people were fully informed about what was going on.[7]

_____

7. See: *Die Konstitution der Allgemeinen Anthroposophischen Gesellschaft und der Freien Hochschule für Geisteswissenschaft—der Wiederaufbau des Goetheanum* (CW 260a) [The Constitution of the General Anthroposophical Society and the Free High School for Spiritual Science—the rebuilding of the Goetheanum (not translated)].

Because of this immense overburden and the severe illness that commenced in the autumn of 1924, only the first of the intended three classes and one or two of the intended scientific and artistic sections could be established. How the second and third class would have been arranged, and whether the ritual element would have been a part of it, has only been hinted at. Marie Steiner mentions much later, in a letter, that he had said to her in this respect: "In Class II much of what he had given us in the M.E. [Mystica Aeterna] would flow into it imaginatively and that in Class III this would have been transformed into moral strength."[8] And in her notes for an address to be given at a memorial ceremony for the anniversary of Rudolf Steiner's death on March 30, 1926, it is stated:[9] "He has left us before he was able to complete the work which he had started, before he was able to give us what he described as the second and third class. In the second he had wanted to give us the ritual, which would have corresponded with what were the revelations that flowed out of the imaginations of the supersensible School of Michael in the ...[end of the 18th and beginning of the 19th centuries]."[10]

Rudolf Steiner died a few months after giving these indications. Long exhausted, he succumbed on March 30, 1925, to the excessive strain that he had endured since Christmas 1923 as a result of his decision to take upon himself the task of renewing the Society and the Esoteric School under his sole responsibility. Thus the abyss between the aristocratic principle of the spirit and the ever-growing demands for democracy by the new age, about which he had spoken in the esoteric lesson on October 27, 1923, as of a "heroic tragedy in human history," could be bridged. Destiny did not allow him to complete this mightily conceived work for the future. Nevertheless, in line with a passage in his Mystery Drama, it: "... as an example for humanity would have—just once—been

---

8. Letter from November 8, 1947, to Helga Geelmuyden, Norway.
9. Notebook, Archive No. 133.
10. Cf. p. 127.

placed upon Earth. In spirit it will work on, even if it does not survive in earthly life. And it will contribute to the Earth a small part of the power, which will one day bring about the marriage of spiritual goals with earthly deeds."[11]

---

11. *The Soul's Awakening*, Scene I, Hilary speaks. (Translation by Michael Hedley Burton and Adrian Locher, 1994).

DOCUMENTS

Handwritten copy in notebook Archive No. 98
No date, presumably for Christiania (Oslo), December 1921

Der Weltenbau muß werden
Aus Menschen muß er erbaut werden

The creation of the World must come about
From out of the human being it must be built

Brüder der Vorzeit

Euer Schaffen werde unsere Weisheit, wir
wollen des Kreises Rundsinn und der
Geraden Richtkraft aus Euerer königlichen Kunst
gebrauchen; Eure getane Arbeit sei
Kraft unsere Seele, sei Kraft unserer
Hände.

Brüder der Gegenwart

So Ihr weiser seid als wir, lasset
strömen Eure Weisheit in unsre
Seelen, auf daß wir Glieder
werden Eurer Gottesgedanken.

Brüder der Zukunft

So Ihr des Baues Plan in Eurem
Willen traget, lasset strömen Euere
Kraft in unsere Glieder, auf daß
wir Leib werden den großen Seelen.

Brothers of Ages Past
May your creative activity become our wisdom,
We would make use of the sense of roundness
of the circle and the upright force of the straight
line belonging to the Royal Art;
May your completed work be the strength of our soul,
be the strength of our hands.

Brothers of the Present Time
Since you are wiser than we, let your wisdom
radiate into our souls, so that we become
members of your divine thoughts.

Brothers of the Future
Since you bear the building plan
in your will, let your strength stream
into our limbs so that we may become
the body for the great souls.

———————

M.E.
[Mystica Aeterna]

2

Meister der Vorzeit:
In schaudernder Ehrfurcht
Erblickt mein Geistesauge
Eure lichte Weisheit
In Eure Regionen strebe
Mein Seelensinn
Mit Euch zu bauen an dem Menschen-Welten-Bau.

Meister der Gegenwart:
In williger Andacht
Erhöre mein Seelenohr
Euer schaffend Weltenwort
Daß nicht ewiglich verloren
Der Mensch dem Weltenziele
Und Lucifer verfallen müsse.

Meister der Zukunft:

Im lieberfüllten Wollen	Im lieberfüllten Wollen
Verbind ich Eigen-Ich	Verbinde sich das Eigen-Ich
Mit eurem Weltenwollen	Mit Eurem Weltenwollen
Es soll vereinen sich	In ihm nur darf er hoffen
Des Menschen Willenskraft	Von Ahrimans Seelenkälte
Mit Kraft erzeugendem *Weltenwort.*	Verschont sich selbst zu finden.

Lehrling   der Welt und des Lebens
                Verlieren uns selbst.

Genosse   der Menschen
                Finden den Andern

Meister   seiner Selbst.

Die wankende Lichtvolle Säule
Die feste dunkle Säule

Masters of the Ages Past:
Shaking in awe
The eye of my spirit
Perceives your radiant wisdom
May the aim of my soul
Be to enter your regions
To build with you the world-building of humanity.

Masters of the Present Time:
In willing devotion
May the ear of my soul
Hear your creative universal word
So that human beings be not forever lost
To the world-aims
And succumb to Lucifer.

Masters of the Future:

In love-filled will	In love-filled will
I unite my individual "I"	May my individual "I"
With your universal will	Unite with your universal will
Humankind's strength of will	Only through that may it hope
Must unite with the universal Word	To find itself protected
Engendering strength.	From Ahriman's coldness of soul.

Apprentice of the world and of life
     Losing the self.

Companion of humankind
     Finding the other person

Master of the self

     The wavering luminous pillar
     The steadfast dark pillar.

*The Solemn Disbandment of the Cognitive-Ritual Work Group,
Norway, December 1921*

Report from memory by Ingeborg Möller-Lindholm
in a letter from Föllebü of February 20, 1952

In 1923 Rudolf Steiner gave an Esoteric Lesson but it was not an M.D. [Misraïm-Dienst—previously F.M.]. But he gave an M.D. in 1921 when he visited Norway again, seven years after the outbreak of the First World War (he had been separated from us during the war and in the first post-war years). At that time he collected all the earlier members of the M.D. together but without ritual and without ritual vestments. During this lesson he ceremoniously disbanded the old M.D.—it would not have been possible at that time (for a number of reasons) to have gone on working according to the earlier instructions. The changed conditions demanded something different. But the old would come to life again in a changed form, with us too, he said. Probably he meant by that the second and third classes, which however, never made an appearance on Earth, because death claimed him before that could happen.

As far as I remember, the Temple Legend was not told at that time, 1921. That took place only at the inception into the First Class, not later.

I have no notes from the Esoteric Lesson in Oslo (called E.S. and not to be confused with M.D.)—we were not allowed to take notes.

Esoteric Lesson in Christiania (Oslo), May 18 or 20, 1923
Undated account by Helga Geelmuyden set down later from memory

On Dr. Steiner's visit to Oslo—his last one—in May 1923—he held an M.E. meeting.[1]

During the meeting he continued to recount the Temple Legend in a very impressive way. And he went on to speak about how the Sons of Abel found their way to the Sons of Cain when the theologians asked him for the new ritual. That aroused growing enmity on the part of the Sons of Abel and the Sons of Cain in the outside world. (What he meant was the Jesuits and the Occult Brotherhoods—as I understand it, at least).

And he said further that the fire that destroyed the Goetheanum was started in the same hall in which the new ritual was given to the theologians.

Following on the Temple Legend it was further reported that it would be necessary to rebuild the Goetheanum. It was expressed somewhat as follows: Solomon's Temple never existed in a physically material form. But it had to be on the earth at some time. (The Doctor once told me on a previous occasion that the Sons of Abel might not be admitted to the M.E. This was said in connection with the fact that someone had wanted to introduce a woman possessing atavistic clairvoyant faculties into the gathering).

The things which the Doctor said regarding the rebuilding of the Goetheanum made a deep impression on me. Later—in the summer—I was present at the General Meeting of the Goetheanum Association [in Dornach], which was dealing with the question of the rebuilding. I asked him on that occasion if he would not repeat what he had told us in Norway. He shook his head and said abruptly: quite impossible.

Now I must confess: the new Goetheanum was never able to satisfy me against the background of this vivid memory. It is especially

---

1. The designation "M.E.—meeting" for the Esoteric Lesson is explained by the fact of its similarity to an M.E. Instruction Lesson.

painful for me to see the Christ Statue completely isolated. In 1916 when I spoke to the Doctor in Berlin as I was passing through on my way to Dornach, he said to me: "Whenever you visit the building you must imagine the whole time the carved group in its place."—I did that too, and a living movement was set in motion along all the pillars and architraves and what caused the movement was the Christ-"I" as it manifests in the carving. The old Goetheanum died without having quite embodied this "I"—it was still outside. In the new Goetheanum there is no possibility of an organic merging.

The union of the Sons of Abel with the Sons of Cain has also not been completely realized.[2]

---

2. A supplementary remark to this statement can be read in the following (type-written by Paul Michaelis from a diary entry quoting Dr. Steiner by Ludwig Polzer-Hoditz after his last visit to the sick bed of Rudolf Steiner, March 3, 1925):

"'... always keep in mind, however: The Jesuits have taken away religiousness and piety from humankind, they are identical with the authority of the Roman State. The battle, i.e. the sin against the Spirit, is their means of enforcing their authority, the only sin of which the Bible says it cannot be forgiven. And yet the Spirit cannot be entirely eliminated, but only a few people will carry it forward into the future.' This current is also strongly evident in the Society and he hopes that he may have paralyzed it by means of the Christmas Conference (c.f. CW 260). For it was not without reason that he tried to strike a balance between male and female spirits among the members of the Committee (Vorstand), as the tendencies were clearly visible that showed that the female spirit was to have been excluded because of old relationships. 'I emphasized that to begin with when I spoke about the Temple Legend. But it was clearly not understood. Nevertheless it is an important undercurrent within the Society.'"

Sketch by Rudolf Steiner for Professor Wohlbold, Munich (undated, ca.1923)

SPIRITUAL WORLD

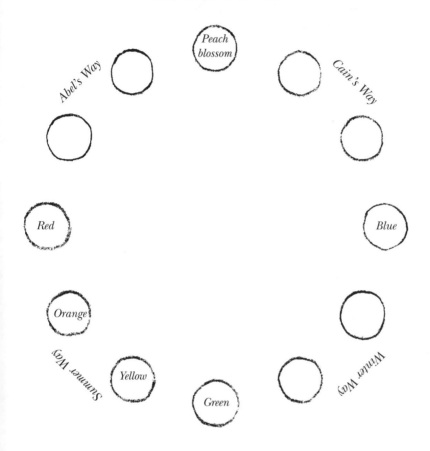

EARTHLY WORLD

The summer way is the way of the Christian Community in memory of a community (pre-natal) in the spiritual world (Abel's way).

The winter way is the way of anthroposophists through cold solitude to knowledge (Cain's way).

Three Esoteric Lessons with Subject Matter from Earlier Cognitive-Ritual Work Connections

Held in Dornach on May 27, 1923; October 23, 1923; and January 3, 1924 for the Wachsmuth-Lerchenfeld Group.[3]

Text by Maria Röschl-Lehrs "from memory written down immediately afterwards."

I

By way of introduction it was told how it is again possible to have such a group. Clear consciousness is a necessity. Earlier one had approached the anthroposophical affairs with too little consciousness, too little spiritual awareness.

If what was given in those old esoteric connections had been published, many rituals would have come into existence in the world. But as it was not published the whole thing aroused hatred and betrayal.

The people here have not been summoned by him, they have come together of their own accord. In the sight of the spiritual world he had rejected the founding of further groups—one must not be arrogant! There are more people who would be considered for such a thing, also some who have progressed further! Here there are only those who came together of their own free will. About meditating. It is not only a personal matter, but one of world importance. The cosmos is interested in the fact of whether we carry it out or not.

O human ...[4]

Legend [Temple Legend] new supplement

---

3. Called that by Rudolf Steiner (see p. 481) because the initiative sprang from the two Wachsmuth brothers, Count Lerchenfeld and Harriet von Vacano. Named participants that have been recorded: Marie Steiner, Dr. Ita Wegman, Dr. Elisabeth Vreede, Albert Steffen, Dr. Günther Wachsmuth, Wolfgang Wachsmuth and wife, Dr. Kurt Piper, Dr. Otto Palmer, Dr. von Baravalle, Dr. Maria Röschl, Count Lerchenfeld, Harriet von Vacano, Jürgen von Grone, Margarita Woloschin.

4. This mantra was later incorporated into the mantras of the First Class of the Free High School of Spiritual Science.

Two directions—in John the middle. Recognise what comes from the two directions. The burning [of the Goetheanum] because both were united against the middle. Hate against the continuation of this middle.

Wake up! Be awake in respect of these two directions, but also in general. Wake up through proper meditation! Goethe was very much awake, Schiller only half awake, Herder and Lessing were fast asleep.

Before the Mystery of Golgotha the words of an initiate were: Salem. Now the reverse: Melas ... the circle is complete.

Supplement: Formerly Mach ben ach—earthly son of sorrow or the bodily-physical has separated from the soul-spiritual.

Vowel practice—pilgrimage to the "I" [5]

O A J A O : "I" between light and space

A J O J A : Space for 'I' and light

J O A O J : Light through space and m[e].

I am

Only now about the two directions and the fire.[6]

---

5. See original sketch p. 491.

6. Note here by Maria Röschl-Lehrs: "Here only very sparse notes. Sequence not clear."

The Temple Legend—1923 Version

The wording of the Temple Legend from the Esoteric Lesson May 27, 1923, was afterwards written down from memory by several different participants and reconstructed out of texts from earlier cognitive-ritual work. The title "new version given in spring 1923" under which it was distributed is actually only appropriate to the final ending (referred to in the notes of Maria Röschl-Lehrs as "new supplement"). The text of the first part of the Legend corresponds exactly to the written copy by Rudolf Steiner from 1906 (p. 379). The description of the casting of the brazen sea and Hiram's death, which follows on immediately from that, shows, on the other hand, some variations from earlier accounts. The story in the version of 1923 that follows the sentence in Rudolf Steiner's copy (p. 381): "Only Hiram owns a truly human 'I,'" runs as follows:

...

From this moment onwards a violent jealousy took hold of King Solomon against his architect Hiram Abiff. The latter had three apprentices for the work of building the temple, who demanded the Master's degree from him. But they had demonstrated their lack of efficiency by having cut the mighty irreplaceable beam of the temple building too short. Hiram, by using his special powers, had corrected the damage by stretching the beam to the right length. The apprentices were henceforth the opponents of Hiram Abiff, because they were refused by him when they asked him for the Master's degree and the Master Word, for which they were unfit. The three perfidious apprentices found no difficulty in gaining the ear of the king for a deed by which they wished to destroy Hiram Abiff.

The completion of the temple was to have been crowned by a work by which Hiram Abiff hoped to reconcile the tension and enmity between the Sons of Cain and the Sons of Abel. It was the brazen sea, of which the casting from the seven metals (lead, tin, iron, gold, copper, quicksilver and silver) and the earth-metal, water, were to be so mixed together that the finished casting would be completely transparent. The thing was complete except for a final infusion, which was to be made in the presence of the assembled court and also in front of the Queen of Sheba and which was to transform the still dull substance into complete lucidity.

But now the three perfidious apprentices who had the task of adding the last ingredient, added the wrong amount of water and instead of it becoming transparent the casting spurted up in devastating flames. Hiram Abiff tried to quench the flames but he did not succeed. The flames burst out in all directions.

But Hiram heard a voice coming out of the flames and from the glowing mass: "Throw yourself into the sea of flames, you are immune from harm." He threw himself into the flames and noticed that his pathway was taking him to the center of the Earth. Midway on his course he met his ancestor Tubal-Cain, who led him to the center of the Earth where his great ancestor Cain, was in the state he had been in before the sin of Abel's murder. Cain gave him the golden triangle with the Master Word. Midway on his return journey Tubal-Cain presented him with a mallet and told him to touch the casting of the brazen sea with it. Hiram Abiff received the information from Cain that the energetic development of human earthly forces would ultimately lead to the peak of initiation and that the initiation acquired in this way would replace the old clairvoyance in the course of evolution and that the latter would disappear. Hiram returns with the mallet to the surface of the earth and touches the brazen sea with the mallet. The casting succeeds and Hiram Abiff is able to prepare for its complete transparency.

Hiram wanted to take a last look at his building of the temple and went there during the night. The three treacherous apprentices were lying in wait for him there. The first of them gave him a blow on his left temple at one of the gates, so that the blood trickled down to his shoulder. Hiram Abiff turned to the second gate, in order to get out of the temple. Then the second apprentice gave him a blow on the right temple so that the blood flowed down to his shoulder. He turned to the third gateway. There he was met by a blow to the forehead by the third apprentice so that he collapsed. He dragged himself out till he came to a well into which he sank the golden triangle. The three apprentices buried his body. Before dying Hiram was able to submerge the golden triangle with the Master Word into a deep well. On his grave there grew up a cassia tree [acacia]. It was known to those with insight that when an initiate dies a cassia tree grows out of his grave. When his corpse was discovered the new Master Word sounded forth: "Mach ben ach."[7] That signifies: The soul-spiritual has become separated from the bodily-physical.[8] The golden triangle was then sought and was found in the well. A stone cube on which the ten commandments were inscribed was placed on the triangle and it was hidden by being walled up in the temple.

The foregoing symbolism gives us that which raises the inner essence of human development on Earth to imagination during meditation. The brazen sea can be looked upon as what humankind would have become had not the three conspiratorial powers found entrance into its soul. These three powers are: doubt, superstition, and illusion about oneself.

Hiram Abiff was reborn as Lazarus and through that he was the first person to be initiated by Christ. With him begins the reconciliation of the strife existing between the Cain and Abel streams.

---

7. In this account the connecting section of the usual versions is missing: Solomon gave instructions for Hiram's body to be sought. As it was believed that the murderers would have extorted the Master Word from Hiram, it had been agreed not to mention the search. The first word that one of the Masters inadvertently let fall during the excavation should pass for the new Master Word. When, after long endeavor the body was found, the words "Mach ben ach" escaped from one the searchers. This was accepted as the new Master Word.

8. Another explanation of this is: "earthly son of suffering."

According to a different version "the new supplement" runs as follows:

Hiram Abiff was reborn as Lazarus and through that he was the first to be initiated by Christ. With him the middle stream was inaugurated, the stream that stood between that of Cain and that of Abel. In the course of time the Cain stream was represented mainly as F. (Freemasonry-stream), while the stream of Abel was expressed by the priestly current of the (Catholic?) Church. Both of these streams within humankind remained strictly at war with one another. They only once united in concord: in their hate of the middle stream. The result of this concerted action of the otherwise opposing directions was the destruction of the John Building (the Goetheanum).

II

To begin with the Indian mantra was given for the first time, the translation [also] for the first time.[9] After the Indian mantra the invocation was regularly made: "Brothers of ..."[10]

True esotericism is incomprehensible to begin with. As an example for this visualize a living human being who outwardly betrays no indication of expressing a spiritual existence. The life of the spirit is directed solely within.—Nevertheless an intensive inner life.

Concerning the vowels: the hierarchies are involved in them.

I.A.O.   Seraphim, Cherubim and in part the Thrones.

U.   Kyriotetes, Exusiai, Dynamis.

E.   Archai, Archangeloi, Angeloi

All of this together signifies the primordial sacred word of Jahve in place of the I-am. To create this Jahve-word from the hierarchies signifies a deed. The putting into practice of this deed on Earth: The Butterfly Meditation:

---

9. See p. 491 et seq.
10. See p. 488.

Fange den Falter
Sende ihn in eisige Höhen
Wo die Weltenträume walten.
Wird er dir zum Vogel
Dann hast du der Arbeit
Hälfte vollbracht.
Den Vogel tauche
In Meerestiefen
Wo der Weltenwille wirket.   J A O U E
Ertrinkt der Vogel,
Dann bleibt dir noch zu tun,
Die Vogelleiche
Im Feuer läuternd zu verbrennen.
Dann verzehr'die Asche
Und du bist
Das Licht im Weltendunkel. –

Catch the butterfly
Send it into icy heights
Where cosmic dreams hold sway.
If it becomes for you a bird
Then you have performed half the work.
Plunge the bird
Into the depths of the sea
Where cosmic will works.   J A O U E
If the bird drowns
Then there remains still
For you to burn purifying in fire
The corpse of the bird.
Then consume the ash
And you are
The light in cosmic darkness.[11]

---

11. English translation of above with acknowledgement to Virginia Sease.

The imagination of the Butterfly Meditation has an etheric effect. Only a simple explanation.—Search the memory with the "three-and-half-years" span with reference to the Butterfly Meditation. One of its etheric effects is that it causes one to look into one's own will-impulses and in retrospective assessment of these one can find a point in one's life that impelled one to a particular task. One often finds that in one's search for such a moment, the failure to comply with which caused dissatisfaction, a point is reached lying about three and a half years in the past (hindrance through outer circumstances, e.g. the Threefold Movement).

When this point has been ascertained then it becomes a question of fostering the contents of such a desire, not by seeking in any way to put it into action, but by nurturing the content in the best fashion. Then the possibility of realizing one's desire will present itself again after three and a half years from the time one first became conscious of it. And at that point it will become a question of carrying out a selfless deed with no connection to the original starting point of seven years previously. That could be a quite insignificant deed looked at from without.

Description of time, position in time. The present lectures and this lesson, when compared with the ruling fanaticism at the height of democracy outside, are the very antithesis of the latter; they represent the height of aristocracy and hierarchy. A huge abyss over which evolution has to leap if it is to overcome this antithesis. Descriptions of this abyss across which some courageously leap, others are dragged and others torn. It is all a heroic tragedy in the history of humankind.

> Butterfly Meditation [p. 474 and p. 497]
>
> Invocation [p. 488]
>
> Indian mantra [p. 491 et seq.]

III

Brothers of ...
Indian mantra

Reference to the new [Anthroposophical] Society, which had been founded successfully without mention of the esoteric basis. (He said earlier that the Founding had an esoteric background). Esotericism cannot bear trifling, everything previous to that had been trifling [had been taken lightly]. Esotericism must now be proclaimed openly and seriously in the world, spreading out from its center in Dornach. There must no longer be any playing about with esotericism. Modesty is necessary in that, especially modesty in face of the ego.

For that reason be wakeful! Become aware of the fact that we are sleeping! Every time we wake up we come into a new cosmic sphere, for we live entirely surrounded by cosmic spheres, only we are asleep and know nothing of them. Up till now everything to do with humankind took place in dreams. Importance of the Butterfly Meditation (about which he said previously that all he divulges about the effect of this meditation and its connection with the twice three-and a half-years only applies to people over 28). Reading of the same – J A O U E.

Something must be given that strengthens the effect of the Butterfly Meditation:

4 stages of sleep: in the thinking, feeling , willing, in the "I."
4 stages of waking: in the thinking, feeling , willing, in the "I."

Thinking:

The head is like a fruit, the heart like a shining chalice. We should experience our head, self-illuminating, stretching down to the heart. We should experience our thinking as an etheric organ tenderly reaching out to what it should lay hold of. The esotericist can be distinguished from the non-esotericist by the fact that the former is conscious of this organ raying out into the etheric world. We should experience ourselves like a snail stretching out its tentacles. Thinking has to become a delicate reaching out! Help for this:

Awaken in thinking: you exist in the spirit light of the world.

Experience yourself as shining, reaching out towards what is shining.

Through this kind of thinking the whole of nature is illumined. Stone and plant light up in the earth-realm, ... as animal and human ... in the moral realm. Through experiencing thinking as a reaching out we develop something akin to a consciousness of touch: we behold a dandelion blossom and experience it as velvet, we look at a chicory plant and experience it as silk, a sunflower as a prickly animal.

Feeling:

This is still a deep dreaming. We should experience our heart as shining, but so that it receives light from the whole of its surroundings and reflects it outwardly like the Moon. We should experience the world quite differently through our awakening feeling; the Earth as a sentient being that laughs and cries. The withering of autumn is a kind of weeping of nature, but a delight among ahrimanic beings. In the spring there is joy among the luciferic beings. Natural processes as the deeds of spiritual beings! Trees—in winter they are just physical body, the etheric is outside them. One can advance so far as to see how the trees carry out tasks in the etheric.

If one awakens in thinking one stretches oneself to infinity. If one awakens in feeling one sets oneself in motion, comes out of oneself.

Awaken in your feeling: you exist within the spirit deeds of the world.

Experience yourself, feeling the spirit-deeds.

Willing:

In this sphere deep sleep prevails in humanity today. In our will, however, we are thrown back upon ourselves. We have our thinking in this earth-life alone, we take nothing of it with us into the life after death. Our thinking is needed by the Gods, our feeling and willing are not required by them. A person may be a genius, perhaps, but only because the Gods need it that way. Geniuses are the lamps needed by the Gods. Our thinking capacity returns to the Gods at death.

Our willing, on the other hand, accompanies us during our incarnations, it is a product of them, we work upon it during our lives on earth. In our co-operation in the shaping of the world our will is the most essential characteristic. Willing is the property of humans, whereas human thinking belongs to the Gods. Jealousy of the Gods!

There is individual life in our will. But we are still asleep in our will. People like the will because they always believe that what they "will" is always right. But through our will we co-operate in the shaping of the world. We wake up in our will when we become aware of the fact that we are not there for ourselves alone, but are responsible for the deeds of others. Take the example of Kully: for that which he does, for just that which upsets us most, we ourselves are responsible, we actually accompany that; the Goesch-affair = maya.[12] When we feel ourselves no longer separated as individual beings, but as bound up in the general activity, then we awaken in our will, only then we arrive at a living will, then we think the spiritual beings:

Awaken in your will: you exist within the spirit-being of the world.

Experience yourself in thinking the spirit beings.

---

12. Kully and Goesch: two active opponents of that time.

Awaken in your "I":

We are asleep in our "I." We only use the word "I" because the Gods once spoke it for us—our Angels—and human beings now speak it in imitation thereof. But we must awaken in our "I"! The imagination for this: Altar, the sun above it. We approach the altar and experience ourselves wholly as shadow, as completely being-less. Formerly we said: I am. Now we say consciously: I am not. A divine being then descends from the sun above the altar and fills the shadow with life. We are like a chalice that receives the light of the divine being that descends out of the sun—through grace we receive this Divinity, it bestows itself on us—that was what Fichte experienced, but in a completely shadowy way. Therefore, what he says about it is completely abstract.

Awaken in your "I": you are within your own spirit being.

Experience that, receiving from the Gods and bestowing it on yourself.[13]

Then was spoken:

      The stones are mute ... [p. 484 et seq.]

      Brothers of ... [p. 488]

      Indian mantra [p. 491 et seq.]

---

13. C.f. handwriting on p. 495.

27. Mai 1923 Dornach die Wachsmuth-
Lehrenfeld-gruppe:

_____

mit gewinn des Efot. dann ?

1) Auseinandersetzung des Ernstes = | Das Efot.
                                      | räigen

2.) Hass, Ehrgeiz, verweigerte Liebe —
astrales Licht —

3.) Die Legende —

4.) Die Aktifen.

heute = man hat guten Ich und dem
(Worte den Gedanken verloren. —

Melas

S l m ch

Salem

Concerning the Three Esoteric Lessons for the "Wachsmuth-Lerchenfeld-Group"

Rudolf Steiner's notebook entries, notebook Archive No. 281. Some of it could also have been given at the Esoteric Lesson in Christiana (Oslo) on May 18 or 20.

May 27, 1923, Dornach the Wachsmuth-Lerchenfeld-Group:

esoteric enjoyed at first, then

1.) Emphasizing seriousness = esoteric forgotten

2.) Hate, ambition, denied love –
    astral light –

3.) The Legend –

4.) The intentions

today = one has lost the thought which
belongs to the "I" and the Word. –

perceiving thinking

Melas

s l m ch

spoken rightly
so that the Word
is effective

Salem

Mastery over
oneself

Esot. M.E.

1.) Invocation.

2.) The Temple Legend   Elohim Eve Cain Jehovah

                           Eve Abel

                           Sons of Fire – Sons of Earth

                           Enoch

                           Irad

                           Methusael T

                           Tubal-Cain

                           Hiram – Solomon

                                       Balkis

                               Temple

                             Brazen Sea

                               |

                           Lazarus-John

                               |

                           Now in the present

Epil. M. E.

1.) Anrufung.

2) Die Tempellegende: Elohim Eva Kain Jehovah

Eva Abel

Söhne des Feuers - Söhne der Erde.

Enoch

Irad

Methusael T

Tubalkain.

Hiram —   Salomo

                          Balkis.

Tempel

Ehernes Meer.

|

Lazarus - Johannes.

|

Nun in der Gegenwart.

The Divine is revealed through Symbols

The Human is conveyed through Touch

The Sub-human is averted through the Word

3.) The stones are mute; I have placed and hidden the eternal Creator-Word in them; chaste and modest they hold it in the depths.

Materia prima. Matter hardens in itself

The plants live and grow. I have placed the eternal Creator-Word in them; sprouting and thriving they carry it into the depths.

Materia secunda. Matter opens itself to the spirit

The animals feel and will. I have placed the eternal Creator-Word in them; shaping and molding they hold it in the depths.

Materia tertia. Matter shines in the light of the soul

Das göttliche wird geoffenbart durch die Zeichen.

Das Menschliche wird vermittelt durch die Berührung

Das Untermenschliche wird abgewendet durch das Wort.

3.) Die Steine sind stumm; ich habe das ewige
Schöpferwort in sie gelegt und verborgen;
Keusch und schamvoll fallen sie es in den Tiefen.
  Mat. prima. Die Materie verhärtet in sich

Die Pflanzen leben und wachsen. Ich habe das
ewige Schöpferwort in gelegt; sprießend
und gedeihend tragen sie es in die Tiefen.
  M. s. Die Materie öffnet sich dem Geist

Die Tiere empfinden und wollen. Ich habe das
ewige Schöpferwort in sie gelegt; formend
und bildend halten sie es in den Tiefen.
  M. t. Die Materie glänzt im
    Licht der Seele.

The human being thinks and acts; I have placed the eternal Creator-Word in him; he should fetch it from the depths.

Spiritus tertius. The "I" finds itself in the world

The soul knows and is devoted; I shall release my eternal Creator-Word from her, that she may carry it into the heights of purity and piety.

Spiritus secundus. The "I" sacrifices itself to God

The spirit releasing itself loves the Universe. I speak it in my eternal Creator-Word, awakening and liberating the world in purity.

Spiritus primus. The "I" works in God[14]

---

14. With acknowledgements to Virginia Sease.

Der Mensch denkt und handelt ; ich habe das
ewige Schöpferwort in ihn gelegt; er soll es
holen aus den Tiefen.

      s. t. <u>Das Ich findet sich in der Welt</u>

Die Seele erkennt und giebt sich frei ; ich
~~habe~~ löse mein ewiges Schöpferwort
aus ihr, dass sie es trage in die
Höfen der Reinheit und Frömmigkeit.

      s. s. <u>Das Ich opfert sich dem Gotte</u>

Der Geist liebt sich lösend das All - Ich
spreche in ihm mein ewiges Schöpferwort, weckend und erlösend in
Reinheit die Welt.

      s. p. <u>Das Ich wirkt in dem Gotte</u>

1)

<u>Brothers of Ages Past</u>: May your creative activity become our wisdom; we take the circumference and plumb line of the heights from your hands; may your accomplished work be strength for our soul, be strength for our hands.

<u>Brothers of the Present Time</u>: Since you are wiser than we, let your wisdom radiate into our souls, so that we become revealers of your thoughts of God.

<u>Brothers of the Future</u>: Since you bear the building plan in your will, let your strength stream into our limbs, so that we may become the body for the great souls. ————

I

Brüder der Vergil: Euer Schaffen werde unsere
Weisheit, wir nehmen den Umkreis und das
Lot der Höhe aus Euren Händen; Eure
getane Arbeit sei Kraft unserer Seele, sei
Kraft unserer Hände.

Brüder der Gegenwart: So Ihr weiser seid als
wir, lasset leuchten Eure Weisheit in unsere
Seelen, auf dass wir Offenbarer werden
Eurer Gottesgedanken.

Brüder der Zukunft: So Ihr des Willens Baues Plan
in Eurem Willen traget, lasset strömen Eure
Kraft in unsre Glieder, auf dass wir
Leib werden den Grossen Seelen. —

"Brothers of ... " (another version)
In Rudolf Steiner's handwriting, from Notebook Archive No. 281

Göttliche Bildner des Weltenalls
Erfühlet den Seelen-Opferrauch
Den wir in Eure Lichtes-Höhen
Verehrend möchten strömen lassen.

Göttliche Denker des Weltenalls
Nehmet auf in Euer Denken das Opferwort
Das wir den Luftkreisen vertrauen
Die Euch begegnen, wenn Euere Kräfte
Welten durch den Raum hindurch führen.

Göttliche Schöpfer des Weltenalls
Nehmet hin in Euer Wesen unser eignes Wesen
Daß wir in Eurem Schutze gedeihen
Wenn Ihr aus den Erdentiefen
Eine Welt gegen die Lichteshöhen wachsend hebt.

Divine Architects of the Universe
Take into your feelings the smoke of sacrificing souls
Which we would let stream in reverence
Into your light-filled heights.

Divine Imagers of the Universe
Take up into your thinking the sacrificial Word
Which we entrust to the circles of air
Which meet you when your powers
Lead worlds through space.

Divine Creators of the Universe
Take our own being into your Being
So that we may prosper under your protection
When you raise up from the depths of Earth
A world growing towards the light-filled heights.

Meditation from the Esoteric Lesson, Dornach May 27, 1923
(See pp. 469, 473)

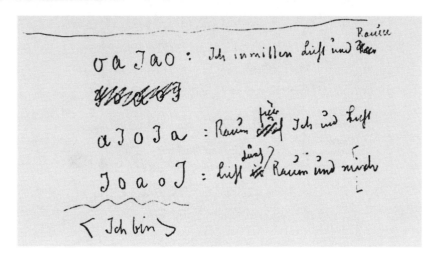

The Indian Mantra
The text has not been preserved

Among Rudolf Steiner's handwritten notes to these esoteric lessons there are two Indian mantras:

> Yasmat jatam jagat sarvam, yasminn eva praliyate
> yenedam dhriyate caiva, tasmai jnanatmane namah.

> From Him out of Whom the whole world evolves, to Him
> to Whom it returns again,
> by Whom it is firmly supported,
> to Him the Self, Who knows, be Glory and Honor.

The other Indian mantra is entered as follows in the notebook:

Translation of above:

External Existence, Eternal Feeling, Eternal Life = Brahma
Revelation's Beauty, Revelation's Happiness, Revelation's Splendor
Immeasurably extended harmony, Innumerable forces of growth, Incomprehensible unity of endless multiplicity "I," O immeasurably extended harmony, – , –

The Power of Existence, Might of Blessing, Fullness of Grace.
Brightness of Joy, Love, Heart of Will
Peace, Essence of Becoming, Unity.

The Indian text not included by Rudolf Steiner

Satyam	gnanam		anantam	Brahma
ananda	rupam		amritam	vibharti
Shantam		Shivam		advaitam
Shanti		Shanti		Shanti

Fange den Falter

Sende ihn in eisige Höhen

Wo die Weltenträume walten

Wird er dir zum Vogel

Dann hast du der Arbeit

   Hälfte vollbracht:

Den Vogel tauche   JAOUE

   In Meerestiefen

Wo der Weltenwille wirket

Ertrinkt der Vogel

Dann bleibt dir noch zu tun,

Die Vogelleiche

   Im Feuer läuternd zu verbrennen

Dann vergeh' die Affe

Und du bist

Das Licht im Weltendunkel —

See p. 474 for translation.

Im Denken erwache: du bist im Geistes licht
          der Welt -
Erlebe dich als leuchtendes das Leuchtende tastend.

Im Fühlen erwache: du bist in den Geistes-Taten
          der Welt.

    Erlebe dich die Geistes Taten fühlend.

Im Wollen erwache: du bist in den Geistes-Wesen
          der Welt.

    Erlebe dich die Geistes wesen denkend.
Im Ich erwache: du bist in deinem
              eignen Geistes Wesen.

    Erlebe dich sein von Göttern empfangend
    und dir selbst gebend.

Translation of foregoing:

Awaken in thinking: you exist in the spirit light

of the world –

Experience yourself as shining reaching out

towards what is shining.

Awaken in feeling: you exist within the spirit deeds

of the world.

Experience yourself, feeling the spirit-deeds.

Awaken in the will: you exist within the spirit-being of the world.

Experience yourself in thinking the spirit beings.

Awaken in your "I": you are within your own

spirit-being.

Experience yourself, receiving from the Gods

and bestowing on yourself.

The text of the two apparently contemporaneous pieces of writing by Rudolf Steiner come from the estate of the English sculptress Edith Maryon, who helped Rudolf Steiner with the wooden carving of the "Group" and who became ill after the burning of the Goetheanum. Rudolf Steiner, who often visited her during her illness, must have told her about the Esoteric Lesson of May 27, 1923, and written down for her the two mantras.

Page of notes from Archive No. 5852

Translation of facsimile on next page:

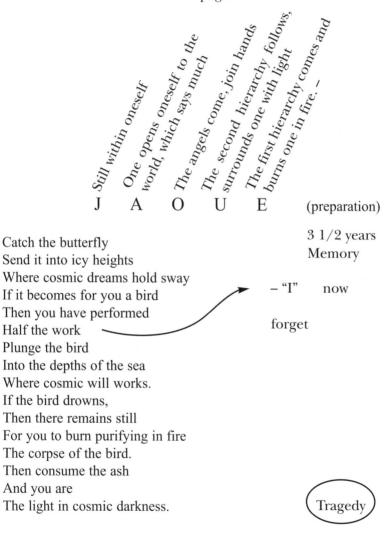

J   A   O   U   E   (preparation)

Catch the butterfly
Send it into icy heights
Where cosmic dreams hold sway
If it becomes for you a bird
Then you have performed
Half the work
Plunge the bird
Into the depths of the sea
Where cosmic will works.
If the bird drowns,
Then there remains still
For you to burn purifying in fire
The corpse of the bird.
Then consume the ash
And you are
The light in cosmic darkness.

3 1/2 years
Memory

– "I"   now

forget

Tragedy

J A O U E... (Vorbereitung)

Fange den Falter
Sende ihn in eisige Höhen
Wo die Wellenträume walten
Wird er dir zum Vogel
Dann hast du die Arbeit
 Hälfte vollbracht
Den Vogel taufe

In Meerestiefen
Wo der Wellenwille wirkt
Ertränkt den Vogel
Dann bleibt dir noch zu tun
Die Vogelleiche
Im Feuer läuternd zu verbrennen
Dann verzieh... die alte
Und du bist
Das Licht im Wellendunkel.

On the back of the page, in Edith Maryon's handwriting the following notes appear, which are obviously directions given by Rudolf Steiner for the carrying out of the meditation:

"First think about thinking—only the eyes move as he reads.

Then the content, the letters connect him with the hierarchies.

Then say: JAOUE

Butterfly = thought

3 1/2 years months or weeks or days

3 1/2 later step forth with enthusiasm

Experience alternately democracy with one's fellow human beings and the loneliness and tragedy of the aristocracy of thinking.

Loneliness penetrates to the contents."

———— ———— ————

Page of notes from Archive No. 5853

Translation of the foregoing:

If the Gods had merely consumed themselves in pleasure,

the World would never have come into existence;

They would only have scattered

their own being into the atmosphere of the Earth:

They became sad about that

And embraced their own being lamenting

And out of the lamentation

The holy sanction arose

The world-creating Word.

EPILOGUE

For the first anniversary of Rudolf Steiner's death, on March 30, 1926, a memorial celebration of symbolic-ritual character within the framework of the First Class of the Free High School for Spiritual Science was inaugurated by Marie Steiner-von Sivers, who was not only the co-founder and co-leader of the cognitive-ritual work circle, but had also occupied a special position therein, owing to her inner ability.[1] On the black-draped stage of the hall in the workshop building of the Goetheanum, where all Dornach performances took place at that time, she had arranged three altars, the one on the East being the one where she had officiated by the side of Rudolf Steiner. The following outlines of her address express what the life's work of Rudolf Steiner meant to her: namely the realization of the Temple Legend in his own biography.

Marie Steiner

We have gathered here to commemorate him who departed from life one year ago, who worked for us and with us in this place, who gave us instructions for our dealings in life, who served at the altars of wisdom, beauty and strength, as a sign whereof we have erected these altars to symbolize his work. As a symbol of his creative practical deeds we have laid these tools on the altars. With them he carved the new forms into the wood. They include his compasses, rule, trowel and mallet. They are still ensouled with the fire of his hands. They speak to us and demand deeds.

---

1. A participant commented on this theme as follows: "At the top, as Head of the School and as mediator for spiritual realities stood Rudolf Steiner. At his side and as companion and co-worker was Marie von Sivers. ... At a ritual of a higher degree, which only a small number of participants might attend, it was announced by Rudolf Steiner himself that Marie Steiner's co-operation should be taken in a fully justified sense—not in a symbolic sense, as with all of us others. And it was indeed the case that this referred to a reality which extended beyond birth and death." Reported by Adolf Arenson in a circular letter to the members of the Anthroposophical Society in October 1926.

In memory of him and of what we have to do we light these candles:

1. May the light which he kindled in our hearts shine brightly and become wisdom.
2. Let it rise up to him in purity, as purely as he imbued our souls with it.
3. May it find strength in him in active creativeness so that our deeds serve his spirit, our spirit grow strong in penetrating into the Christianizing of the "I."

—————

We stand in this room of sadness, thinking of the great one who has left us. The three altars stand before us as symbols and seal of his activity. The leader, who presided at this turning-point of humanity served continually at these altars. He was able to call them up from the depths of the temple, where they had rested since Mysteries existed, and he was able to hand them over to humanity. He bestowed them upon us in pictures, in art, by incorporating them into his Mystery Dramas in the stages of development of the spiritual pupils. He gave us them through his word by placing the ideals of wisdom, beauty and strength in the center of his work and continually before our eyes their single effects and their interplay with one another. He was able to permit the two most outstanding poets among his pupils to portray the Legend in words and pictures for the public. You know them for their works of art.[2] We shall consider them only insofar as they have been made artistically available to the public. And may Rudolf Steiner be remembered by the mallet stroke with which he linked

—————

2. Albert Steffen's drama *Hiram and Salomo* and the poems of Kurt Piper. See Supplementary Notes, p. 515.

the foundation stone celebration to the eternal spirit.[3] We will unite with him and place ourselves under his protection, to serve the powers to whom he led us in service.

How is it that Rudolf Steiner was permitted to perform a deed which signified a turning point for humanity and also a break and a new direction for esotericism?

When something great is close to us we do not see it, the cliff-wall overhangs us, it crushes the one, it obscures the view of the other. We cannot see over it, we can only feel that it is something very great.

It takes a long time until we reach the summit of the mountain and attain the wider view; but during the laborious climb we now and again catch a glimpse beyond and parts of the immense panorama fall into place.

Observing was made easy for us, we were able to experience it, but the light was perhaps too bright for us to discern it exactly.

We experienced the building, we experienced how Rudolf Steiner lifted his mallet while at work, and how his pupils flocked towards him to serve the project; the temple had risen sublime and radiant through the strength of his spirit and the skill of his hands and we were allowed to learn and participate in the work. But we too had the three treacherous apprentices alongside our weaknesses and imperfections, who went so far as to betray and wish to destroy. The seed of hate bore its fruit. The building stood

---

3. It is the laying of the foundation stone for the forming of the General Anthroposophical Society at Christmas 1923 which is referred to. Adolf Arenson reports about it thus: "Rudolf Steiner did not open the Christmas Conference with words, but with symbolic mallet strokes, by which he demonstrated the law of continuity. For to everyone who belonged to this institution, which Rudolf Steiner describes in the 36th chapter of his *Autobiography*, these mallet strokes signified: 'the new thing which I give to you, I now attach to what formerly existed, true to the laws of esotericism.' ... It hardly needs to be emphasized that this attachment to what existed earlier does not preclude the possibility of introducing something new, even something that bridges a gap such as is illustrated by the plant developing blossoms from leaves and yet producing something completely new therewith." Letter from Adolf Arenson to Albert Steffen, December 24, 1926.

in flames as once did the brazen sea. Rudolf Steiner lived out the Legend in his own life; he realized it through a physical deed; he became the Legend. He made it known to humanity through his own life.

And Rudolf Steiner threw himself into the scorching flames at the center. We were his scorching flames, we, the Children of Cain. He took our destiny upon himself so that we would be more free to serve. But our destiny was too hard and too heavy for him to bear and it broke his physical strength almost immediately after he had concluded the union. His last year of life was a mighty out-breathing of his spirit ...

When we come together as we do today, it is because we are conscious of the fact that we have experienced a moment of world history that is a cardinal point, not merely a turning point in time. The Spirit descended into undreamed of currents, through a human being who had prepared himself to receive it into his spirit, soul and body. We do not intend to do anything more today than let the spirit hold sway in the words he left with us as the well-head of life and strength, the words and music inspired by him in the room hung with black, which is the physical color of the spirit, at the three altars, the significance of which is known to you through the Mystery Plays by the light of the three candles that illuminate these altars.

Our thoughts are raised to him who departed from us a year ago. To him who poured his wisdom into our hearts with inexhaustible and never-ending gentleness and kindness, whose love united us all and took our souls upon himself, whose strength raised up our earth from the clutches of Ahriman's material hooks and snares, by which it was in danger of being suffocated, who bore it aloft to the Spirit on the wings of the Christianizing of the "I," which he taught and exemplified in his life. "Christ in me"—that was his life, his work and his word.

Through his word he created a building of indestructible strength, clarity and beauty. That the word may remain alive among us is the aim to which our thinking, feeling and willing must aspire!

We have placed upon the altars of wisdom, beauty and strength at which he served, the tools which he used in his work. Tools which are still ensouled by the warming fire of his hands, which encompassed the future in their grasp. With these tools he worked into matter until it became a revelation of the spirit through art, thus laying bare for us the most hidden truths of nature, forcing itself upon us in the beauty of outward manifestation. These are his compasses, his measuring rule, his trowel, his mallet and the mallet he used when carving the forms of the sculpted Group—: (Three mallet strokes: long short short; long short short; long short short).

We meet today in his spirit, asking that he may draw a veil over our weaknesses and inadequacies, through the radiance of his being. In his name we call upon the Archangel, to whose service he has dedicated us, striving to recognise the Guardian who stands at the temple's threshold into the realms beyond: (Three mallet strokes: long short short, long short short; long short short). We seek to draw near to this Guardian in the sign of his love, his love which, radiating wisdom, becomes for us the bestowing virtue of his word, his word which, transmitted into deed, becomes for us the directing, active sword of Michael, of his pervading life which, by inducing knowledge, leads us back to our original state and, overcoming space and time, becomes our future. We invoke these existing, active, ruling powers: the ones newly created by him: Anthroposophia,

Him whom he bade us follow: Michael

The comprehensive primeval beginning which bears the future within it: Jehovah-Adonai

Life – Love – Logos

Christ in me

Ex deo nascimur / In Christo morimur / Per spiritum sanctum reviviscimus.

(Three mallet strokes: long short short; long short short; long short short).

SUPPLEMENTARY NOTES

To page 32

Schuster, Hugo (1876-1925)

Swiss. As a young merchant in St. Gallen, 1903/04, he shared in the initiative of building up the anthroposophical work in Switzerland, notably in the founding of Branches in St. Gallen, Berne and Basel. As a result of Rudolf Steiner's portrayal of Christ, he felt impelled towards the priesthood. In 1918 he became a priest in the Old Catholic Church and held his first office in Basel. He received the Ritual for Burial from Rudolf Steiner at the beginning of 1919. Rudolf Steiner had indeed often given memorial addresses at the funerals of members of the Anthroposophical Society, but he had never treated it as a ritual, because, as Marie Steiner once formulated it, he was as little inclined to take up the priesthood as he was to become a medical doctor. But, because a member of the Society functioned as a priest, they were able to work together. On the occasion of such a death the Rev. Schuster held the new service which he had been given by Rudolf Steiner. This took place in Arlesheim on January 14, 1919, and was concluded by Rudolf Steiner's memorial words. From a telegram in Rudolf Steiner's handwriting preserved in the Archives of the Rudolf Steiner Nachlaßverwaltung [Trusteeship of Rudolf Steiner's literary estate], it can be gathered that, on the death of a member in May 1920, the Rev. Schuster was asked by Rudolf Steiner himself to arrange the funeral ceremony. Also in October 1920, a similar shared ceremony can be attested to. According to what Marie Steiner expressed in a letter, Rudolf Steiner spoke on the occasion of funerals or cremations of members "when the family requested it. To begin with it was on isolated occasions only. As these gradually became ever more frequent, and as meanwhile the priests (of the Christian Community) who had turned to him were given the ritual by him, he wanted it to be carried out in such a way that he would just as little be engaged in the priestly profession as he was in the medical profession." Because Schuster had to give up his activity already in 1921 owing to illness, the burial service was taken over by the Christian Community.

Rudolf Steiner had newly conferred the Mass ritual on the Rev. Schuster in 1919. On April 20, 1919, immediately prior to his departure for Stuttgart, where next day a meeting of the signatories of the "call to the German Nation and the Civilised World," the people's movement of the Threefold Commonwealth, was taking place for the first time, Rudolf Steiner sent Schuster the first parts of the Mass—the Gospel and the Offertory—the accompanying letter runs as follows: "Dornach, April 20, 1919. My dear Rector Schuster, To begin with please find all that is completed of the Mass that can be made available. But I will take it with me on my journey and it is my intention to place all in your hands very soon, now that I have finished my book (*The Threefold Social Order...*). Do not be angry with me that you only get so little to begin with; but the thing will continue. With cordial greetings Rudolf Steiner." The further installments followed a little later. The exact date is not known.

To p. 43

Egyptian Masonry (Rite of Memphis-Misraim)

This type of Masonry, which is not acknowledged by the ordinary Masonic orders, has no documented historical foundation. On the basis of divers literary records the following picture presents itself:

Under the name of Egyptian Masonry the Misraim Rite is commonly understood, whereas the Memphis Rite, as such, is reputed to be a copy of the latter, originating in the nineteenth century. Both rites became united, but are said, nevertheless, to have been worked separately, so that under the title "Memphis-Misraim" not one rite but two separate rites are to be envisaged.

The Misraim Rite was widely distributed in France during the first half of the nineteenth century. It was banned several times until, in the course of the second half of the nineteenth century, it more or less disappeared from the horizon. In some way or other it reached America and from there Yarker obtained his charter for these two rites for Great Britain and Ireland. He combined the Memphis, the Misraim and the Scotch 33° Cerneau Rite into one organization. Reuß, Hartmann and Klein received a charter from Yarker in 1902 to introduce this United Scotch-Memphis and Misraim Rite into Germany. The man who instigated and arranged this was the Austrian industrialist tycoon and inventor Karl Kellner (1850-1905) who, according to Möller/Howe was one of "the most remarkable esotericists in the German-speaking world at that time," conceived the idea of an Academy of Freemasonry and believed he could realise this project best by means of the system of Egyptian Masonry. The name "Oriental Templar Order" (O.T.O.) can be traced to him. All these names, however, do not really signify anything. They were continually being changed. One should only consider, for instance, what variety is present in the documents of Reuß. All of this was of no concern to Rudolf Steiner. He had merely acquired from this current, out of a sense of ritual obligation to preserve the historic continuity, the nominal right to arrange and carry out his own symbolic-ritual work in the way he wished. For everyone in the know it is obvious that the ritual texts by him are his own independent creation. Whoever wants documentary evidence of this fact is referred to the published translation of the *Rituals of the Misraim Rite (Rite Egyptien dit de Misraim)* of Bernh Beyer, printed in: The Freemasonry Museum. Archive for the study of Freemasonry Ritual and Historical Research. Appearing at no fixed dates. Published by the History Department of the Bayreuth Freemasonry Museum. Editor: Dr. Bernh. Beyer. Vol. 7, Bernhard Sporn Publishing Company, Zeulenroda / Leipzig 1932.

To p. 43

Sellin, Albrecht Wilhelm (Berlin-Ludwigslust, 1841-1933, Munich)

Brazilian colonist, later wholesale merchant in Hamburg. Was involved in preparing and co-founding the Society for Experimental Psychology of Berlin. In this capacity he experimented with Max Dessoir and Albert Moll among others, 1888-92, in order to find an answer to the question of the difference between animal magnetism and hypnosis. Also got to know of Blavatsky's *Theosophy* at that time, which, however, did not satisfy him. From 1902 onwards he was the editor of the Freemasonry periodical: *Bundesblatt* [Union Paper] the organ of the National Mother Lodge of the Grand Lodge of the Three Globes in Berlin and was later the Grand Archivist of this order. When he heard Rudolf Steiner lecturing in Hamburg in 1904 he immediately joined the German Section and became an esoteric pupil of Rudolf Steiner. As he soon afterwards received his pension, he devoted himself thenceforth completely and wholly to the study of Anthroposophical spiritual science and was still active, already as a septuagenarian, taking leading parts in Rudolf Steiner's Mystery Plays in Munich in the years 1910-1913.

See A.W. Sellin, *Erinnerungen aus dem Berufs- und Seelenleben eines alten Mannes*, Constance, 1920. [Reminiscences of the professional life and Soul-experiences of an old man].

To p. 48

Yarker, John (1833-1913)

Originally having high degrees in ordinary Freemasonry, but resigning from this because he had learned from experience that "as the Masonic fraternity is now governed, the Craft is fast becoming the paradise of the bon vivant; of the 'charitable' hypocrite ... the manufacturer of paltry Masonic tinsel...the Masonic 'Emperors' and other charlatans who make power or money out of the aristocratic pretensions ..."[1] he founded several high-degree systems of Masonry on a mystical basis. Since 1872 he was the representative of the Egyptian Rites of Great Britain and Ireland. According to H.P. Blavatsky he was one of the highest Masonic authorities of his day, of great learning and true knowledge.[2] He was an honorary member of the Theosophical Society, having been engaged in the founding of the same (c.f. p. 50 of present volume). After the appearance of H.P. Blavatsky's first big work, *Isis Unveiled* (1877) he conferred the highest adoption degree of Egyptian Freemasonry on her. In 1902 he gave her a Charter for the introduction of the same into Germany (c.f. note on Egyptian Masonry).

To p. 48

Reuß, Theodor (Augsburg, 1855-1923, Munich)

It is almost impossible to gain a clear insight into this abstruse personality, even though a description of his life has become available lately in which much material has been collected. See Helmut Möller/Ellic Howe: *Merlin Peregrinus. About the "underground" of the West*, Würzburg, 1986. The life of Reuß was for the most part spent in a setting made up of politics, writing and Freemasonry. Casual writings of a political or Masonic turn are of no importance, evidence concerning them is contradictory and unverified. What is sure, however, is that he was always in financial difficulties and that his Freemasonry activity served as a source for his livelihood. In his later years his Masonic interests outweighed everything else. He shared in the activities of numerous groups, which, however, sometimes only existed on paper. He received a Charter from Yarker in 1902 along with Franz Hartmann

---

1. H.P. Blavatsky: *Isis Unveiled*, Vol. II, p. 376 (facsimile edition).

[John Yarker: *Notes on the Scientific and Religious Mysteries of Antiquity; the Gnosis and Secret Schools of the Middle Ages; Modern Rosicrucianism; the Various Rites and Degrees of Free and Accepted Masonry*, London 1872, Quoted by H.P. B.].

2. H.P. Blavatsky: *Isis Unveiled*, Vol. II, p. 376 (facsimile edition).

and Heinrich Klein for the introduction of the "United Scotch-, Memphis- and Misraim-Masonry" into Germany (c.f. note on Egyptian Masonry). Rudolf Steiner who, for reasons of historical continuity, wished to link his own symbolic-ritual work-group to the ancient Egyptian Mystery-current, had dealings with Reuß from the end of 1904 until the turn of the following year 1905/06 to arrange terms by which his circle would be nominally allowed to run its affairs independently and therewith contractually insuring that the management of the Misraïm Rite would devolve upon him alone as soon as the hundredth member had been enrolled (see document on p. 86). This was the main reason why he had conferred with the German representative of Egyptian Masonry. Upon being reproached for having entered into a contract with such a man as Reuß, Rudolf Steiner made the following reply in his *Autobiography*:

> Of course it is easy afterwards to make the observation that it would have been more "intelligent" not to have made connections with something that provided opportunities for slanderers. But I may remark in all modesty that at the period of my life under consideration I still belonged to those who assume uprightness and not crookedness in the people with whom they deal. The ability of spiritual perception does not in the least alter one's trust in people. Spiritual perception should not be misused for the purpose of investigating the inner intentions of another person, unless requested by the person. Otherwise, to investigate the inner life of others is something forbidden for the spiritual investigator just as the unauthorised opening of a letter is something forbidden. Thus one's reaction to others is the same as for someone who has no spiritual cognition. There is the difference, though, that one must assume people to be honorable till the opposite has been proved or else be distrustful of the whole world. In the latter case it becomes impossible to work in partnership with others, as this must be based on a foundation of mutual trust.

To p. 51

Adoption-Masonry and Annie Besant

Up to the end of the seventeenth century women were totally excluded from Freemasonry. Only when, at the beginning of the eighteenth century, unions arose in France comparable to Freemasonry, which admitted women, did the so-called Adoption Lodges arise, women's lodges, which were subordinate to the men's lodges; that is to say that every female dignitary, was adopted by a male member. The first such Adoption Lodge—issuing from the Grand Orient de France—was founded in Paris in 1775. At that time Cagliostro had accepted women into his Egyptian Masonry. As the first woman to be admitted, 100 years later, into a regular men's lodge, one usually cites the French Women's Rights campaigner, Marie Deraismes (1828-1894). After her admission she gave a speech in which she said: "For what reason has Freemasonry excluded us women? Does it possibly possess some higher truths, which are only accessible to an enlightened elite? Does it occupy itself with abstract transcendental problems that require preparatory studies? No. One is accepted without any patent or final certificate. Can Freemasonry perhaps offer any secrets, arcana or mysteries that can only be confided to a small number of chosen people? No; for the time of mysteries, secrets and arcana is finally at an end!" Quoted from A. Mellor in *Logen, Rituale, Hochgrade* [Lodges, Rituals, High Degrees] German edition, 1985.

But as her acceptance into a regular men's lodge in 1882 still remained an exception, she founded a new order in Paris in 1882 together with some Masons of the Scotch 33°—Rite, the "Ordre Maçonnique Mixte International" [International Mixed Freemasonry] known under the name of the French Grand Lodge "Le droit humain," the authenticity of which has been disputed.

It was into this order that Annie Besant was admitted in 1902. She was given a charter permitting her to found lodges in London and this enabled her, alongside her theosophical activities, to help the order to spread throughout the English-speaking world, where it became known as the Order of Universal Co-Masonry. According to a statement made by Emil Adriányi to Rudolf Steiner, Reuß had replied to his question about whether Annie Besant was a member of the Memphis-Misraïm Rite with the explanation that she had certainly applied for membership to both Yarker and Reuß, but had been refused by both.

To p. 379

The Temple Legend

According to Rudolf Steiner's lecture in Berlin, November 4, 1904, the Legend goes back to Christian Rosenkreutz, the founder of the Rosicrucian Movement in the fourteenth/fifteenth century. In what ways the necessarily Rosicrucian legend became the basis for Freemasonry he did not say, but he mentioned in his lecture in Berlin, November 11, 1904, that Freemasonry linked up to Rosicrucianism. Through that we have an explanation of the name "Rosicrucian-Freemason," used in some of Rudolf Steiner's ritual texts (c.f. p. 238).

According to Masonic literature the origin of the Temple Legend is assigned to the early eighteenth century, because that was when it first appeared in print. True, it is assumed to have been part of the doctrine of Freemasonry before that time, but this is not supported by documentary evidence. There is no unequivocal draft of the text. In the different versions there are always some variations.

Outside Freemasonry it first became known in the nineteenth century, on the one hand through the literary amendment by Gerard de Nerval (pseudonym for Gerard Labrunie, Paris, 1828-1858), which appeared in Paris in the mid-nineteenth century; on the other hand by Charles William Heckethorn in his work: *Secret Societies of All Ages and Countries*, London, 1875. The version he gives was used by Rudolf Steiner in his lectures published in the volume called *The Temple Legend, Freemasonry and Related Occult Movements*.

In connection with the Esoteric Lesson for the Wachsmuth-Lerchenfeld Group in 1923 Rudolf Steiner incited the two participating writers, Kurt Piper and Albert Steffen, to give an artistic rendering of the Legend. Through that, Albert Steffen produced his drama *Hieram uns Salamo,* before the death of Rudolf Steiner (March 1925) in which he also worked in parts of The Golden Legend. Its first publication appeared in 1925 in the weekly periodical: *Das Goetheanum.* In 1935 it was produced for the first time by Marie Steiner on the Goetheanum stage. In 1937 it was given as a guest performance at the World Exhibition in the Théatre des Champs Elysées in Paris. Kurt Piper worked up the Legend into a cycle of poems: "Cain and Abel-Seth. Mystery Legend inscribed on ten tablets at the grave of Rudolf Steiner," [meant in a figurative sense] published in the monthly magazine: *Die Drei,* 6th year, 1926/27, No. I.

To p. 355

The Golden Legend

This Legend was recounted and explained on several occasions in lectures to members since the preparing of the cognitive-ritual work groups. See lectures in Berlin, May 29, 1905; Leipzig, December 15, 1906; Berlin, December 17, 1906; Munich, May 21, 1907; Cassel, June 29, 1907; Basel, November 25, 1907; Dornach, December 19, 1915. On its first mention in the lecture in Berlin, May 29, 1905, it was called "The Wood of the Cross Legend of the Middle Ages," but from then onwards it was called "The Golden Legend." This appellation was surely not given to it on account of the name of the collection of legends by Jacobus de Voragine in the thirteenth century, called by him *Legenda Aurea,* but was more likely to have had an esoteric origin, for according to the explanations, the pictures of the Legend are an expression of the fourth step of the Rosicrucian initiation, which corresponds to the finding of the Philosopher's Stone, also called the "Golden Stone."

In the collection *Legenda Aurea* the legend is called "The finding of the Holy Cross"—the corresponding section expressed it as follows:

When Adam fell ill, his son Seth went to the gate of the Earthly Paradise and begged for oil from the Tree of Mercy, so that he might anoint the body of his father Adam and heal him. Thereupon the Archangel Michael appeared to him and said: "Do not try to obtain the oil from the Tree of Mercy and do not weep because of it, for that may not be realized by you until five thousand and five hundred years have passed." And yet one thinks that from the time of Adam until the time of Christ's suffering was only five thousand one hundred and ninety nine years. One also reads that the Angel gave Seth a twig of the tree and asked him to plant it on Mount Lebanon. According to a Greek story, which, however, is apocryphal, we are told that the Angel gave Seth some of the wood of the tree by which Adam sinned and said to him: "When this branch brings forth fruit your father will be healed." Now when Seth arrived home his father had already died; so he planted the branch on his father's grave and it grew to become a large tree and lasted until the days of Solomon. As to whether this is true or not we let the reader decide, for it is not recorded in any history book or chronicle. Now when Solomon saw how beautiful the tree was he ordered it to be cut down and used for the building of a forest house. But the wood did not fit any part of the house, as is recounted by Johannes Beleth, for it was always either too long or too short and when it had been shortened according to the correct measurements it was then too short, so that it would never fit. For that reason the workmen became angry and discarded it and laid it across a pond to serve as a footbridge for those who wanted to cross over. But as the Queen of Sheba had heard of Solomon's wisdom and wished to go to visit him across the lake she beheld in spirit vision that the Savior of the World would one day hang from this wood; therefore she did not want to cross over it, but knelt down and worshipped it. But in the *Historia Scholastica* it tells us that the Queen of Sheba saw the wood in the dwelling house and as she was about to return to her native country she summoned Hiram and told him that One should hang from that wood through whose death the Kingdom of the Jews should be destroyed. Therefore Solomon took the wood and ordered it to be buried deep in the bowels of the earth. After many years the Sheep's Pool was built over the place where the Nathanites washed the sacrificial animals; and thus the moving of the waters was occasioned and the healing of the sick, not merely on account of the arrival of the Angel, but also on account of the power of the wood. But as the suffering of Christ was approaching, the wood floated to the surface and when the Jews noticed it they took it and constructed the Cross of the Lord from it.

The oldest source of the Legend in the history of literature is reputed to be from the Alexandrian Church Father Origen of the second century, who gave us the tradition of the burial of Adam on Golgotha; to which was added from the third century Gospel of Nicodemus the story of the sending of Seth to Paradise, the original version of which was that Seth brought the Oil of Mercy from the Tree of Life for his sick father Adam. Only in later centuries was the genealogical connection made between the wood of the Paradise Tree and that of the Cross in its several varied forms. "The Saga of the Three Seeds" forms one of a group of such tales from an unusually complicated confusion of sagas from the twelfth century onwards. (c.f. the religious-historical research of Otto Zöckler: *Das Kreuz Christi* [The Cross of Christ], chapter entitled: "Die Kreuzholzlegenden des Mittelalters." [Medieval Legends about the Wood of the Cross], Gütersloh, 1875)

Rudolf Steiner—who freely made use of this material and of elements that went beyond it in his various recountings of the Legend, but especially in the one in which Seth collects the seeds from the two intertwined paradise-trees—derives the source of the Legend from a far more distant past of pre-Christian Mysteries.

When he was asked, on the occasion of his first discussion of the Legend in the lecture in Berlin, May 29, 1905, if it was very ancient, he replied that it indeed only appeared in a literary-historical form during the Middle Ages, but that it originated out of the Mysteries without having been previously written down. It was connected with the Adonis Mysteries of Antioch in which already the Crucifixion, Burial and Resurrection were celebrated as an outward picture of an inner initiation. The lamenting women beside the Cross were also depicted at that time, which are represented in Christianity by Mary and Mary Magdalene. Similar things took place in the Apis-, Mithras- and Osiris- Mysteries. What was still apocalyptic in those days has been fulfilled in Christianity. Just as John describes the future in his Apocalypse, in a similar fashion the old apocalypses pass over into new legends. The Queen of Sheba was the one possessing deeper insight, who had the real wisdom. In the Cassel lecture, too, (June 29, 1907), the Legend is characterized as the teaching material of esotericism since primeval times. Of Seth it is said that "his mission" was always seen as envisaging what was to occur "at the end of time": the balancing of the two principles in the human being. With the two principles is here meant the trees of the red and the reddish-blue blood, symbolized in the two pillars.

These did not only play a part in the Cognitive-Ritual, but were also an essential element in the arrangements for the Munich Congress at Whitsuntide 1907. They were placed in front of the stage and were also represented in the fourth of the seven seals of the Apocalypse, in which the apocalyptic rainbow in its seven colors is depicted uniting the two pillars. Since the first performance of the third Mystery Play, "The Guardian of the Threshold" (1912), they belong as part of the scenery of the last scene (Temple Scene), following Rudolf Steiner's stage directions.

When it is said in the lecture in Munich, May 21, 1907, about the decoration of the Congress Hall that the red pillar (on the left from the point of view of the audience) was inscribed with J and the blue (on the right from the point of view of the audience) was inscribed with B, and that these letters were the initial letters of two words which he was not allowed to pronounce under the present circumstances, he certainly did not thereby refer to the names Jachin and Boaz, known from the Bible (1 Kings, 7.21), which had been adopted by Freemasons. This is evident from the report of the Congress for the periodical *Lucifer-Gnosis*, according to which these letters on the pillars denote an evolutionary secret "known only to initiates" and elaborated by Rudolf Steiner in a fashion appropriate to modern spiritual science. All explanations given in published works or within certain Societies, remained a purely superficial exoteric interpretation.

Such an explanation will be cited here, however, because it illuminates the significance of the pillars in the history of civilization. In the *Vergleichenden Handbuch der Symbolik der Freimaurerei mit besonderer Rucksicht auf die Mythologien und Mysterien des Altertums* [Comparative handbook to the mythologies and mysteries of Freemasonry with especial reference to the mythologies and mysteries of antiquity] by Joseph Schauberg, Schaffhausen, 1861 (contained in Rudolf Steiner's library) it affirms in Vol. I, p. 205 et seq., "that it was not without significance in Masonic lodges that the rising sun and the setting moon were placed opposite the two pillars. Their significance as eternal interchange of 'day and night, light and shade, becoming and passing away, life and death, good and evil, pure and impure, true and false' belonged to the greatest antiquity of the Egyptians and Semites and presumably the twin spires of the Teutonic Christian Churches and Cathedrals of the Middle Ages have been derived from that ... in Egypt two high obelisks were often erected in front of the Temple entrance, which in Egyptian language were called the 'sun-rays' ... Among the Semitic peoples, especially among the Syrian races and the Phoenicians, two pillars of wood, metal or stone appeared as divine symbols in the Sanctuary of the Gods. Two famous pillars—one of pure gold erected by Hiram, contemporary and friend of King Solomon, the other of emerald, which gleamed lustrously at night—stood in Tyre in the ancient Temple of Melkarth (i.e. the "City's monarch"), a temple shining with gold as symbol of the brightness of the sunlight. Also in the Temple of Melkarth in

Gades two brazen pillars stood eight ells high [30 ft.] on which the building-expenses of the Temple were inscribed. But the largest pillars of all were the ones which God himself had built at the end of the Earth, the rocky heights of Calpe and Abylyx in the Straights of Gibraltar. According to coins that have been discovered, there also seem to have been two trees at the entrance to some of the temples in Syria, especially two cypresses, as a symbol of the sun and Moon. Before the eastern front of the Solomonic Temple stood the two pillars Jachin and Boaz, the names of which have been transmitted to the pillars of the Masonic lodges. *Movers* interprets Jachin as derived from Phoenician, meaning 'stable,' 'upright,' Boaz as something that is moving or progressing ...

The pillars are also called Seth or 'Seth's Pillars' after the Sun-God; for Seth, according to Bunsen: *Egypt's Place in World History*, Vol. V, p. 291, is the oldest authentic name of the Sun-God ... Seth, by the way, means the pillar itself in Hebrew, as also in the Egyptian language, and signifies in general something which is upright, erected or high ..."

In Vol II, p. 203 the following extract from the deed of the constitution of the York Rite from the year 926 is quoted as follows: "Cain's son Enoch was in particular a great architect and astronomer. He foretold in advance from the stars that the world would be destroyed once by water and another time by fire, and he therefore erected two large pillars, one of stone and the other of clay, on which he inscribed the basic tenets of the arts, so that the sciences of Adam and his descendants might not be lost."

"These are therefore 'Seth's Pillars', or the 'Pillars of Enoch', as the pillars Jachin and Boaz are also known, without further use being made in present-day Masonry of this Jewish-Masonic Myth ..."

An explanation, akin to this, of the pillars as "World-Pillars," pillars of birth and death, and the names Jachin and Boaz is given by Rudolf Steiner in the lecture, Berlin, June 20, 1916: "Humankind descends into birth through Jachin, being reassured by Jachin: What is outside in the cosmos is now within you, you are now a microcosm, for that is what Jachin means: the divine in you which is spread out over the universe. Boaz, the other pillar, the entry into the spiritual world through death. What is summarized in the word Boaz signifies more or less: What I formerly sought within myself, strength, I shall now find spread out over the whole universe in which I shall now live."

After this characterization there now follows the essential indication that the pillars, nevertheless, only represent life in a one-sided way, for life only exists in the equilibrium between the two: "Jachin is not the life, for it is the transition from the spiritual to the body, neither is Boaz the life, for it is the transition from the body to the Spirit. The balance is that on which it depends." This equilibrium was vividly portrayed by Rudolf Steiner—in contradistinction to the traditional view of it being a new element—as the rainbow of the fourth apocalyptic seal which connects the two pillars.[3]

To p. 467

Abel's way—Cain's way

The difference between these two paths is succinctly and clearly characterized by Jan K. Lagutt in his writing: *Grundstein der Freimaurerei,* Zurich, 1958 (Foundation Stone of Freemasonry) in the section "The nature of Priesthood and the Nature of Initiation," thus:

The priestliness of all religions [Abel's way] rests on consecration. By means of that higher, impersonal powers are bestowed

---

3. For information about the two pillars see *Rosicrucianism Renewed: The Unity of Art, Science, and Religion. The Theosophical Congress of Whitsun 1907* (CW 284). Also the lectures Nuremberg, June 25 and 26, 1908, in *The Apocalypse* (CW 104); Berlin, June 20, 1916 in *Cosmic Being and Egohood* (CW 169) (typescript); Dornach, December 29, 1918, in *How Can Mankind Find the Christ Again?* (CW 187); further—the artistic representation of the I-A-O motif in the painting of the large cupola of the First Goetheanum in "Twelve sketches for the paintings of the large cupola of the First Goetheanum," an art-satchel, Dornach 1930; also in *Das Farbenwort* by Hilde Raske, Stuttgart, 1982.

upon the bearer, the priest, which can be regarded as the outflow-ing of divine grace. Consecration brings it about that divine effects of grace can be carried into the physical world through the priest. Clearly expressed, the consecrated priest becomes a channel through which divine effects can flow into the earthly world.

There could thus, at least in theory, be a priest of doubtful per-sonal morality, who nevertheless could produce effects because these would not issue from his own personal sphere, but from a superhuman divine source. By that the priest would become a magician who, on the strength of his ordination and by the use of certain sacral formulae, could force the Godhead to bestow its heavenly favors. Such an extreme interpretation of the priest-hood as now and again surfaces, is certainly a long way from the truth. Nevertheless, it points to the distant origin of the priest-hood, to a past epoch of humankind, which one designates an epoch of magic.

No criticism is intended by this account. It is only concerned with giving an explanatory characterization.

That current to which Freemasonry, among other movements, belongs leads in a different direction [Cain's way]. In this, no ordination in the sense of conferring higher powers occurs, but an initiation or awakening takes place, the nature of which is marked by an activation of powers that are already inherent in the human being. The symbolic-ritual actions usually associated with initiation have the sole intention of awakening latent powers and bringing them into activity.

In Christianity, as in all great religions and cultures of antiquity, two currents run alongside one another, the priestly and the initia-tory. It is as though the two currents, which are very ancient, flow together in Jesus in order to flow out again from Him with renewed vitality.

When Jesus sends out his disciples (Mark 6. 7, Luke 9. 1) He confers new powers on them, which lie entirely along the priestly line and do not originate in the personal-human sphere of the disciples themselves. "... and gave them power and authority..."

In the John Gospel Jesus stands out clearly as the Great Initiator, the Initiate par excellence. This is indicated already in the first chapter of the Gospel, in which He summons Nathaniel to discipleship. In the sense of initiation He speaks to Nathaniel in a special manner and the latter recognizes Him immediately as the higher Initiate. In complete openness Jesus comes forward as the Great Initiate, as Hierophant in the sense of the Ancient Mysteries, when He performs the rite of raising Lazarus (Chapter XI). Jesus reawakens the life of Lazarus who was already rigidified in the sleep of death. And alongside the "outward" resurrection process there is another deeper process taking place in Lazarus "whom the Lord loved." And this immortal thing is the Life, of which Jesus says that it is HE. In whatever place the Spirit, the Immortal part of humankind, the Higher Self breaks through or, to express it differently, wherever we, in our striving endeavor, draw near to the source of our being, we experience the great awakening.

Is it then to be wondered at that the Gospel of John occupies such a central position within the current of esoteric Christianity?

If at the start of true priesthood there is grace of a superhuman kind, so should true initiation end in grace. If impersonal powers of a higher kind are lent to the priest on ordination, so must it rest with him to become worthy to awaken through them and simultaneously to depersonalize those same powers. Initiation, insofar as it is not empty ceremony, calls on our deepest individual powers. And through them we must become ripe to enter those spheres where divine grace resides.

The highest, therefore, is the priest who has become an initiate. Conversely, an initiate gains priestly dignity when his deepest human qualities, which are divine, unfold within him. Then he becomes endowed with grace.

Here the circle of seeming opposites comes together and is completed. The one does not exclude the other. Both are paths along the great highway of humanity towards our true being. And that is God.

CHRONOLOGICAL REGISTER OF LECTURES
REFERRED TO IN THE TEXT
with date, place and editors' (CW) reference number

Date   Place   Title in English (if translated) or German with CW ref.

1902

15 Mar.	Berlin	Unpublished notes

1904

4 Jan.	Berlin	Spirituelle Seelenlehre und Weltbetrachtung, CW 52
1 June	Berlin	Unpublished notes
8 July	Berlin	as above
25 July	Berlin	as above
11 Nov.	Berlin	The Temple Legend and the Golden Legend, CW 93
9 Dec.	Berlin	as above
16 Dec.	Berlin	as above
23 Dec.	Berlin	as above

1905

16 Feb.	Berlin	Ursprung und Ziel des Menschen, CW 57
5 May	Berlin	as above
15 May	Berlin	The Temple Legend and the Golden Legend, CW 93
29 May	Berlin	as above
22 Oct.	Berlin	Members News Sheet (in German) No 34-35, 1945
23 Oct.	Berlin	The Temple Legend and the Golden Legend, CW 93
25 Oct.	Berlin	Foundation of Esotericism, CW 93a
16 Nov.	Berlin	Die Welträtsel und die Anthroposophie, CW 54
23 Nov.	Berlin	as above

1906

2 Jan.	Berlin	The Temple Legend and the Golden Legend, CW 93
29 Jan.	Berlin	Ursprungsimpulse der Geisteswissenschaft, CW 96
15 Mar.	Berlin	Die Welträtsel und die Anthroposophie, CW 54
9 April	Bremen	Unpublished notes
6 June	Paris	An Esoteric Cosmology, CW 94

8 Oct.	Berlin	Ursprungsimpulse der Geisteswissenschaft, CW 96
13 Oct.	Leipzig	Das christliche Mysterium, CW 97
4 Nov.	Munich	An Esoteric Cosmology, CW 94
30 Nov.	Cologne	Das christliche Mysterium, CW 97
2 Dec.	Cologne	as above
15 Dec.	Leipzig	as above
17 Dec.	Berlin	Ursprungsimpulse der Geisteswissenschaft, CW 96

1907

21 May	Munich	Bilder okkulter Siegel und Säulen, CW 284
29 June	Cassel	Menschheitsentwickelung und Christus-Erkenntnis CW 100
7 Oct.	Berlin	Mythen und Sagen. Okkulte Zeichen und Symbole, CW 101
25 Nov.	Basle	Menschheitsentwickelung und Christus-Erkenntnis CW 100
27 Dec.	Cologne	Mythen und Sagen. Okkulte Zeichen und Symbole, CW 101
28 Dec.	Cologne	as above
29 Dec.	Cologne	as above

1908

1 June	Berlin	The Influence of Spiritual Beings upon Man, CW 102
15 Aug.	Stuttgart	Universe, Earth and Man, CW 105
16 Aug.	Stuttgart	as above
12 Sept.	Leipzig	Egyptian Myths and Mysteries, CW 106
23 Oct.	Berlin	Geisteswissenschaftliche Menschenkunde, CW 107
24 Oct.	Berlin	Wo und wie findet man den Geist, CW 57
26 Oct.	Berlin	Geisteswissenschaftliche Menschenkunde, CW 107
22 Dec.	Berlin	Die Beantwortung von Welt- und Lebensfragen, CW 108
28 Dec.	Berlin	No text available.

1909

6 Jan.	Munich	No text available.
21 Jan.	Heidelberg	Goethes geheime Offenbarung. Dornach, 1982.
6 May	Berlin	Wo und wie findet man den Geist, CW 57
4 July	Cassel	No text available.
7 July	Cassel	The Gospel of Saint John (Cassel), CW 112
4 Dec.	Munich	Die tiefere Geheimnisse des Menschheitswerdens im Lichte der Evangelien, CW 117

1910

8 Feb.	Berlin	The Christ Impulse and the Development of Ego-Consciousness, CW 116
28 Nov.	Hamburg	Unpublished notes.

1911

5 Jan.	Mannheim	Die Mission der neuen Geistesoffenbarung, CW 127
27 Sept.	Neuchâtel	Das esoterische Christentum, CW 130
28 Sept.	Neuchâtel	as above
13 Oct.	Karlsruhe	From Jesus to Christ, CW 131
14 Dec.	Berlin	Concerning the History and the Contents of the First Section of the Esoteric School 1904-1914, CW 264

1912

23 April	Berlin	Earthly and Cosmic Man, CW 133
22 Dec.	Berlin	Life between Death and a new Birth, CW141

1913

6 Feb.	Berlin	Ergebnisse der Geistesforschung, CW 62

1914

6 Jan	Berlin	The Fifth Gospel, CW 148
13 Jan	Berlin	as above
16 July	Norrköping	Christ and the Human Soul, CW 115

1915

2 March	Berlin	Menschenschicksale und Völkerschicksale, CW 157
6 July	Berlin	as above
11 Oct.	Dornach	The Occult Movement in the 19th Century, CW 254
19 Dec.	Dornach	Die geistige Vereinigung der Menschheit, CW 165

1916

4 April	Berlin	Gegenwärtiges und Vergangenes im Menschengeiste, CW 167
20 June	Berlin	Weltwesen und Ichheit, CW 169

20 Sept.	Dornach	Bauformen als Kultur- und Weltempfindungsgedanken, Dornach, 1934.
26 Nov.	Dornach	The Karma of Vocation, CW 172
27 Nov.	Dornach	as above

1917

| 20 Feb. | Berlin | Cosmic and Human Metamorphoses, CW 175 |

1918

6 Jan.	Dornach	Alte Mythen und ihre Bedeutung, CW 180
29 April	Heidenheim	Der Tod als Lebenswandlung, CW 182
9 Oct.	Zurich	as above
20 Dec.	Dornach	The Challenge of the Times, CW 186
27 Dec.	Dornach	How can Mankind find the Christ again? CW 187
29 Dec.	Dornach	How can Mankind find the Christ again? CW 187

1919

| 11 Jan. | Dornach | Der Goetheanismus, ein Menschen-Umwandlungsimpuls und Auferstehungsgedanke, CW 188 |
| 15 June | Stuttgart | Geisteswissenschaftliche Behandlung sozialer und pädagogischer Fragen, CW 192 |

1920

23 Jan.	Dornach	Architektur, Plastik und Malerei des ersten Goetheanum, Dornach 1972 and 1982
11 Feb.	Dornach	Incorrect date. Source cannot be identified.
25 Sept.	Dornach	In "Blätter für Anthroposophie", 1955. 7th year, No 3.

1921

14 June	Stuttgart	Erster Theologen-Kurs, CW 342
2 Oct.	Dornach	Zweiter Theologen-Kurs, CW 343
16 Nov.	Stuttgart	Konferenzen mit den Lehrern, CW 300

1922

| 5 March | Berlin | Unpublished notes |

29 Sept.	Dornach	Die Grundimpulse des weltgeschichtlichen Werdens der Menschheit, CW 216
9 Dec.	Stuttgart	No written record
23 Dec.	Dornach	Man and the World of the Stars, CW 219
30 Dec.	Dornach	as above
31 Dec.	Dornach	as above

1923

3 March	Dornach	Awakening to Community, CW 257
11 July	Dornach	The History and Regulations of the Anthroposophical Movement, CW 258
5 Aug.	Ilkley	A Modern Art of Education CW 307
31 Aug.	Penmaenmawr	The Evolution of Consciousness, CW 227
11 Sept.	Dornach	Rythmen im Kosmos und im Menschenwesen, CW 350
2 Sept.	London	Rudolf Steiner und die Zivilisationsaufgaben der Anthroposophie, Dornach, 1943.

1924

5 April	Prague	Karmic Relationships, V, CW 239
9 April	Stuttgart	as above
4 June	Dornach	Die Geschichte der Menschheit und die Weltanschauungen der Kulturvölker, CW 353
27 June	Dornach	Karmic Relationships, II, CW 236
8 July	Dornach	Karmic Relationships, III, CW 237
20 Aug.	Torquay	True and False Paths in Spiritual Investigation, CW 243
16 Sept.	Dornach	Karmic Relationships, IV, CW 238
28 Sept.	Dornach	as above

RUDOLF STEINER'S COLLECTED WORKS

The German Edition of Rudolf Steiner's Collected Works (the Gesamtausgabe [GA] published by Rudolf Steiner Verlag, Dornach, Switzerland) presently runs to over 354 titles, organized either by type of work (written or spoken), chronology, audience (public or other), or subject (education, art, etc.). For ease of comparison, the Collected Works in English [CW] follows the German organization exactly. A complete listing of the CWs follows with literal translations of the German titles. Other than in the case of the books published in his lifetime, titles were rarely given by Rudolf Steiner himself, and were often provided by the editors of the German editions. The titles in English are not necessarily the same as the German; and, indeed, over the past seventy-five years have frequently been different, with the same book sometimes appearing under different titles.

For ease of identification and to avoid confusion, we suggest that readers looking for a title should do so by CW number. Because the work of creating the Collected Works of Rudolf Steiner is an ongoing process, with new titles being published every year, we have not indicated in this listing which books are presently available. To find out what titles in the Collected Works are currently in print, please check our website at www.steinerbooks.org, or write to SteinerBooks 610 Main Street, Great Barrington, MA 01230 :

Written Work

CW 1	Goethe: Natural-Scientific Writings, Introduction, with Footnotes and Explanations in the text by Rudolf Steiner
CW 2	Outlines of an Epistemology of the Goethean World View, with Special Consideration of Schiller
CW 3	Truth and Science
CW 4	The Philosophy of Freedom
CW 4a	Documents to "The Philosophy of Freedom"
CW 5	Friedrich Nietzsche, A Fighter against His Own Time
CW 6	Goethe's Worldview
CW 6a	Now in CW 30
CW 7	Mysticism at the Dawn of Modern Spiritual Life and Its Relationship with Modern Worldviews
CW 8	Christianity as Mystical Fact and the Mysteries of Antiquity
CW 9	Theosophy: An Introduction into Supersensible World Knowledge and Human Purpose
CW 10	How Does One Attain Knowledge of Higher Worlds?
CW 11	From the Akasha-Chronicle
CW 12	Levels of Higher Knowledge
CW 13	Occult Science in Outline

Paralipomena on the Four Mystery Dramas
CW 45   Anthroposophy: A Fragment from the Year 1910

Public Lectures

CW 51   On Philosophy, History and Literature
CW 52   Spiritual Teachings Concerning the Soul and Observation of the World
CW 53   The Origin and Goal of the Human Being
CW 54   The Riddles of the World and Anthroposophy
CW 55   Knowledge of the Supersensible in Our Times and Its Meaning for Life Today
CW 56   Knowledge of the Soul and of the Spirit
CW 57   Where and How Does One Find the Spirit?
CW 58   The Metamorphoses of the Soul Life. Paths of Soul Experiences: Part One
CW 59   The Metamorphoses of the Soul Life. Paths of Soul Experiences: Part Two
CW 60   The Answers of Spiritual Science to the Biggest Questions of Existence
CW 61   Human History in the Light of Spiritual Research
CW 62   Results of Spiritual Research
CW 63   Spiritual Science as a Treasure for Life
CW 64   Out of Destiny-Burdened Times
CW 65   Out of Central European Spiritual Life
CW 66   Spirit and Matter, Life and Death
CW 67   The Eternal in the Human Soul. Immortality and Freedom
CW 68   Public lectures in various cities, 1906-1918
CW 69   Public lectures in various cities, 1906-1918
CW 70   Public lectures in various cities, 1906-1918
CW 71   Public lectures in various cities, 1906-1918
CW 72   Freedom – Immortality – Social Life
CW 73   The Supplementing of the Modern Sciences through Anthroposophy
CW 73a   Specialized Fields of Knowledge and Anthroposophy
CW 74   The Philosophy of Thomas Aquinas
CW 75   Public lectures in various cities, 1906-1918
CW 76   The Fructifying Effect of Anthroposophy on Specialized Fields
CW 77a   The Task of Anthroposophy in Relation to Science and Life: The Darmstadt College Course
CW 77b   Art and Anthroposophy. The Goetheanum-Impulse
CW 78   Anthroposophy, Its Roots of Knowledge and Fruits for Life
CW 79   The Reality of the Higher Worlds
CW 80   Public lectures in various cities, 1922

Lectures to the Members of the Anthroposophical Society

CW 229   The Experiencing of the Course of the Year in Four Cosmic Imaginations

CW 230   The Human Being as Harmony of the Creative, Building, and Formative World-Word

CW 231   The Supersensible Human Being, Understood Anthroposophically

CW 232   The Forming of the Mysteries

CW 233   World History Illuminated by Anthroposophy and as the Foundation for Knowledge of the Human Spirit

CW 233a   Mystery Sites of the Middle Ages: Rosicrucianism and the Modern Initiation-Principle. The Festival of Easter as Part of the History of the Mysteries of Humanity

CW 234   Anthroposophy. A Summary after 21 Years

CW 235   Esoteric Observations of Karmic Relationships in 6 Volumes, Vol. 1

CW 236   Esoteric Observations of Karmic Relationships in 6 Volumes, Vol. 2

CW 237   Esoteric Observations of Karmic Relationships in 6 Volumes, Vol. 3: The Karmic Relationships of the Anthroposophical Movement

CW 238   Esoteric Observations of Karmic Relationships in 6 Volumes, Vol. 4: The Spiritual Life of the Present in Relationship to the Anthroposoph-ical Movement

CW 239   Esoteric Observations of Karmic Relationships in 6 Volumes, Vol. 5

CW 240   Esoteric Observations of Karmic Relationships in 6 Volumes, Vol. 6

CW 243   The Consciousness of the Initiate

CW 245   Instructions for an Esoteric Schooling

CW 250   The Building-Up of the Anthroposophical Society. From the Beginning to the Outbreak of the First World War

CW 251   The History of the Goetheanum Building-Association

CW 252   Life in the Anthroposophical Society from the First World War to the Burning of the First Goetheanum

CW 253   The Problems of Living Together in the Anthroposophical Society. On the Dornach Crisis of 1915. With Highlights on Swedenborg's Clairvoyance, the Views of Freudian Psychoanalysts, and the Concept of Love in Relation to Mysticism

CW 254   The Occult Movement in the 19th Century and Its Relationship to World Culture. Significant Points from the Exoteric Cultural Life around the Middle of the 19th Century

CW 255   Rudolf Steiner during the First World War

CW 255a   Anthroposophy and the Reformation of Society. On the History of the Threefold Movement

CW 255b   Anthroposophy and Its Opponents, 1919-1921

CW 256   How Can the Anthroposophical Movement Be Financed?

CW 256a   Futurum, Inc. / International Laboratories, Inc.

CW 256b   The Coming Day, Inc.

Volumes. Vol. 1: Faust, the Striving Human Being

CW 273   Spiritual-Scientific Commentary on Goethe's "Faust" in Two
Volumes. Vol. 2: The Faust-Problem

CW 274   Addresses for the Christmas Plays from the Old Folk Traditions

CW 275   Art in the Light of Mystery-Wisdom

CW 276   The Artistic in Its Mission in the World. The Genius of
Language. The World of the Self-Revealing Radiant Appearances
– Anthroposophy and Art. Anthroposophy and Poetry

CW 277   Eurythmy. The Revelation of the Speaking Soul

CW 277a   The Origin and Development of Eurythmy

CW 278   Eurythmy as Visible Song

CW 279   Eurythmy as Visible Speech

CW 280   The Method and Nature of Speech Formation

CW 281   The Art of Recitation and Declamation

CW 282   Speech Formation and Dramatic Art

CW 283   The Nature of Things Musical and the Experience of Tone in
the Human Being

CW284/285 Images of Occult Seals and Pillars. The Munich Congress of
Whitsun 1907 and Its Consequences

CW 286   Paths to a New Style of Architecture. "And the Building
Becomes Human"

CW 287   The Building at Dornach as a Symbol of Historical Becoming
and an Artistic Transformation Impulse

CW 288   Style-Forms in the Living Organic

CW 289   The Building-Idea of the Goetheanum: Lectures with Slides
from the Years 1920-1921

CW 290   The Building-Idea of the Goetheanum: Lectures with Slides
from the Years 1920-1921

CW 291   The Nature of Colors

CW 291a   Knowledge of Colors. Supplementary Volume to "The Nature
of Colors"

CW 292   Art History as Image of Inner Spiritual Impulses

CW 293   General Knowledge of the Human Being as the Foundation of
Pedagogy

CW 294   The Art of Education, Methodology and Didactics

CW 295   The Art of Education: Seminar Discussions and Lectures on
Lesson Planning

CW 296   The Question of Education as a Social Question

CW 297   The Idea and Practice of the Waldorf School

CW 297a   Education for Life: Self-Education and the Practice of Pedagogy

CW 298   Rudolf Steiner in the Waldorf School

CW 299   Spiritual-Scientific Observations on Speech

CW 300a   Conferences with the Teachers of the Free Waldorf School in
Stuttgart, 1919 to 1924, in 3 Volumes, Vol. 1

SIGNIFICANT EVENTS
IN THE LIFE OF RUDOLF STEINER

1829: June 23: birth of Johann Steiner (1829-1910)—Rudolf Steiner's father—in Geras, Lower Austria.

1834: May 8: birth of Franciska Blie (1834-1918)—Rudolf Steiner's mother—in Horn, Lower Austria. "My father and mother were both children of the glorious Lower Austrian forest district north of the Danube."

1860: May 16: marriage of Johann Steiner and Franciska Blie.

1861: February 25: birth of *Rudolf Joseph Lorenz Steiner* in Kraljevec, Croatia, near the border with Hungary, where Johann Steiner works as a telegrapher for the South Austria Railroad. Rudolf Steiner is baptized two days later, February 27, the date usually given as his birthday.

1862: Summer: the family moves to Mödling, Lower Austria.

1863: The family moves to Pottschach, Lower Austria, near the Styrian border, where Johann Steiner becomes stationmaster. "The view stretched to the mountains...majestic peaks in the distance and the sweet charm of nature in the immediate surroundings."

1864: November 15: birth of Rudolf Steiner's sister, Leopoldine (d. November 1, 1927). She will become a seamstress and live with her parents for the rest of her life.

1866: July 28: birth of Rudolf Steiner's deaf-mute brother, Gustav (d. May 1, 1941).

1867: Rudolf Steiner enters the village school. Following a disagreement between his father and the schoolmaster, whose wife falsely accused the boy of causing a commotion, Rudolf Steiner is taken out of school and taught at home.

1868: A critical experience. Unknown to the family, an aunt dies in a distant town. Sitting in the station waiting room, Rudolf Steiner sees her "form," which speaks to him, asking for help. "Beginning with this experience, a new soul life began in the boy, one in which not only the outer trees and mountains spoke to him, but also the worlds that lay behind them. From this moment on, the boy began to live with the spirits of nature...."

1869: The family moves to the peaceful, rural village of Neudorfl, near Wiener-Neustadt in present-day Hungary. Rudolf Steiner attends the village school. Because of the "unorthodoxy" of his writing and spelling, he has to do "extra lessons."

1870: Through a book lent to him by his tutor, he discovers geometry: "To grasp something purely in the spirit brought me inner happiness. I know that I first learned happiness through geometry." The same tutor allows him to draw, while other students still struggle with their reading and writing. "An artistic element" thus enters his education.

1871:   Though his parents are not religious, Rudolf Steiner becomes a "church child," a favorite of the priest, who was "an exceptional character." "Up to the age of ten or eleven, among those I came to know, he was far and away the most significant." Among other things, he introduces Steiner to Copernican, heliocentric cosmology. As an altar boy, Rudolf Steiner serves at Masses, funerals, and Corpus Christi processions. At year's end, after an incident in which he escapes a thrashing, his father forbids him to go to church.

1872:   Rudolf Steiner transfers to grammar school in Wiener-Neustadt, a five-mile walk from home, which must be done in all weathers.

1873-75: Through his teachers and on his own, Rudolf Steiner has many wonderful experiences with science and mathematics. Outside school, he teaches himself analytic geometry, trigonometry, differential equations, and calculus.

1876:   Rudolf Steiner begins tutoring other students. He learns bookbinding from his father. He also teaches himself stenography.

1877:   Rudolf Steiner discovers Kant's *Critique of Pure Reason*, which he reads and rereads. He also discovers and reads von Rotteck's *World History*.

1878:   He studies extensively in contemporary psychology and philosophy.

1879:   Rudolf Steiner graduates from high school with honors. His father is transferred to Inzersdorf, near Vienna. He uses his first visit to Vienna "to purchase a great number of philosophy books"— Kant, Fichte, Schelling, and Hegel, as well as numerous histories of philosophy. His aim: to find a path from the "I" to nature.

October 1879-1883: Rudolf Steiner attends the Technical College in Vienna— to study mathematics, chemistry, physics, mineralogy, botany, zoology, biology, geology, and mechanics—with a scholarship. He also attends lectures in history and literature, while avidly reading philosophy on his own. His two favorite professors are Karl Julius Schröer (German language and literature) and Edmund Reitlinger (physics). He also audits lectures by Robert Zimmerman on aesthetics and Franz Brentano on philosophy. During this year he begins his friendship with Moritz Zitter (1861-1921), who will help support him financially when he is in Berlin.

1880:   Rudolf Steiner attends lectures on Schiller and Goethe by Karl Julius Schröer, who becomes his mentor. Also "through a remarkable combination of circumstances," he meets Felix Koguzki, an "herb gatherer" and healer, who could "see deeply into the secrets of nature." Rudolf Steiner will meet and study with this "emissary of the Master" throughout his time in Vienna.

1881:   January: "… I didn't sleep a wink. I was busy with philosophical problems until about 12:30 a.m. Then, finally, I threw myself down on my couch. All my striving during the previous year had been to research whether the following statement by Schelling was true or not: *Within everyone dwells a secret, marvelous capacity to draw back from the stream of time—out of the self clothed in all that comes to us from outside—into our innermost being and there, in the immutable form of the Eternal, to look into*

ourselves. I believe, and I am still quite certain of it, that I discovered this capacity in myself; I had long had an inkling of it. Now the whole of idealist philosophy stood before me in modified form. What's a sleepless night compared to that!"
Rudolf Steiner begins communicating with leading thinkers of the day, who send him books in return, which he reads eagerly.

July: "I am not one of those who dives into the day like an animal in human form. I pursue a quite specific goal, an idealistic aim—knowledge of the truth! This cannot be done offhandedly. It requires the greatest striving in the world, free of all egotism, and equally of all resignation."

August: Steiner puts down on paper for the first time thoughts for a "Philosophy of Freedom." "The striving for the absolute: this human yearning is freedom." He also seeks to outline a "peasant philosophy," describing what the worldview of a "peasant"—one who lives close to the earth and the old ways—really is.

1881-1882: Felix Koguzki, the herb gatherer, reveals himself to be the envoy of another, higher initiatory personality, who instructs Rudolf Steiner to penetrate Fichte's philosophy and to master modern scientific thinking as a preparation for right entry into the spirit. This "Master" also teaches him the double (evolutionary and involutionary) nature of time.

1882: Through the offices of Karl Julius Schröer, Rudolf Steiner is asked by Joseph Kurschner to edit Goethe's scientific works for the *Deutschen National-Literatur* edition. He writes "A Possible Critique of Atomistic Concepts" and sends it to Friedrich Theodore Vischer.

1883: Rudolf Steiner completes his college studies and begins work on the Goethe project.

1884: First volume of Goethe's *Scientific Writings* (CW 1) appears (March). He lectures on Goethe and Lessing, and Goethe's approach to science. In July, he enters the household of Ladislaus and Pauline Specht as tutor to the four Specht boys. He will live there until 1890. At this time, he meets Josef Breuer ((1842-1925), the coauthor with Sigmund Freud of *Studies in Hysteria,* who is the Specht family doctor.

1885: While continuing to edit Goethe's writings, Rudolf Steiner reads deeply in contemporary philosophy (Edouard von Hartmann, Johannes Volkelt, and Richard Wahle, among others).

1886: May: Rudolf Steiner sends Kurschner the manuscript of *Outlines of Goethe's Theory of Knowledge* (CW 2), which appears in October, and which he sends out widely. He also meets the poet Marie Eugenie Delle Grazie and writes "Nature and Our Ideals" for her. He attends her salon, where he meets many priests, theologians, and philosophers, who will become his friends. Meanwhile, the director of the Goethe Archive in Weimar requests his collaboration with the *Sophien* edition of Goethe's works, particularly the writings on color.

1887: At the beginning of the year, Rudolf Steiner is very sick. As the year progresses and his health improves, he becomes increasingly "a man

of letters," lecturing, writing essays, and taking part in Austrian cultural life. In August-September, the second volume of Goethe's
Scientific Writings appears.

1888: January-July: Rudolf Steiner assumes editorship of the "German
Weekly" (*Deutsche Wochenschrift*). He begins lecturing more intensively, giving, for example, a lecture titled "Goethe as Father of a New
Aesthetics." He meets and becomes soul friends with Friedrich
Eckstein (1861-1939), a vegetarian, philosopher of symbolism,
alchemist, and musician, who will introduce him to various spiritual
currents (including Theosophy) and with whom he will meditate and
interpret esoteric and alchemical texts.

1889: Rudolf Steiner first reads Nietzsche (*Beyond Good and Evil*). He
encounters Theosophy again and learns of Madame Blavatsky in the
Theosophical circle around Marie Lang (1858-1934). Here he also
meets well-known figures of Austrian life, as well as esoteric figures
like the occultist Franz Hartman and Karl Leinigen-Billigen (translator of C.G. Harrison's *The Transcendental Universe.*) During this
period, Steiner first reads A.P. Sinnett's *Esoteric Buddhism* and Mabel
Collins's *Light on the Path.* He also begins traveling, visiting Budapest,
Weimar, and Berlin (where he meets philosopher Edouard von
Hartman).

1890: Rudolf Steiner finishes volume 3 of Goethe's scientific writings. He
begins his doctoral dissertation, which will become *Truth and Science*
(CW 3). He also meets the poet and feminist Rosa Mayreder (1858-
1938), with whom he can exchange his most intimate thoughts. In
September, Rudolf Steiner moves to Weimar to work in the Goethe-
Schiller Archive.

1891: Volume 3 of the Kurschner edition of Goethe appears. Meanwhile,
Rudolf Steiner edits Goethe's studies in mineralogy and scientific
writings for the *Sophien* edition. He meets Ludwig Laistner of the
Cotta Publishing Company, who asks for a book on the basic question
of metaphysics. From this will result, ultimately, *The Philosophy of
Freedom* (CW 4), which will be published not by Cotta but by Emil
Felber. In October, Rudolf Steiner takes the oral exam for a doctor-
ate in philosophy, mathematics, and mechanics at Rostock
University, receiving his doctorate on the twenty-sixth. In November,
he gives his first lecture on Goethe's "Fairy Tale" in Vienna.

1892: Rudolf Steiner continues work at the Goethe-Schiller Archive and on
his *Philosophy of Freedom. Truth and Science,* his doctoral dissertation, is
published. Steiner undertakes to write introductions to books on
Schopenhauer and Jean Paul for Cotta. At year's end, he finds lodg-
ing with Anna Eunike, née Schulz (1853-1911), a widow with four
daughters and a son. He also develops a friendship with Otto Erich
Hartleben (1864-1905) with whom he shares literary interests.

1893: Rudolf Steiner begins his habit of producing many reviews and articles. In March, he gives a lecture titled "Hypnotism, with Reference
to Spiritism." In September, volume 4 of the Kurschner edition is

completed. In November, *The Philosophy of Freedom* appears. This year, too, he meets John Henry Mackay (1864-1933), the anarchist, and Max Stirner, a scholar and biographer.

1894: Rudolf Steiner meets Elisabeth Förster Nietzsche, the philosopher's sister, and begins to read Nietzsche in earnest, beginning with the as yet unpublished *Antichrist.* He also meets Ernst Haeckel (1834-1919). In the fall, he begins to write *Nietzsche, A Fighter against His Time* (CW 5).

1895: May, *Nietzsche, A Fighter against His Time* appears.

1896: January 22: Rudolf Steiner sees Friedrich Nietzsche for the first and only time. Moves between the Nietzsche and the Goethe-Schiller Archives, where he completes his work before year's end. He falls out with Elisabeth Förster Nietzsche, thus ending his association with the Nietzsche Archive.

1897: Rudolf Steiner finishes the manuscript of *Goethe's Worldview* (CW 6). He moves to Berlin with Anna Eunike and begins editorship of the *Magazin für Literatur.* From now on, Steiner will write countless reviews, literary and philosophical articles, and so on. He begins lecturing at the "Free Literary Society." In September, he attends the Zionist Congress in Basel. He sides with Dreyfus in the Dreyfus affair.

1898: Rudolf Steiner is very active as an editor in the political, artistic, and theatrical life of Berlin. He becomes friendly with John Henry Mackay and poet Ludwig Jacobowski (1868-1900). He joins Jacobowski's circle of writers, artists, and scientists—"The Coming Ones" (*Die Kommenden*)—and contributes lectures to the group until 1903. He also lectures at the "League for College Pedagogy." He writes an article for Goethe's sesquicentennial, "Goethe's Secret Revelation," on the "Fairy Tale of the Green Snake and the Beautiful Lily."

1888-89: "This was a trying time for my soul as I looked at Christianity. . . . I was able to progress only by contemplating, by means of spiritual perception, the evolution of Christianity . . . . Conscious knowledge of real Christianity began to dawn in me around the turn of the century. This seed continued to develop. My soul trial occurred shortly before the beginning of the twentieth century. It was decisive for my soul's development that I stood spiritually before the Mystery of Golgotha in a deep and solemn celebration of knowledge."

1899: Rudolf Steiner begins teaching and giving lectures and lecture cycles at the Workers' College, founded by Wilhelm Liebknecht (1826-1900). He will continue to do so until 1904. Writes: *Literature and Spiritual Life in the Nineteenth Century; Individualism in Philosophy; Haeckel and His Opponents; Poetry in the Present;* and begins what will become (fifteen years later). *The Riddles of Philosophy* (CW 18). He also meets many artists and writers, including Käthe Kollwitz, Stefan Zweig, and Rainer Maria Rilke. On October 31, he marries Anna Eunike.

1900: "I thought that the turn of the century must bring humanity a new light. It seemed to me that the separation of human thinking and willing from the spirit had peaked. A turn or reversal of direction in human evolution seemed to me a necessity." Rudolf Steiner finishes *World and Life Views in the Nineteenth Century* (the second part of what will become *The Riddles of Philosophy*) and dedicates it to Ernst Haeckel. It is published in March. He continues lecturing at *Die Kommenden*, whose leadership he assumes after the death of Jacobowski. Also, he gives the Gutenberg Jubilee lecture before 7,000 typesetters and printers. In September, Rudolf Steiner is invited by Count and Countess Brockdorff to lecture in the Theosophical Library. His first lecture is on Nietzsche. His second lecture is titled "Goethe's Secret Revelation." October 6, he begins a lecture cycle on the mystics that will become *Mystics after Modernism* (CW 7). November-December: "Marie von Sivers appears in the audience...." Also in November, Steiner gives his first lecture at the Giordano Bruno Bund (where he will continue to lecture until May, 1905). He speaks on Bruno and modern Rome, focusing on the importance of the philosophy of Thomas Aquinas as monism.

1901:   In continual financial straits, Rudolf Steiner's early friends Moritz Zitter and Rosa Mayreder help support him. In October, he begins the lecture cycle *Christianity as Mystical Fact* (CW 8) at the Theosophical Library. In November, he gives his first "Theosophical lecture" on Goethe's "Fairy Tale" in Hamburg at the invitation of Wilhelm Hubbe-Schleiden. He also attends a tea to celebrate the founding of the Theosophical Society at Count and Countess Brockdorff's. He gives a lecture cycle, "From Buddha to Christ," for the circle of the *Kommenden*. November 17, Marie von Sivers asks Rudolf Steiner if Theosophy does not need a Western-Christian spiritual movement (to complement Theosophy's Eastern emphasis). "The question was posed. Now, following spiritual laws, I could begin to give an answer...." In December, Rudolf Steiner writes his first article for a Theosophical publication. At year's end, the Brockdorffs and possibly Wilhelm Hubbe-Schleiden ask Rudolf Steiner to join the Theosophical Society and undertake the leadership of the German section. Rudolf Steiner agrees, on the condition that Marie von Sivers (then in Italy) work with him.

1902:   Beginning in January, Rudolf Steiner attends the opening of the Workers' School in Spandau with Rosa Luxemberg (1870-1919). January 17, Rudolf Steiner joins the Theosophical Society. In April, he is asked to become general secretary of the German Section of the Theosophical Society, and works on preparations for its founding. In July, he visits London for a Theosophical congress. He meets Bertram Keightly, G.R.S. Mead, A.P. Sinnett, and Annie Besant, among others. In September, *Christianity as Mystical Fact* appears. In October, Rudolf Steiner gives his first public lecture on Theosophy ("Monism and Theosophy") to about three hundred people at the Giordano Bruno Bund. On October 19-21, the German Section of the Theosophical Society has its first meeting; Rudolf Steiner is the general secretary, and Annie Besant attends. Steiner lectures on practical karma studies. On October 23, Annie Besant inducts Rudolf Steiner into the Esoteric School of the Theosophical Society. On October 25, Steiner begins a weekly series of lectures: "The Field of Theosophy." During this year, Rudolf Steiner also first meets Ita Wegman (1876-1943), who will become his close collaborator in his final years.

1903: Rudolf Steiner holds about 300 lectures and seminars. In May, the first issue of the periodical *Luzifer* appears. In June, Rudolf Steiner visits London for the first meeting of the Federation of the European Sections of the Theosophical Society, where he meets Colonel Olcott. He begins to write *Theosophy* (CW 9).

1904: Rudolf Steiner continues lecturing at the Workers' College and elsewhere (about 90 lectures), while lecturing intensively all over Germany among Theosophists (about a 140 lectures). In February, he meets Carl Unger (1878-1929), who will become a member of the board of the Anthroposophical Society (1913). In March, he meets Michael Bauer (1871-1929), a Christian mystic, who will also be on the board. In May, *Theosophy* appears, with the dedication: "To the spirit of Giordano Bruno." Rudolf Steiner and Marie von Sivers visit London for meetings with Annie Besant. June: Rudolf Steiner and Marie von Sivers attend the meeting of the Federation of European Sections of the Theosophical Society in Amsterdam. In July, Steiner begins the articles in *Luzifer-Gnosis* that will become *How to Know Higher Worlds* (CW 10) and *Cosmic Memory* (CW 11). In September, Annie Besant visits Germany. In December, Steiner lectures on Freemasonry. He mentions the High Grade Masonry derived from John Yarker and represented by Theodore Reuss and Karl Kellner as a blank slate "into which a good image could be placed."

1905: This year, Steiner ends his non-Theosophical lecturing activity. Supported by Marie von Sivers, his Theosophical lecturing—both in public and in the Theosophical Society—increases significantly: "The German Theosophical Movement is of exceptional importance." Steiner recommends reading, among others, Fichte, Jacob Boehme, and Angelus Silesius. He begins to introduce Christian themes into Theosophy. He also begins to work with doctors (Felix Peipers and Ludwig Noll). In July, he is in London for the Federation of European Sections, where he attends a lecture by Annie Besant: "I have seldom seen Mrs. Besant speak in so inward and heartfelt a manner...." "Through Mrs. Besant I have found the way to H.P. Blavatsky." September to October, he gives a course of thirty-one lectures for a small group of esoteric students. In October, the annual meeting of the German Section of the Theosophical Society, which still remains very small, takes place. Rudolf Steiner reports membership has risen from 121 to 377 members. In November, seeking to establish esoteric "continuity," Rudolf Steiner and Marie von Sivers participate in a "Memphis-Misraim" Masonic ceremony. They pay forty-five marks for membership. "Yesterday, you saw how little remains of former esoteric institutions." "We are dealing only with a 'framework'... for the present, nothing lies behind it. The occult powers have completely withdrawn."

1906: Expansion of Theosophical work. Rudolf Steiner gives about 245 lectures, only 44 of which take place in Berlin. Cycles are given in Paris, Leipzig, Stuttgart, and Munich. Esoteric work also intensifies. Rudolf Steiner begins writing *An Outline of Esoteric Science* (CW 13). In January, Rudolf Steiner receives permission (a patent) from the Great Orient of the Scottish A & A Thirty-Three Degree Rite of the Order of the Ancient Freemasons of the Memphis-Misraim Rite to direct a chapter under the name "Mystica Aeterna." This will become the "Cognitive Cultic Section" (also called "Misraim Service") of the Esoteric School. (See: *From the History and Contents of the Cognitive Cultic Section* (CW 264). During this time, Steiner also meets Albert Schweitzer. In May, he is in Paris, where he visits Edouard Schuré. Many Russians attend his lectures (including Konstantin Balmont, Dimitri Mereszkovski, Zinaida Hippius, and Maximilian Woloshin). He attends the General Meeting of the European Federation of the Theosophical Society, at which Col. Olcott is present for the last time. He spends the year's end in Venice and Rome, where he writes and works on his translation of H.P. Blavatsky's *Key to Theosophy*.

1907: Further expansion of the German Theosophical Movement according to the Rosicrucian directive to "introduce spirit into the world"— in education, in social questions, in art, and in science. In February, Col. Olcott dies in Adyar. Before he dies, Olcott indicates that "the Masters" wish Annie Besant to succeed him: much politicking ensues. Rudolf Steiner supports Besant's candidacy. April-May: preparations for the Congress of the Federation of European Sections of the Theosophical Society—the great, watershed Whitsun "Munich Congress," attended by Annie Besant and others. Steiner decides to separate Eastern and Western (Christian-Rosicrucian) esoteric schools. He takes his esoteric school out of the Theosophical Society (Besant and Rudolf Steiner are "in harmony" on this). Steiner makes his first lecture tours to Austria and Hungary. That summer, he is in Italy. In September, he visits Edouard Schuré, who will write the introduction to the French edition of *Christianity as Mystical Fact* in Barr, Alsace. Rudolf Steiner writes the autobiographical statement known as the "Barr Document." In *Luzifer–Gnosis*, "The Education of the Child" appears.

1908: The movement grows (membership: 1150). Lecturing expands. Steiner makes his first extended lecture tour to Holland and Scandinavia, as well as visits to Naples and Sicily. Themes: St. John's Gospel, the Apocalypse, Egypt, science, philosophy, and logic. *Luzifer-Gnosis* ceases publication. In Berlin, Marie von Sivers (with Johanna Mücke (1864-1949) forms the *Philosophisch-Theosophisch* (after 1915 *Philosophisch-Anthroposophisch*) *Verlag* to publish Steiner's work. Steiner gives lecture cycles titled *The Gospel of St. John* (CW 103) and *The Apocalypse* (104).

1909: *An Outline of Esoteric Science* appears. Lecturing and travel continues. Rudolf Steiner's spiritual research expands to include the polarity of Lucifer and Ahriman; the work of great individualities in history; the Maitreya Buddha and the Bodhisattvas; spiritual economy (CW 109); the work of the spiritual hierarchies in heaven and on Earth (CW 110). He also deepens and intensifies his research into the Gospels, giving lectures on the Gospel of St. Luke (CW 114) with the first mention of two Jesus children. Meets and becomes friends with Christian Morgenstern (1871-1914). In April, he lays the foundation stone for the Malsch model—the building that will lead to the first Goetheanum. In May, the International Congress of the Federation of European Sections of the Theosophical Society takes place in Budapest. Rudolf Steiner receives the Subba Row medal for *How to Know Higher Worlds*. During this time, Charles W. Leadbeater discovers Jiddu Krishnamurti (1895-1986) and proclaims him the future "world teacher," the bearer of the Maitreya Buddha and the "reappearing Christ." In October, Steiner delivers seminal lectures on "anthroposophy," which he will try, unsuccessfully, to rework over the next years into the unfinished work, *Anthroposophy (A Fragment)* (CW 45).

1910: New themes: *The Reappearance of Christ in the Etheric* (CW 118); *The Fifth Gospel; The Mission of Folk Souls* (CW 121); *Occult History* (CW 126); the evolving development of etheric cognitive capacities. Rudolf Steiner continues his Gospel research with *The Gospel of St. Matthew* (CW 123). In January, his father dies. In April, he takes a month-long trip to Italy, including Rome, Monte Cassino, and Sicily. He also visits Scandinavia again. July-August, he writes the first mystery drama, *The Portal of Initiation* (CW 14). In November, he gives "psychosophy" lectures. In December, he submits "On the Psychological Foundations and Epistemological Framework of Theosophy" to the International Philosophical Congress in Bologna.

1911: The crisis in the Theosophical Society deepens. In January, "The Order of the Rising Sun," which will soon become "The Order of the Star in the East," is founded for the coming world teacher, Krishnamurti. At the same time, Marie von Sivers, Rudolf Steiner's coworker, falls ill. Fewer lectures are given, but important new ground is broken. In Prague, in March, Steiner meets Franz Kafka (1883-1924) and Hugo Bergmann (1883-1975). In April, he delivers his paper to the Philosophical Congress. He writes the second mystery drama, *The Soul's Probation* (CW 14). Also, while Marie von Sivers is convalescing, Rudolf Steiner begins work on *Calendar 1912/1913*, which will contain the "Calendar of the Soul" meditations. On March 19, Anna (Eunike) Steiner dies. In September, Rudolf Steiner visits Einsiedeln, birthplace of Paracelsus. In December, Friedrich Rittelmeyer, future founder of the Christian Community, meets Rudolf Steiner. The *Johannes-Bauverein*, the "building committee," which would lead to the first Goetheanum (first planned for Munich), is also founded, and a preliminary committee for the founding of an independent association is created that, in the following year, will become the Anthroposophical Society. Important lecture cycles include *Occult Physiology* (CW 128); *Wonders of the World* (CW 129); *From Jesus to Christ* (CW 131). Other themes: esoteric Christianity; Christian Rosenkreutz; the spiritual guidance of humanity; the sense world and the world of the spirit.

1912: Despite the ongoing, now increasing crisis in the Theosophical Society, much is accomplished: *Calendar 1912/1913* is published; eurythmy is created; both the third mystery drama, *The Guardian of the Threshold* (CW 14) and *A Way of Self-Knowledge* (CW 16) are written. New (or renewed) themes included life between death and rebirth and karma and reincarnation. Other lecture cycles: *Spiritual Beings in the Heavenly Bodies and the Kingdoms of Nature* (CW 136); *The Human Being in the Light of Occultism, Theosophy, and Philosophy* (CW 137); *The Gospel of St. Mark* (CW 139); and *The Bhagavad Gita and the Epistles of Paul* (CW 142). On May 8, Rudolf Steiner celebrates White Lotus Day, H.P. Blavatsky's death day, which he had faithfully observed for the past decade, for the last time. In August, Rudolf Steiner suggests the "independent association" be called the "Anthroposophical Society." In September, the first eurythmy course takes place. In October, Rudolf Steiner declines recognition of a Theosophical Society lodge dedicated to the Star of the East and decides to expel all Theosophical Society members belonging to the order. Also, with Marie von Sivers, he first visits Dornach, near Basel, Switzerland, and they stand on the hill where the Goetheanum will be. In November, a Theosophical Society lodge is opened by direct mandate from Adyar (Annie Besant). In December, a meeting of the German section occurs at which it is decided that belonging to the Order of the Star of the East is incompatible with membership in the Theosophical Society. December 28: informal founding of the Anthroposophical Society in Berlin.

1913: Expulsion of the German section from the Theosophical Society. February 2-3: Foundation meeting of the Anthroposophical Society. Board members include: Marie von Sivers, Michael Bauer, and Carl Unger. September 20: Laying of the foundation stone for the *Johannes Bau* (Goetheanum) in Dornach. Building begins immediately. The third mystery drama, *The Soul's Awakening* (CW 14), is completed. Also: *The Threshold of the Spiritual World* (CW 147). Lecture cycles include: *The Bhagavad Gita and the Epistles of Paul* and *The Esoteric Meaning of the Bhagavad Gita* (CW 146), which the Russian philosopher Nikolai Berdyaev attends; *The Mysteries of the East and of Christianity* (CW 144); *The Effects of Esoteric Development* (CW 145); and *The Fifth Gospel* (CW 148). In May, Rudolf Steiner is in London and Paris, where anthroposophical work continues.

1914: Building continues on the *Johannes Bau* (Goetheanum) in Dornach, with artists and coworkers from seventeen nations. The general assembly of the Anthroposophical Society takes place. In May, Rudolf Steiner visits Paris, as well as Chartres Cathedral. June 28: assassination in Sarajevo ("Now the catastrophe has happened!"). August 1: War is declared. Rudolf Steiner returns to Germany from Dornach— he will travel back and forth. He writes the last chapter of *The Riddles of Philosophy*. Lecture cycles include: *Human and Cosmic Thought* (CW 151); *Inner Being of Humanity between Death and a New Birth* (CW 153); *Occult Reading and Occult Hearing* (CW 156). December 24: marriage of Rudolf Steiner and Marie von Sivers.

1915:   Building continues. Life after death becomes a major theme, also art. Writes: *Thoughts during a Time of War* (CW 24). Lectures include: *The Secret of Death* (CW 159); *The Uniting of Humanity through the Christ Impulse* (CW 165).

1916:   Rudolf Steiner begins work with Edith Maryon (1872-1924) on the sculpture "The Representative of Humanity" ("The Group"—Christ, Lucifer, and Ahriman). He also works with the alchemist Alexander von Bernus on the quarterly *Das Reich*. He writes *The Riddle of Humanity* (CW 20). Lectures include: *Necessity and Freedom in World History and Human Action* (CW 166); *Past and Present in the Human Spirit* (CW 167); *The Karma of Vocation* (CW 172); *The Karma of Untruthfulness* (CW 173).

1917:   Russian Revolution. The U.S. enters the war. Building continues. Rudolf Steiner delineates the idea of the "threefold nature of the human being" (in a public lecture March 15) and the "threefold nature of the social organism" (hammered out in May-June with the help of Otto von Lerchenfeld and Ludwig Polzer-Hoditz in the form of two documents titled *Memoranda*, which were distributed in high places). August-September: Rudolf Steiner writes *The Riddles of the Soul* (CW 20). Also: commentary on "The Chemical Wedding of Christian Rosenkreutz" for Alexander Bernus (*Das Reich*). Lectures include: *The Karma of Materialism* (CW 176); *The Spiritual Background of the Outer World: The Fall of the Spirits of Darkness* (CW 177).

1918:   March 18: peace treaty of Brest-Litovsk—"Now everything will truly enter chaos! What is needed is cultural renewal." June: Rudolf Steiner visits Karlstein (Grail) Castle outside Prague. Lecture cycle: *From Symptom to Reality in Modern History* (CW 185). In mid-November, Emil Molt, of the Waldorf-Astoria Cigarette Company, has the idea of founding a school for his workers' children.

1919:   Focus on the threefold social organism: tireless travel, countless lectures, meetings, and publications. At the same time, a new public stage of Anthroposophy emerges as cultural renewal begins. The coming years will see initiatives in pedagogy, medicine, pharmacology, and agriculture. January 27: threefold meeting: " We must first of all, with the money we have, found free schools that can bring people what they need." February: first public eurythmy performance in Zurich. Also: "Appeal to the German People" (CW 24), circulated March 6 as a newspaper insert. In April, *Toward Social Renewal* (CW 23)—"perhaps the most widely read of all books on politics appearing since the war"—appears. Rudolf Steiner is asked to undertake the "direction and leadership" of the school founded by the Waldorf-Astoria Company. Rudolf Steiner begins to talk about the "renewal" of education. May 30: a building is selected and purchased for the future Waldorf School. August-September, Rudolf Steiner gives a lecture course for Waldorf teachers, *The Foundations of Human Experience (Study of Man)* (CW 293). September 7: Opening of the first Waldorf School. December (into January): first science course, the *Light Course* (CW 320).

1920: The Waldorf School flourishes. New threefold initiatives. Founding of limited companies *Der Kommenden Tag* and *Futurum A.G.* to infuse spiritual values into the economic realm. Rudolf Steiner also focuses on the sciences. Lectures: *Introducing Anthroposophical Medicine* (CW 312); *The Warmth Course* (CW 321); *The Boundaries of Natural Science* (CW 322); *The Redemption of Thinking* (CW 74). February: Johannes Werner Klein—later a cofounder of the Christian Community—asks Rudolf Steiner about the possibility of a "religious renewal," a "Johannine church." In March, Rudolf Steiner gives the first course for doctors and medical students. In April, a divinity student asks Rudolf Steiner a second time about the possibility of religious renewal. September 27-October 16: anthroposophical "university course." December: lectures titled *The Search for the New Isis* (CW 202).

1921: Rudolf Steiner continues his intensive work on cultural renewal, including the uphill battle for the threefold social order. "University" arts, scientific, theological, and medical courses include: *The Astronomy Course* (CW 323); *Observation, Mathematics, and Scientific Experiment* (CW 324); the *Second Medical Course* (CW 313); *Color.* In June and September-October, Rudolf Steiner also gives the first two "priests' courses" (CW 342 and 343). The "youth movement" gains momentum. Magazines are founded: *Die Drei* (January), and—under the editorship of Albert Steffen (1884-1963)—the weekly, *Das Goetheanum* (August). In February-March, Rudolf Steiner takes his first trip outside Germany since the war (Holland). On April 7, Steiner receives a letter regarding "religious renewal," and May 22-23, he agrees to address the question in a practical way. In June, the Klinical-Therapeutic Institute opens in Arlesheim under the direction of Dr. Ita Wegman. In August, the Chemical-Pharmaceutical Laboratory opens in Arlesheim (Oskar Schmiedel and Ita Wegman, directors). The Clinical Therapeutic Institute is inaugurated in Stuttgart (Dr. Ludwig Noll, director); also the Research Laboratory in Dornach (Ehrenfried Pfeiffer and Gunther Wachsmuth, directors). In November-December, Rudolf Steiner visits Norway.

1922: The first half of the year involves very active public lecturing (thousands attend); in the second half, Rudolf Steiner begins to withdraw and turn toward the Society—"The Society is asleep." It is "too weak" to do what is asked of it. The businesses—*Die Kommenden Tag* and *Futura A.G.*—fail. In January, with the help of an agent, Steiner undertakes a twelve-city German tour, accompanied by eurythmy performances. In two weeks he speaks to more than 2,000 people. In April, he gives a "university course" in The Hague. He also visits England. In June, he is in Vienna for the East-West Congress. In August-September, he is back in England for the Oxford Conference on Education. Returning to Dornach, he gives the lectures *Philosophy, Cosmology, and Religion* (CW 215), and gives the third priest's course (CW 344). On September 16, The Christian Community is founded. In October-November, Steiner is in Holland and England. He also speaks to the youth: *The Youth Course* (CW 217). In December, Steiner gives lectures titled *The Origins of Natural Science* (CW 326), and *Humanity and the World of Stars: The Spiritual Communion of Humanity* (CW 219). December 31: Fire at the Goetheanum, which is destroyed.

1923: Despite the fire, Rudolf Steiner continues his work unabated. A very hard year. Internal dispersion, dissension, and apathy abound. There is conflict—between old and new visions—within the society. A wake-up call is needed, and Rudolf Steiner responds with renewed lecturing vitality. His focus: the spiritual context of human life; initiation science; the course of the year; and community building. As a foundation for an artistic school, he creates a series of pastel sketches. Lecture cycles: *The Anthroposophical Movement; Initiation Science* (CW 227) (in England at the Penmaenmawr Summer School); *The Four Seasons and the Archangels* (CW 229); *Harmony of the Creative Word* (CW 230); *The Supersensible Human* (CW 231), given in Holland for the founding of the Dutch society. On November 10, in response to the failed Hitler-Ludendorf putsch in Munich, Steiner closes his Berlin residence and moves the *Philosophisch-Anthroposophisch Verlag* (Press) to Dornach. On December 9, Steiner begins the serialization of his *Autobiography: The Course of My Life* (CW 28) in *Das Goetheanum*. It will continue to appear weekly, without a break, until his death. Late December-early January: Rudolf Steiner refounds the Anthroposophical Society (about 12,000 members internationally) and takes over its leadership. The new board members are: Marie Steiner, Ita Wegman, Albert Steffen, Elizabeth Vreede, and Guenther Wachsmuth. (See *The Christmas Meeting for the Founding of the General Anthroposophical Society* (CW 260). Accompanying lectures: *Mystery Knowledge and Mystery Centers* (CW 232); *World History in the Light of Anthroposophy* (CW 233). December 25: the Foundation Stone is laid (in the hearts of members) in the form of the "Foundation Stone Meditation."

1924: January 1: having founded the Anthroposophical Society and taken over its leadership, Rudolf Steiner has the task of "reforming" it. The process begins with a weekly newssheet ("What's Happening in the Anthroposophical Society") in which Rudolf Steiner's "Letters to Members" and "Anthroposophical Leading Thoughts" appear (CW

26). The next step is the creation of a new esoteric class, the "first class" of the "University of Spiritual Science" (which was to have been followed, had Rudolf Steiner lived longer, by two more advanced classes). Then comes a new language for Anthroposophy—practical, phenomenological, and direct; and Rudolf Steiner creates the model for the second Goetheanum. He begins the series of extensive "karma" lectures (CW 235-40); and finally, responding to needs, he creates two new initiatives: biodynamic agriculture and curative education. After the middle of the year, rumors begin to circulate regarding Steiner's health. Lectures: January-February, *Anthroposophy* (CW 234); February: *Tone Eurythmy* (CW 278); June: *The Agriculture Course* (CW 327); June-July: Speech [?] Eurythmy (CW 279); *Curative Education* (CW 317); August: (England, "Second International Summer School"), *Initiation Consciousness: True and False Paths in Spiritual Investigation* (CW 243); September: *Pastoral Medicine* (CW 318). On September 26, for the first time, Rudolf Steiner cancels a lecture. On September 28, he gives his last lecture. On September 29, he withdraws to his studio in the carpenter's shop; now he is definitively ill. Cared for by Ita Wegman, he continues working, however, and writing the weekly installments of his *Autobiography* and *Letters to the Members/Leading Thoughts* (CW 26).

1925: Rudolf Steiner, while continuing to work, continues to weaken. He finishes *Extending Practical Medicine* (CW 27) with Ita Wegman.

On March 30, around ten in the morning, Rudolf Steiner dies.

INDEX